THE WALL OF SEPARATION

FRANK J. SORAUF

The Wall of Separation

The Constitutional Politics of Church and State

For Fred Morrison —
from an 'intruder' into
the temple —

Frank Sorauf

PRINCETON UNIVERSITY PRESS, PRINCETON, NEW JERSEY

To four of my teachers,
to whom this book and its author
owe a great deal:

LEON D. EPSTEIN
DAVID FELLMAN
RALPH K. HUITT
WILLIAM H. YOUNG

PREFACE

This project has been "in progress" for an inordinately long time. On occasion, in fact, the progress was almost imperceptible. To the best of my recollection it all began in 1962, and the field interviewing extended intermittently between 1963 and 1972. Work was interrupted by a departmental chairmanship and a venture into academic administration, as well as by the usual academic responsibilities. I mention this little bit of history chiefly to indicate how much I often depended on the help of others to keep the project moving forward. It will also explain in part how I came to be obliged to so many people.

My debts in this study are of many kinds. Not the least of them is to the agencies that supported it, especially its considerable field research. The John Simon Guggenheim Foundation and the College of Liberal Arts at the University of Minnesota, through its McMillan funds, both supported me generously. The Graduate School of the University of Minnesota was both generous and patient, making more research grants to this project than anyone might wish to remember. I am especially grateful to those Graduate School committees for their continuing confidence.

A number of undergraduate and graduate assistants helped me in many important ways over the years. They worked chiefly in the library data-gathering tasks and in the coding and management of the data. Some of them worked so long ago that they must surely have forgotten about the project. In alphabetical rather than chronological order they were Gary Engstrand, John Erickson, Eugene Gaetke, Caroline Wolf Harlow, Michel Nelson, R. Chris Perry, Rolf Sonnesyn, Louis Vincent, and Herbert Weisberg. The late Frank Ashman worked courageously and all too briefly.

The field interviewing was entirely my responsibility, and in it I met an encouraging helpfulness everywhere I traveled. Busy people interrupted their schedules to talk with me, and their candor and cooperation contributed enormously to this volume. Their friendliness, interest, and hospitality remain very pleasant memories. I could not begin to mention all of these individuals, and so

I will mention none. Should any of them read this preface, I hope they will accept these thanks as if they were more personal.

My researches carried me repeatedly to the files and archives of the American Civil Liberties Union, the American Jewish Congress, and Americans United for Separation of Church and State. The various librarians at all were unfailingly helpful. For additional assistance and courtesies I should like to record special thanks to Franklin Salisbury of AU and to Leo Pfeffer and Joseph Robison of AJC. Augusta Winkler and Sophie Zerlanko of the AJC were also kind far beyond the call of duty.

As this manuscript began to materialize, Gloria Priem typed two drafts in her usual calm and reliable way. My secretary, Gloria Thayer, helped in many ways. Jeanna Struthers helped tremendously in reading the page proofs. Leo Pfeffer and Joel Grossman read the first of those drafts and saved me from many inaccuracies and misjudgments. I am especially obliged to them for their careful and thoughtful readings. Those shortcomings which remain do so despite their warnings. Finally, I am also grateful for the patience of Sanford Thatcher and the Princeton University Press in waiting through those last, very slow years.

CONTENTS

LIST OF TABLES

THE WALL OF SEPARATION

I | THE CONSTITUTION AND THE SEPARATION

Aphorisms about the growth and exposition of the American Constitution center largely on the judges. In the famous words of Charles Evans Hughes, "We are under a Constitution, but the Constitution is what the judges say it is." The Supreme Court itself is, depending on the commentator, "the living voice of the Constitution" or "almost . . . a continuous constitutional convention."[1] It is as if we reveal all of constitutional politics when we part the veils that surround the judges and their judgments.

Yet if the Constitution is what the judges say it is, it is also true that the range of the judges' options is sharply limited. They are not roving Robin Hoods in search of injustice, nor are they constitutional draftsmen in pursuit of constitutional ambiguity or anomaly. They are, above all, prisoners of the cases brought to them, trapped in the facts and the arguments of the litigants who bring the cases. It advances the cause of realism in American constitutional law to say that the Constitution is what the judges say it is. But it also advances that cause to recognize that the Constitution is both what others permit the judges to say it is, and what they recognize the judges to have said it was.

In no way does it denigrate the appellate courts to explicate the roles of other actors in the judicial process. It is a commonplace that the appellate courts are passive instruments, that they are largely limited to deciding the issues others bring to them. If it is important to understand the passive actors, it is also useful to study the active initiators. Groups and individuals decide—sometimes purposefully, sometimes willy-nilly—which issues will appear on the judicial dockets and which ones will not. They and their attorneys decide in what form questions will come to the

---

[1] The Hughes words apparently came from a speech made in 1907 in Elmira, New York; President Franklin Roosevelt "immortalized" them by quoting them in a fireside chat on March 9, 1937. The next two quotations, in order, belong to James Bryce, *The American Commonwealth,* rev. ed. (New York: Macmillan, 1931), vol. 1, 273; and to Robert H. Jackson, *The Struggle for Judicial Supremacy* (New York: Vintage, 1941), pp. x–xi.

courts, in what facts and argument they will be encased. Others in this subtle interplay will assess the judicial decision, gauge its impact, even assure its enforcement and, perhaps, also take the next step in the process by posing a new constitutional question.

In looking at the colloquy between constitutional litigators and the courts, one can imagine it as an episodic, almost random dialogue. A much-vexed taxpayer or a heavily pressured school board, for example, reacts to purely local conditions and precipitates action that raises constitutional issues. The courts eventually decide, and that body of constitutional law then awaits the more or less random occurrence of another controversy—related perhaps only distantly to the previous one—to come to it or to the high court of another jurisdiction. In some areas of American constitutional law, however, the process is considerably less haphazard. Large national groups have organized and structured the litigation of constitutional questions with a considerable degree of proficiency. In these instances the initiating groups have raised the quality of their interchange with the courts to something approaching a Socratic dialogue on some clause of the constitution. Probing question preceeds precise—perhaps even cagey—answer, which in turn suggests—even invites—the next artful query. And in the dialogue, even when it is far more fragmented and discontinuous, one must understand the questions and the questioners if one is to understand the answers.

Even a full accounting of the actors and the actions within the judicial process, however, does not wholly depict the politics of constitutional growth and interpretation. Constitutional issues and actors wander freely across the unmarked borders between the judicial process and political processes in the other branches of government. Litigants often, indeed, try to convert losses or inattention in those other processes into victory in the courts. Decisions in the courts, moreover, have impacts and consequences far beyond the judiciary. Constitutional decisions, especially, have a forceful impact on the subsequent making of public policy; they may also spur constitutional amendments and battles over compliance and enforcement. So although it is true that the authoritative constitutional interpretations are the work of the courts, the broader politics of constitutional development can touch virtually any point or institution in the entire political process.

This is the point of view from which this study departs. In more specific terms, it is the story of litigating one area of constitutional law—that on the separation of church and state—in American appellate courts from 1951 to 1971. It portrays the plaintiffs, attorneys, and the groups bringing the litigation, their strategies and goals, their successes and failures. It suggests, as well, something of the community context and group conflict in which the litigation develops, and of the broader policy problems and social attitudes behind it. It is an attempt to chronicle the entire process and politics of litigating one area of American constitutional law, and in so doing, to say something more generally about the politics of constitutional growth.

At the same time, it is the story of some of the most anguished constitutional controversies of the time. Only the furor over desegregation and the rights of racial minorities rivaled the intensity of feeling on prayer in the public schools, or public aid to private religious schools. These were not only constitutional questions of baffling complexity and closely matched equities. They were also issues of public policy to excite the most fervent beliefs and to test the resilience of American religious heterodoxy. It is, too, a story whose plot is matched by its dramatis personae. Madalyn Murray O'Hair's assaults, first against prayer in the city schools of Baltimore and then against virtually all public religious influences in American society, made her perhaps the best known of all constitutional plaintiffs. But she was not alone. There were at all points dozens of other committed individuals, and an impressive array of local and national litigating groups.

THE CONSTITUTIONAL CASES

From 1951 through June of 1971, high American appellate courts decided a total of sixty-seven cases primarily concerned with constitutional issues of church-state separation. They are the subject of this book, for it is their origin, their issues, their sponsorship, their decision, and their aftermath that form the recent development of this one area of American constitutional law. The great majority of these cases, fifty-nine in all, originated in state courts. All of them reached the highest state appellate courts, and six of them were ultimately decided by the United States Supreme Court. The remaining eight originated in the federal courts; four progressed only as far as a court of appeals, and four went to the Supreme Court for substantive decision. All of these cases, in other words, have reached either a high state appellate court or a federal appellate court. Furthermore, they are the only cases between 1951 and 1971 to have raised substantial constitutional questions of church-state separation in those courts. They are the universe of constitutional cases in that period, and taken together they are the constitutional precedents—the known, reported, and final decisions—available to judges and legal scholars.[2]

While the sixty-seven cases all raise questions of church-state relationships, some raise them under state constitutions, some under the U.S. Constitution, and many under both. In general those questions can be embraced by the enduring metaphor of the wall of separation between church and state; under the U.S. Constitution they are the cases argued under the "no establishment" clause of the First Amendment.[3] As a matter of logic rather than constitutional law, these separation cases fall easily into two subcategories. There are those that involve public aid or support to some religious practice or institution: aid to religious schools or hospitals, for example. And there are issues of religious influence in public life—questions, for instance, of prayer or Bible-reading in public schools or crosses in public parks.

Even within one carefully defined area of American constitutional law there is, however, a rich diversity of conflict that the two subcategories do not begin to disclose. The largest single number of the cases (12) touched on questions of transporting pupils in religious schools at public expense. (In the 1950s, one must remember, "busing" was an issue of separation of church and state!) Another 10 cases involved prayer or Bible-reading in the public schools. Indeed, the overwhelming majority of the cases (43 of the 67) in some way or another involved the elementary and secondary schools, either public or private religious schools. The nonschool cases included those questioning tax exemptions for religious buildings, aid for buildings at religious colleges and universities, a cross on public property, and the reference to the Deity in the pledge to the flag.[4]

The settings of the sixty-seven cases are equally diverse. They

[2] Appendix I describes at greater length the criteria used in identifying this universe of cases.

[3] The reader will note, therefore, that there are no cases concerned with issues of religious freedom (such as those arising under the "free exercise" clause of the First Amendment); see Appendix I.

[4] Some of the cases fall into more than one fact category, and some of these fact categories must be refined additionally. These matters will be further developed.

came from every part of the country: from Maine to Florida, and from Washington to Arizona and California. Two originated in Alaska, and one in Hawaii. They came from New York City and other metropolitan centers, but they also came from small towns in isolated Appalachian valleys. They came from the areas of heaviest Roman Catholic strength—the states of Connecticut and Rhode Island—and from areas of Southern Protestant fundamentalism. There are cases from areas of greatest Jewish population, as well as from the special religious strength of Buddhists and Shintoists in Hawaii and Mormons in Utah.

The diversity of the sixty-seven cases extends, furthermore, to differences in their importance in the fabric of American constitutional law. Among them are the "great" cases, those that produced a vast and public impact, and dot the casebooks and the commentaries. Among them would certainly be the prayer and Bible-reading decisions of 1963 and 1964 (*Engel* v. *Vitale, Schempp* v. *School District,* and *Murray* v. *Curlett*) and the clutch of decisions in 1971 ruling on direct state aid to religious schools (especially *Lemon* v. *Kurtzman* and *DiCenso* v. *Robinson*).[5] But also included are cases of little or no note. There is one man's quixotic attack on the national motto "In God We Trust," a case decided with the briefest possible per curiam paragraph (*Aronow* v. *U.S.*). There is also a case (*Miller* v. *Cooper*) charging religious influences in the public schools of Lindrith, an unincorporated and virtually uninhabited town in the northwest section of New Mexico. Obviously, no criterion of intrinsic "importance" has governed the selection of the cases. All cases decided in the time period and in the specified appellate courts, and that raised substantial issues of church-state relations, are here.

THE INTERESTS AND THE PARTIES

It is in the nature of the adversary conflict in these cases that the plaintiffs generally acted on behalf of a "separationist" interest. They were objecting to some government program of aid to religion, some entanglement of government with religion, or some religious influence in public life. The public policy against which they acted seemed not to keep church and state sufficiently apart. Occa-

---

[5] The sixty-seven cases are listed with full citations at the end of Appendix I. They will be footnoted in the text only where more specific notation or comment is necessary.

7

sionally the plaintiffs were "accommodationists"—that is, they sought closer cooperation (or a less distant relationship) between church and state. Plaintiffs in West Virginia argued, for example, that private school pupils were discriminated against by a school board decision to bus only children going to the public schools (*State ex rel. Hughes* v. *Board of Education*). But there were only ten accommodationist suits out of the sixty-seven.

Also as a matter of the logic of these adversary cases, the accommodationist defendants were usually a governmental body. They were, in other words, the governmental authorities that had in some way brought (or permitted the bringing of) church and state together. Not surprisingly, the most common defendant was a local school board or district; these appeared as the defendant (or one of the defendants) in thirty of the cases. In many of these cases, of course, the defendant may have acted only as a proxy in wedding church to the state. Consider the case of school boards that appeared as defendants in cases challenging the transportation of children to private religious schools. In the majority of those cases the school boards were merely providing bus service at the insistence of a mandatory state law. In some instances, indeed, the members of the boards may have been personally and collectively opposed to the law, either because of convictions about church-state separation, or because they preferred to spend school funds for other programs. Thus "interests" in these cases were not as clearly defined as one might suspect. The nature of the case or controversy in the American court system casts the action in adversary terms, and often "creates" a sharper or different confrontation of interests than exists in reality.

We thus have two broad categories of interest in church-state relationships: the "separationists" and the "accommodationists." Each, however, contains a wide range of positions on church-state relationships. The lines dividing the two camps shift from case to case. A little-known case from Seattle (*Calvary Bible Presbyterian Church* v. *Regents of University of Washington*) illustrates the problem. Ministers of the Bible Presbyterian Church charged that a course on the Bible as literature taught at the University of Washington reflected only one or some theologies of the Bible, and by reason of that selectivity amounted to an establishment of religion. The state affiliate of the American Civil Liberties Union, whose views are usually strongly separationist, supported the university and its interpretation of academic freedom. Nomi-

8

nally, at least, the ACLU unexpectedly found itself in an accommodationist camp.

Part of the problem, of course, is in the easy use of the "separationist" and "accommodationist" labels. Both cover and embrace a considerable range of views. The "separationist" tag, at least, has some philosophical or constitutional point of reference in the Supreme Court's explications of the "no establishment" clause. But the "accommodationists" have little more in common than their collective role as defendants in most of this litigation. It would certainly be unfair and inaccurate to imply that their position is 180 degrees opposite that of the separationists. In many instances, indeed, they are only some small distance away from the separationists; but even small ideological distances can foster substantial constitutional conflict. Writers and scholars in the field of church-state law have been notably uncertain what to call these interests and groups on "the other side." On behalf of the term "accommodationist"—awkward though it surely is—one can at least say that it is more defensible than "antiseparationist," and that it is winning the slow battle of general usage.

THE SETTING

On one day in late June, 1971, the Supreme Court, in a veritable frenzy of judgment, disposed in one way or another of eight church-state cases. Most prominent among them were the challenges to direct aid to religious schools in Pennsylvania and Rhode Island, and to Congress's construction grants for religious colleges and universities. As a terminal date for the cases of this study, that day marks, if not the end, at least a point of culmination in several decades of increasingly feverish litigation on the constitutional separation of church and state.

And feverish it was by any standards. The pace of the litigation accelerated steadily from 1951 to 1971; over half of the cases—thirty-four of the sixty-seven—were decided in the last third of the period, the years between 1965 and 1971. And it overshadowed any earlier period of church-state litigation. The eight cases decided in the United States Supreme Court in the period were, for example, more than the Court had decided in its entire prior history. Church and state came very late to the U.S. Supreme Court. The entire body of major precedents in the area contains only two decided before 1951, and both of them were decided

9

in the 1940s: the New Jersey bus case (*Everson* v. *Board of Education*), and the released-time case from Champaign, Illinois (*McCollum* v. *Board of Education*).[6]

Behind such swiftly moving constitutional litigation were the events of a very turbulent period in American religious history. The period from 1951 to 1971 includes, quite incredibly, both a period of religious revival and a time of religious decline. Paradoxes and ironies abound. For Roman Catholics they were decades that saw Bishop Fulton Sheen become a television celebrity, and John F. Kennedy become president of the United States; and yet the period culminated in the decline of a parochial school system that had been the envy of Catholics in the rest of the world. For Protestants the years were rife with reform and change; it was a time of ecumenical movements and church mergers, of theological and doctrinal change, of radical social ethics and involvement. But for all of that, at least by the 1970s, it was, ironically, the conservative and fundamentalist Protestants, the groups least touched by the currents of the period, that seemed to flourish most.

Above all, these were the years of the dismantling of the "Protestant Establishment." There had indeed been an implicit or silent American religious establishment, and it had been Protestant. The American social, economic, and political elites had been largely Protestant, and public piety—whether in the schools, in the public calendar, or in celebrations and occasions—had been largely Protestant. But all of that came to an end in the years after World War II. Catholics and Jews challenged it, and so did nonbelievers and secular humanists. Both those challenges and the public policies to which they led eventually found their way to the courts. They ultimately led to the first fully sustained development of an American constitutional law of church-state relations.

[6] 330 U.S. 1 (1947) and 333 U.S. 203 (1948). There had, of course, been earlier church-state decisions (see, for example, *Bradfield* v. *Roberts*, 175 U.S. 291 [1899]), but the Court's decisions in those cases were either narrowly or ambiguously framed.

II | THE LEGAL AND RELIGIOUS CONTEXT

The period from 1951 to 1971 was for almost every major religion in the United States a period of questing and questioning. Virtually every tradition and orthodoxy came under fire, and the settled conventions were challenged by movements as diverse as ecumenism and the use of popular music in religious services. It was also a time of rapid, confusing, enormously disconcerting change. In the early 1950s, for example, religious denominations were noting impressive gains in memberships, in Sunday worshippers, and in financial resources. Not much more than a decade later church attendance began to fall off, and national denominations admitted a crisis in declining contributions.

Perhaps no religious group or body better illustrates the changes in these two decades than the Roman Catholic church. Long one of the strongest and most thriving of the national churches in Catholicism, it saw the departure of large numbers of priests and nuns, and by the late 1960s its once affluent system of parochial schools was deep in financial crisis. Changes in the forms of worship and religious obligation—away from the Latin mass and the ban against meat on Friday, for instance—were only one indication of the winds of change set loose by Pope John XXIII, the Vatican Council, and young American priests and theologians. Never the authoritarian monolith that many Protestants (and some Catholics) had imagined, the American Catholic church went through perhaps the greatest challenges to the authority of the hierarchy it had known since the Reformation. Lay groups began to question the power of the bishops and win a growing voice in the management of the Catholic schools, the parishes, and even the dioceses. Councils of priests even began to be formed, and by the 1970s they had in a few celebrated instances expressed votes of "no confidence" in the hierarchy.

That such a period of religious change and crisis should have been the period during which we had such extensive litigation of church-state relations is no accident. In some instances the relationship between these trends and constitutional litigation is transparent. The problems of organized religion became public problems; the crisis of the parochial schools gave rise to public aid, and that in turn led to constitutional litigation. In other instances the tie is less obvious. Perhaps a time of religious controversy and change exacerbates latent religious conflict by publicizing differences and dissatisfactions. Perhaps, too, each erosion of religious authority and solidarity invites a challenge.

Whatever the explanation, the two decades from 1951 to 1971 also saw the growth of an impressive body of constitutional law on the separation of church and state. Many of its most perplexing problems were decided by appellate courts for the first time in the period. The nine church-state cases the Supreme Court decided from 1962 to 1971 were more than it had decided previously in its entire history. There is probably no avoiding the treatment of these sixty-seven cases as more or less bleeding chunks of litigation ripped from the contexts both of our religious life and the broader political conflicts over public policy. But one should at least know something of the context from which they are taken.

ORGANIZED RELIGION, 1951–1971

The change and diversity that mark American religious life in the 1950s and 1960s complicate the task of making quick but intelligible summary statements about it. To some extent the currents and countercurrents, the little eddies, and even the backwaters that one saw depended where one stood in the stream. From the viewpoint of eventual constitutional litigation on church-state issues, however, one could identify four significant trends.

The Return to Religion

In the less churchly days of the 1970s it is difficult to remember that less than a generation earlier Americans talked widely, and with no little self-satisfaction, of a "return to religion." There was considerable confidence that the materialism of the 1930s and the war years had been overcome, and preachers such as Bishop Fulton Sheen and the Reverends Billy Graham and Norman Vincent Peale became national celebrities. The "return" was symbolized for many Americans by the election in 1952 of Dwight D. Eisenhower to the presidency. A somewhat late convert to the strengths of organized religion himself, President Eisenhower put the stamp

12

of officialdom on the religious revival with prayer breakfasts, regular church attendance, and homely exhortations at press conferences.

A good deal of popular culture also reflected the return. Religious works dotted and even dominated the nonfiction best seller lists in the early 1950s. In 1953, for instance, the top ten sellers for the year included the new Revised Standard Version of the Bible (about three million sold in that year and the preceding one), Norman Vincent Peale's *Power of Positive Thinking,* Bishop Sheen's *Life Is Worth Living, A Man Called Peter* (a biography of a young and noted minister by his widow), and *The Greatest Faith Ever Known.* The Peale volume, in fact, made the top ten list for all four years between 1952 and 1955, one year more than did the Revised Standard Version.[1] Popular magazines such as the *Reader's Digest* became the medium—if not the message itself—of the revival. From 1951 through 1954 Episcopal Bishop Henry Knox Sherrill, Rabbi Louis Finkelstein, Bishop Fulton J. Sheen, Bishop Otto Dibelius, Pope Pius XII, the Archbishop of Canterbury, and the Reverend Billy Graham all graced different covers of *Time* magazine.

The religious revival did not, however, proceed without criticism. One conspicuous and much-published critic deplored the "piety along the Potomac."[2] Serious religious thinkers and theologians deplored it as middle-class, simplistic religion; distinctions appeared between piety and piousity. And indeed, at its most banal, the new religious renaissance was an inviting target. Much of it (the power of positive thinking, for instance) seemed to have more to do with Dale Carnegie, a revival of Couéism, or the psychology of success than it did with theology or serious ethical thought. Much of the criticism also pointed out—quite correctly in many cases—that the return to religion was bound up with the contemporary crusade against domestic and international communism. Indeed the enemy came to be known—positively, if a bit redundantly—as "godless atheistic communism." A somewhat nationalist religion in some quarters justified the excesses of Senator Joe McCarthy's search for domestic communists. And a good

[1] The listings come from Alice Payne Hackett, *Seventy Years of Best Sellers* (New York: Bowker, 1967); it relies in turn on the sales data of *Publishers' Weekly.*

[2] See, for example, William Lee Miller, "Religion, Politics, and the 'Great Crusade'," *Reporter* (July 7, 1953), pp. 14–16; and "Piety along the Potomac," *Reporter* (August 17, 1954), pp. 25–28.

deal of the public religiosity of the time had as its rationale the strengthening of the moral fiber of American youth against the seductions of godless alien doctrines.

The policy consequences of religious education expanded as young students trouped for an hour or two every week from their public schools to local churches, parish houses, and synagogues for religious instruction. Public educators explored new ways of teaching moral and spiritual values, and of teaching "about" religion in the public schools. And prayer and Bible-reading entered the public schools in parts of the country in which those practices had earlier been rare or unknown. Even into the sixties and seventies, indeed, the fragments of this movement for public religiosity struggled to the verge of success in writing into the U.S. Constitution an amendment permitting prayer in the public schools.

The Crisis in Religious Education

For signs of the crisis it is again easiest to take the Roman Catholic schools and institutions of higher education as examples. The parochial school system, less than a generation earlier the pride of American Catholicism, was by 1971 closing fifty elementary schools a month. Pressures mounted in the late 1960s for aid to keep religious schools open; the alternative, proponents warned, was the closing of the parochial schools and the dumping of millions of new pupils onto the public education system. Signs on religious schools in various parts of the country proclaimed them "the taxpayer's best friend." And a national interest group, Citizens for Educational Freedom, grew to maturity in the fight for state legislative aid for religious schools.

To be sure, the crisis in the religious schools extended beyond Roman Catholic institutions. But by sheer bulk the problem was largely a Catholic problem. About ninety percent of the pupils enrolled in religious schools, elementary and secondary, were Catholic. Furthermore, by general agreement, the problems of the Catholic schools were qualitatively, as well as quantitatively, more severe than those of Lutheran, Reformed, Jewish Orthodox, Episcopal, or other schools. And Catholic colleges and universities tended to maintain closer ties with the church, in contrast, say, to the attenuated relationships that characterized the nominally Congregationalist or Presbyterian colleges. Most important, the crisis in the religious schools and the search for public aid were perceived in terms of Roman Catholicism by many Americans.

14

Certainly it is no secret that the struggles over state aid to religious schools awakened some identifiable old anti-Romanism.

The reasons for the crisis in the religious schools are not easy to sort out. Certainly the Catholic parochial schools were caught in a cost squeeze, and one component of the squeeze was the increasing inavailability of nuns, priests, and brothers to staff the schools. In 1970 a majority of the teachers in Catholic elementary schools were lay people, while only a decade earlier they had been a third. Catholic schools were also troubled in many of the older cities with deteriorating physical plants and with families migrating out of the area to the suburbs. Part of the cost squeeze, too, resulted from lower levels of Catholic support for the schools, part of the phenomenon of generally lower levels for all religious giving.

The crisis gave rise directly and clearly to a remarkable campaign for state aid to religious schools. (That form of aid came to be called "parochaid." In some quarters the term has pejorative connotations, but none is suggested here.) By the time of the Supreme Court's decision in mid-1971 eleven state legislatures had passed some form of parochaid. On June 28th the U.S. Supreme Court struck down three of the first state laws, but the battle continued in the courts and legislatures to find some form of aid that could pass muster under the First and Fourteenth Amendments. And to that search for a modus operandi Richard Nixon pledged himself in the summer of 1971 in a public assurance of help and good will to Terence Cardinal Cooke of New York. His opponent in the 1972 election, Senator George McGovern, pledged his help later in the campaign.

Internal Change and Innovation

The shifting theologies, doctrines, and styles within most American religious denominations in the fifties and sixties disturbed and confused even the most devout. Novel and unorthodox theologies sprang up, and in many congregations great gulfs yawned between the preaching of those recently come from the seminaries and theological schools on the one hand, and the multitude's simple faith and belief in a personal God on the other. Old truths and regularities came under question. Some theologians even proposed aphoristically that God was dead.

At the same time substantial minorities, especially among the clergy, developed new social concerns. Priests, nuns, rabbis, and ministers marched with Southern blacks in the freedom marches

15

of the fifties and early sixties. Later they led a substantial segment of the peace movement and opposition to the war in Vietnam. A heightened social ethic led to new social action, even to radicalism; the Berrigan brothers, both Roman Catholic priests, languished in jail for assaults on selective service records, and were even accused of complicity in a bizarre plan to kidnap Henry Kissinger, then President Nixon's adviser on foreign affairs.

The religious upheaval was manifested in a number of other ways. Priestly rebellions against bishops exemplified the Catholic challenges to religious authority. Protestant seminaries encountered new demands for freedom, and some of their national conventions were wracked by doctrinal debates. And everywhere laymen sought a greater role in the governance of denominations that had had traditions of clerical rule. Ecumenical movements produced new junctures; Congregationalists, for example, joined the Evangelical and Reformed church to make the United Church of Christ. And new forms of religious worship shook the more traditional liturgies. Roman Catholics dropped Latin from the mass, and the sounds of folk and rock music became more common in the new ways of worship.

The political result of all of these changes has been a further splintering of the political voice of organized religion. It had always been the case that denominations differed in public policy debates; now it was increasingly the case that single denominations were also divided. There were Roman Catholics opposed to aid to religious schools, as well as those in favor of it. Protestants were increasingly divided on the wisdom of tax exemptions for religious property, and the social concerns of the National Council of Churches embroiled it in continuing controversy with more conservative Protestants. There were new internal pressures within almost all denominations in favor of cutting ties with public authority; the possibility of legalizing prayer in public schools drew increasing opposition from within the churches. In short, organized religion began to speak with an ever more divided voice, and with a voice robbed of some ring of authority by criticism and opposition from within.

New Moralities and Ethics

The twenty years of this study were years in which the Protestant domination of American life and culture largely ended. In the immediate sense, much of the public religiosity that was ended in

16

that period was Protestant in nature. But in more general matters of morality, too, it was the end of the dominant Protestant ethic in American life; gone was the ethic of work and industry, of frugality, and of a stern sexual morality. Just as organized religion in the United States endured substantial internal convulsions in the fifties and sixties, it also faced enormous external challenges to its prevailing ethic.

It was above all a time of loosening the old moral constraints. So great was freedom in the arts—all of them—that by the early seventies one could seriously wonder if terms such as "obscenity" or "pornography" could any longer sustain any meaning. Nudity and sexual explicitness became art forms in themselves and, indeed, captured a substantial part of the book and movie market. The open, serious discussion of birth control, sexual love, and abortion that was common in 1971 would have been unthinkable twenty years earlier. One cannot, of course, group all of the new moralities together. They ranged from the brittle and casual hedonism of *Playboy* magazine to the earnest debates over such issues as abortion reform. They nonetheless shared a common challenge to the traditional Judeo-Christian morality.

At the same time, millions of Americans by the late sixties and early seventies increasingly rejected traditional, organized religion. Church attendance and financial collections declined. A Gallup poll in early 1972 showed weekly church-going down to 40 percent in 1971 from 49 percent in 1958. Opinion polls also indicated that belief in the old verities—a God, personal salvation, eternities in heaven or hell—had also declined. A *Newsweek* poll in mid-1971 disclosed that 58 percent of American Catholics thought that a good Catholic could ignore the church's position on contraception, and 53 percent thought priests should be permitted to marry.[3] An increasing percentage of Americans did not identify with any religious denomination, and young Americans were especially wary of traditional religion. The impressive denominational centers that ringed the campuses of most large American universities fell on especially bad times.

These developments also had their political ramifications. They built a contrareligious sentiment, while they challenged the prevailing religious consensus and hegemony. They provided support for a new American secularism, and perhaps they were also the beginning of a vague, still inarticulate American anticlericalism. Ameri-

[3] *Newsweek,* October 4, 1971.

17

can society had always had a small but vocal group of humanists and atheists—sons and daughters of Voltaire, perhaps, or Robert Ingersoll—but they gained new support in the sixties. They threw their weight against attempts to write traditional Christian morality into law, and into legal attempts to broaden the definition of religious freedom. Above all they rejected the influence of traditional Christianity in American public schools.

It was, then, a time of trouble for organized American religion. The changes in American religion, diverse as they were, echoed through American political and legal controversy. Opposition grew up even within the organized religions. The faithful became estranged from their religious leaders. What else is one to make of the vote in the House of Representatives in November 1971 on the constitutional amendment to permit prayer in public places? Despite the opposition of virtually every major religious denomination and a good many religious federations (such as the National Council of Churches), the amendment carried a majority in the House of 240 to 162.[4]

THE CONSTITUTIONAL LAW OF SEPARATION

Almost 150 years in its history passed before the United States Supreme Court confronted the First Amendment. Congress legislated only rarely in areas touching it, and the Bill of Rights had no force against state action.[5] In the mid-1920s, however, the Court finally began interpreting the due process clause of the Fourteenth Amendment to incorporate some of the protections of the Bill of Rights against the states. In 1940, in a case involving the Jehovah's Witnesses, the Supreme Court incorporated the "no establishment" and "free exercise" clauses into the Fourteenth Amendment.[6] For the first time issues of state involvement with religion could easily reach the Court.

The Supreme Court wrote, therefore, on something very close to a clean slate as it decided *Everson* v. *Board of Education* in 1947. Between 1790 and 1945, in fact, it had decided only three cases touching in any substantial way on church-state relationships. In 1899 it held that Congressional payments to a religious hospital

---

[4] Since the constitutional amendment had to be passed by a two-thirds majority, it was, of course, defeated. See Chapter XIII for a fuller account of the attempts at amendment.

[5] *Barron* v. *Baltimore,* 7 Pet. 243 (1833).

[6] *Cantwell* v. *Connecticut,* 310 U.S. 296 (1940).

18

in the District of Columbia—the payments were for the care of the poor—did not violate the First Amendment. The sisters of the hospital were merely providing a public service, the Court held; hence there was no aid to religion. Nine years later the Court upheld payments under a treaty to Roman Catholic schools on an Indian reservation on the ground that they came from treaty funds merely held by the government in trust for the Indians themselves. Then, in 1930, it upheld Louisiana's purchase of nonsectarian textbooks for pupils attending all schools, including parochial schools run by religious denominations. The decision was notable both for announcing the "child benefit" theory—aid was to the child rather than the religious institution, and hence no problem—and for being the only pre-*Everson* establishment case to deal with state action.[7] None of these three early decisions, however, explained in any substantial way what the Court considered an impermissible joining of church and state.

The modern constitutional law of separation begins with *Everson*. New Jersey had authorized local school boards, if they chose, to reimburse parents of children going to private schools for the cost of bus transportation to and from school. The township of Ewing elected to do so, and a challenge to its payments to parents of children attending religious schools eventually reached the U.S. Supreme Court. In a 5–4 decision the Court upheld the reimbursement. The majority opinion, written by Justice Hugo Black, reached back to *Cochran* for the child benefit theory. But while the decision upheld the bus rides for parochial school children, it was enveloped in the language of the most absolute doctrine of the separation of church and state. In construing the "no establishment" clause of the First Amendment for the first time in the Court's history, Justice Black revived the Jeffersonian metaphor of the wall of separation. The clause, wrote Justice Black, means "at least this":

Neither a state nor Federal Government can set up a church. Neither can pass laws which aid one religion, and all religions, or prefer one religion over another. Neither can force nor

[7] The citation to *Everson* is 330 U.S. 1 (1947). The three earlier cases, in the order discussed here, are: *Bradfield* v. *Roberts,* 175 U.S. 291 (1899); *Quick Bear* v. *Leupp,* 210 U.S. 50 (1908); and *Cochran* v. *Louisiana Board of Education,* 281 U.S. 370 (1930). The *Cochran* case came to the Supreme Court on the assertion that Louisiana was taking private property for a private purpose in violation of the Fourteenth Amendment.

19

influence a person to go to or to remain away from church against his will or force him to profess a belief or disbelief in any religion. No person can be punished for entertaining or professing religious beliefs or disbeliefs, for church attendance or non-attendance. No tax in any amount, large or small, can be levied to support any religious activities or institutions, whatever they may be called, or whatever form they may adopt to teach or practice religion. Neither a state nor the Federal Government can, openly or secretly, participate in the affairs of any religious organizations or groups and *vice versa*. In the words of Jefferson, the clause against establishment of religion by law was intended to erect 'a wall of separation between church and state.' . . . That wall must be kept high and impregnable. We could not approve the slightest breach. New Jersey has not breached it here.[8]

The majority had succeeded, if "succeeded" is the right word, in combining the strictest separationist rhetoric with an accommodationist outcome.

The *Everson* result pleased very few. The four-man minority on the Court rejected the dichotomy between aid to the child and aid to the school. And for the gulf between rhetoric and outcome, Justice Jackson had only scorn. It reminded him of Byron's Julia, who "whispering 'I will ne'er consent'—consented."[9] Separationists not on the Court were displeased with the outcome, and Catholics, although pleased with the legitimizing of bus transportation, quickly saw the greater loss they suffered in the explication of the First Amendment's few words on establishment.

Just a year later, in the *McCollum* case, the Court confirmed the worst suspicions of the accommodationists.[10] At issue was the "released-time" program of the Champaign (Illinois) schools, in which students were released from their usual classroom responsibilities for an hour every week for instruction in the religion of their preference. The Court held that the public aid to the program of religious instruction—especially the free use of school buildings, and administration and supervision of the program—constituted a degree of aid forbidden by the "no establishment" clause. Only Justice Reed dissented, although a concurring opinion was at pains

[8] 330 U.S. 18.
[9] *Ibid.*, p. 19.
[10] *McCollum* v. *Board of Education*, 333 U.S. 203 (1948).

to point out that the decision was not a rejection of any and all varieties of released-time programs.

That, in substance, was where the constitutional law of church-state relationships under the U.S. Constitution stood in the late 1940s, when the earliest of the sixty-seven cases under scrutiny here began to reach trial court hearings. The corpus of constitutional litigation included only five cases; and only two of those came from the contemporary court. The legal aftermath of *Everson* and *McCollum* was one both of debate and uncertainty. The Court reaped more than a full measure of criticism for the two decisions: Justice Black, in a dissent in 1952, confessed, "I am aware that our *McCollum* decision . . . has been subjected to a most searching examination throughout the country. Probably few opinions from this Court in recent years have attracted more attention or stirred wider debate."[11] Litigating groups, or anyone else searching the two decisions for auguries, found that the cues were mixed. There was much rhetoric and rationale that encouraged the separationists and discouraged their opponents; a very sizable majority of the Court seemed agreed, at least in principle, on an unqualified, absolute separation of church and state. And yet the willingness to separate aid to individuals from aid to religious institutions left doubts about the application of the separationist words to real cases.

Between 1951 and 1971 the Court did clarify its intentions and stake out the major outlines of a constitutional law of church-state relations. In that period it decided ten cases bearing directly on the "no establishment" clause, exactly twice the number it had decided in the preceding 162 years of activity. Indeed, only one of the ten—the decision in *Zorach* v. *Clauson,* the New York released-time case—came between 1951 and 1961, leaving the 1961–1971 period as the time of major development.[12]

The ten Supreme Court cases fall into a small number of categories of fact. The first of them, *Zorach* v. *Clauson,* held in 1952 that the New York City released time differed enough from that in Champaign to pass the litmus tests of constitutionality. Religious groups held their classes in places other than the public schools, and they, rather than public school authorities, selected teachers and administered the program. A second case, *Walz* v. *Tax Com-*

---

[11] *Zorach* v. *Clauson,* p. 317.
[12] Citations to the cases of 1951 to 1971 (and thus the data of this study) can be found in Appendix i.

21

mission, brought to the Court for the first time (in 1970) the issue of tax exemptions. The Court held that the granting of a tax exemption was not an aid or subsidy to organized religion but simply a legislative decision not to force the church to support the state.

The eight remaining cases fall into two groups of four apiece. Four of them, all decided between 1962 and 1964, dealt with religious observances in the public schools. In 1962 the Court, in *Engel* v. *Vitale,* struck down the saying of a prayer written and recommended to local school districts by the New York Board of Regents:

> Almighty God, we acknowledge our dependence upon Thee, and we beg Thy blessings upon us, our parents, our teachers and our country.

A year later it ruled against reading the Bible and saying the Lord's Prayer in the public schools (the *Schempp* and *Murray* cases). The fact that the observances were formally voluntary did not save them; the Court appeared to take the position that any act of religious instruction or devotion in the public schools would fall. Only Justice Potter Stewart dissented in the three cases. The fourth case in this set was little more than a summary application of these full-length decisions to a case (*Chamberlin* v. *Dade County*) challenging a number of religious practices and observances in the schools of Miami.

The final set of four cases all came within the years 1968 to 1971, and all dealt with government aid to religious schools. The first of the cases, *Board of Education* v. *Allen,* upheld the New York state program in which textbooks for secular subjects were lent to pupils in religious schools. The Court followed the spirit of the *Everson* decision, to hold that the loan program benefitted the children and their parents rather than the religious schools. On June 28, 1971—the end point of this study—the Court disposed of the other three cases. In one set of opinions it voided both the Pennsylvania and Rhode Island programs of aid to private secondary and elementary schools; Pennsylvania proposed to purchase secular educational services for nonpublic schools, and Rhode Island planned to pay salary supplements to some teachers in private schools whose per pupil expenditure fell below the public school average.[13] In both instances the Court found, with only Justice White dissenting in the Rhode Island case, that the

---

[13] The two cases are: *Lemon* v. *Kurtzman* from Pennsylvania and *DiCenso* v. *Robinson* from Rhode Island.

programs advanced the cause of religion, and that the result of the programs was to foster an excessive entanglement between government and religion.

Then, on the same day and by the narrowest of margins—a vote of 5–4—the justices upheld in *Tilton* v. *Richardson* the Higher Education Facilities Act, which the Congress had passed in 1963. It provided construction grants for secular buildings on the campuses of religious colleges. Plaintiffs in Connecticut had challenged the grants to four Catholic institutions for libraries, science buildings, and language laboratories in that state. In certifying the constitutionality of that law the Court distinguished between elementary and secondary schools on the one hand and colleges and universities on the other. Religious education and indoctrination was the chief mission of most of the former, but not of the latter; students in the former, too, were more susceptible to religious influence than were college students. In short, they said, the religious influences, mission, and control of the religious colleges and universities were considerably less marked and less important.

The pattern of these ten Supreme Court cases relates directly to the currents and concerns of their time in American religious life. The first of them, *Zorach* v. *Clauson,* may be considered a follow-up to the *McCollum* decision, and the attempt of released-time advocates to fashion a constitutionally acceptable program in its aftermath. The four prayer and Bible-reading cases of the early 1960s follow the public piety of the 1950s, with its heightened attention to religious training in the schools. The four cases testing aid to religious schools and universities follow the emerging financial crisis in religious education and the political pressures in Congress and state legislatures to act on it. And, just as surely, one can anticipate that the next wave of cases in the 1970s will involve new attempts to find constitutionally acceptable ways of aiding those same schools and universities.

Apart from their obvious importance as the prevailing law of the American Constitution, the ten Supreme Court decisions were in effect a succession of cues and hints to litigating groups and individuals in the period. The first of them, in fact, the New York released-time case, chilled the enthusiasm of the separationists for more test cases. Not only was the decision a retreat from the absolutist implications of the *McCollum* case, but the opinion of Justice Douglas was laced with a language far removed from the separationist severity of *Everson:* "The First Amendment, however, does not say that in every and all respects there shall be a separation of Church and State. Rather, it studiously defines the manner, the specific ways, in which there shall be no concert or union or dependency one on the other. That is the common sense of the matter. Otherwise, the state and religion would be aliens to each other— hostile, suspicious, even unfriendly."[14] Furthermore, noted Mr. Douglas, "We are a religious people whose institutions presuppose a Supreme Being. . . . When the state encourages religious instruction or cooperates with religious authorities by adjusting the schedule of public events to sectarian needs, it follows the best of our traditions."[15] Reasonable men could and did assume that the Court was signalling a sharp turn away from the direction of *Everson* and *McCollum.*

With the advent of the prayer cases a decade later, the Supreme Court began to piece together a more expanded series of tests or doctrines with which to give concrete meaning to the establishment clause of the Constitution. In *Schempp* the Court turned to a double test of the purpose (or intent) and the primary effect of the governmental action. For a law "to withstand the strictures of the Establishment Clause there must be a secular legislative purpose and a primary effect that neither advances nor inhibits religion."[16] In *Walz,* the New York tax exemption case, the Court added another test: whether the end result of the program, the church-state alliance—whatever its intent or purpose—was an "excessive government entanglement with religion."[17] That "entanglement," the Court made clear, must be more than mere aid; it must include a range of possible effects as marked as the setting of state standards in religious schools or the exacerbation of church-state conflict in American politics.

These two tests became the Court's chief guidance in the aid cases in the late sixties and early seventies. Finally, in *Tilton* v. *Richardson,* the Chief Justice pulled them together for the Court, adding another one in passing. Four questions must be considered, he wrote: "First, does the Act reflect a secular legislative purpose? Second, is the primary effect of the Act to advance or inhibit religion? Third, does the administration of the Act foster an excessive entanglement with religion? Fourth, does the implementation of the Act inhibit the free exercise of religion?"[18] The extent to which

[14] *Zorach* v. *Clauson,* p. 312.
[15] *Ibid.,* pp. 313–314.
[16] At p. 222.
[17] At p. 674.
[18] *Tilton* v. *Richardson,* p. 678.

words such as those provide much of a test in constitutional law is a matter of conjecture. Constitutional doctrines by their nature flirt with platitude or circularity; perhaps it is enough if they re-word the central questions in more easily applicable terms. But there is no gainsaying that the words of the Court seemed to many separationists a suggestion of pre-*Zorach* attitudes. That reading, plus a generalized confidence in the libertarianism of the Warren Court, certainly encouraged the pressing of test cases in the 1960s.

Yet, at the same time, the Court assumed a general posture of uncertainty and confusion about the establishment clause. The de-cisions of the 1960s are full of judicial hand-wringing over the difficulties of giving concrete meaning to the clause. Justice White noted in *Board* v. *Allen* that "the line between state neutrality and state support of religion is not easy to locate."[19] Chief Justice Burger wrote in *Walz* that the First Amendment's two clauses deal-ing with religion "are not the most precisely drawn portions of the Constitution."[20] Then in *Lemon* v. *Kurtzman,* the Pennsylvania parochaid case: "Candor compels acknowledgement . . . that we can only dimly perceive the lines of demarcation in this extraordi-narily sensitive area of constitutional law. . . . The line of separa-tion, far from being a 'wall,' is a blurred, indistinct, and variable barrier depending on all the circumstances of a particular relation-ship."[21] It was that sense of judicial groping, plus the seriousness of the financial plight of religious schools, that invited the next wave of litigation in the 1970s on new forms of aid, such as tax credits and tuition payments.

The law of the United States Constitution is not, of course, the totality of American constitutional law. Each of the fifty states has at least one section in its constitution affecting church-state relations. Those sections are as diverse as they are frequent. By far the most usual are clauses that state more fully than the U.S. Constitution a concept of no support for religious groups. For example:

> No money shall ever be taken from the public Treasury, directly or indirectly, in aid of any church, sect, or denomination of reli-gionist, or of any sectarian institution.
>
> (Article I, sec. 1, ch. 2–114 of the
> Georgia constitution)

[19] *Board* v. *Allen,* p. 242.
[20] At p. 668.
[21] *Lemon* v. *Kurtzman,* pp. 612, 614.

In other instances the prohibition against establishment is put in terms of the rights of the individual:

> no man ought to, or of right can be compelled to attend any religious worship, or erect or support any place of worship, or maintain any minister, contrary to the dictates of his conscience.
>
> (Chapter I, art. 3 of the Vermont constitution)

In many of the state documents one also finds more specific clauses prohibiting aid to religious schools, either through a specific sanction or through a protected public school fund.

In any event, the diverse state provisions on church and state could not and have not developed apart from the growth of the First Amendment. Both the state and federal constitutional questions are usually pressed in the same cases. Furthermore, the same social and religious currents shape them, and in the shaping process the sheer intellectual force and the greater visibility of the U.S. Supreme Court's decisions mark them for leadership. Finally, of course, the U.S. Constitution is the supreme law of the land, supreme even over the constitutions of the states. The states may, if they wish, erect a higher wall of separation between church and state, but they are prevented by the U.S. Constitution from setting a lower one. Thus, if policy A violates the U.S. Constitution and policy B does not, the states have no choice but to abandon A, but they may also abandon B, if they choose.

In reality, the law of the state constitutions closely follows the interpretations of the Supreme Court under the U.S. Constitution. Several state decisions on parochaid anticipated both the direction and the rationale of the Supreme Court's decisions in June of 1971. And perhaps because of the force of accommodationist pressure, few states have raised the wall of separation much, if any, above the federal minimum height. Only on the question of transportation and textbooks for children attending religious schools have some states been more separationist than the U.S. Constitution. At least six states prohibit such transportation under the terms of their state constitutions, and several ban the purchase of texts.[22]

[22] See Chapter XIII for a fuller reference to these states; Alaska, Delaware, Hawaii, Missouri, Oklahoma, and Washington do not permit bus rides; New Mexico and Oregon have rejected textbooks. Also for a fuller treatment of the state constitutional provisions, see Anson Phelps Stokes and Leo Pfeffer, *Church and State in the United States* (New York: Harper and Row, 1964) pp. 420–425, and Walter Gellhorn and R. Kent Greenawalt, *The Sectarian College and the Public Purse* (Dobbs Ferry, N.Y.: Oceana, 1970), appendix B.

RELIGIOUS MEMBERSHIPS AND LOYALTIES

These sixty-seven cases have a more literal context and setting, a setting in specific states and localities and in their specific mix of religious traditions and loyalties. Many of the sixty-seven, indeed, grew out of that mix, and more especially out of the public policies those different religious loyalties and interests shape. It is certainly no accident, for instance, that the earliest and most lavish state programs of aid to nonpublic schools came largely from those states of the northeastern United States with large numbers of Roman Catholics and Catholic schools. For in a very immediate way the legal explication of the constitutional relationship between church and state in the United States begins with the translation of religious values and loyalties into public policy claims for some kind of aid or preferred position for the dominant religious tradition or denomination.

In religious composition, the fifty states largely fall into three main groups. There are those states with substantial numbers of Roman Catholics among mixed Protestant populations; they are concentrated heavily in the industrial states of the Northeast and Great Lakes. They range from a state such as Rhode Island, commonly said to be about two-thirds Catholic, to states such as Wisconsin, with Roman Catholic percentages around 25 or 30. Then there are the overwhelmingly Protestant states. Concentrated chiefly in the South, they tend as well to homogeneous Protestant conservatism and fundamentalism; Baptists and Methodists predominate. Thirdly, a group of states concentrated West of the Mississippi are marked by diverse mixtures, both of Catholics and Protestants, and of the assorted Protestant denominations. Within such sweeping generalizations, of course, there is room for considerable diversity and many subtypes. There are also some very notable special cases: the state of New York with its substantial concentration of Jews (probably about 30 percent of the state's population), Utah with its dominant Mormonism, Louisiana with its unique combination of Catholicism in the southern part of the state and Southern Protestantism in the north, and Hawaii with its very special combination of Buddhism and Shintoism on the one hand and Yankee Congregationalism on the other.

The judicial battles described here often do not develop on a statewide level, however. The context or site is frequently a city or a county, and one must therefore be alert to special mixtures

27

and concentrations within the states. New York City's relatively equal division among the three major religious traditions is the most significant case in point. Dade County, Florida, locale of Miami and Miami Beach, similarly has a relatively high percentage of Jews. Within a Southern Protestant state such as Kentucky, one also finds counties in which there are large numbers of Roman Catholics. And there are Protestant counties in heavily Catholic Connecticut.

Thus a fight over bus rides for students going to private religious schools rings and resonates differently from state to state. In Hawaii "private religious school" tends to mean the Congregationalist schools that for so long educated the dominant white, Anglo-Saxon elite of the islands. In Connecticut or Maine bus rides largely mean rides to Roman Catholic schools. Similarly, aid to religious colleges and universities in many states of the country is aid to a mixture of Catholic and Protestant colleges of varying strengths of denominational ties. In South Carolina, however, there is not a single Roman Catholic institution of higher education, and a substantial number of the Protestant colleges were founded as Negro colleges.

Take, for fuller illustration, the context out of which grew the challenge to Louisiana's 1970 statute that assisted private schools in the state with salary supplements for teachers of nonreligious subjects. In most other states such legislation would have been simply an attempt to rescue financially strapped religious schools. But in Louisiana it was passed in the aftermath of court orders in 1969 and 1970 intended to hasten desegregation in the public schools. Private academies were springing up, and public school pupils and teachers were moving to them. Many superintendents, principals, and teachers who attempted to carry out the court orders faced mounting public criticism, even dismissal in some cases. Others who remained in the public schools were demoralized by the new tensions and educational problems resulting from the integration. And yet, at the same time, the Catholics of the state were maintaining an extensive parochial school system that shared the financial problems of parochial systems all over the country.

Not surprisingly, perhaps, such a complex setting gave rise not to one, but to two court challenges to the salary supplements. The local American Civil Liberties Union and NAACP affiliates brought suit in 1970 in federal district court under the First and Fourteenth Amendments, raising both the church-state and the

28

equal protection issues. At approximately the same time a group of public school leaders, working through the Louisiana Teachers Association, organized a challenge to the aid program in the state courts. Although it, too, raised issues of separation (under the Louisiana constitution), its separationist position rested far less than did that of the federal court suit on convictions about separation of church and state. The public school leadership feared that in a relatively poor state such aid to nonpublic schools signaled the end of committed support for the public schools. It was sure that declining appropriations would match declining enrollments and confidence in the public schools. It was this latter suit in which the state Supreme Court struck down the statute by a 4–3 vote.[23]

The context in which these sixty-seven cases arose was, therefore, of many dimensions—contitutional, religious, demographic—and of great diversity within dimensions. But constitutional conflict is made not of background and context but of specific individuals and groups seeking redress of particular wrongs. Dominating the aggrieved actors in these cases are three national litigating groups: the American Civil Liberties Union, the American Jewish Congress, and Americans United for Separation of Church and State. Their activities in these cases dwarf those of all other participants. One quite properly begins an account of church-state litigation with them.

[23] *Seegers* v. *Parker.*

III | THE SEPARATIONIST GROUPS

There is often in constitutional litigation an initiating role in search of an initiator. The judicial drama may go on with the role essentially unfilled—or with it filled willy-nilly. Plaintiffs come to the court to seek redress or to enforce a law, and in doing so they raise, more or less in passing, the broader questions of public law. But this is a sporadic, even haphazard way of bringing constitutional issues to appellate courts. Furthermore, it is often done badly. Counsel in such cases are often inexperienced in constitutional law, the trial court record on the constitutional issues is nonexistent or terribly thin, and the plaintiff and his attorney may be willing to jettison the constitutional question if it conflicts with the immediate goal of redress or remedy. Small wonder, therefore, that organized interests have in certain areas of constitutional litigation increasingly seized the initiative and started to bring constitutional litigation in an orderly, purposeful way. Probably at no other point in the judicial process—except perhaps at the initial selection of the judges—can group activities have such an impact.

Not all groups enjoy equal opportunities for these agenda-setting initiatives, however. The "fates" of adversary litigation determine largely which interest, and thus which groups, are cast in the plaintiff role and which must undertake the defense. The major initiatives rest with those cast in the plaintiff's role, and in civil liberties cases it is usually the minority interests that enjoy that advantage. Those minorities, having failed to stop some public policy in the more usual political processes—be it a ban on some form of speech or aid to nonpublic schools—assert that the policies violate their constitutionally granted rights. It is that access to the judiciary as a plaintiff with all the options and initiatives of a plaintiff, just as much as the sympathy of judges for minority rights, that lies at the root of minorities' success in the judicial forum.

In these 67 church-state cases it is chiefly the separationist interests that enjoy the plaintiff's position. In 53 of them (79.1 percent) the plaintiffs are separationists, and if one eliminates the 9 friendly

30

suits, 91.4 percent (53 of 58) had separationist plaintiffs. By logical necessity, the defense position is overwhelmingly accommodationist. Furthermore, the defense in church-state cases almost invariably falls either to a government official or officials, or to some governmental body whom the plaintiffs accuse of making an unconstitutional alliance with religion. Both because of the limitations of the defense role and because of the domination of the defense in these cases by governmental bodies and officials, group activities on behalf of accommodationist interests have been less persistent and pervasive than those of the separationist groups.[1]

Three groups have dominated separationist activity in these cases: the American Civil Liberties Union and its affiliates, the American Jewish Congress, and Protestants and Other Americans United for Separation of Church and State, lately known as Americans United.[2] In only sixteen of these sixty-seven cases, indeed, are there no signs of activity by at least one of the three. No other groups or individuals have been remotely as influential in shaping the direction of church-state law in recent years.

THE THREE LEADING GROUPS

Beyond the shared national reference in their names, the three leading separationist groups have little in common, ideologically or organizationally. Both the American Civil Liberties Union and the American Jewish Congress originated in the turmoil of World War I, the ACLU to guard the liberties of Americans against a repetition of the incursions of that period, and the AJC to work for the goal of a Jewish homeland in the negotiations at Versailles. Whie the goals and missions of both have shifted with new times and events, they both sustain missions that extend far beyond church-state issues. Americans United, on the other hand, has from its origin in 1947 been exclusively concerned with questions of separation. The groups' clienteles and membership obviously differ sharply, and their organizational styles vary from the somewhat casually decentralized operations of the ACLU to the centralized, even autocratic style of Americans United.

The agreement of the three groups on church-state issues in

---

[1] Accommodationist group activity will be discussed in Chapter VIII.

[2] POAU formally became AU in 1972 after using the AU name informally for some years before then. The name change reflects the broadening membership and outlook of the organization.

31

American courts is all the more remarkable in view of these differences. In the cases raising issues of separationism in the American appellate courts, the ACLU, AJC, and AU are virtually always on the separationist side; in only two instances have they not been. A state affiliate of the ACLU supported the University of Washington against Protestant fundamentalist charges that its course in the Bible as literature amounted to the establishment and support of a particular theological view of the Bible, and AU opposed a challenge in the Supreme Court to tax exemptions for places of religious worship.[3] In short, the three groups are united by the consistent and virtually absolutist approach they share to the separation of church and state.

To put the point another way, it is not easy to find concrete issues on which the three groups differ. They do differ on questions of tax exemptions for religious bodies. The ACLU takes the absolute position: no exemptions on any property held by religious groups. AU favors exemptions on the property used for religious purposes, and AJC is unofficially divided and uncertain, officially mute. As a consequence, the ACLU and AU ended up on different sides in the tax exemption case before the U.S. Supreme Court, *Walz* v. *Tax Commission*. That case was, in fact, the only one of the sixty-seven in which two of these three groups disagreed. While the groups have also differed on the question of nuns and other religious persons teaching in public schools—AU taking the absolutist position contra, and the other two opposing only the wearing of religious garb—those differences have not resulted in division in a case.

While the separationist position may not differ, the underlying separationist philosophies and motives do. The ACLU's separationism grows out of a number of traditions. It has within it the separationism of Madison and Jefferson and other children of the Enlightenment, today most evident in the New England tradition of the Congregationalists, Unitarians, and Universalists. Within the ACLU one also finds the separationism of agnosticism and militant atheism, with its rejection of religion in all kinds and forms. Between and close to these two traditions—and perhaps forming the

---

[3] The two cases are *Calvary Bible* v. *Board of Regents* and *Walz* v. *Tax Commission*. The ACLU position in the former was in defense of academic freedom; AU in the latter maintained that while property owned by churches and used for nonreligious purposes ought to be taxed, places of worship ought not to be.

ACLU mainstream—is the separationism of secular humanism. It is skeptical and freethinking, searching for universals other than those of conventional religion, and often finding them in a humanism that merges comfortably into social and political liberalism. It is the tradition of the Ethical Culture Society, of the more liberal Unitarian societies, and of untold numbers of unorganized but unbelieving Americans. Taken together, it is a separationism tied closely to the rejection of dogmatic and authoritative religions, especially when their power is coupled to the coercive power of the state.

The separationism of the American Jewish Congress springs directly from the experience of Reform and Conservative Judaism. The public alliances with religion in the United States have almost invariably been alliances with Christian religions. Jewish separationism is, in short, impelled by the vulnerabilities of a religious minority that understands that accommodations between church and state have in the past too often served as vehicles of majority religious intolerance. Even though Orthodox Jews, whose lives are more fully contained within a homogeneous Jewish community, reject such a separationism, it clearly remains the dominant point of view of the rest of American Judaism.

In contrast to these separationist traditions based on minority logic and theological liberalism, Americans United speaks the separationism of conservative, traditionalist, and fundamentalist Protestantism. Unifying this varied and complex separationism is an underlying, pervasive fear of Roman Catholic social and political power. Whether it takes the shape of fundamentalist "antipopery" or a more muted concern about the implications of Catholic majorities, the fear persists and recurs. It may also be viewed as a fear of the loss of Protestant hegemony in American society, for a good deal of traditional separationism has buttressed that superiority— in the Protestant domination of American elites, in the Protestant authorship of statute law touching moral matters, and in the prevailing Protestantism of public religiosity. Indeed, the initial name of the organization—*Protestants* and Other Americans United— bespeaks something of the tradition and its implications.

That fear of Catholic power, and the resulting charges of bigotry, has made the separationism of Americans United more vulnerable and contentious than that of the ACLU and the AJC. Of the historic fear of Catholicism in AU there can be no doubt. For a number of years Paul Blanshard, whose *American Freedom and*

Catholic Power[4] was unquestionably the most widely read anti-Catholic polemic of the post-World War II years, was a long time POAU staff member. The organization's periodical, *Church and State,* has long targeted the Roman Catholic Church as the prime enemy, and both AU staffers and members are fond of citing "Spain" as the horrible example of church-state alliance. During the chilliest years of the Cold War, a few conservative local POAU worthies could even be heard allowing that Catholic power actually constituted a greater threat than communism to the American democracy.

All of this is not to suggest that the fear of Catholicism was petty, petulant, or devious. It was unquestionably founded on honestly held, if somewhat outdated, views of monolithic Catholic power. Much of the depth of passionate feeling, too, reflected the most deeply held moral and theological views. Countless AU members did profoundly resent the use of their tax monies to serve in any way the advantage of a church they believed to have perverted the tenets and practice of Christianity. Nor can it be denied that this fear of Catholicism ebbed through the 1950s and 1960s. That change may have resulted in part from a reaction to the criticism of more liberal Protestants who resigned their early membership. In part, too, it reflected the changing stance of the Roman Catholic church in the days of Pope John and the Vatican Council. And yet AU does retain some of the old shrill anti-Catholic tone; it still appeals (however covertly and through "code" phrases such as "Spain") to fears of Catholicism rather than to a separationist commitment. And even into the 1970s the editors of *Church and State,* the AU magazine, retain a fondness for pictures of public officials kissing episcopal rings.[5]

These are questions of underlying value, of motivation, even of rhetorical nuance. More serious and immediate for the business of litigating church-state issues is the widely held belief that AU applies its church-state convictions with varying degrees of fervor. It is indeed true that AU has not found it easy to challenge Protes-

[4] Boston: Beacon Press, 1949. The substance of Blanshard's argument appeared earlier in articles in *The Nation.* The articles were serialized in twelve segments published between November 1, 1947, and June 5, 1948, in vols. 155 and 156.

[5] On POAU and the charges of anti-Catholicism, see "POAU in Crisis," *Newsweek* (October 5, 1964), pp. 102–103, and Richard E. Morgan, "Backs to the Wall: A Study in the Contemporary Politics of Church and State," Ph.D. dissertation, Columbia University, 1967.

tant influences in public institutions—the classic instance being prayer and Bible-reading in public schools. In fact, in an early Kentucky case challenging the hiring of nuns as public teachers, the local POAU attorney, a U.S. Congressman, included in his complaint the objection that the nuns failed to read the then-mandated daily chapters from the Bible. (National POAU leadership did, however, move quickly to alter the complaint.)[6] In such instances AU came perilously close to accepting Protestant alliances with the state while condemning those of Catholicism. By the 1960s, however, AU had struck a more consistent position. It supported—albeit with considerable internal grumbling—the Supreme Court's decisions on prayer in the public schools, and it opposed attempts to reverse the decision by constitutional amendment.

DIVERSITY AND INTENSITY IN SEPARATIONISM

The definitions and applications of separationism by the three groups differ with differences in their clienteles. Furthermore, each has within it considerable diversity of views. Within the ACLU the differences generally are those of the statewide affiliates. For example, affiliates have differed on both sides of national ACLU policy that nuns may be hired as public school teachers but that they may not teach in religious garb. At least one affiliate has argued that nuns ought not to be hired under any circumstances, and another has objected to the qualification about religious garb and would hire without it. The AJC, too, has periodically faced opposition to its absolute separationism within the Jewish community. Some Jewish parents, for instance, find no objections to religious holidays being observed in the public schools, so long as Channukah is celebrated on a "free and equal" basis. AU has in the 1960s opposed amendments to the Constitution that would permit prayer in public schools, even though that stand has brought a steady stream of resignations and letters of concern about AU's succumbing to the Red Peril and ecumenical heresies.

For whatever reasons, the ACLU and the AJC have maintained their separationist position with fewer compromises than has AU. The special problem of AU may be related to a number of factors. As an organization devoted exclusively to separationism, its membership is uniformly and intensely interested in church-state mat-

---

[6] The complaint mentioned was the one filed in *Rawlings* v. *Butler.*

ters. In an organization such as the ACLU, members with less than absolutist positions on church-state matters may well have a greater interest in other civil liberties issues. Furthermore, AU has very special problems in conflicting clienteles. Its main membership comes from conservative and fundamentalist Protestantism; local AU leaders very frequently are local Protestant pastors, very often Baptist or Methodist pastors. And it gets a good share of additional support from the Southern Jurisdiction of the Scottish Rite Masons. Those influences dispose it to one kind of separationism, but its desire to maintain good working relationships with other Protestant groups (especially the National Council of Churches) and with the ACLU and the AJC pull it to another.

While the separationist commitments of AU may strike even some allies as excessively emotional, those of the national ACLU appear to others to be too casual. The enthusiasm for and commitment to church-state litigation on the part of the national ACLU has unquestionably declined since the early 1960s. One can search in vain for even the smallest tidbit of church-state news in most issues of the Union's monthly, *Civil Liberties*. A number of recent annual reports have also failed to touch on church-state issues. Not even the new controversies over state aid to religious schools in the late sixties and early seventies rekindled any substantial passion for the question. Viewed broadly, it is a problem of priorities, of the choice among competing organizational goals. AU, having no other concerns, does not face the issue. The ACLU, as a general civil liberties organization, does. Unity of goal thus creates one set of problems for AU, and diversity fosters another within the ACLU.

The downgrading of church-state issues in the ACLU reflects its strong recent move to something approaching political activism. That in itself has been a controversial move, and one that has taken the ACLU away from its traditional concerns.[7] Its new involvements increasingly center around more contemporary questions, the "now" issues, such as the draft, new forms of dissent, opposition to the war in Southeast Asia, abortion, surveillance, poverty, election law, minority rights, and sexual freedom and equality. At the same time, questions of church-state relations have

[7] On that controversy see the articles of Joseph W. Bishop, Jr., "The Reverend Mr. Coffin, Dr. Spock, and the ACLU," *Harper's* 236 (May 1968), 57–60ff.; "Politics and ACLU," *Commentary* 52 (December 1971), 50–58.

36

become low-priority, if not passé, concerns. Indeed, at least one national official considers the church-state issue to be as quaintly irrelevant and dated as prohibition.

The ACLU's demotion of church-state concern has been made possible, or at least more palatable, by two mitigating circumstances. The national officers and legal staff know that the American Jewish Congress will continue to patrol this area of constitutional concern with a fervor, a policy, and a competence that is more than merely acceptable to the ACLU. Furthermore, the national ACLU's loss of interest in church-state coincided with a decentralization of decisions on litigation to the local affiliates, and those affiliates are far more enthusiastic than the national headquarters in pursuing church-state issues. A simmering dispute between the national ACLU and a number of local affiliates on the priority given church-state issues has thus been easily resolved. It can at the same time be a low-priority item for the national organization and a high-priority item for a number of affiliates, especially those in states where public policy most invites action.

None of this, however, appears to have been decided formally within the ACLU. Like priority decisions in any other large organization, this one was set in the course of making a number of other specific decisions. In particular, the makers of the immediate decisions allocating time and energy, especially the legal director, Melvin Wulf, and the three general counsel, shaped the shift in priorities. Certainly at no time had either the Church-State Committee or the national board confronted the issue in any explicit way. Had the organization not had the alternate avenue of action—the affiliates—it would, like any multipurpose organization, have had to face a most divisive and difficult set of decisions.

POLICY MAKING IN THE THREE GROUPS

Nothing illustrates the organizational differences among the ACLU, AJC, and AU as clearly as the ways in which they go about making policy. And no policy crisis involved all three of them in reevaluation and indecision as deeply as the one in the late 1960s over tax exemptions for places of religious worship. The *Walz* case, the occasion for the decision, began so quietly as to catch the groups unprepared, but ultimately it opened up the one issue that most threatened their internal cohesion and their external agreement.

37

Within AU, Franklin Salisbury, the organization's general counsel, prepared and printed an amicus curiae brief for the U.S. Supreme Court that was pro-Walz. Before he could file it, however, Dr. Glenn Archer, AU's first and only executive director, decided not to file it. The Supreme Court's deadline for filing was extended, Salisbury redrafted and reprinted a brief, and AU submitted it— this time against Walz and in favor of tax exemptions for church property used for religious purposes! The decision was apparently Archer's, perhaps after consultations with AU leaders. All evience suggests an Archer decision, and it would have been consistent with other reports on the autocratic decision making within AU.

All questions concerning what AU will do or what positions will be taken are decided in Archer's office. From his desk he gets in touch with those people whose importance to the organization requires that they be consulted. If there is divergence of opinion or objection to what he proposes, it can usually be adjusted before the proposal comes before the board or the executive committee.[8] Very possibly the sober second thoughts in *Walz* had been occasioned by the realization that a number of AU's most loyal supporters, such as the Seventh Day Adventists, favored tax exemptions for places of worship. Since early publicity on the case had indicated that Walz consented to the filing of an amicus brief on his side, interested parties within AU may well have taken the opportunity to speak for themselves to Archer.

At AJC headquarters in New York, counsel and organization officers were early alerted to the emerging issue. Leo Pfeffer, long the AJC's leading church-state attorney and probably the country's leading church-state expert, advised staying out of the case entirely. So did Will Maslow, the AJC general counsel. Pfeffer probably opposed tax exemptions for any property held by religious organizations, but realized that such a position would be hypocritical as long as the AJC itself held a tax exemption. Other AJC leaders, both in and out of New York, favored the exemption, some arguing, in fact, that to deny it would infringe the religious freedom of religious groups. ("The power to tax is the power to control," wrote one AJC activist.) In short, the AJC was badly divided on the question; in the middle of the indecision, for example, its Commission on Law and Social Action divided 5–4 in favor

[8] Morgan, "Backs to the Wall," p. 143.

of opposing exemptions. It also became increasingly apparent that the AJC's major competitor groups, the American Jewish Committee and the Anti-Defamation League of B'nai B'rith, would not oppose tax exemptions. Thus the decision to abstain, apparently arrived at by consensus after discussions among AJC counsel and the organization's leadership, was a logical one.

While the AJC was undergoing its agonies of decision in 1969, the national American Civil Liberties Union was being literally whipsawed by the issue. The openness and democracy of ACLU decision making brings all major disagreement into view, and the emergence of the *Walz* case caught it without a comprehensive policy on tax exemption for religious property. Worse, it caught the ACLU between regular meetings of its board of directors, the body that usually sets such policies. Faced with the issue in mid-1969, the executive committee of the board first took a "soft" and very pragmatic position. Reckoning that the Supreme Court was "almost doubtless going to affirm the lower court," it voted to take a stand against tax exemption under the establishment clause, but to urge the Court, if it was inclined to permit exemptions, to permit them only on the ground that the counterthrust of the free exercise clause sanctioned them. On September 4th the ACLU staff reported to the executive committee that it could not enlist a knowledgeable church-state attorney to write a brief incorporating that "two-pronged" position. Leo Pfeffer of the AJC was among those in attendance, and he argued that the position was indefensible both intellectually and tactically. To take a separationist position and at the same time to suggest an acceptable ground for the contrary position, he argued, was to invite the latter. The executive committee reversed itself, and in early October the board ratified the decision after heated debate and by a vote of 33 to 24. The ACLU thus supported Walz's challenge to exemptions, and Pfeffer helped write the brief.

As the separate reactions to the emerging *Walz* case indicate, policies are set within the AJC and AU a good deal less formally and less democratically than in the ACLU. Decision-making in AU tends to be very greatly concentrated in the strong person of its executive director, Glenn Archer. Both in the detail and breadth of his concern, it is not much of an exaggeration to say that all major operating decisions are his. His role in policy decisions is strengthened by the fact that he is a lawyer and former dean of the Washburn University Law School in Topeka, Kansas. The decision-making elite is broader at the American Jewish Congress, with informal influence and consultation the watchword. But it is at the ACLU that pluralism and formal democratic processes flourish; they are, of course, an integral part of the ethos to which the ACLU is dedicated. The national board remains the final decision-making center for ACLU policy, supplemented at times (such as those in *Walz*) by its executive committee.[9]

The ACLU, alone of the three groups, also experimented with bringing church-state experts into the policy-making process. Its Church-State Committee (known earlier as the Religion Panel) was active chiefly in the middle 1950s, but fell into inactivity by the late fifties, a period of mounting criticism of the ACLU's absolutist position on church-state matters.[10] Perhaps in response to the criticism, the committee was reactivated in 1960. It was also reconstituted, for in addition to continuing separationist members such as Pfeffer and Kenneth Greenawalt (the ACLU's attorney before the U.S. Supreme Court in the New York released-time case), it also counted a number of members more closely identified with religious groups and with a less rigorous separationism. By the next year, indeed, the committee had at least four Roman Catholic members, and the shift in policy preferences on the committee had become so marked that Pfeffer resigned in a public letter to Patrick M. Malin, the ACLU's executive director. Among the issues that impelled his resignation was a committee decision that the religious composition of the community ought to be a factor in determining the observance of religious holidays in the schools.

The reconstruction of the Church-State Committee thus led generally to a reconsideration of ACLU separationist policy—as it was probably intended to. It did not lead to an alteration of that policy; that was prevented by staunch support from a combination of local affiliates and the national board for the traditional absolutist position. In 1962 the board rejected by votes of 13–1 and 14–0 the committee's recommendations that bus rides and textbooks for parochial school pupils not be considered a violation of constitutional separation. (The committee itself was badly divided on the

[9] These accounts of decision making in the three organizations at the time of *Walz* depend chiefly on my examination of the files and papers of the organizations.

[10] See, for example. Robert F. Drinan, "Religion and the ACLU," *America* (September 27, 1958), pp. 663–665.

recommendations, having approved them 6–5 and 5–4.) However representative the committee was of the religious communities and constituencies, it clearly was not representative of ACLU membership or leadership. The 1964 biennial conference, indeed, concerned about national drift on church-state policy, resolved that "We need a clear articulation of the goals and principles of the ACLU in the area of government and organized religion and with all deliberate speed." The committee set about drafting that "articulation" for the 1966 conference; from there it went to board meetings several times in 1967. Ultimately the board referred it back to the committee for further work and consideration, and thus to a quiet and unceremonious burial. So it was that the ACLU, for all its elaborate policy-making machinery, faced the *Walz* case without either a comprehensive church-state policy or a policy on tax exemptions, and was forced to make ad hoc policy.

The ACLU's exercise in reconsideration underscores the thoroughness and openness of its deliberative processes. It indicates, too, the overwhelming strength of an absolutist separationism within its membership and affiliates. The Church-State Committee of the early 1960s brought to ACLU deliberations an expertise and a breadth of informed opinion that it had not earlier known on church-state questions. Aside from distinguished counsel, such as Pfeffer and Greenawalt, the committee at various times in the early 1960s included the associate editor of *Commonweal*, professors at Villanova and Fordham, an executive of the National Council of Churches, several ministers, the religion editor of a publishing house, a chaplain at Columbia University, and a professor of religion. But it was the values of the vast membership that prevailed, just as surely as they prevailed at the AJC and AU. Decision-making styles and apparatuses differ greatly among the three organizations, but in their separate ways they all reflect membership views on church-state separation. It is a common sensitivity to those views that has kept all three on relatively unchanging separationist courses over recent decades.

DECISION MAKING ON LITIGATION

Important as general policy issues are, specific decisions on litigation—the origination of a case, entry into an ongoing case, and the subsequent control of the organization's role in it—are even more important for constitutional change and the judicial process.

41

Again, the patterns of decision making in the three leading separationist groups differ. The American Civil Liberties Union decentralizes litigation decisions to local affiliates; the American Jewish Congress and Americans United do not.

The three groups, however, do have in common the problem of limited resources, and thus the need to choose among possibilities for litigation. Their organizational names carry an impressive ring, and as interest-group activity in litigation grows, "devil" theorists imagine great legal behemoths leading assaults on the judiciary with unlimited resources. The truth of the matter is vastly less impressive. AU has recently functioned with one legal counsel, aided of course by the legal experience of the executive director. The legal staffs of both the national ACLU and the AJC's Commission on Law and Social Action (which handles the AJC role in this litigation) number no more than three or four. Both have general counsel and prominent attorneys who give legal aid and advice, but the full-time working staffs are not large, and in both cases they are handling much more than church-state questions. The entire annual budget of the legal staff of the national ACLU during the 1960s was not a great deal more than $50,000.

Scarce resources, therefore, force hard choices among possible cases. So do the strategies of the groups as they try to pick and frame litigation to maximize their separate, often diverse, goals. So also does the need to sustain satisfactory relationships within the group, especially with local members and chapters, and with external, tangent groups.

Litigation decisions within the ACLU in the decade of the 1960s and into the 1970s were by far the most decentralized of the three separationist groups. It was not always so, however; in the 1950s most decisions to inaugurate or enter cases were made in New York, in the legal department. The inability of the national staff to manage the growing volume of legal business, combined with growing pressures from the local affiliates for greater freedom, produced a rapid decentralization. By the 1970s, ACLU policy was to permit the affiliates to litigate on their own initiative, with the one great reservation that the national organization was to approve appeals to the U.S. Supreme Court. Says the *Guide for ACLU Litigation* of March 1970: "No affiliate or chapter of the Union shall file any petitions for certiorari, jurisdictional statements, or briefs in the United States Supreme Court, except to initiate review when time requires it, without prior opportunity for review by the

42

national legal office."[11] Furthermore, the *Guide* recognizes that the national office has "a special interest" in certain types of cases:

a. cases in which federal statutes or federal executive officers are involved, particularly if they concern new, untested, controversial, or complicated federal statutes;
b. cases involving novel applications of the Constitution;
c. cases which, though seemingly of local application, draw into issue important matters of ACLU policy that are of interest to other affiliates;
d. cases raising unusual civil liberties issues not previously faced by the Union.

In these instances the national ACLU reserves the right to initiate litigation, and must be informed when an affiliate decides to litigate. The national organization reserves the right to act when a case is interstate in character and involves a number of affiliates, when an affiliate asks it to, and when an affiliate fails to act in a matter the national organization thinks important. The *Guide*, finally, suggests policy limits to the affiliates' freedom to litigate, but these are more in the nature of hortative admonitions. It urges them, for example, to be selective and use their resources on "cases which have some reasonable promise of having broad impact on other cases," and it counsels them to make prudent, tactical judgments.

In reality—at least in the area of church and state—only the limitation on action in the U.S. Supreme Court really limits the freedom of ACLU affiliates. The national legal office, given its lower level of concern for church-state questions, is rarely in a position of trying to jog an affiliate into action. More commonly it tries to discourage action, although discouragement is not always easy or successful. In the celebrated test case over the reading of the New York Regents' Prayer in the schools of Mineola (*Engel v. Vitale*), the New York Civil Liberties Union sponsored the case. Leo Pfeffer of the American Jewish Congress and some national ACLU leaders tried to squelch the case because they thought the facts of the case, the unchurched plaintiffs, and the quality of local counsel promised a debacle in the courts. They did not succeed,

[11] The *Guide* is a mimeographed ACLU document dated March 1970. Note that in the *Guide* it is only the "affiliates," usually statewide or metropolitan in scope (e.g., The Greater Pittsburgh Civil Liberties Union and The Minnesota Civil Liberties Union), that are granted autonomy. The ACLU "chapters" are not.

43

of course, and it went forward to an eventually successful outcome in the U.S. Supreme Court.

The effective decentralization of ACLU litigation in church-state cases becomes apparent when one looks at the national and affiliate involvement by seven-year periods between 1951 and 1971. The shift has been virtually total. All four ACLU interventions between 1951 and 1957 were national, but six of seven between 1958 and 1964 were by affiliates, and so were eighteen of nineteen in the period from 1965 to 1971. That does not mean that the national legal office had no contact with the cases. In some instances local attorneys, executive directors, or legal directors sought legal help; more often they sought financial help. In most instances, the national office found out about the litigation either after the decision was made to litigate, or after the suit was filed. Thus a letter from Spencer Coxe, director of the Philadelphia affiliate, to Melvin Wulf, national ACLU legal director, about the origin of the testing (*Lemon* v. *Kurtzman*) of the Pennsylvania parochaid statue:

> In view of the nation-wide importance of this suit, I believe you should be fully notified of our intention, and I would value any suggestions you, Marvin Karpatkin, or anyone else might care to make, now or later. Once the lawyer has been chosen, I am sure he would welcome suggestions from New York; in this regard, the American Jewish Congress will be soliciting Leo Pfeffer's help, but our plans at the moment are that the case should be run by Pennsylvania counsel.[12]

The opportunities for the national ACLU office to shape litigation are, in general, sporadic, limited, and even unpredictable. In view of its preoccupation with other legal issues, it does not object.

To some extent, the decentralization of litigation within the ACLU springs naturally from its dependence on local cooperating attorneys who serve in ACLU cases without fee. They are generally active in the affiliate, or at least known to the affiliate's officers and legal director. Often the affiliate has a legal committee that makes the decision to litigate in the first place, and the cooperating attorneys often serve on it. Their ties, recruitment, and loyalty are local, and the national Union has little leverage over them. Even when they seek help from the national legal office, it is able to do little more for them than review the draft of a brief, send them

[12] Letter of July 3, 1968, in ACLU archives, Princeton University Library, Princeton, N.J.

44

copies of old briefs, and direct them to the expertise of the American Jewish Congress.

In contrast, the major decisions on litigation in both the AJC and AU are centralized in the national organization. In both instances, too, the dominant decision maker was in that position for the entire 1951–1971 period—Leo Pfeffer with the AJC, and Glenn Archer in AU. Both organizations have local chapters or organizations in various localities around the country, but these have no authority to bring litigation in the name of the organization. But aside from the central fact of centralization, there are other differences in decision-making on litigation between AJC and AU. Within the AJC national organization, Pfeffer's voice on basic litigation decisions was the dominant but not the only voice; the AJC hierarchy is a complex and well-institutionalized one. AU, on the other hand, remains very much a one-man organization— smaller, more single-minded, and in many ways an extension of the will of its one executive director. Formally, decisions on litigation do rest with AU's national board, and some may indeed be made there. But the board and the legal department notwithstanding, Archer maintains a very tight control.[13]

Once the major decision to begin or enter a case has been made, however, AU and AJC policies diverge. Within the American Jewish Congress control over litigation rests with the national organization and its staff in New York. Local contacts, field representatives, and ordinary members often carry some of the load; in some instances they may even furnish the attorney of record. But legal direction—and often the major legal work—remained primarily in the hands of the CLSA staff in the period between 1951 and 1971, especially in the hands of Leo Pfeffer and his successor as head of CLSA, Joseph Robison. Americans United, once it has decided to involve itself, more customarily retains local counsel and entrusts legal decisions to him. National AU officials—Glenn Archer in particular—do not completely abdicate control of the litigation, especially in decisions whether or not to appeal the case. (Often those decisions are, in fact, made in terms of whether to continue AU financial support or general involvement in the litigation.) But local attorneys make a greater percentage of the legal decisions in AU cases. It is one reason why AU has been able to get along for most of the time since 1951 with a legal staff of one.

[13] Again, see Morgan, "Backs to the Wall," pp. 146 and 201.

45

So neither the AJC nor AU has the problem the ACLU has with litigating local units. Yet each does have substantial problems with its local chapters. For AU the problem is most often one of aggressive, deeply involved local members and leaders. Local AU members may be outraged at some immediate incident, as, for example, the decision of a county commission to contract with Roman Catholic nuns for the management of the local publicly owned hospital. They want immediate AU help in seeking immediate relief or remedy, and it does not in the least dull their passion or satisfy their complaint to be told that the constitutional issue is either settled or unpromising. Alternatively, the "scenario" may go another way. Local AU members and leaders may in the same circumstance form an ad hoc organization, hire an attorney, and bring a suit. Having read of AU's legal activities in *Church and State,* they then go to the national organization with a plea for support. In either case national headquarters finds itself under considerable pressure from the membership to be involved.

The AJC's problem with its locals is quite the opposite: the hesitance of local Jews and Jewish communities, even of local AJC members, to be involved in the litigation that the national AJC would like to undertake. As a member of the National Community Relations Advisory Council, a coordinating organization of national and local Jewish organizations, the AJC subscribes to its policy that member organizations will clear any actions they wish to take in a locality with the local Jewish Community Relations Council or some other body representative of the local Jewish community. On a number of occasions the local community has demurred in response to AJC soundings. When Pfeffer inquired about possible AJC involvement in a challenge to Bible-reading in the schools of Nashville, one local Jewish leader responded: "We have a very small Jewish population in this county with less than one percent of all the children in the public schools. . . . My own particular attitude is that . . . I feel we, who are the People of the Book, surely should not object to the Bible being read in the schools." Another wrote, "I am certain that the local Jewish community would not support, certainly not with any unanimity of feeling, any action." As a result the case went ahead without AJC participation, and certainly at a far lower level of legal sophistication than Pfeffer and the AJC would have brought to it.[14]

[14] *Carden* v. *Bland.* The letter quoted is in the files of the AJC.

Local Jewish communities most frequently believe that litigation will disturb the modus vivendi they have struck with Christian majorities. Their objections repeatedly reflect the fear that a suit will unleash or exacerbate anti-Semitism. Coupled with those concerns are the more general tactical differences between the AJC and other groups representing Jewish interests. The American Jewish Committee and the Anti-Defamation League of B'nai B'rith reject what they believe to be the AJC's excessive willingness to resort to litigation. Their preference is for lower-profile negotiations and conciliations. The combination of fears within the local Jewish community and the organizational opposition of the two organizations constitutes major limits to national AJC decisions on litigation. About them, Will Maslow, general counsel of the AJC, has written:

> If the plaintiff is identified as a Jew or his cause is publicly sponsored by a Jewish organization, the local Jewish community council may fear that other Jews, not involved in the litigation, may become the targets of ostracism or boycott or that latent anti-Semitism may erupt or even that the harmonious relations existing between Christians and Jews in a community may be disrupted.
>
> AJC has always believed that such fears are exaggerated and reflect a basic psychological insecurity of a minority group. We are convinced that whatever hostile reactions occur will quickly subside and that in the long run a religiously-oriented community will respect a courageous and principled defense of religious liberty by a Jewish organization.[15]

Local resistance to litigation persists, however, and so too does the persistent tension, even feuding, between the AJC and the other two groups. In part those disagreements relate to personal antagonisms and real or imagined insults, but in part they reflect very basic disagreements over the use of litigation to achieve group objectives.[16]

[15] Maslow, "The Legal Defense of Religious Liberty—The Strategy and Tactics of the American Jewish Congress," mimeographed paper presented at the annual meeting of the American Political Science Association in St. Louis, Mo. (September 6–9, 1961), p. 5.

[16] The American Jewish Committee and the Anti-Defamation League withdrew from early membership in the NCRAC, at least in part because of that organization's decision to assign to the American Jewish Congress major responsibility for litigating the rights and interests of American Jewry.

OTHER SEPARATIONIST GROUPS

While no groups in the separationist camp put all of their efforts into litigation, the ACLU, AJC, and AU have individually and collectively made by far the greatest commitment to action in the judicial process. Other separationist groups, however, dip occasionally into the judicial process. Some do so with a fierce abandon; others do so cautiously and only in the company of more experienced litigators. None of them has had an impact on the litigating of church-state issues even remotely approaching the impact of the three leading groups. It is probably no exaggeration to say that their efforts taken together did not really match those of any one of the leading three between 1951 and 1971.

The Atheists

Especially in the years before the Second World War, Joseph Lewis and the Freethinkers of America made numerous separationist forays into the courts of New York. The complete canon of Lewis litigation is not easy to establish, but its targets ranged from the inclusion of a reference to God in the pledge of allegiance to the flag, to the presence of a chapel at the state prison at Clinton (see box). Lewis apparently won none of them. Although he is represented in this set of cases only by his attempt to alter the pledge to the flag,[17] his most important contribution to the litigation of the period may well have been his aborted challenge to the New York City released-time program. The AJC and ACLU were appalled at the case—Lewis was an atheist, had no children in the city's schools, and did not even reside in the city. They pleaded with him to withdraw it, and Lewis agreed on the condition that they bring a test case of their own. And so was born the case of *Zorach* v. *Clauson,* in which the Supreme Court eventually upheld the program.

As little more than an extension of Lewis's forceful personality, the Freethinkers of America has declined into inactivity since his death in 1968. It is presently housed in a second-floor office on the shabby edge of midtown Manhattan, crowded between a discount radio store and an emporium of cheap orientalia. Its mail goes unanswered, and it has no telephone. Most of the atheist organizations, for that matter, are organizationally insubstantial and often little more than one-person crusades. The National Lib-

---

[17] *Lewis* v. *Allen.*

eral League and the American Association for the Advancement of Atheism both appeared as amicus curiae in the *Walz* tax exemption case. The *Encyclopedia of Organizations*[18] lists both organizations (the former under its reincarnation as the National League for Separation of Church and State) at the same post office box in San Diego. The same person presides over both, and together they claim a total of 270 members.

More recently, but in the same tradition, Madalyn Murray O'Hair founded or resuscitated a series of organizations from which she launched her crusades. The Society of Separationists has been the most durable. In its brief in the *Walz* case she claimed 30,000 families "in affiliation," and listed her husband, Richard O'Hair, as its president. At other times she has been identified with the Freethought Society of America and Other Americans, Inc. (Whether that latter organization's title is a calculated variation on Protestants and Other Americans United is not easy to determine.) Such organizations, in any event, rarely have an independent decision-making capacity of their own. They are only nominally "groups." It may be more accurate to think of them as institutionalized personalities. And, like their predecessors, they operate independently of other litigating groups. Groups such as the AJC and AU avoid them as a "kiss of death," both for their impact on the courts and the site involved in a case, and because of the reaction of their own members to alliances with the aggressively godless.

The Educators

As the states have increasingly appropriated public funds for religious schools and colleges, the public education "establishment" has become increasingly involved in the politics of church-state relations. In the most general terms, it fears that such aid undermines the favorable position of public education, and to some extent rejects its values. More specifically, it sees the public "pie" for education as more or less fixed in size, and fears that as aid for private education increases, funds for public schools will stabilize or decrease.

The education groups still concentrate their activities in legislative and administrative politics, but occasionally they venture into the judicial arena. The Louisiana Teachers Association organized and sponsored the successful attack on the Louisiana legislature's

---

[18] Seventh edition (Detroit: Gale Publishing Co., 1972), vol. 1.

49

THE JOSEPH LEWIS FILE

The extent of Joseph Lewis's litigation on behalf of a scrupulously absolute separation of church and state probably defies a definitive cataloging. The main elements, however, were certainly the reported cases he brought in the New York courts:

1) *People ex rel. Lewis* v. *Graves,* 156 NE 663 (1927), to stop the released time program of the schools of White Plains.

2) *Lewis* v. *Board of Education,* 179 NE 315 (1932), to halt the purchase of Bibles, hymnals, and other religious books by the public schools of New York City.

3) *New York League for Separation of Church and State* v. *Graves,* 10 N.Y.S.2d 142 (1939), to prevent a Jesuit from showing a film about the Arctic (for an admission charge) in the auditorium of the state education building.

4) *People ex rel. New York League for Separation of Church and State* v. *Lyons,* 21 N.Y.S.2d 250 (1940), to remove the chapel from the grounds of Clinton prison.

5) *Lewis* v. *LaGuardia,* 27 NE2d 44 (1940), to stop broadcasts of religious breakfast speeches on the New York City radio station (WNYC).

6) *Lewis* v. *Spaulding,* 85 NE2d 791 (1949), to halt the released-time program in the City of New York (a suit eventually withdrawn in favor of *Zorach* v. *Clauson*).

7) *Lewis* v. *Mandeville,* 107 N.Y.S.2d 865 (1951), to stop Jewish and Catholic congregations from using a town fire house for services while their places of worship were being built or repaired.

8) *Lewis* v. *Allen,* 252 N.Y.S.2d 80 (1964), to challenge the pledge of allegiance to the American flag, especially the phrase "one nation under God" (this case is included in the universe of 67 in this book).

All of these suits ended in defeat. In addition, other sources (largely the *New York Times*) indicate that Lewis at other times commenced, or threatened to commence, suits to end the routine circumcision of male babies in public hospitals, transportation of crippled children to parochial schools, erection of a chapel at Idlewild (later John F. Kennedy) airport, religious instruction in Mt. Vernon Schools, withholding of birth control information in New York City hospitals, and New York City's unwillingness to collect taxes on a hotel owned by the Knights of Columbus.

program of aid to religious schools.[19] In other states education associations, teachers unions, and associations of administrators and school boards have entered alliances with other groups to challenge similar programs of parochaid. Their allies generally include one or more of the three leading groups. In other instances they have entered omnibus ad hoc "umbrella" organizations that involve themselves occasionally in litigation. The various state Committees on Public Education and Religious Liberty (better known by their acronym PEARL) afford the best example. In New York State, it is a statewide alliance of some twenty-nine groups, a large number of which are education groups; the American Jewish Congress and the New York Civil Liberties Union also belong.

Among these assorted groups of educators, the Horace Mann League stands apart because of its special concern for separation. It "supports the belief that public schools should be free, classless, nonsectarian and open to all children, and opposes the use of public funds for parochial schools."[20] Its guiding spirit in the 1960s was Edgar Fuller, the executive secretary of the Council of Chief State School Officers. It claimed a membership of some five hundred public school educators, and former officers of the National Educational Association and the American Association of School Administrators were active in its work. The League organized and

[19] *Seegers* v. *Parker.*
[20] *Encyclopedia of Associations,* seventh edition, vol. 1, p. 554.

sponsored a successful challenge in 1965 to the Maryland legislature's appropriations for buildings to religious colleges.[21] The organization itself was the chief plaintiff in this case, and it retained Leo Pfeffer as its attorney. But following that success, the officers' promise of continued legal activity has not been fulfilled. Fuller, an old friend and admirer of Pfeffer and something of a constitutional law "buff," retired from his executive secretaryship, and at about the same time the League's vigor began to decline once again.

The Churches

It would be hard to find a Protestant denomination with no concern for church-state questions, but the concern of two is sufficiently great to note here. The Seventh Day Adventists have long taken a virtually absolutist position on separation issues. Where they have their own elementary schools, they customarily refuse offers of state aid, such as textbooks or bus rides for their students. They also have opposed prayer and other religious influences in public schools at times and places in which other Protestant denominations wavered or compromised. Their record in litigation is not extensive, but their periodical *Liberty* (actually the publication of the International Religious Liberty Association, an SDA affiliate) publicizes the legal fight with articles by Pfeffer, Archer, and Stanley Lowell, the associate director of AU.

The Southern Baptists, too, have long held to an unyielding separationism. A number of their state conventions in the 1960s, in fact, ordered their colleges and universities to refuse available federal funding, a principled stand that cost them substantial sums for construction. The Southern Baptists have not themselves engaged in litigation on church-state issues, but they have been close to those who do. A number of state conventions are said to contribute presently to AU, and local churches have in a number of instances contributed to local litigation. Several of these sixty-seven cases were begun by local Baptist ministers, and ministers and the faithful constitute a substantial portion of AU's most loyal individual members. Individual Southern Baptists, moreover, played a prominent role in the founding of POAU. Joseph M. Dawson of the Baptist Joint Committee on Public Affairs organized several of its founding conferences, and served temporarily as its executive secretary until the hiring of Glenn Archer.

[21] *Horace Mann League* v. *Board of Public Works.*

52

The Baptist Joint Committee itself has also become a major advocate of separationism since World War II. Founded in 1939, it is maintained by nine sponsoring Baptist bodies as a Baptist voice in Washington on policy issues of the day. Throughout its life it has represented the Baptist commitment to a strict separation of church and state. It was, for instance, one of the first Protestant groups to support the Supreme Court's decisions on prayer and Bible-reading in the public schools, and to oppose the Constitutional amendments that would have overturned them. Its role in constitutional litigation has, however, been limited to sporadic briefs as an amicus curiae and to participation in broad consortia of separationists trying to plan major litigation.

Finally, a word about the National Council of Churches—or more formally, the National Council of the Churches of Christ in the United States of America, the major American alliance of Protestant denominations. Its Commission on Religious Liberty, headed by Rcv. Dean M. Kelley, has been the center of its church-state involvements. Kelley has been active in New York separationist circles and has been the NCC's usual representative in intergroup conferences and consortia on church-state issues. He also served as a member of the ACLU's Church-State Committee. Although his commission and the NCC generally have continued the major share of their public activity outside of the judicial process, since the early 1960s they have filed an increasing number of amicus briefs in church-state and religious freedom cases. That remains, however, the extent of their involvement in the judicial process, and in the sixty-seven cases of this study they filed a brief only in the *Walz* tax exemption case. Their position in favor of tax exemptions in that case illustrates their less-than-absolute separationist position. In the 1960s, however, the NCC did stand in the forefront of opposition to constitutional amendments to restore prayer and Bible-reading to the public schools.

The Masons

If the connotations of the metaphor are not too inappropriate, one can think of the Scottish Rite Masons (Southern Jurisdiction) as the eminence grise of church-state litigation.[22] They do no liti-

---

[22] The Southern Jurisdiction includes the South and all of the country beyond the Mississippi. The Northern Jurisdiction embraces only fifteen states of the Northeast, and it has not been active in church-state issues. The reasons for the differential concern of the two jurisdictions are not clear, but one can at least suppose that the small number of Roman Catho-

gating, but their impact through their ties to AU is important and of long standing. The Scottish Rite Masons were—along with the Baptists and other founders—present at its creation. Their national temple in Washington housed at least one organizational meeting, and Joseph Dawson recalls that the Sovereign Grand Commander "advanced a gift to cover modest operations for the first year" of the fledgling POAU.[23] The aid continued to some unknown— but more than nominal—extent throughout the 1950s and 1960s.[24]

The ties between the Scottish Rite and AU extend beyond financial help. Both Glenn Archer and Stanley Lowell of AU are 33rd-degree members of the Scottish Rite, and both often write for its Southern Jurisdiction in the early 1970s was Henry C. Clausen magazine, *The New Age.* The Sovereign Grand Commander of the of San Francisco, an old AU attorney and west coast stalwart for many years. Clausen writes for *Church and State,* the AU organ, and his works (such as *Hear the Pounding Hoofbeats!,* a "brilliant dissection" of tax credit proposals for aid to religious schools) have been offered by AU as inducements for financial contributions. Various state officials of the Scottish Rite have also helped the AU arrange for leadership and local attorneys in test cases. They have also helped organize local ad hoc organizations; in the 1950s those organizations often bore a name that was some variant of Friends of the Public Schools. Their assistance also involves the little aids—AU meetings held in local Scottish Rite temples, for example. For their part, AU officials often advise financially strapped local litigators to tap the local Masons.

Yet one sees only the flickerings on the wall of the cave, shadowy reflections of Scottish Rite activities. The full picture and dimensions of its role are wrapped in its own veiled, enigmatic style. Even in personal interviews its officers respond to pointed inquiries with hortative homilies. (It is, one should add, probably a general organizational style rather than one adopted particularly for the church-state mission.) And yet two conclusions are clear.

---

lics in the states of the Southern Jurisdiction makes their separationism less contentious and threatening for the organization.

[23] Quoted in Morgan, "Backs to the Wall," p. 45.

[24] See, for example, the publication of the Southern Jurisdiction, *The New Age,* 77 (October 1969), 43ff. It lists the annual POAU budget for that year at $640,000, with 20 percent ($128,000) coming from churches and institutions such as Masonic bodies. The article concludes that the Supreme Council supports POAU "because the work it is doing is a service to our American Way of Life, Constitutional Government, and our Heritage of Freedom."

Scottish Rite (Southern Jurisdiction) involvement in church-state litigation is of long standing; it dates at least back to its defense in the 1920s of an Oregon statute requiring children between the ages of eight and sixteen to attend public schools.[25] And the role continued throughout the 1951–1971 period, never as a solo role, but always in concert with AU action or the action of an AU-inspired ad hoc group.

The Local Groups

With few exceptions—such as the Louisiana Teachers Association—the groups described so far have been national in organization and scope. Their impact on the litigation of the constitutional separation has been the major one. But there is a myriad of local groups—groups of statewide scope or less—that complement, even buttress the initiatives of the national groups. In some instances they have provided the main initiative in organizing constitutional litigation. The Louisiana Teachers Association did exactly that in successfully challenging the state's parochaid program. A group of local separationists in Eugene, Oregon, organized themselves as Citizens in Support of Religious Liberty and Civil Authority to seek the removal of a concrete cross on public lands overlooking the city of Eugene.[26]

Local groups in this litigation are of two types: the existing, ongoing groups, and ad hoc groups formed for the single purpose of the litigation. The Louisiana Teachers Association typifies the ongoing group; similarly, in the Pennsylvania parochaid case, the Pennsylvania Education Association, the Pennsylvania Conference of the NAACP, the Pennsylvania Council of Churches, and Pennsylvania Jewish Community Relations Conference all sponsored the case.[27] The majority of these local ongoing groups are, in fact, affiliated in some way with national groups. The Eugene, Oregon, group typifies the ad hoc organization. So also do groups with such more or less explicit names as the Citizens' Committee for a Community Operated Hospital (of Ketchikan, Alaska), and the Kentucky Free Public Schools Association.

[25] The statute was invalidated in the U.S. Supreme Court in the landmark case of *Pierce* v. *Society of Sisters,* 268 U.S. 510 (1925). For a full narrative of Scottish Rite activities in those events, see Clement E. Vose, *Constitutional Change: Amendment Politics and Supreme Court Litigation since 1900* (Lexington, Mass.: D. C. Heath, 1972), chapter 6.

[26] The case was *Lowe* v. *City of Eugene.* The Louisiana case referred to was *Seegers* v. *Parker.*

[27] *Lemon* v. *Kurtzman.*

The ad hoc groups take many forms. Some are little more than the formalizing of a small, self-selected group of separationists in the community. At other times they may be "fronts" for or organizational embellishments of the efforts of a single individual or organization. Madalyn Murray O'Hair has often used them, and the early POAU chapters often tried to broaden support by setting up ad hoc bodies whose very names suggested both a broad coalition of support and the specific nature of the current battle. At still other times ad hoc litigating groups are really coalitions of local organizations or organizational elites. Leading Baptists, Seventh Day Adventists, Unitarians, Scottish Rite Masons, and officials of the PTA and local ACLU affiliate came together in Hawaii in an ad hoc organization (Hawaii Committee for the Preservation of Church-State Separation) to fight the state program of bus rides for pupils attending religious schools.[28]

While local groups dominate the litigating of a few cases, they do not in the aggregate match the impact of the national groups. They lack the skills and resources, the organizational span of attention, even the litigating tradition or self-image, of groups such as the ACLU, AJC, and AU. And by their very nature—the ad hoc groups especially—their involvement in constitutional litigation rarely extends beyond a single case.

GROUPS IN CONSTITUTIONAL LITIGATION

The activity of these separationist groups unfolded in the 1950s and 1960s in a context of the growing visibility of group activity in the litigation of constitutional questions. To say that, however, is not to suggest that group activity was new in the postwar period. Groups had brought or supported some of the "great" cases in earlier American constitutional history.[29] Nor is it even to assert that the total of such group activity increased markedly in the years after World War II. That may or may not be the case, and it is a question for later consideration. What was clearly new was the openness and visibility, the diminishing embarrassment, and even the pride of groups pursuing their goals through judicial politics.

The growing acceptance of group litigation was both symbolized and consolidated in the period between 1951 and 1971 by a decision of the United States Supreme Court. In voiding a Virginia

[28] *Spears* v. *Honda.*
[29] See Vose, *Constitutional Change.*

statute that limited the role of litigating groups by an expansion of the statutory definition of improper solicitation of legal business, the Court held in 1963 that the offending statute infringed First Amendment freedoms of political expression. Speaking for the majority of the Court in the case (*NAACP* v. *Button*), Justice William Brennan conferred new legitimacy on group litigation:

> In the context of NAACP objectives, litigation is not a technique of resolving private differences; it is a means for achieving the lawful objectives of equality of treatment by all government, federal, state, and local, for the members of the Negro community in this country. It is thus a form of political expression. Groups which find themselves unable to achieve their objectives through the ballot frequently turn to the courts. Just as it was true of the opponents of New Deal legislation during the 1930s, for example, no less is it true of the Negro minority today. And under the conditions of modern government, litigation may well be the sole practicable avenue open to a minority to petition for redress of grievances.[30]

The traditional common-law crimes of barratry, maintenance, and champerty, the Court held, all involved "malicious intent," a term or concept it did not believe appropriate for attempts to secure one's constitutional rights through litigation. As Mr. Justice Brennan summarized, "Resort to the courts to seek vindication of constitutional rights is a different matter from the oppressive, malicious, or avaricious use of the legal process for purely private gain."[31] The *Button* decision was, in short, a charter of legitimacy and respectability for the litigating groups, a buttress against the lingering concerns—even among attorneys of the litigating groups themselves—that they were trimming the corners of traditional legal ethics.

Thus within this single area of constitutional litigation on separation, a well articulated set of separationist groups and individuals operated throughout the entire period from 1951 to 1971. In an approximate but important way the major varieties of separationism all had their advocates. The AJC, AU, and ACLU represented, in order, a Jewish, conservative Protestant, and secular humanist separationism. More liberal Protestant separationism

[30] 371 U.S. 415 (1963), pp. 429–430.
[31] *Ibid.*, p. 443; the entire discussion of "malicious intent" begins at p. 439.

57

found its spokesmen in part through the ACLU and its affiliates, and in part through the National Council of Churches and some state councils. Joseph Lewis and then Madalyn Murray O'Hair spoke for the more aggressive atheist and antireligious separationism. The informal "system" of separationist groups that developed did not necessarily represent all the nuances of separationism. It did not, perhaps, even represent the major ones in proportion to their strength in the American society. It is notable and important, however, that no major current of separationism went through the period without an organized spokesman.

These groups do not monopolize the litigating of church-state issues in American courts. They do, however, dominate it. The ACLU, AJC, and AU, in turn, dominate the totality of group activity. The way in which they do so—that is, the nature and extent of all of the exertions by interest groups in litigating these constitutional questions—will be the central concern of the next chapter.

IV | THE SEPARATIONISTS IN LITIGATION

With a number of groups involved in the litigation of church-state issues, the potential for legal chaos is considerable. One could imagine a fragmented judicial politics not unlike legislative politics under multiparty or multifactional systems. It would be characterized by groups promoting single causes or short-run goals in litigation. Groups would enter and leave the field, and there would be no continuity of opposing interests, no pursuit of stable and long-run goals, no necessary continuity of issues from one case to the next. Such fragmentation is not, however, the case here. The strength and involvement of the American Civil Liberties Union, the American Jewish Congress, and Americans United have imposed an impressive degree of order and stability on church-state litigation.

To say that the ACLU, AJC, and AU dominate the group activities in this church-state litigation is not to suggest that they act as a monolith. They cooperate in some instances, but they compete in others, occasionally even to the extent of setting up their own test cases and racing each other to court. They participate in some of the same cases, but to some extent they differ in how they enter cases, reflecting their different goals and their different clienteles. One might say that in the combination of cooperation, competition, and division of labor in these cases there are the outlines of an interest-group "system" at work. The workings and relationships of the three groups, that is, display many of the characteristics of party systems.

THE CASES OF THE LEADING THREE

Of the entire set of 67 church-state cases decided in American appellate courts between 1951 and 1971, at least one of the three groups participated in 51 (76.1 percent), or more than three out of four. In fact, in 23 of the 67 (34.3 percent) at least two of three groups were involved. Individually, the records of participation are these: the ACLU and its affiliates, 30 cases (44.8 percent of the total 67 cases); the AJC, 22 cases (32.8 percent), and AU, 30 cases (44.8 percent). No other national or local group begins to approach that record; most, in fact, do not appear in more than one case.

The pattern of group participation in these cases indicates that AU staked out a more "national" role than the ACLU or AJC. The latter two groups were much more heavily involved in those cases originating in the northeastern states (Table 4–1, section II). Not surprisingly, therefore, they tended to support litigation that began in a metropolitan area—specifically, in one of the Census Bureau's standard metropolitan statistical areas (Table 4–1, section III). AU's cases originated more frequently in the nonmetropolitan sites. Those differing geographical patterns reflect, in part, organizational strength and membership; AJC strength and involvement tends to be greater in those areas of greater Jewish populations, and the ACLU affiliates of the northeast have long been the ACLU's largest and strongest. In part, too, the ACLU and AJC concentrations may simply reflect the convenience of proximity to headquarters. Communication is better and involvement is easier: one can travel easily to the site, confer with attorneys, interview plaintiffs.

More significant by far are the differences apparent in the kinds of cases the three groups cultivated. To a very surprising degree AU was interested only in those cases in which Roman Catholic interests were involved—cases dealing with bus rides to parochial schools and nuns teaching in public schools, for instance (Table 4–1, section IV). It is precisely in these figures—AU participation in 72 percent of the cases in which Roman Catholic interests were involved, but in only 7 percent of the other cases—that the suspicions of AU's anti-Catholic animus are most deeply grounded. For in constitutional litigation, as in any other form of political activity, it is the action rather than the motive or intention that is crucial. It does indeed appear that AU has come down to an operational definition of breaches of separation that confirms the worst suspicions of its critics. At the very least, AU has had considerable difficulty in dividing the issue of church-state separation from that of Roman Catholic social and political power.

Even more significant for the broader question of church-state litigation is the gravitation of all three groups to cases involving some aspect or another of elementary or secondary education

60

TABLE 4-1
Participation of Three Leading Groups in Church-State Cases,
by Character of the Cases

The Cases	ACLU	AJC	AU	At Least 1 of the 3
I. Total number (67)	30 (44.8%)	22 (32.8%)	30 (44.8%)	51 (76.1%)
II. Regions of cases				
Northeast (26)	16 (61.5%)	13 (50.0%)	12 (46.2%)	23 (88.5%)
North central (8)	3 (37.5%)	1 (12.5%)	4 (50.0%)	6 (75.0%)
South (19)	6 (31.6%)	5 (26.3%)	8 (42.1%)	13 (68.4%)
West (14)	5 (35.7%)	3 (21.4%)	6 (42.9%)	9 (64.3%)
total (67)	30	22	30	51
III. Urban site of cases[a]				
in SMSA (37)	20 (54.1%)	16 (43.2%)	16 (43.2%)	30 (81.1%)
not in SMSA (20)	6 (30.0%)	3 (15.0%)	11 (55.0%)	15 (75.0%)
total (57)	26	19	27	45
IV. Involvement of Roman Catholic interests				
involved (39)	16 (41.0%)	13 (33.3%)	28 (71.8%)	34 (87.2%)
not involved (28)	14 (50.0%)	9 (32.1%)	2 (7.1%)	17 (60.7%)
total (67)	30	22	30	51
V. Involvement of schools				
involved (43)	24 (55.8%)	18 (41.9%)	21 (48.8%)	37 (86.0%)
not involved (24)	6 (25.0%)	4 (16.7%)	9 (37.5%)	14 (58.3%)
total (67)	30	22	30	51
VI. Year of final substantive decisions				
1951–1957 (11)	4 (36.4%)	4 (36.4%)	6 (54.5%)	9 (81.8%)
1958–1964 (22)	7 (31.8%)	6 (27.3%)	9 (40.9%)	15 (68.2%)
1965–1971 (34)	19 (55.9%)	12 (35.3%)	15 (44.1%)	27 (79.4%)
total (67)	30	22	30	51

Note: See Appendix III for the explanation and definition of categories used here (regions, involvement of Catholic interests, etc.).

[a] Section III of the table reflects a universe of only 57 cases (all other sections being based on the full set of 67 cases). In this one instance, ten cases were dropped because in this sense they had no "site"; they were tests of state policy that had no specific locale.

(Table 4–1, section v). That concentrated effort results from a conjunction of several goals and tendencies. In part it reflects the AU preoccupation with things Catholic; a good share of those cases involve the private schools. In part, too, it reflects the desire of the American Jewish Congress (and to a lesser extent the ACLU) to maintain a strong public education system. The AJC is especially sensitive to the dilemma of young Jewish children who, when confronted by any kind of Christian religiosity in the public schools, face the wrenching choice of either the social dangers of nonconformity or participation in religious observances other than their own. Will Maslow, the general counsel of the AJC, writes, "we believe that financial grants by the state to religious institutions are less significant than government coercion, whether blatant or subtle, to profess a religious faith that is not one's own. The most important battleground for us is the public school system because immature children are involved and because the state compels their attendance."[1] Church-state issues touching the schools, in other words, often raise troubling questions of conscience and pressures to conform to alien traditions, and both the ACLU and the AJC are sensitive to those issues.

This preoccupation with cases touching on elementary and secondary education has another fascinating side. The outcomes in the church-state cases involving schools are vastly more proseparation than the outcomes in other cases. Of that more later; it suffices to note here that all but one of the separationist victories come in school cases. ACLU, AJC, and AU activity, in other words, is greatest in those cases in which the probability of victory is the greatest. Did the groups select them for that reason—did they have an implicit strategy in which the potential for winning weighs heavily and by reason of which they avoid the likely "losers"? Or is it possible that the greater separationist success in the school cases results from the group participation—that their skill in organizing and arguing them and their identification with them enhance the legal weight of their cause? A better-informed answer to those questions will have to await a number of additional explorations.

Finally, as the percentages of Table 4–1 show, the general outlines of major group activity in church-state cases remain fairly

---

[1] "The Legal Defense of Religious Liberty—The Strategy and Tactics of the American Jewish Congress," mimeographed paper presented at the annual meeting of the American Political Science Association in St. Louis, Mo. (September 6–9, 1961), p. 9.

stable over time. There was some collective dip in involvement in the years between 1958 and 1964, which one may attribute to the rapid expansion of the number of cases that began in that period. The groups were sluggish in meeting the challenge of the new pace of litigation. One of the three groups, the ACLU, did register a marked jump in activity in the final seven-year period. This resulted largely from the decentralization of ACLU litigation to its affiliates, and the consequent "unleashing" of many new litigators.

All of this suggests, to reiterate, that there was an informal, implicit division of effort among the three major litigating groups. To some extent their kinds of separationism, their clienteles, and the nature of their organizations impelled them to different kinds of church-state cases. AU's almost exclusive concern with cases involving Catholic interests best illustrates that point. (The greater similarity of AJC and ACLU concerns also suggests the relative ease with which they cooperate in litigation.) But group participation in these cases differed in quality as well as quantity. It ranged in extent from the filing of a hurriedly drafted amicus brief to the full sponsorship of a constitutional test case. It extended, in other words, from the most insubstantial contribution in an appellate court case to the fullest possible shaping of the facts, the participants, and the strategies of an entire case.

THE LEADING THREE: ROLES IN LITIGATION

Litigating groups initially accelerated their activity by transforming the amicus curiae brief "from neutrality to partisanship, from friendship to advocacy."[2] Its increasing use in the late 1940s, in fact, occasioned considerable legal disapproval and several shifts in the U.S. Supreme Court's policy on the admission of amici. Critics referred to group submission of amici briefs as "lobbying" before the appellate courts,[3] and, to be sure, the more egregious instances of repetitious, poorly-crafted briefs did appear to be little more than attempts to identify a group with an interest or policy position. Only slowly have practitioners, scholars, and judges come

[2] Samuel Krislov, "The Amicus Curiae Brief: From Friendship to Advocacy," *Yale Law Journal* 72 (March 1963), 704.
[3] For example, see Fowler Harper and Edwin Etherington, "Lobbyists before the Court," *University of Pennsylvania Law Review* 101 (June 1953), 1172–1177.

to accept the amicus brief as an appropriate instrument of group access to the judicial process.

Ironically, as the groups won the battle over the respectability of the amicus role, they began to realize its limitations and to shift to a fuller, more active role in litigation. The ACLU's 1970 litigation guide describes the advantages of the more active role (which it calls "direct representation"): "There are often substantial advantages to be gained by direct representation. They include the opportunity to establish and preserve an appropriate record related to the civil liberties issue which is of interest; the possibility of raising new or additional civil liberties issues which would not otherwise be necessarily involved in a case; and, in some cases, the possibility of securing affirmative relief with a broad effect."[4] The ACLU claims are unnecessarily modest. The basic problem with the amicus role is that it divorces the group's legal (constitutional) argument from the conduct of the case—choosing the plaintiffs, building the record of fact, selecting a court or remedy, shaping the legal arguments, indeed making virtually all the decisions of strategy and tactics. The likelihood of influencing the judicial outcome increases as the group controls more of the factors affecting that outcome. The trouble with the amicus brief is that it attempts to influence only one: legal argument.

The ACLU, AJC, and AU entered the 1950s essentially committed to the role of amicus. The AJC is the possible exception to that rule; it had begun to move to a more active role in church-state litigation before 1951, as witness its willingness to organize an alternative to Joseph Lewis's test of the New York City released-time program. The ACLU, for its part, shifted away from reliance on the amicus brief much more slowly. As late as 1961 its legal director wrote:

> The ACLU traditionally has appeared in key cases as amicus curiae. We are not a general legal defense agency and have felt that we could be most effective by highlighting civil liberties issues on the appellate level, once the facts have been established by evidence in the trial courts. This approach has certain obvious disadvantages in that we cannot control the method of production of evidence and thus the establishment of an adequate appeal record in the trial courts. . . .

[4] *Guide to ACLU Litigation,* mimeographed paper (March 1970), p. 1.

We have not sought test cases, although some of them have come our way.[5]

The 1970 *Guide to ACLU Litigation,* however, notes that "although the Union formerly did most of its legal work in an *amicus curiae* capacity, in recent years direct representation has come to play an increasingly important role for both the National organization and the affiliates."[6] AU, too, has shifted its emphasis; it seeks increasingly to initiate litigation in its own name as an organizational plaintiff, and litigation reports in its magazine *Church and State* take pride in noting AU sponsorship in cases.

The shift of litigating groups to roles beyond the amicus curiae is not, of course, limited to the church-state field. The increasing importance of the "test case" has been widely noted.[7] Its greater importance stems in part from the increased aggressiveness of interest groups and their growing awareness of the limits of the amicus role. It also stems from the greater receptiveness of both bench and bar, as in the Supreme Court's landmark decision in *NAACP* v. *Button.*[8] Since then, group counsel have in several ways pushed the courts "beyond" *Button.* Some state and federal courts increasingly permit the groups themselves to be plaintiffs in suits; Americans United and the Horace Mann League have each given their name to one of these sixty-seven cases. And by the 1970s, groups—especially those involved with consumer and environmental interests—were pressing for standing to bring suits on behalf of general social interests, even though they themselves were not directly affected or injured.

The trend to a direct or sponsoring role in litigation has not gone without challenge. Within the ACLU a number of attorneys have questioned its wisdom, although it would appear that in part the issue has been confused with the debate in the Union over what the civil liberties mission of the organization is to be. The direct ACLU representation of Dr. Spock and his codefendants in their Boston trial on charges of counselling draft evasion struck some

[5] Roland Watts, "The Role of the American Civil Liberties Union—In the Courts and Thereafter," mimeographed paper presented at the annual meeting of the American Political Science Association in St. Louis, Mo. (September 6–9, 1961), p. 2.

[6] P. 1.

[7] See, for example, Fred P. Graham, "The Test Case at the Bar," *New York Times* (January 21, 1968), sec. 4.

[8] 371 U.S. 415 (1963).

of the traditionalist members of the ACLU as a commitment somewhat beyond the traditional range of civil liberties. Furthermore, concern over the greater role stems from a professional concern that an attorney engaged in such a case will find it difficult to serve both the interests of his client and the constitutional goals of his organization.[9] (Those latter concerns, however, apply most often to instances of a group's representing a defendant in a criminal proceeding; they are less frequent in church-state litigation because the individuals are usually asserting the same constitutional rights and positions as the group representing them.) Some older attorneys, too, are uncomfortable with group litigation for the changes it implies in the role of the attorney, and for what they see as an unwholesome politicizing of the courts. Their qualms reflect a generational difference in legal education, professional goals, and even implicit understandings of the law and the judicial process.

Despite the *Button* decision and the growing frequency of group litigation, some trial court judges are also not comfortable with it. Even after the *Button* decision in 1963, several judges in these cases evidenced a resistance to group litigation that was distinctly "pre-*Button*." Judge Joseph H. Stamler of the New Jersey Superior Court for Morris County had before him in mid-1970 a challenge to the state's law authorizing bus rides for children in religious schools. The West Morris Regional Board of Education brought the suit with the assistance of the New Jersey Civil Liberties Union. Incensed by newspaper reports of NJCLU activity (which were, in fact, exaggerated) and by the fact that the NJCLU had sponsored another test case of the same legislation (the *McCanna* case), Judge Stamler summoned Stephen Nagler, executive director of the affiliate, for lengthy and less than friendly questioning. Despite Nagler's clarifications and assurances, the judge's ruling in the case makes his displeasure evident:

> I don't question here the right of the A.C.L.U. to assist an individual where civil rights are being imposed upon, as described by Mr. Negler (sic). But here we are dealing with the West Morris Regional Board of Education and two members of that Board, a public body of the State of New Jersey, certainly capable of securing the funds, if necessary, to pay counsel. The payment of the expenses by the A.C.L.U. in a case of this kind

[9] See the four-way debate in *Civil Liberties*, no. 254 (March-April 1968), pp. 6–7ff.

while McCanna was still going on comes very close to the common law crime of maintenance and champerty. . . .

I would hope that this Court or other Courts in our state would not have to impose sanctions or cite for contempt persons who participate in litigation and are yet not controlled by the Court . . . and I suggest to the American Civil Liberties Union that in the future, at least in this Court, it make itself known as a participant.[10]

One year earlier a federal district court judge in Pittsburgh took similar exception to the local ACLU affiliate's role in a suit brought by a parent to force the schools his sons attended to comply with the Supreme Court's prayer decisions of five and six years earlier. During the proceedings Judge Louis Rosenberg pursued the ACLU role, especially in the origin of the case, with the ACLU attorney representing the plaintiff:

Judge Rosenberg: "Did you invite him (the plaintiff), or did he come of his own volition?"

Louis Kushner, the attorney: "He came of his own volition. We had never known or had contact with him before."[11]

Later in his opinion in the case the judge dismissed the affiliate's listing of itself as a plaintiff: "Neither am I inclined to allow grievance party status to groups of individuals who professionally seek to inculcate themselves into litigation for the sake of litigation itself, or who seek to induce litigation by persons, remote from them, which litigation is totally unrelated to the personal rights of such individuals."[12] It is possible to make too much of such hostility to group litigation. For one thing the ACLU affiliates in both cases went a step beyond the usual group role—in New Jersey

[10] Decision of Judge Stamler in *West Morris Regional Board* v. *Sills,* 110 N.J. Super 234 (1970); transcript on file in the office of the clerk of the New Jersey Supreme Court as a part of the record for 279 A2d 609 (1971).

[11] Transcript of trial of *Mangold* v. *Gallatin* (October 2 and 3, 1969); on file in the office of the Clerk of the District Court for Western Pennsylvania in Pittsburgh (at 307 F. Supp. 639).

[12] *Mangold* v. *Gallatin,* 307 F. Supp. 637 (1969). The suspicion of group litigation persisted beyond the 1971 cutoff date for this study. In his dissent in *PEARL* v. *Levitt,* a 1972 case, Judge Palmieri explains in a footnote, "This comment and those immediately following are not intended to reflect upon my esteemed colleagues but are directed to those who appear to be making a career of this type of destructive litigation." See 342 F. Supp. 439 at p. 445.

67

by bringing a second challenge of the same statute, and in Pennsylvania by serving as an organizational plaintiff. And two judicial storms do not make a hostile judicial climate. Nonetheless, they do reflect a lingering view, especially among trial court judges, that groups ought to function in the judicial process more or less in the role of a legal aid society. But that view negates the major purpose of group involvement. The legal aid society pursues personal justice for an individual, and the judicial interest group pursues broader policy goals.

In view of both the stated intentions of the groups themselves and the general trends to more than merely amicus involvement, it is surprising *not* to see a shift in the kind of group involvement in these sixty-seven church-state cases between 1951 and 1971 (Table 4–2). Even when one looks at the total number of group roles (in Table 4–3; note that Table 4–2 uses the cases as the unit of analysis), it becomes clear that the three leading groups have only slightly shifted the nature of their activities in these church-state cases. Only the ACLU shows an increase in the sponsorship role, a shift that may result as much from increasing affiliate activ-

TABLE 4-2
Maximum Degree of Involvement in Cases by Three
Leading Groups by Seven-Year Periods

| | Cases Decided in | | |
	1951–1957	*1958–1964*	*1965–1971*
Maximum involvement of three leading groups[a]			
amicus curiae	1	0	9
intermediate	4	10	7
sponsorship	4	5	11
total (51)	9	15	27
Total number of all church-state cases (67)	11	22	34
Percentage of cases with some involvement by three leading groups	81.8%	68.2%	79.4%

[a] These aggregate totals record only the highest level of group involvement in a case. Thus, if in one case one of the three groups sponsored the litigation and the other two were involved at a lower level of participation, the case would be recorded among the "sponsored." In other words, the unit of analysis here is the case, not the participating group.

TABLE 4-3
Total Number and Kinds of Roles of the Three Leading
Groups by Seven-Year Periods, 1951-1971

	1951–1957 ACLU AJC AU			1958–1964 ACLU AJC AU			1965–1971 ACLU AJC AU		
Roles of three leading groups									
amicus curiae	2	0	0	0	1	0	7	2	6
intermediate	1	2	3	3	4	8	2	6	6
sponsorship	1	2	3	4	1	1	10	4	3
totals	4	4	6	7	6	9	19	12	15
Total roles for three groups combined (82)	14			22			46		
Total cases in study (67)	11			22			34		
Ratio of groups' roles to cases (roles divided by cases)	1.3			1.0			1.4		

ity as from conscious policy to move away from the amicus role. (Its amicus activity has, after all, also grown.) In short, the ACLU, AJC, and AU had largely developed their pattern of activity beyond the amicus role by the early years of the 1951–1971 period.

If the kinds of activity have not changed drastically, the quantity has. The three leading groups have more than kept up with the accelerating pace of church-state litigation. They have, with the exception of a slight dip between 1958 and 1964, consistently been active in some way in about eighty percent of the church-state cases (Table 4–2) despite the sharp and steady increase in the number of those cases. In fact, the increase in the ratio of total roles to cases in the three seven-year periods (Table 4–3) shows that their activity increased after 1964 at a rate greater than the increase in litigation. That increase suggests, in fact, that the groups themselves had something to do with the growth of litigation.

Of the various categories of group activity, only that of the amicus curiae is self-evident. It is a role that is defined by the

69

court, and that the group itself formally chooses. In these tables and narratives, "sponsorship" refers to the group's initiation and management of a case. That role involves group presence at the actual origination, the acceptance or location of plaintiffs, the provision of counsel, a voice in general strategy and tactics (especially in decisions to appeal), and responsibility for at least part of the costs. Increasingly the groups themselves accept and apply a concept of sponsorship to themselves; group sponsorship of cases is, for example, noted in the *Litigation Docket* published by the American Jewish Congress. The "intermediate" role that appears in the text and tables is something of a residual category. It includes all group activity beyond (but not necessarily including) that of the amicus, but short of sponsorship. It generally involves providing funds, legal advice, help in drafting complaints or briefs, argument in an appellate court, some general encouragement and support, or some combination of these. More often than not, the group involved "intermediately" comes to the case after its initiation, and frequently after its trial. Typically, and at the least, the group enters in the appellate court a case that had originated locally, and provides some degree of help with the printed brief and the oral argument. At the maximum, the intermediate role is perhaps typified by AU activity in an obscure Kentucky case that challenged a county contract with an order of Roman Catholic nuns to operate the county-owned hospital.[13] The local originators of the case—ministers and laymen in some of the local fundamentalist Protestant churches—consulted with AU before filing the action; AU gave a general blessing and promises of help. It redeemed that promise with a small sum to help with trial costs, gave more money and advice in the Kentucky Court of Appeals (although the decision to appeal was made by the local originators), and then took over the case in an unsuccessful plea for certiorari in the United States Supreme Court. (The ACLU's term "direct representation," incidentally, includes the concept of sponsorship and probably a good many of what I have called "intermediate" roles.)

In many ways the assignment of roles here has been a cautious one. The minimum criterion for "assistance" requires giving some specialized help in that case specifically; instances of groups' referring a plaintiff or attorney to another group or merely of sending copies of past briefs did not qualify them for the "intermediate"

---

[13] *Abernathy* v. *City of Irvine*.

category. Most significantly, perhaps, the criterion eliminated instances of the group "nonrole." In two instances of suits by the State of New Jersey to compel local school districts to comply with the Supreme Court's prayer decisions,[14] the New Jersey ACLU affiliate threatened suit if the state did not act. In at least one of those cases, ACLU and AJC representatives conferred with state officials about the strategy of forcing compliance. Thus, even though there is no recorded role in these cases for any of the three leading groups, it seems certain that the leverage of a threatened suit helped stiffen the resolve of state officials to take action.

To illustrate further the role of the three leading groups beyond the cases in which they have formal roles, one need only look at the Hawaii bus ride case.[15] A number of individuals and group leaders successfully challenged the public provision of bus rides to children attending private schools, including religious schools. Formally, none of the three groups had even so much as an amicus role in the case; but consider the following aspects of the case. Donald Beck of Honolulu, the plaintiff's attorney, quickly located Leo Pfeffer's books and articles on separation in his researches for the case; by his own word he admired them and relied heavily on them. Beck also wrote AU to ask for materials, and received the briefs AU had filed in several earlier bus cases in other states. Leaders of the local ACLU affiliate were also active in the ad hoc organization that sponsored the case, and one even served as a plaintiff. And the ACLU affiliate would have filed a supporting brief as an amicus curiae had Beck not decided as a matter of tactic to discourage all overt group support. One can thus see that the estimates of ACLU, AJC, and AU influence on this body of litigation are conservative ones.

Granted the distinctions and indistinctions among various group roles, are there times and events in which the groups are more apt to choose one role or another? The groups differ in the quantity of their involvement, but do they differ as well in the depth of that involvement? As the data of Table 4–4 suggest, the depth tends to vary with the quantity. That is to say, depth of involvement, as measured by the relative frequency of the sponsorship role, tends to be greater precisely in those kinds of cases in which the quantity of the involvement (Table 4–1) tends to be the greatest—in cases involving elementary and secondary education, and

[14] *Sills* v. *Board of Education*, and *State Board* v. *Netcong.*
[15] *Spears* v. *Honda.*

71

TABLE 4-4
Highest Level of Group Role in Church-State Cases

| Aggregate Role of Three Groups | Region | | | |
	Northeast	North Central	South	West
Amicus curiae	5	1	3	1
Intermediate	4	3	7	7
Sponsorship	14 (60.9%)	2 (33.3%)	3 (23.1%)	1 (11.1%)
Total (51)[a]	23	6	13	9

| Aggregate Role of Three Groups | Do Facts of Case Concern Elementary or Secondary Schools? | |
	yes	no
Amicus curiae	6	4
Intermediate	14	7
Sponsorship	17 (45.9%)	3 (21.4%)
Total (51)[a]	37	14

Note: This table again records the highest level of involvement of any of the three groups in a case; the lesser roles of one or both of the other groups are therefore not recorded. The unit of analysis is the case, not the group roles.

[a] The 51 cases here are those in which at least one of the three leading groups was involved.

in cases brought in the northeastern states. Thus it appears that considerations of proximity and priority—those cases closest to the group headquarters and highest on its priorities—influence the kinds of involvements. Quite understandably, the kinds of immediacy necessary for finding and establishing a role of any kind are heightened when the role is as complex and demanding as the sponsorship role. To a considerable extent, too, these data reflect the very understandable desire of the groups to pick and establish test cases near home base. Groups may also pick the locale because of the sympathy of state and federal courts in the Northeast to civil liberties claims in general, and to church-state claims in particular.

THE THREE GROUPS: THE ABILITY TO ACT

The recruitment of any group or individual into any form of political activity presupposes both the opportunity for action and the capacity to act. So it is, too, with interest groups in the judiciary. Opportunity for them is defined by the pace, the properties, and the participants in the judicial process. Their capacity for action is not easy to assess. One certainly cannot assume it from the very fact of action. But for litigating groups, at least four considerations are central to their ability to affect the course and outcome of constitutional litigation: control of information, cohesion of the group, its litigation resources, and skill in managing its various resources.

Especially if the group wishes to act in any role other than that of amicus, its effectiveness depends on the earliest possible information about an emerging case. The earlier the intervention, the more aspects of the case the group can influence. The sponsorship role requires by definition that the group enter at the origin of a case or very soon thereafter. But the ACLU, AJC, and AU involve themselves early even when their role is less than sponsorship. In 60 of the total of 82 appearances that the three groups made in these 67 cases—in 73.2 percent—they entered the cases before trial. For the ACLU and AU, it was 20 of 30 instances (66.7 percent), and for the AJC 20 of 22 (90.9 percent). That early participation results in part from explicit group policy. The files of all three are full of correspondence indicating a great reluctance to join litigation already fully shaped. But it also reflects in part the excellence of the groups' information and communications systems.

These systems are not, however, identical among the three groups, and the little differences in the timing of their participations reflect the differences in their systems. The AJC's early involvement is especially remarkable when one remembers that the AJC, unlike the ACLU, does not permit autonomous litigation by local affiliates. It does, however, enjoy excellent and early information from its local members, field representatives, officials of other Jewish organizations, and local or national ACLU leaders. Pfeffer's preeminence in the field also brings early inquiries and contacts. And the growing disposition of ACLU activists to work through the AJC adds a second informational network to its own. The AJC, in its conscious efforts to increase its information, has also relied extensively on the releases of the Religious News Service. For the ACLU there is a fully articulated network of local affiliates and chapters, but its need for a national information-gathering capacity was ended with its decision to decentralize the litigating of cases. For its part, AU hears of cases primarily from local originators and/or plaintiffs—some of whom, of course, are AU members or activists. Its capacity for gathering word of incipient or emerging litigation is less effective than the AJC's. The AU, as a consequence, more commonly enters a case after the origination (as marked, say, by the filing of legal papers), though still before the trial, while the AJC and ACLU are more commonly involved at the time of origin.[16]

The general pattern of information is, therefore, expressed in patterns of group litigation. In the case of AU, local plaintiffs, activists, and organizers of litigation typically come together to plan a legal challenge to local policy. After they make the initial commitment to act, they seek the help of AU, both for funds and for church-state expertise. They tend to be familiar with AU activities in the field and sympathetic, too, with AU's kind of separationism. The AJC, on the other hand, makes a concerted attempt to sense the developing case. Its representatives and contacts, as well as those of the ACLU, are also more conditioned to seek AJC guidance before carrying any litigation even into initial stages. In part that conditioning reflects the greater AJC insistence on the national, central control of litigation in which it is involved; its style of litigation thus demands a highly developed network of communication. The looser AU rein on litigation permits it to operate within a less effective information network.

The capacity of groups to litigate successfully depends, secondly, on the degree of cohesion they maintain—within the national organization, within the local affiliates or chapters, and in the relationships between national and local. And those problems in cohesion, hard as they are to identify, do crop up in about twenty-five percent on the cases the three groups were involved in. The sources of discord are of various kinds. Occasionally it may be a dispute within the national organization over fundamental policy; the ACLU's painful division over tax exemptions for religious property is illustrative. In a few cases there are instances of local organizations' reluctance to enter cases; that especially may force the AJC to keep a low or hidden profile in the case. But all three groups

[16] The publication of the AJC's *Litigation Docket* since 1966 has also added to the circulation of information about church-state litigation. But because it contains only information about litigation under way, it comes too late for short-run decisions. It undoubtedly contributes, however, to the effectiveness of the groups' long-range strategy and coordination.

have had occasional difficulties of the opposite kind—local pique over the national office's unwillingness to enter a case or carry it all the way to the U.S. Supreme Court. For example, AU supported the New Mexico suit to exclude nuns in habits from public school employment.[17] When the local organizers of the case won a substantial, if partial, victory in the trial, the locals and national POAU divided sharply on whether or not to appeal the decision. The locals wanted to appeal in hopes of full vindication; the national office was happy to settle for the limited success and feared a loss of even that in a hostile appellate court decision.

Of these instances of internal disagreements, a number of things, none of them conclusive, can be said. First, it is hard to imagine a body of litigation such as this, which brings together so many people and subtle shades of interest, proceeding in total harmony. Furthermore, the fact that instances of disagreement of whatever kind do occur regardless of the role of the group suggests that the disharmonies do not seriously disturb the litigation. But most important, and most inconclusively, the record here is a record of the action, the participation of the three groups. There is no record of the instances in which discord and disagreement prevented action—not only in these sixty-seven cases, but in other litigation that might have been but wasn't. It is the tantalizing problem, perhaps one of the most tantalizing in the social sciences, of identifying and explaining nonbehavior. All one can say, perhaps, is that with all but sixteen of the sixty-seven cases touched by one or more of the three groups, they were clearly not greatly restrained from acting in the cases that happened. Of those "cases" that did not "happen," all is silence.

Thirdly, the capacity for action depends on the group's resources. Chief among them are its legal skills. Leo Pfeffer's talents and experience established the AJC's preeminent legal reputation. But it should be noted that other legal work at AJC headquarters also met the highest standards. The reputation of AU's legal staff among its peers throughout the 1950s and 1960s was less flattering. Morgan wrote that the AU legal department

has never been very careful about the technical development of its cases; one has the sense that it cares more about *having* cases on particular issues in particular places than about quality

[17] *Zellers* v. *Huff.*

of craftsmanship or even chances of success. This casual and haphazard style is a continuing scandal to lawyers for more precedent-conscious groups (notably the AJ Congress), and there is a strong feeling within the separationist community that the POAU wastes much of the money it spends on litigation.[18]

It is a harsh judgment, but it is one that students of separationist litigation hear repeatedly. In the days before ACLU decentralization of its litigation, the work of its national staff occasioned neither the awed respect accorded to AJC legal work nor the criticism directed at AU's. (The quality of the local attorneys of record in these group-sponsored cases is indeed a relevant aspect of the groups' capacities; their performance will be assessed in Chapter VII.)

In litigation, as in all other forms of political activity, money is an important resource. But just how much money is necessary is hard to say. There exists a good deal of conventional wisdom that sets it at $10,000 or $15,000 for a constitutional case carried to the U.S. Supreme Court. But those are at best approximations or modal figures for the 1950s and 1960s. Many of these church-state cases were litigated for far less, and some, indeed, cost less than $1,000. Some cost a good deal more, and several ran into the range of $50,000 to $75,000. These figures, it should also be noted, cite only cash outlay. They would be considerably increased if one included contributed time and skills, lost income or income opportunities, and other noncash costs.

Above all, the cost of constitutional litigation varies with the nature of the litigation itself, with the presence or absence of a trial, the number of appellate courts hearing the case, and the quantity and quality of counsel. The style of litigation the major groups prefer—especially in their desire to build a complete trial court record of fact—unquestionably costs a good deal more than some of the "minimal" nongroup litigation. Nothing escalates the cost of litigation so much as a long trial with a number of witnesses, a battery of attorneys, and substantial transcripts and printing bills. While they are hardly affluent, the three groups are able

---

[18] Richard E. Morgan, "Backs to the Wall: A Study in the Contemporary Politics of Church and State," Ph.D. dissertation, Columbia University, 1967, p. 264. In a footnote to this observation Morgan records that "this opinion was expressed by seven respondents, each of whom requested that it not be attributed."

and willing to bear the costs or part of the costs of such litigation. Indeed, the financing of substantial constitutional litigation is so low in priorities of even wealthy individuals that it falls to the litigating groups on that ground alone.

Finally, the group's capacity depends on its ability to manage resources and schedule activities. The major shortcoming of this sort was the ACLU's difficulty in meeting its commitments in a number of cases. One early scenario went this way. The legal office in New York got word of a rural Missouri case that involved the transformation of a local Catholic school into the local public school.[19] Roland Watts, the ACLU legal director, wrote to a cooperating attorney in St. Louis for details and a progress report. The attorney responded with the papers in the case, including the stipulated facts. Watts and his staff decided on an amicus brief that would take the ACLU's consistent position about the freedom of nuns to accept public employment so long as they wore no religious symbols and engaged in no religious activities. They conveyed their wishes to the St. Louis Civil Liberties Committee, and half a year later they received word that it was too late to file a brief.

That misadventure was duplicated in at least four or five other ACLU cases in the period. The ACLU's national legal staff was clearly carrying more commitments than it could manage, and at the same time the local cooperating attorneys, working without fee, repeatedly put ACLU business aside as they became burdened with their own practices. The combination of overextended national staff and distant, unsupervised cooperating attorneys repeatedly unhorsed the ACLU. One suspects that this problem contributed to the ACLU decision to decentralize litigation responsibilities to the local affiliates.

So when information, resources, cohesion, and management skills are all considered, it is evident that the AJC stands apart in capacity for litigation. Its problems in intragroup cohesion are probably no worse than those of the ACLU and AU, and it surpasses them in the other three criteria. Yet it is important to note that the role the AJC in litigation has chosen demands a generally higher level of capacity. The centralization of its litigation and its overwhelming concern with the outcome of the legal decision demand that level of skills. AU, by contrast, has maintained less central control over litigation, and it has been willing to settle for

[19] *Berghorn* v. *School District.*

77

the organizational pay-offs in litigation. Its capacities fit its litigation role. Overall level of capacity in litigation thus appears related to the litigation role the groups assume. One would like to think that there is a parsimonious strategy at work here, in which groups develop only those skills and only as much of them as they need. Yet the possibility also exists that the role chosen reflects in part the ability of the group to develop the capacity for litigation.

OPPORTUNITIES FOR ACTION

A group's ability to act depends on its opportunities for action. The nature of the controversy, of the other actors, and of the judicial forum must be such as to offer the groups the chance to participate if they choose. A major enemy of group activity is speed in litigation. Consider a recent case in West Virginia. Roman Catholic parents in Charleston and Fairmont, angered that the school boards of their counties were not exercising the statutory option to provide bus rides for children attending parochial schools, brought suit to compel them to do so. They argued the somewhat novel proposition that denial of the bus rides denied them and their children the equal protection of the laws under the Fourteenth Amendment. Beyond being a new argument, it was one fraught with sweeping consequences for the entire church-state controversy, and one supposes that the separationist groups surely wanted to be involved. But the suit was brought in the original jurisdiction of the West Virginia Supreme Court (a writ of mandamus was sought) on October 23, 1969. On November 3rd the court agreed to hear the case, and it did so on the next January 14th, less than three months later. Decision came on April 14th, 1970, a decision for the plaintiffs.[20] Only AU managed to enter as an amicus curiae.

There are other instances of cases more or less exploding in this way, many of them cases in the late sixties and early seventies. The ACLU, assisted by Leo Pfeffer, brought suit in Federal District Court in New Orleans to challenge the Louisiana parochaid statute, both on separationist and on equal protection (that is, racial equality) grounds. After that suit was filed, the Louisiana Teachers Association filed its challenge in a state court in Baton

[20] *State ex rel. Hughes* v. *Board of Education.*

78

Rouge on September 8, 1970.[21] The time sequences of the two cases tell their own stories (all dates are in 1970):

STATE COURT CASE		FEDERAL COURT CASE	
		Aug. 28	suit filed in New Orleans
Sept. 8	suit filed in Baton Rouge	Sept. 8	three-judge court named
Sept. 17	parties seek certiorari to La. Supreme Ct.		
Sept. 21	certiorari granted	Sept. 21	hearing set for Oct. 2
		Sept. 22	intervenors supported by Archdiocese of New Orleans admitted
		Sept. 24	Leo Pfeffer admitted as associate counsel; Oct. 2 hearing postponed
Sept. 25	oral argument in La. Supreme Ct.		
		Oct. 16	plaintiff motion for temporary restraining order denied
Oct. 19	decision of La. Supreme Court	Oct. 19	action stayed pending outcome in similar cases before U.S. Supreme Court

The U.S. Supreme Court eventually denied certiorari, and the decision of the Louisiana Supreme Court (by a 4–3 vote) invalidating the state aid program stood. It had been the first state court challenge to a statewide parochaid statute, and of the three leading separationist groups, only AU participated in it with some covert advice and encouragement. Certainly the speed of the proceedings—the bypassing of the trial court and the elapsed time of only six weeks from filing to final decision—limited opportunities for participation. So fast did the case come and go, in fact, that it was never even accorded a listing in the AJC's *Litigation Docket*.

Such speedy proceedings clearly trouble the national groups. Information comes to them late, and then the pace of the case gives them only a fast-moving target to hit. It is a bit like trying to catch a ring on the whirling carousel. But despite it all, the three groups appear just as frequently in the speedy cases as in the slow ones. Even in those cases—such as the ones in Louisiana and West

---

[21] *Seegers* v. *Parker*. The case in federal court was *Rodney* v. *Dodd* (Civil calendar 70–2381 in U.S. Dist. Court for Louisiana).

TABLE 4-5

Participation of Three Groups in Adversary
and "Friendly" Cases

Maximum Involvement of Three Leading Groups	Adversary Cases	Friendly Cases
None	11 (19.0%)	5 (55.6%)
Amicus curiae	8 (13.8%)	2 (22.2%)
Intermediate	19 (32.8%)	2 (22.2%)
Sponsorship	20 (34.5%)	0
Total	58	9

Note: This table again records the highest level of involvement of any of three groups in a case; the lesser roles of one or both of the other groups are therefore not recorded. The unit of analysis is the case, not the group roles.

Virginia—that have been expedited in some unusual way,[22] group activity by the leading three does not fall off. That fact suggests that the groups' information and communications networks—and more generally their capacity for action—have kept step with the faster pace of litigation.

In fact, only one variable in "opportunity" appears to deter the ACLU, the AJC, or AU. It is the absence of an adversary proceeding (Table 4–5). There are, in other words, nine among the sixty-seven cases in which friendly parties, parties with really no differences of interests, contrived the litigation to speed the settling of a legal issue. By their nature the friendly cases discouraged the participation of the three leading groups. Exactly how they did so awaits the fuller treatment of Chapter XI. For the moment it is enough to record that as a group these cases in themselves are the chief barrier to group activity in the constitutional politics of church and state.

RELATIONSHIPS AMONG THE THREE GROUPS

The rate of activity in church-state litigation of the three leading groups inevitably brings them into frequent contact. To some ex-

[22] The specific forms of expedition were these: in West Virginia, the filing of the case in the original jurisdiction of the highest appellate court; in Louisiana, the removing of the case before hearing in the trial court to the state supreme court by writ of certiorari. "Expediting" in general will be fully discussed in Chapter XIV.

tent they maintain a division of labor—different types of cases in different parts of the country. But their interventions in these sixty-seven cases overlap and produce a complex set of two and three-way relationships. Those relationships mix trust and suspicion, competition and cooperation, informal ties and formal organization.

One fact governs and colors virtually all of the intergroup contacts: the relatively low esteem in which other groups hold AU. It is not new, and it is not limited to the ACLU and AJC. State councils of churches have, for instance, dissociated themselves from AU in at least two of these cases. The suspicion of AU is grounded in part in an unhappiness with AU's anti-Catholicism (or perhaps, one might say, with its commitment to a Protestant hegemony in American life and culture)—unhappiness both with the fact of the obsession and with the public relations problems it creates. The low regard reflects also what the other groups believe to be AU's reckless litigation and substandard legal work. It may also reflect an awareness elsewhere of AU's socio-political conservatism; AU simply is not a part of the generally "liberal" style, rhetoric, and fraternalism that characterize the other separationist groups.

The distance between AU and the other separationist groups obviously does not completely sour the relationships.[23] A number of the ACLU affiliates, especially those in states of lower Roman Catholic population percentages, work well with AU. But while the gulf does not obliterate intergroup relations, it does strain them. The other groups, for example, have more than once kept AU out of "their" sponsored litigation. The rejection is rarely explicit or overt. More commonly it takes the form of the unanswered letter, the delayed response, or the postponed decision. In the case in which the Rhode Island affiliate of the ACLU challenged that state's law providing textbooks to religious school pupils, the affiliate's attorney effectively blocked an amicus role for AU by his repeated failure to respond to AU letters until after the case was decided.[24] When in late 1970 a local ACLU attorney in Michigan again balked AU participation by failures to respond, Franklin Salisbury, then the AU general counsel, exploded in an

[23] I think, therefore, that Morgan's term for AU, an "organizational pariah," may suggest a degree of ostracism that really isn't there. See his "Backs to the Wall," p. 318.
[24] The case was *Bowerman* v. *O'Connor*.

intraoffice memo: "This illustrates the utter futility of dealing with ACLU attorneys on matters of church-state relations. We did everything that we could to keep up to date and to do what Mr. Ellman [the ACLU attorney] requested. The result was simple. Whether it was planned by ACLU or not, we were not represented."[25] Thus the unhelpfulness of one group sharply limited the opportunities for participation by another.

These intergroup tensions manifest themselves in another way: the attempt of the groups to set up competing cases. In five of these sixty-seven cases AU planned or sponsored one suit that competed with a suit set up either by the AJC, the ACLU, or both. Perhaps the most dramatic instance of competition, *Dickman* v. *School District,* centered around an Oregon law authorizing free textbooks for students in religious schools. The then-POAU and local Masons (who provided the attorney) organized a test case, but it combined a challenge to the textbook law with one testing bus rides for the same pupils. ACLU, relying on Leo Pfeffer's advice, urged separation of the issues; the case against the texts was stronger, they thought, because the Supreme Court precedent was older and vaguer, and because texts were more central to the educational mission than bus rides, and less clearly covered by the "child benefit" doctrine. Beyond the differences in strategy, each side also wanted the credit and publicity of a test case. Local ACLU leaders additionally shied away from the shrillness of the POAU-Masonic separationism. National POAU officials, caught between the fervor of its locals and the arguments of Pfeffer, waffled and finally supported the judgment of local counsel in Oregon. Then, despite all of the effort and preparation, its suit stalled when its plaintiffs pulled out at the last minute. The ACLU took the opportunity to rush to litigation, locating plaintiffs and filing its case within forty-eight hours. POAU and the Oregon Masons never reorganized their suit.

In two more of these five instances of competition, the AU suits were also not filed. In one of those instances, the test of the Pennsylvania parochaid statute,[26] AU early located a plaintiff and attorney in Harrisburg and threatened a suit. AU did later join with a group of organizations in bringing a different suit, but it used the threat of its own suit for bargaining leverage in the alliance

---

[25] The case was the test of the Michigan constitutional amendment to block aid to religious schools, *In Re Proposal C.*

[26] *Lemon* v. *Kurtzman.*

to assure the listing of AU as an organizational plaintiff. In the remaining two of the five, the competing suits were filed and ultimately consolidated.[27]

These five instances of intergroup competition, however, are not solely attributable to the holding of AU at arm's length. In part they stem from the groups' desires to have their own cases, both for reasons of strategic freedom and for full group publicity. Competition among the groups, therefore, may be unrelated to any unusual tensions or antipathies. Furthermore, in two other instances the AJC and an ACLU affiliate set up or threatened to set up competing cases. In one instance the AJC, beaten to court by the NYCLU, dropped its plans; in the other, the separate suits were consolidated at the trial.[28] But for all the qualifications and exceptions, the fact remains that in five of seven instances of planned or real competing cases, it was AU against the other two.

Although tensions and competition among the "big three" are substantial, so too is their cooperation. The contacts among them have always been important. The informational ties between the ACLU and AJC were perhaps the strongest, but there have always been ties between the AJC and AU as well. The network of these informal ties had essentially developed around the leadership of the AJC and Leo Pfeffer. Both the ACLU and AU have long relied on AJC judgment; both recognize Pfeffer's scholarly and legal mastery in the field, and both are more than a little in awe of it. But these informal contacts began to diminish in the early 1960s. The decentralization of ACLU litigation was one reason, although Melvin Wulf, the national organization's legal director, continued to funnel inquiries to the AJC and to tap its judgment on litigation strategies. The desire of AU to go its own way and to increase its involvement in litigation, especially entering cases as an organizational plaintiff, was another reason. In any event, the informal ties eroded just at the time at which group activity and shoulder-rubbing began to increase sharply.

By the middle and late 1960s the ACLU, AJC, and AU began to formalize their relationships. The formalization began, ironically, at an informal, unpublicized, and very much off-the-record Legal Conference on the Establishment Clause held in September of 1965. Organized by a number of leaders actively concerned with

[27] *Rhoades* v. *School District* and *Americans United* v. *School District*.
[28] The two cases, in order, were *Board of Education* v. *Allen,* and *Chamberlin* v. *Dade County*.

church-state litigation, it brought together about fifty attorneys and organization representatives (including those of the ACLU, AJC, and AU) to consider litigation goals and strategy. The assemblage discussed the full range of church-state issues, including the emerging ones of antipoverty aid to religious institutions, direct aid to religious schools, and aid for housing and hospital construction. It was at that conference that it was agreed that the AJC, ACLU, and AU would coordinate and exchange information about their litigation.

By 1966, accordingly, the three groups had set up a litigation consortium. It was, however, slow to move into formal action. Initially it involved little more than more frequent communications among Pfeffer, John Adams of the AU legal staff, and officials of the national ACLU. By late 1967 or 1968 the consortium had begun formal meetings and formal agreements. A meeting in 1968, for instance, produced a memo of July 20, 1968, which outlined a set of "guiding principles" (see box). The memo concluded with a set of proposed courses of action. High priorities were attached to tests of the Pennsylvania parochaid statute and Congress's Higher Education Facilities Act. (Both priorities were eventually realized in *Lemon* v. *Kurtzman* and *Tilton* v. *Richardson,* in which all three groups were involved.) The consortium also agreed to initiate a surplus property case, but declined to pursue the poverty program because of fear of adverse public response. The memo concluded with general principles, among them the need to pursue legal victories, and thus to avoid "borderline" cases.

The consortium met at least three more times through 1968 and 1969. Typically, a dozen to twenty individuals were present, representing a number of groups besides the three—groups such as the National Council of Churches (whose Dean Kelley was one of the consortium's founders), the Baptist Joint Committee, and assorted educational groups. In October of 1968, for example, with Pfeffer presiding, it discussed the *Tilton* case. It also urged AU to postpone its Dayton, Ohio, suit on textbooks and secondary services in view of the Supreme Court's decision in *Board* v. *Allen.* It did, however, encourage an AU suit on the issue of tax exemptions for religious bodies earning—by holdings such as vineyards and spaghetti factories—"unrelated religious income." After May of 1969 the consortium apparently stopped meeting. The groups continued to meet (usually in New York) over specific litigation in which they were involved, but they had always done that. The

THE LITIGATION CONSORTIUM

The first formal meeting of the separationist litigation consortium drafted a series of guiding principles and proposed courses of action that were then circulated in a mimeographed memo of July 20, 1968. The four "guiding principles" were these:

A. It is especially important that the next decision by the Supreme Court be in favor of the separation principle. It is also more important than usual at this time to have victories rather than losses in the lower courts. This suggests that borderline cases should not be pressed at this time.

B. Every effort should be made to prevent cases from going to the Supreme Court on a bare record. In the *Allen* decision, the Court made it plain that such a record is proper and desirable. [The reference here is clearly intended to be a full record rather than a "bare record."] Our complaints, therefore, should contain such detailed and complete allegations concerning the religious nature of the operations involved and concerning the extent of aid to the institutions that it will be unprofitable for the other side to move to dismiss.

C. In selecting cases, efforts should be made to find and name as defendants schools in which there is a high level of religious activity.

D. It would be desirable if the next case to come to the Supreme Court dealing with aid to sectarian schools showed a substantially higher degree of aid than busses or textbooks. We should avoid making it easy for the Court to move by a series of small steps all the way down the road to full aid. Our best chance of turning it away from that road is to pose an issue requiring a large step or none. This suggests a case involving a clear, substantial increase in the total assets of the institution, particularly in assets usable for religious as well as nonreligious activities, or one involving the infusion of public funds directly into the treasury of the institution.

consortium had been an attempt to plan mutually their longer-range litigation priorities and strategies.

Perhaps the short life of the consortium was the result of the motives behind its origins. It was in part an attempt to limit AU's litigation "recklessness." A number of the participants, probably including AU, recognized this. And whether or not it was so intended, it soon became a vehicle for Leo Pfeffer's judgments and preferences. He was, at least, its dominant figure, and its decisions almost invariably reflected his views. The statement of "guiding principles," for instance, was certainly "pure" Pfeffer. In part, too, the consortium was doomed by the rising levels of AU litigation and by the new freedom of ACLU affiliates to litigate. It was, in short, erected on a flawed premise: that a national consortium could control the full range of church-state litigation.

THE TOTAL PATTERN OF GROUP ACTIVITY

Despite the dominance of the three leading groups, separationist litigation does attract a few other national groups and a number of local ones. At least on the surface, their interventions are substantial. Local separationist groups participated in 35 of the 67 cases, assuming a sponsorship role in 12 of them. National groups other than the ACLU (or its affiliates), the AJC, and AU were in 18 of the 67, and in 4 of them as sponsors. All of that activity suggests that these groups supplement the work of the leading three in some important way. For a number of reasons, however, there is less to their activity than meets the eye.

For one thing, the "other" separationist groups, both national and local, are often not very substantial groups. Often, too, they are allied with one of the "big three." An analysis of these groups sponsoring litigation is instructive. Four national groups (other than the major three) sponsored cases, but in two instances the group was Mrs. O'Hair's Other Americans, and in one it was Joseph Lewis's Freethinkers of America—both of them little more than extensions of those two powerful personalities. The fourth was the smallish Horace Mann League, which in its test of Maryland's aid to colleges relied heavily on the expertise of the AJC's Leo Pfeffer. Of the twelve local groups acting as sponsors, six were local AU chapters or ad hoc groups closely tied to AU members. Another four were ad hoc groups without national ties; plaintiffs and local organizers of litigation formed them for the purpose of

86

that litigation, or for earlier policy disputes from which the litigation grew. Such groups operate as mechanisms for raising funds locally, for mobilizing community support, and for making decisions about goals and strategies. Finally, two of the twelve local sponsoring groups—but only two—were existing, ongoing, independent local organizations: the Louisiana Teachers Association and the South Carolina College Council. The latter of these two really had accommodationist interests, and acted as a separationist in a friendly suit only to test South Carolina's tuition grants to students attending religious colleges.[29]

Something of the flavor of this kind of local group may be conveyed by the example of the Public Funds for Public Uses committee, sponsor of a Missouri case in 1960.[30] A group of St. Louisans formed it as a vehicle for opposing a plan to sell land parcels in the Mill Creek redevelopment area to St. Louis University, a Roman Catholic institution. They were convinced that the purchase price was so low as to amount to an unconstitutional subsidy for a religious institution. Through all of the public dispute and into the litigation, PFPU functioned as the agent of the local POAU chapter, one of the nation's largest and most active at the time. The distance between the local POAU chapter and PFPU was never great. The chairman of the ad hoc organization was secretary of the local POAU unit, and an old POAU attorney in Missouri was active in PFPU. Both organizations also had ties to local Masonic groups, and both solicited the Masons for money. After the litigation, PFPU, its one mission ended if not accomplished, died the usual quick death of ad hoc organizations.

When one contrasts the litigating capacity of the national groups—especially the ACLU, AJC, and AU—with these local groups, the disparity is as wide as it is understandable. The local groups lack the legal experience, the sources of information, the organizational skills, and the long-range concern for church-state issues of the national groups. In the perceptive words of Richard Morgan,

In the states and localities, church-state conflicts are much less structured, and the techniques of political action differ from those of the first two arenas [both national in scope]. The

---

[29] *Hartness* v. *Patterson,* in which the South Carolina Supreme Court struck down the grants.
[30] *Kintzele* v. *City of St. Louis.*

emphasis is not on long-range planning and carefully established access to key decision-makers, but rather on rapid marshaling of community sentiment and support for one highly moralized battle—to stop a particular bill in a state legislature, or to force a school board to refrain from doing something. Typically, ad hoc group coalitions develop quickly, activity rises to a climax, some decision is taken and the coalitions dissolve—leaving more or less serious community relations wounds.[31]

Their concern is short and sporadic precisely because their concern is with immediate remedies rather than with the elaboration of a plan of constitutional development. Their community relations problems arise primarily out of their moralistic fervor, but they result, too, from an inability to restrain their often overzealous adherents. Every member of the group is more or less free to be its spokesman; there is little of the discipline or specialization of roles one finds in more settled groups. Local groups struggle with other problems, too. Their collective span of attention is short; it is difficult for them to maintain morale and effort through long and drawn-out legal sparrings. And their problems in fund raising are chronic. What begins with a brash confidence of ability to sustain costly litigation often ends in negotiated partial payments to attorneys.

So, very little of the group activity outside of that by ACLU, AJC, and AU represents activity by ongoing groups with substantial clienteles or even a moderate life span. Furthermore, that activity occurs in the same cases in which the leading three groups participate (Table 4–6). In only one of the sixteen cases in which none of the three major groups acted was another national group involved, and in only two was a local group active. In sum, therefore, in only three of the sixteen cases in which the three major groups were absent did some other group intervene. Furthermore—as a close look at Table 4–6 reveals—the likelihood of some other group intervening in the other fifty-one cases increased with the greater depth of involvement by one or more of the major three. By any measure, therefore, the other groups participated in the same litigation in which the ACLU, AJC, and AU did. They did not complement the activity of the three; at the most they supplemented it.

Finally, as a footnote to group activity apart from the three

[31] *The Politics of Religious Conflict* (Pegasus: New York, 1968), p. 95.

TABLE 4-6

Relationship of Activity of Three Major Groups to Activity of
Other National and Local Separationist Groups

Cases Defined by Participation of Three Leading Groups (N = 67)	Participation of Other National Groups		Participation of Local Groups	
	no	yes	no	yes
None (16)	15 (30.6%)	1 (5.6%)	14 (43.8%)	2 (5.7%)
Amicus curiae (10)	8 (16.3%)	2 (11.1%)	7 (21.9%)	3 (8.6%)
Intermediate (21)	16 (32.7%)	5 (27.8%)	5 (15.6%)	16 (45.7%)
Sponsorship (20)	10 (20.4%)	10 (55.6%)	6 (18.8%)	14 (40.0%)
Totals (67)	49	18	32	35

Note: Following the convention observed in the earlier tables of this chapter, the cases here are classified by the major role any one of the three major groups played in it. The cases and not the group roles are the units of analysis.

major groups, it should be noted that it, too, is becoming "nationalized." While activity by the "other" national groups increased slowly in the years between 1951 and 1971, local group activity dropped sharply. Seen by seven-year periods, the record of local group activity looks thus:

Years	Total Cases	Cases in Which Local Groups Were Involved
1951–1957	11	10 (90.9%)
1958–1964	22	11 (50.0%)
1965–1971	34	14 (41.2%)
Totals	67	35

That dropoff is not easily explained. It does seem clear, however, that some of it can be attributed to the growing centralization of litigation initiatives in AU and the consequent reduction in the activity of its local chapters and their ad hoc litigating organizations. It may additionally mark the preemption of litigation by the three major groups. Perhaps as the availability and interest of national litigating groups becomes better known, potential local litigants increasingly turn to them. As they say in the rhetoric of the right, all those national resources may be undermining local initiative.

The sheer quantity, depth, and constancy of ACLU, AJC, and AU appearances over two decades dwarf the activities of other separationist groups. Other groups entered the same cases they did, adding largely a supplementary ornament to their initiatives. And yet as they reduced any competing litigators to secondary roles—or, perhaps, even to oblivion—they managed to accommodate or embrace a wide range of separationist goals. Only the atheists and militant nonbelievers maintained any substantial role in church-state litigation outside of their ambit.

But it is an oligopoly and not a cartel that we describe. There are competitions and differentiations that in many ways suggest a stable three-group system. The patterns of their relationships are definable and fairly constant—the ACLU-AJC axis, the apartness of AU, and the focus of information channels and leadership expectations on the AJC. The three maintain a division of effort and responsibility in which they work in different cases in different parts of the country, a division that reflects differences in their clienteles, their separationist commitments, their skills and capacities, and even their styles of managing litigation. These differences all have profound consequences for litigating church-state issues, most especially for the differing goals and strategies they pursue in litigation. To those differences and their consequences we turn in the next chapter.

V | GOALS AND STRATEGIES OF THE SEPARATIONIST GROUPS

The connoisseurs of rationality in the political process might well expect the separationist groups to raise the litigating of constitutional issues to new levels of strategic sophistication. Groups enter the judicial process, after all, largely because they perceive the need to pursue their goals in an orderly, systematic way. Their impact on the judicial process results from an enduring interest that enables them to set continuing goals, and from the resources and expertise that enable them to reach them. Their very raison d'etre depends on their possessing the capacity for purposeful, orderly development of a body of constitutional law.

But it is easy to expect too much of the litigating groups, even the most experienced of them. It is true that they operate in a complex process, in which a maze of alternate routes and legal culs-de-sac throws advantage to the side of the shrewd and skillful. But they have little or no impact on extensive portions of the judicial process, especially on the judicial decision itself. Much of their goal-setting and strategy hinges on the very precarious business of predicting decisions they really cannot affect. Nor can they control, even with the greatest effort, the initiatives and access of other plaintiffs. One recluse can attack the tax exemption on churches, and in invoking the power of the Supreme Court (with its unexpected acquiescence), undo the priorities of a whole consortium of litigating organizations. Those organizations, therefore, operate with limited information, limited options, and limited influence, and thus with limited strategic effectiveness.

There is, in other words, no great master battle plan for litigating church-state issues. The increment in strategic effectiveness that the groups have brought to the litigation of church-state issues has the flavor of the ad hoc. Theirs is often short-range or short-term strategy, frequently a strategy that sees no further than the case at hand. Frequently it is little more than the tactical shrewdness that a skilled attorney brings to his case. In quantity and even in quality, however, it does represent a level of sophistication beyond what individual plaintiffs bring to constitutional litigation. There is at least a sense of constitutional objectives, and the need—however imperfectly seen or realized—to reach them. It is a simple advance, perhaps, but in constitutional litigation it is the crucial one.

THE GOALS OF LITIGATION

A good many of the differences in litigating strategies between major groups and the individual plaintiff or the ad hoc group grow from differences in the objectives they pursue. Strategy differences among even the American Civil Liberties Union, the American Jewish Congress, and Americans United reflect divergence in their goals, in fact. Strategy is rooted in the goals the plaintiffs pursue, and all of the plaintiffs in these sixty-seven cases may—with a little simplification—be grouped by three main categories of goals. There are those pursuing remedy, those pursuing ideological or organizational goals, and those pursuing constitutional goals.

It is the individual plaintiffs and the local groups who most often typify the pursuit of litigation for immediate remedy. Theirs is the traditional or conventional litigation that has no real goal beyond the facts of the instant controversy. The plaintiffs tend to be exercised by some alliance of church and state of which they disapprove—whether it is the permission granted a churchless Roman Catholic parish to use a public school building temporarily, or the practice of opening a New England town meeting with a prayer. Their more dispassionate attorneys may counsel against litigation—both did, for instance, in the cases just mentioned.[1] But they are often not dissuaded. They know no other way to end the offending practice, and, if need be, they are willing "to carry the case all the way to the Supreme Court." They have little desire to litigate broader issues, to settle more general principles, to affect more widespread practices. They have a very simple system of priorities among church-state issues; the issue at hand and which is offending is paramount, all others are unimportant. They may, indeed, even play down the church-state issues in a case if that will help to win it.

Madalyn Murray O'Hair presents the classic instance of the second group of goals: litigation for organizational, ideological,

[1] *Southside Estates Baptist* v. *Board of Trustees* and *Lincoln* v. *Page.*

92

even publicity purposes. The courts serve as a vehicle for publicizing the cause, and litigation spurs the necessary contributions to keep the movement going. (Perhaps "movement" is indeed a better term than "organization," for there is the crusading fervor and the absolutism of a social movement.) The very adversary nature of litigation seems to capture, even to "write large," the elemental nature of the struggle, with its overtones of good against evil. And if one litigates carefully, it is an inexpensive and unfailing source of publicity. In that respect, the perennial litigator is much like the perennial candidate in local elections.

Such litigation goals do not foster selectivity in litigation, nor do they lead to pragmatic alliances with groups of different ideology. The result is the kind of staggering record of litigation (most of it dead at the trial level) that Joseph Lewis and Mrs. O'Hair have spawned. And if it is lonely litigation, it is so often by choice of goal. Mrs. O'Hair and the ACLU separated in her suit against the saying of the Lord's Prayer in Baltimore schools over her insistence on being the only plaintiff, and thus in having it "her" case. The ACLU wanted a broader group of plaintiffs, some of whom might be more religious and less iconoclastic than Madalyn Murray. The point here is that the difference of opinion in Baltimore was only superficially over the strategy of plaintiff selection; it was basically over the goal or purpose of the litigation.

Litigation for constitutional development—the third category—is typified by the American Civil Liberties Union and the American Jewish Congress. The litigation guide of the ACLU notes:

> The ACLU cannot take every case where there is a civil liberties question being raised. Rather, it should direct its efforts to cases which have some reasonable promise of having broad impact on other cases. Thus, it is always appropriate to take a case which offers the possibility of establishing new civil liberties precedents which will control other cases. . . .
>
> The case should involve a determination of the civil liberties issue in such fashion as to have an impact on other cases beyond the particular one in question, either by establishing a new legal precedent, or by tending to increase significantly the recognition of existing precedent in practice. Particular attention should be paid to this point where direct representation of a defendant is contemplated, since it may be difficult or impossible for the

93

organization's attorney to withdraw if it turns out that the civil liberties issue is not in fact involved.[2]

It is the long-range precedent, not the immediate remedy or organizational publicity, that is the goal. If anything, the AJC exceeds the ACLU in its constitutional purism. Leo Pfeffer has long considered litigation for any reason other than the purely legal to be irresponsible. This is not to suggest, of course, that these two organizations have no commitment to a separationist ideology, or no concern for the impact of litigation on publicity or for its organizational pay-offs. It is a question of the ultimate, guiding consideration in litigation, and in the main the ACLU and AJC litigate to secure favorable precedents and to avoid unfavorable ones.

So much for the three "pure" types of litigating goals. The goals of AU fall somewhere in between the second and the third, for AU gives evidence of trying to achieve both organizational and constitutional goals. Especially through the 1950s and early 1960s, it was common for AU to support local separationists and their litigation with a modest sum of money and its seal of approval, to send speakers such as Paul Blanshard, Glenn Archer, or Stanley Lowell to raise money and enthusiasm for the suit, and at the same time to start a local chapter of POAU in the area. And so AU early discovered that litigation

> is also an excellent tool for organization-building and constituency mobilization, and in cases where the law suit has proved a washout, POAU has left a chapter and a group of new members behind. The suit draws attention; it focuses tensions within a community, and it encourages people to take sides. It gives the interest group representative something to enlist supporters *for,* and provides a sense of action and immediacy. As Louie Newton put it, . . . it is a "vehicle for arousing people."[3]

Indeed, the files of AU contain more than one reference to "milking" litigation for "what it's worth." The same motivation also increasingly led AU to appear as an organizational plaintiff in the 1960s. In sum, AU depends to a greater extent than the ACLU or AJC on funds and contributions from individuals; and all of

[2] *Guide for ACLU Litigation,* mimeographed paper (March 1970), pp. 1–2.

[3] Richard E. Morgan, "Backs to the Wall: A Study in the Contemporary Politics of Church and State," Ph.D. dissertation, Columbia University, 1967, p. 264. The Newton quote is from a letter of his to Morgan.

its appeal, unlike theirs, rests on church-state issues. AU must, apparently, enlist its members with reports of continuing activity and crisis; both its special mailings and its *Church and State* certainly convey that beleaguered image.[4]

At the appellate stage, and especially in the Supreme Court, however, AU has always tried to shift its goals to the constitutional. At this point, indeed, it has often relied heavily on the judgment of Leo Pfeffer. Yet a shift in goals is often difficult. By this time the people on the scene have been rallied and solicited for funds, and their disposition is to total victory and vindication. In church-and-state terms they want the offending breach of separation stopped, and they want to exhaust all possible remedies to do so. AU has repeatedly found it difficult to prevent legally improvident appeals—which risk repeated hostile precedents in appellate courts—brought by excited local plaintiffs and organizers and their ad hoc organizations. One can only say that while the problem is still a problem for AU, it is diminishing somewhat as AU centralizes more of the decisions on litigation in its Washington offices.

Regardless of goal or purpose, of course, all litigating groups and individuals want to "win" their cases. But "winning" depends on what goals one pursues. Depending on the goal, one can win the suit and obtain the remedy without in any way creating a useful precedent for future cases. One may, indeed, even win the remedy but lose the constitutional battle. And if one's goals are publicity or organizational solidarity or expansion, one may "win" by losing cases in the legal sense of that word. Those kinds of "victories" raise fears in the ACLU and the AJC about other litigating groups.

DIFFERING GOALS: THE STRATEGIC CONSEQUENCES

Most fundamentally, the pursuit of constitutional precedents produces a deep caution and conservatism in litigation. The ACLU and especially the AJC steer widely clear of cases they feel they have no chance of winning. In such cases the "payoffs" in litigating

---

[4] All of this is not to say that the ACLU and AJC have never profited organizationally from their litigation. They have. The ACLU and NYCLU action in *Engel* v. *Vitale,* the New York Regents' Prayer case, for example, gave rise to an ACLU chapter in Nassau and Suffolk counties. At least three of the *Engel* plaintiffs were founding members, and one was the first chairman. But this was a "serendipitous," not a planned, result of the litigation.

for constitutional goals are less promising than the "payoffs" in litigating for remedies or for organizational goals. For one thing, the likelihood of loss is real, and an unfavorable precedent may adversely affect litigation for years to come and lead to other hostile precedents. If, on the other hand, one litigates for remedies or for organizational purposes, no genuine "loss" or set-back is likely in an appellate court loss. An adverse decision means only that the status quo remains what it was; the marriage of church and state doesn't become worse, nor does the organization usually regress.

Even with better prospects for the litigation, the achievement of constitutional precedents is difficult enough to make the AJC or ACLU cautious. A decision for the plaintiff need not assure the group litigator the rule of law, the precedent, or even the dicta it wants. The plaintiff may even win in a lower court and, if the defense refuses to appeal, the group may find that it cannot get its case into the appellate court it had been aiming for. It is as if all kinds of litigators were given five arrows and a target. The seekers of remedies win if any one hits the target. The constitutional litigators *might* win if an arrow hits the target, and they run the risk of losing points for each miss. The organizational litigators are more apt to win or lose on the style and flair of their shooting than on their success in hitting the target.

For these reasons the AJC, especially, and many of the ACLU affiliates avoid all but the most promising cases. The dimensions of that caution cannot easily be established because the major portion of their rejections never reaches an appellate court. Even so, in at least four of these sixty-seven cases the AJC tried to discourage or refused to enter the litigation, at least in part because it thought the case poorly calculated to achieve constitutional goals.[5] AU may also become cautious about weak litigation, especially if it has not been active in it at the trial stages. In such instances it has little to gain organizationally because it comes so late to the case and therefore becomes primarily a constitutional litigator.

Perhaps nothing illustrates the implications of different litigation goals as well as the specific instances in which they conflict. Philip Carden's early suit in Nashville to halt the reading of the Bible

[5] In several of them (*Engel* v. *Vitale* and *Schempp* v. *School District*, for instance) the AJC did, however, enter at later stages. Regardless of its earlier opinion, the AJC will not ordinarily let a case go to the U.S. Supreme Court without its participation.

and other religious practices in the public schools illustrates the point.[6] Carden was outraged to find his young son's teacher not only reading the Bible but also checking her pupils' attendance at Sunday school. On one Monday, in fact, Mark Carden had had to copy the 100th Psalm because of his failure to go to Sunday school the day before. After his protests to the Nashville School Board came to no avail, Carden, supported largely by the local Unitarian church, brought suit to end the practices. Leo Pfeffer and the American Jewish Congress learned of the case through the Religious News Service, and wrote Carden asking him to have his attorney communicate with them. After investigating the case, the AJC decided not to participate, largely because there had been no trial and thus no record of fact, and because the complaint alleged little more than the specific practices of the one school his son attended. In the words of Pfeffer:

> I think that ultimately a suit will have to be brought to the U.S. Supreme Court to test the constitutionality of Bible reading statutes. I think that it is an inopportune time to bring such a suit. Moreover, I think that when the suit is brought it should be based upon an adequate record after a carefully planned trial which would show the abuses and the various practices engaged in during the course of the Bible reading and prayer recitation. The record in the present suit is entirely bare of these factors. . . . The Supreme Court of the United States would be unable, even if it wished, to examine the actual practices in the public school or to base its decision on those practices.[7]

What was Carden's attempt to alter the specific religious influences in his son's education—and the case was pleaded and argued on those terms and for that specific remedy—simply did not pass muster as a constitutional test case.[8]

More recently, the suit of the Louisiana Teachers Association to invalidate that state's parochaid statute also illustrates how

[6] *Carden* v. *Bland.*
[7] Pfeffer to Louis Silberman of Nashville (March 23, 1956); copy in AJC files, New York, N.Y.
[8] There was also another reason for AJC nonparticipation. Readings of opinion in the local Jewish community showed a good deal of hostility to AJC involvement. In the words of one local Jewish leader: "we, who are the People of the Book, surely should not object to the Bible being read in the schools" (letter in AJC files).

97

different litigation goals lead to different strategies.[9] Even though it was one of the first challenges of a statewide parochaid statute—the suit was brought in September of 1970—the LTA went into state courts rather than federal courts, and argued the case on state constitutional grounds. (Both the ACLU and AU were planning suits in federal court and on the U.S. Constitution, clearly the superior strategy, since a precedent would apply in all fifty states.) Furthermore, the LTA agreed to bypass a trial and the building of a trial record in order to take the case immediately on certiorari to the Louisiana Supreme Court. It sought speed at the expense of the trial record, clearly not what a group interested in constitutional goals would have done. In view of the goals of the LTA, however, the strategy was impeccable. Its interest was entirely in nullifying the program of aid, in preserving the position of the public schools, and in doing so before planning and commitments for the 1970 school year were too advanced. Hence the decisions to accelerate the case at any cost and to argue in state courts under the state constitution. The case was won, and the Louisiana statute invalidated by a 4–3 vote of the Louisiana Supreme Court. But American constitutional development had to wait for the U.S. Supreme Court's decisions on the Pennsylvania and Rhode Island parochaid statutes some eight months later.[10]

These conflicts of goals stand out in the decisions to take a case to an appellate court, especially to the U.S. Supreme Court. And they appear most frequently in the AU cases, both because AU has tried to follow both organizational and constitutional goals, and because AU has permitted at least partial local autonomy in cases it has supported. Local groups generally rely on AU financial help for appeals, especially to the U.S. Supreme Court, and that gives the national office some control over appellate decisions. Yet the pressures from local activists for remedy and vindication rather than some abstract precedent or legal half-victory are tremendous. No case better illustrates AU's ambivalence over conflicting litigation goals than the "captive schools" case from New Mexico, *Zellers* v. *Huff*.

The New Mexico case originated in the dusty town of Dixon, a little commercial crossroads in the irrigated country between Sante Fe and Taos. The town was unusual for that state in one respect: it had a Protestant minority, largely Presbyterian, of

[9] The case is *Seegers* v. *Parker*.
[10] *Lemon* v. *Kurtzman* and *DiCenso* v. *Robinson*.

98

some vigor. The events that sparked the litigation, as *Time* reported them, were these:

> Though Dixon's handful of Protestants had never liked the idea of nuns teaching their children, they kept their peace so long as the church owned the building where classes were held. But two years ago, Dixon's 800 citizens raised $13,000 [*sic!*] to build the community a grade school of its own. Protestant parents were dismayed to discover that the county school board had hired a nun as principal and four nuns as teachers. There were crucifixes on the wall, Catholic prayers before and after class. A delegation of Protestants complained to the state board of education.[11]

The forces in Dixon were led by Mrs. Lydia Zellers, a Presbyterian and keeper of the general store in town, and assisted by attorneys and Protestant ministers in Sante Fe. Failing in their representations before the county and state boards of education, they eventually brought suit to end the hiring of nuns in fifteen different counties of the state. (New Mexico has thirty-two counties, and its population was, by count of the 1936 special census, 80.7 percent Roman Catholic.) Their legal objections were both to the employment of the nuns per se and to the religious influences they introduced into the public schools.

The New Mexico trial court ruling stopped short of barring all nuns from public school employment, but it did ban from New Mexico schools 235 nuns, brothers, and priests for having brought religion into public school classrooms. It also ordered an end to a set of religious influences—from religious symbols and books to the release of pupils for daily mass. The ACLU, AJC, and AU, all involved in some degree, considered it a victory. The Protestants of Dixon, their supporters, and their attorney (Harry Bigbee of Santa Fe) did not. They resolved to appeal the decision to seek the removal of all nuns from all the public schools of New Mexico. The three national groups advised against the appeal in the strongest terms. Pfeffer wrote to Bigbee, urging him not to appeal, and to treat evasions of the trial court judgment in separate suits:

> Irrespective of the merits of your position, it is highly improbable that any state supreme court in the United States would

[11] *Time* (September 29, 1947), p. 70.

99

rule it illegal or unconstitutional for members of a religious order to teach in public schools. It seems to me, therefore, that the probability of success is negligible. On the other hand, by appealing you run the real risk that the Supreme Court [of New Mexico] may clearly weaken the force of Judge Hensley's decision and thus impair the victory which you have won.[12]

Glenn Archer, newly installed as POAU's executive director, also tried his hand at dissuasion by urging contempt proceedings against noncompliant school districts rather than an appeal. The chances of the state supreme court's barring all religious groups from public employment were, he estimated, "mightly slim." To this barrage of advice, Bigbee responded that the appeal was going on as planned. Furthermore, he doubted that national groups could arrive at an intelligent recommendation so far from the scene and without the close advice of people fully informed about the local scene. Finally, he said,

> The appellants in this case are dedicated to the proposition and thoroughly convinced there is no separation of church and state when Catholic Religious teach in the school. This is not a theoretical proposition to them since many of their children have been forced to attend . . . schools taught by Catholic Religious where they saw their children being daily indoctrinated by the Catholic Sisters. . . . [They] are only interested in a determination to try to remove all Catholic Sisters from the schools in New Mexico.[13]

The clash in goals could not have been clearer. It was a "theoretical proposition" versus the reality of the Catholic Sisters teaching their children. For those directly involved, to have won the former without eliminating the latter could hardly be considered a victory. Having failed to stop the appeal, the AJC and AU resolved to do what they could to insure its success. Pfeffer, for instance, weighed in with an intensive, two and one-half page critique of a draft of Bigbee's brief for the New Mexico Supreme Court.

While this pulling and hauling was going on, the defense in the New Mexico case also faced strategic decisions of its own about an appeal. A substantial part of the defense had passed from the

[12] Letter of October 5, 1949; copy in AJC files.
[13] Bigbee to Glenn Archer (undated, probably mid-1950) in AU files.

state and county boards of education to the local Catholic archdiocese, and thence to the National Catholic Welfare Conference,
predecessor of the present U.S. Catholic Conference. It was the
NCWC that arranged for the distinguished Washington attorney
and later federal court judge, Charles Fahy, to lead the defense.
Although the local pressures were great to appeal what the church
and local districts must have considered a defeat in the trial court,
Fahy counselled against it. The greatest risk to an appeal by the
defense, he argued, was to open an avenue to the U.S. Supreme
Court, and "the present time [1949 and only one year after *McCollum*] is not a favorable time on such issues in that Court." Furthermore, "the facts of the case would likely create an unfavorable
impression upon the Court. When the garb issue reaches the
Supreme Court, if it must, it should be unencumbered by such adverse facts as becloud that issue in the present case."[14] When the
plaintiffs appealed, Fahy recommended crossappeal only on selected points.

The New Mexico Supreme Court's decision, despite the AU and
AJC fears, did not greatly alter the trial court decision, and the
victory was not lost. But the local plaintiffs' and organizers' urge
for vindication was not satisfied. Apparently they made no request
for AJC or AU support for an appeal to the U.S. Supreme Court,
knowing, perhaps, what the response would be. Out of funds, they
could not go on their own. So Mrs. Zellers wrote the national
ACLU in 1951, asking for help in an appeal to the Supreme Court.
The ACLU, happy that the New Mexico courts had largely
affirmed its own position, refused the request, and there the case
ended.

The decision whether to go to the appellate court reveals more
than conflicts in the goal of litigation. It is also the central and
most crucial strategic step for all constitutional litigators, for it
is at the appellate court levels that constitutional precedents are
made. Indeed, there is no more powerful argument on the side
of a full sponsoring role in such litigation than the argument that
only in that way can the group make sure an unwise appeal will
not be carried. Once the local plaintiffs or organizers of litigation
have decided to carry an appeal, the ACLU, AJC, and AU really
have no choice but to climb aboard and try to prevent the worst

[14] Undated memo (probably shortly after the trial court decision in March
1949) in files of Joseph Guthman of Santa Fe.

101

from happening. But participation for "damage control" is hardly apt to be constructive or productive, and litigating groups are perfectly aware of that fact.

The groups actually have some leverage on their side beyond that arising from sponsorship of a case. If one of them does not sponsor, there is a good chance that local funds for the litigation will run out by the time an appeal to the U.S. Supreme Court is in order. Then the local litigators often come, hat in hand, to one of the national groups. Furthermore, local attorneys grow timid at the prospect of carrying a case to the nation's high court, and the special legal expertise of the national groups is their second point of leverage. Their greatest ally is, actually, the Court itself. Cases and issues that the major litigating groups regard as frivolous or inappropriate, the Court may regard similarly. Of the ten cases decided by the U.S. Supreme Court between 1951 and 1971, there were only two whose appeal (or petition for certiorari) to the Court did not enjoy the support of at least one of the three leading groups: the tax exemption case of Frederick Walz, and the Lord's Prayer case of Madalyn Murray. The eight others were sponsored by at least one of the three.[15]

SEPARATIONIST STRATEGY: ORGANIZING THE CASE

Litigating groups differ less on matters of strategy and tactic than they do on the broader issues of goal or purpose in litigation. In strategic matters, in fact, groups do not even differ greatly from nongroup plaintiffs. To a considerable extent, matters of strategy are really only considerations of wise and prudent litigation, and they depend not so much on the nature of the plaintiff as on the skills and experience of his counsel. There are areas in which wise attorneys disagree, but the differences characterize individuals among litigators rather than types of litigators.

What follows is a brief discussion of the range of strategy decisions the litigators face in these church-state cases. Since most of the litigators are separationists, we will be speaking here largely of the separationist strategies in litigation; accommodationist interests have brought too few of these cases—only five, when one eliminates the friendly suits—for much generalization. Clearly, too, the range of strategy considerations outlined here should not

[15] The two exceptions are *Walz* v. *Tax Commission* and *Murray* v. *Curlett.*

suggest a checklist that faces every litigator. As an aggregate picture it is far more extensive than any particular case contributing to it. But it does remind one of a crucial, if obvious fact: the number and range of strategic decisions any litigator faces in a case is primarily determined by the extent of his role in the case. Indeed, the amicus curiae confronts so few that he will be considered separately at the end of this strategic catalogue.[16]

Selecting the Issue and the Case

The first strategic question, the central one, is whether the constitutional issue and its manifestation is right—right for the group, right for litigation, right for an appellate court victory. Groups may refuse to become involved in a case if the right issue is set or presented in ways they think unfortunate. Leo Pfeffer, for instance, held the AJC out of the Regents' Prayer case (*Engel* v. *Vitale*) at least in part because atheists and nonbelievers dominated the group of plaintiffs. Nonetheless, the basic decision still remains the appropriateness of the issue itself—its "ripeness," its importance to the constitutional universe of church-state, its relationship to other issues.

Had the litigating groups, either singly or cooperatively, been able to develop some schedule of long-range priorities in litigation, they would have had some guide in the selection of issues. But, with the exception of the brief list of priorities drawn up at one meeting of the litigation consortium, they had none. As a result, they have more or less taken the issues as they came. There have been few attempts to reckon whether, in terms of predicted outcomes, resources could more profitably be invested in one issue than another. And yet, while no explicit, long-run system of priorities reigned on these matters from 1951 to 1971, it is apparent that each of the three groups did have an implicit, if somewhat short-run, set of priorities.

To some extent the kinds of cases in which they were involved

[16] I have used "strategy" and "tactic" synonymously here, even though some usage sees a "means" (tactics) and "ends" (strategy) distinction. That distinction I believe I have introduced in the difference between goals on the one hand and strategy or tactics on the other. For another approach to interest group strategies in the judicial process, see Nathan Hakman's work: "Lobbying the Supreme Court—An Appraisal of 'Political Science Folklore'," *Fordham Law Review* 35 (1966), 18ff.; and "The Supreme Court's Political Environment: The Processing of Noncommercial Litigation," in Joel B. Grossman and Joseph Tanenhaus, *Frontiers of Judicial Research* (New York: Wiley, 1969), pp. 205–206.

reveal something of their priorities: AU in cases in which Roman Catholic interests were involved, for example, and all three of the groups in cases involving primary and secondary education. But these were subject-matter rather than litigation priorities, and as such they reflected the groups' clienteles and definitions of separation. All three also had implicit standards of de minimis for breaches in the wall of separation. None was willing, despite the pleas of offended would-be plaintiffs, to test references to the Deity in the national motto or the pledge of allegiance to the flag. (Both issues were litigated without support from any of the three.) De minimis merges into nonissue, of course, and all three groups were careful to avoid entanglement with facts they believed not clearly in violation of the constitutional separation. The AJC ducked involvement with the St. Louis redevelopment case and its sale of land to St. Louis University, Leo Pfeffer noting dryly that nothing prevented a church from driving a hard bargain.[17] AU declined to become involved in a case questioning Maryland loans for the construction of religious hospitals on the ground that the facts did not appear to indicate a sectarian administration of the hospitals.[18] And for years the ACLU ran away from the entreaties of Alexander Lincoln, who objected to the moderator of his township deciding on his own to open town meetings with a prayer.[19]

Within what the groups considered useful or important issues of separation, there were apparently only fragmentary priorities in the 1951–1971 period. Pfeffer and the AJC clearly operated on one "middle-range" priority: that among issues of aid to religious schools the textbook question should be brought to the Supreme Court before the issue of bus rides. The precedent upholding bus rides, they believed, had been more recently and fully considered than the one on texts.[20] Furthermore, texts were more directly related to education and the religious mission of the schools then were busses. In urging AU to keep one of its bus cases from the U.S. Supreme Court, Pfeffer wrote in 1960:

> I feel strongly that it is highly improbable that the Court today would overrule the *Everson* decision. At some future time it may do so but I do not think it is ready to do it now. For that

[17] The case was *Kintzele* v. *City of St. Louis.*
[18] The case was *Truitt* v. *Board of Public Works.*
[19] *Lincoln* v. *Page.*
[20] The case on texts (*Cochran* v. *Louisiana State Board of Education,* 281 U.S. 370) had been decided in 1930; the one on transportation (*Everson* v. *Board of Education,* 330 U.S. 1) came down in 1947.

104

reason, I would advise against an appeal on the Connecticut bus case [*Snyder* v. *Newtown*].

It is and has been my feeling for a long time that the Court is more likely to overrule the *Cochran* decision before it will overrule the *Everson* decision. It is for that reason we decided not to combine the count against bus transportation in our Oregon suit attacking textbook distribution [*Dickman* v. *School District*].

I feel strongly that an adverse decision on an appeal in the Connecticut bus case will be very damaging to our Oregon textbook case and will postpone for a considerable time the overruling by the Supreme Court of both the *Everson* and the *Cochran* decisions.[21]

That judgment on priorities, indeed, kept the AJC out of most of the bus cases in this period. Among the sixty-seven cases there are eleven in which transportation of children to religious schools at public expense was an issue. The AJC participated in only two of them, and both presented special circumstances. In one the bus issue was secondary to more direct religious influences in the schools; even so, the AJC role was largely limited to covert advice.[22] In the second, AU had its separate case, and the AJC joined a competitive case organized largely by the Philadelphia affiliate of the ACLU.[23] Nonetheless, Pfeffer argued strongly, if in vain, against an appeal of the consolidated cases to the U.S. Supreme Court. And if the case were to go to the Supreme Court, he urged the request be for certiorari so that the Court could refuse without a statement. The AU decision—after some internal disagreement—was to go on appeal, apparently because of the smaller filing fee! The Supreme Court denied jurisdiction, noting the absence of a substantial federal question.

Furthermore, between 1951 and 1971 the three groups, especially the AJC and ACLU, came to want their constitutional issues clear and undiluted. Several cases that challenged omnibus lists of religious practices in the public schools did not fare well in the courts. An expensive and well-prepared suit out of Dade County, Florida, was a case in point.[24] The consolidated ACLU and AJC

[21] Pfeffer to Edward P. Felker, POAU counsel (July 5, 1960); copy in AJC files.

[22] *Rawlings* v. *Butler*.

[23] This case (*Worrell* v. *Matters*) was eventually consolidated with the AU case, *Rhoades* v. *School District*.

[24] *Chamberlin* v. *Dade County*.

cases challenged a series of practices; among others, baccalaureate services, pageants on religious (that is, Christian) occasions, Bible-reading, a religious census of pupils, and religious tests for teachers. The trial court decision was complex—partially a victory, partially a loss—and after desultory foot-dragging in the Florida Supreme Court, the U.S. Supreme Court, as if not knowing what to do with so complicated a set of facts and decisions, merely vacated per curiam and remanded to the state supreme court. In another instance POAU became gradually lost in the tangles of the Bradfordsville, Kentucky, case, which it had once fancied as its "ideal" captive schools case.[25] It turned out, however, that the welter of religious influences and ties to the public schools was only part, and perhaps a secondary part, of the controversy. The people of Bradfordsville really were protesting the closing of the local high school and the busing of their children eight miles away to the high school in the county seat of Lebanon. Ultimately the church-state issue became lost in a local school consolidation conflict. Certainly it was not accidental—nor lost on the groups—that these two ill-starred cases involved longer, more complex, and more expensive litigation than all but a few other of the sixty-seven cases.

Finally, in the same desire to keep church-state issues uncluttered and unalloyed, the AJC disagreed with the ACLU in several parochaid cases over the combination of issues. ACLU affiliates added to the church-state issues in these cases the issue of equal protection under the Fourteenth Amendment. They charged that the state, by supporting largely white private schools and by diverting funds that would otherwise go to racially diverse public schools, is in effect depriving racial minorities the equal protection of the laws. Pfeffer and the AJC opposed the tactic (without, it should be added, necessarily opposing the argument). The difference in strategy may merely reflect the fact that ACLU concerns in civil rights are broader than those of the AJC. It probably also reflects some differences over tactical judgments in constitutional litigation.

Selecting the Plaintiffs

Probably no single strategic decision receives more group or lawyerly attention than the selection of plaintiffs. It is, for one thing, a problem present in virtually all cases. It is also a decision

[25] *Wooley* v. *Spalding.*

106

of immediate importance to the attorney who wishes to make as smooth as possible the passage through the community of what will surely be unpopular litigation. For local communities will personalize even the most abstract of legal issues, and the plaintiffs are the objects of that personalized perception.

Litigating groups and attorneys prefer as plaintiffs reliable, stable, "solid" citizens who will invest the litigation with their status and respectability in the community. The plaintiffs must also be willing to accept a passive role in the litigation and permit attorneys or group spokesmen to monopolize contacts with the media. Plaintiffs with a "passion for anonymity" are the most desirable ones.[26] The AJC and AU, at least, would also like their plaintiffs to be religious—or at least not irreligious. Litigators, in other words, look to the impact their plaintiffs will have on the community and its perception of the litigation. They fear that nonbelieving plaintiffs will suggest an antireligious motive for the litigation. (It is, of course, partly because Madalyn Murray O'Hair meets virtually none of these criteria that the groups have hesitated to assume active roles in her cases.) Finally, a plaintiff of intelligence and composure can endure the experience of a trial and contribute to building the trial court record.

An in-house memo of the national ACLU reveals the care with which an experienced litigating group screens its plaintiffs. The subject is Tessim Zorach, whom the ACLU was considering as a possible plaintiff for its challenge of the New York City released-time program in 1948—the challenge brought as a substitute for Joseph Lewis's original suit. After noting that Zorach was "well-informed on the educational implications of the [released-time] program" and that he had "a number of personal reasons for objecting to it," the report continues:

> Zorach has weighed carefully all the factors involved in assuming the role of plaintiff in this case, so that there is no question of his being overwhelmed by adverse publicity. He is in no sense a publicity seeker, and expressed the hope that this thing would

[26] In a few cases groups have hoped to attract a celebrity plaintiff, but those hopes have never materialized. Celebrities often have the distinct disadvantage of adding another controversial note to the litigation. Paul Blanshard of POAU (and author of *American Freedom and Catholic Power*) at one point considered being the plaintiff in a Vermont tuition grant case, but he was discouraged when it appeared his presence would be inflammatory. A "neutral," unknown, and passive plaintiff was finally found, and the case was finally litigated as *Swart* v. *South Burlington*.

not bring a storm in the press, but he is prepared to withstand whatever adverse propaganda is forthcoming. He is the son of William Zorach, the sculptor, who has been identified with left-wing groups, but the son has no such record. . . . Zorach may not be the ideal plaintiff, but I believe he comes as close to it as we are likely to find.[27]

Care of a different, but equally impressive, kind was apparent in the selection of plaintiffs for the Louisiana Teachers Association attack on the state's parochaid statute.[28] Because the state's supreme court is one of the few in which the justices are elected from separate judicial districts, the LTA organizers selected at least one plaintiff from each district. The plaintiffs were known as supporters of public education—teachers, principals, superintendents, school board members—and were thus known also as people of substance and respectability. At least one was a personal acquaintance of a justice. It was, in short, a plaintiff selection strategy well tailored to the "friends and neighbors" localism of Louisiana politics.

Candor compels one to admit, however, that not all litigators take such scrupulous care in the selection of plaintiffs. AU has in at least one case found its plaintiffs by combing its membership rolls for the county in which it wanted to bring suit.[29] And the ACLU affiliates that "advertise" that they are looking for plaintiffs with whom to bring a test suit often find it difficult to reject the unpromising, if eager, plaintiff. But when the care in picking plaintiffs is less than complete, the reason is rarely carelessness or inadvertence. It is more often desperation, and the consequent need to choose from among so few possibilities. And if the group enters the case after its origin, of course, the plaintiff or plaintiffs are already on board.

In addition to wanting the attractive, steady plaintiff, the groups want more than one—another point of difference with Mrs. O'Hair. Their reasons are several. First, they must protect themselves against a mooting of the case. "If a plaintiff's standing to sue depends upon a particular status, loss of that status before the suit is finally disposed of may render the action 'moot,' i.e.,

[30] Will Maslow, "The Legal Defense of Religious Liberty—The Strategy and Tactics of the American Jewish Congress," mimeographed paper presented at the annual meeting of the American Political Science Association in St. Louis, Mo. (September 6–9, 1961), pp. 12–13.

[31] *Mangold* v. *School District.*

no longer an actual controversy which the courts will decide."[30] Thus the child of the single plaintiff may graduate from the school whose practices he challenges, or the plaintiff may die or move from the jurisdiction. Against the dangers of mootness, therefore, there is safety in numbers.

Secondly, a number of plaintiffs of the right kind, the groups believe, will have a more reassuring effect on the community. They will indicate a breadth of support—both in numbers and in quality—for the litigation. Thirdly, plural plaintiffs divide and disperse hostile reactions; a single plaintiff becomes the one vulnerable object for community backlash and reprisals. When Edwin Mangold came forward to bring suit against prayers in the local schools—some years after the Supreme Court's rulings—in a rural area south of Pittsburgh, the ACLU affiliate tried to protect him by surrounding him with group plaintiffs and a number of Protestant ministers from the Pittsburgh area, even though it was suspected that their standing as plaintiffs was shaky.[31]

The "multiple-plaintiff" strategy becomes something of a "balanced ticket" strategy in the hands of Pfeffer and the AJC. Their preference is not only for religious plaintiffs—and that generally means something more "religious" than a Unitarian—but for representatives of the major religious traditions. It is, perhaps, an expression of an understandable desire not to have litigation appear to be brought by Jews against the community's Christians. In their challenge of the New York City released-time program in the *Zorach* case, the AJC and the ACLU, indeed, hoped to find Protestant, Catholic, and Jewish parents as plaintiffs. A devout Catholic parent with a child in the public schools was, at least at that time, something of an anomaly, and the case commenced with just Protestant and Jewish parents. As times changed and organized religions dropped in influence, the AJC became a little less committed to the "balanced ticket." By the late 1960s one could find Unitarians and nonbelievers as plaintiffs in cases the AJC sponsored or cosponsored.

Finally, of course, it is essential that the plaintiffs have the necessary standing to sue. That much is more a requirement than a strategy. While taxpayer standing is not necessarily a bar to liti-

[27] Memo of June, 1948, in ACLU files, Princeton University Library, Princeton, N.J. Zorach became the first plaintiff in the suit that became *Zorach* v. *Clauson*.
[28] *Seegers* v. *Parker*.
[29] *Rhoades* v. *School District*.

109

gation, it is the most remote interest, and the least secure standing in the state courts. It is hedged with special problems of standing in a few state courts—such as those of New York—and it is everywhere limited, at least potentially, to instances in which litigants can show a significant drain on the public treasury.[32] Furthermore, taxpayers' suits were excluded from federal courts under the old *Frothingham* rule until June of 1968.[33] All in all, the groups generally recognized the desirability of an interest and thus a standing beyond that of the mere taxpayer wherever possible.

But it was not always possible to do so. Potential plaintiffs are not always plentiful, and all groups, especially when they looked for large numbers of plaintiffs in a single case, often had to settle for a sprinkling of taxpayers among the parents, the pupils, the public officials. Often, too, the structure of the dispute limited the groups—and especially AU—to taxpayers. AU had to depend on them simply because of its greater concern for instances of public financial support for religious groups (public aid to religion issues). The AJC and ACLU more often went into cases of religious influence in public, and therefore, as Maslow notes of the AJC, "The plaintiffs in the test cases it [the AJC] has initiated or intervened in have usually been parents of school children or other individuals directly and personally aggrieved who complained not of pecuniary injury but of a violation of religious liberty."[34] Certainly in this set of religion-in-public cases a parent raises a greater range of interests more securely than a taxpayer. Thus the greater reliance of AU on taxpayer standing is largely a result of its brand of separationism, and thus of the kind of cases it worked in. The strategy of litigation, once again, flows from and is shaped by basic group goals and commitments.

One final note on plaintiffs. Not all of them are individuals, and in two instances ACLU affiliates have had sobering experiences with local school boards functioning as plaintiffs. While the legitimacy and respectability they bring are assets, they have one clear

---

[32] On the complicated matter of taxpayer standing see: "Taxpayers' Suits: A Survey and Summary," *Yale Law Journal* 69 (1960), 895–924; Kenneth C. Davis, *Administrative Law and Government* (St. Paul: West, 1960); and Louis L. Jaffe, "Standing to Secure Judicial Review: Public Actions," *Harvard Law Review* 74 (1961), 1265–1314. The authorities disagree, however, even on the question whether states will entertain taxpayer suits; Davis says that no state excludes them categorically, but the *Yale Law Journal* note claims that New York and New Mexico do.

[33] See the decision of that month in *Flast* v. *Cohen,* 392 U.S. 83 (1968).

[34] Maslow, "The Legal Defense of Religious Liberty," p. 11.

liability: their inclination to change their minds. The New Jersey CLU's involvement in the West Morris bus case—and its passage at arms with Judge Stamler—arose out of its earlier sponsorship of a similar test case in Teaneck, in which the board voted only 5–4 to commence litigation, and then wavered as an election approached. Convinced that it was about to lose that plaintiff and thus that test case, the NJCLU accepted a sponsoring role in West Morris.[35] Similarly, the NYCLU worried through its challenge to the New York textbook law as the East Greenbush school board similarly wavered. The board originally went into the case on a 6–3 vote, but after an intervening election brought two new members to the board and a public referendum showed the community opposed to the litigation, the margin shrank to 5–4. Fearful that it was about to lose this plaintiff, the NYCLU sought and found a stauncher board on Long Island to enter the case belatedly as a backup plaintiff.[36] Something of the problem may, indeed, be indicated by the fact that these two cases are the only ones among the sixty-seven in which local governmental bodies were plaintiffs in adversary proceedings.

Selecting the Court and the Site

Before the Supreme Court's decision in *Flast* v. *Cohen* in 1968,[37] access to the federal courts was severely restricted. Not only did the Supreme Court not entertain taxpayers' suits, but it and several lower federal courts had on several occasions expressed their distaste for ruling on the constitutionality of state statutes without prior consideration by state courts. The result, in effect, was to make it "almost impossible to challenge in the courts Federal grants to religious bodies that would appear to be obviously unconstitutional."[38] Perhaps that was at least one reason for the reversal and the new lenience in *Flast*. In any event, between 1968 and 1971 the litigators in these cases often faced the initial choice of going to federal or to state courts.

The majority of attorneys and groups, but by no means all, would appear to prefer the federal courts. Especially for groups whose goal is the constitutional precedent, it is the surest and fastest route to the U.S. Supreme Court. With a trial by a three-judge

[35] *West Morris Regional Board* v. *Sills.*
[36] *Board of Education* v. *Allen.*
[37] 392 U.S. 83 (1968).
[38] Maslow, "The Legal Defense of Religious Liberty," p. 10.

111

panel, the route to the Supreme Court is, indeed, very direct, and with dockets fairly clear, a decision can usually be expected in the next term of the Court. The choice of the federal forum also obviates the problem of the state court deciding on a state constitutional ground and thereby effectively cutting off access to the U.S. Supreme Court. And with most objectionable public policies being national—or at least common to a number of states—it is the single nationwide precedent that is sought.

Furthermore, a number of attorneys feel that their chances both of developing a full trial record and of winning the case will generally be better in the federal courts. Attorneys and groups in Pennsylvania and Rhode Island preferred the federal courts for these reasons when they challenged those states' programs of aid to parochial schools.[39] Such calculations reflect the overall reputation of federal courts for showing greater sympathy for claims of civil rights and greater competence in handling constitutional issues than do state courts. On the specifics of church-state decisions, however, the estimate is not unanimous. Will Maslow of the AJC noted in 1961 that "there is little indication that federal judges are more deeply committed to the principle of separation of church and state or more sensitive to abuses than state judges."[40]

The choice between federal and state courts ultimately hinges on the litigators' estimates of the probable decisions of the U.S. Supreme Court. The go-to-the-federal-court strategy holds only so long as the Supreme Court is a hospitable forum for the cases. And it was hospitable for separationism during the years of the Warren Court. Even in its transition after 1968 (*Flast*) it remained so at least until 1971. Were the Burger Court to become less friendly to separationist interests in the middle or late 1970s, the litigating groups would very likely begin to spot cases in friendly state and lower federal courts. Then, to project a little further, "If victory is achieved at these levels, the role of the civil liberties lawyer (and an uncharacteristic one) will be to try and persuade the Supreme Court to practice 'judicial restraint'—to refuse to review the decisions of these lower courts."[41] By the same token, too, the ACLU's policy decentralizing its litigation was made—and went smoothly—at a time when few negative decisions had

[39] *Lemon* v. *Kurtzman* and *DiCenso* v. *Robinson*.

[40] Maslow, "The Legal Defense of Religious Liberty," p. 14.

[41] Alan M. Dershowitz, "Bracing for the Lean Years," *New York Times*, sec. 4 (December 19, 1971), p. 8.

to be made about taking a case all the way to the U.S. Supreme Court.

There are, nonetheless, instances in which separationist plaintiffs happily choose the state courts. State constitutional provisions may erect a higher wall of separation than the federal courts have found in the U.S. Constitution. Especially if only an immediate remedy is sought, the preference for the state court is obvious, as it was, for example, in the Louisiana parochaid case brought by the Louisiana Teachers Association. Furthermore, local judges' reputations for general civil rights sympathies or for latitude in allowing attorneys to build a trial record may dictate that choice. There are, too, instances in which dockets in the local federal district courts are more crowded than the nearby state courts. In any event, whatever the decision, the chief criteria are clear: sympathy of the judges, relationship of the relevant constitution to the goals of the litigation, and speed of access to both trial and appellate courts.

The strategic decision of selecting the court—where there is an option—often merges imperceptibly with the selection of the site of the litigation. If the practices of which the plaintiff complains are the policies of a local school board, the locale of the case is thus determined. If it is a state law—one, for example, requiring local school boards to provide transportation for children attending private schools—the litigators could theoretically choose any school district in the state. The choice may be made because of a friendly court, or the residence of available plaintiffs, or the locale of a favorable context of fact. On that latter point, in searching for a site for its proposed test of the Pennsylvania state bus law, AU looked for a dramatically impacted school district. It found one in Abington, where the school board had had to add an extra $10,000 for the bus transportation onto a school budget already drafted for the year.[42] On the other hand, the Oregon CLU apparently chose Clackamas County as a site for its test of the Oregon textbook law on a mixture of considerations: a local judge they thought would permit them to shape a full trial record, a county in which plaintiffs could be found, and a locale that had not been the site (unlike both Salem and Portland) of earlier church-state conflict.[43] The Horace Mann League chose Annapolis and Anne Arundel County for its suit on Maryland aid to religious colleges because the county had no Roman Catholic judges, be-

[42] Rhoades v. School District.
[43] Dickman v. School District.

113

cause reporting by the newspapers and other reporters there was good, and because it was away from the Baltimore scene, so recently inflamed by the suits of Madalyn Murray.[44] Sometimes the organizers of litigation will try to move it from a turbid and divided community and the resulting pressure on the court. Litigators of a "captive school" case in Kentucky made the state superintendent of instruction a defendant so that they could bring suit in distant Franklin County (at the state capital, Frankfort).[45]

The strategic decisions of litigators yield only the sketchiest scholarly materials. There are rarely records of them, and one infers them from the histories of cases at the gravest risk. Even participants in the strategic decisions may not report them fully—details about decisions such as these seem to fade more quickly than recollections of legal argument and precedent. But on the basis of participants' reports, one can say that four considerations appear to dominate the selection of the site for litigation. The litigator seeks favorable facts, sympathetic judges, desirable plaintiffs, and low levels of religious conflict in the community. Beyond these criteria there is for national litigating groups the general "convenience" factor in site selection of which we have already spoken. It appears in part to explain the concentration of these sixty-seven cases in the urban centers and in the Northeast.

ESTABLISHING THE RECORD

Midway in the opinion of the Supreme Court in *Board of Education* v. *Allen,* the test of the New York textbook law, Justice Byron White took note of the "meager" record before the Court:

> This case comes to us after summary judgment entered on the pleadings. Nothing in this record supports the proposition that all textbooks, whether they deal with mathematics, physics, foreign languages, history, or literature, are used by the parochial schools to teach religion. No evidence has been offered about particular schools, particular courses, particular teachers, or particular books. We are unable to hold, based solely on judicial notice, that this statute results in unconstitutional involvement of the State with religious instruction.[46]

[44] *Horace Mann League* v. *Board of Public Works.*

[45] *Rawlings* v. *Butler.*

[46] At p. 248. On the other hand, the Florida Supreme Court praised counsel in *Johnson* v. *Presbyterian Homes* for stipulating facts so fully and so ably.

114

Combined with expressions of dismay there may also have been choruses of "we told you so" in the offices of the AJC, ACLU, and AU. For if there is any one general strategic point on which they agree, it is the need for development of a full record of facts in the trial court. Success in building a full record at the trial level, they realize, is usually more important than winning the decision, for the case will be appealed in any event.

Spokesmen for the three separationist groups have often made their preferences for a substantial trial record very explicit. Henry Clausen, an AU stalwart before becoming Sovereign Grand Commander of the Scottish Rite Masons, remonstrated with AU attorneys in an Alaska bus case:

> for many months I have urged the broadening of the pleadings and the injection of factual material which would permit proof of the substantial aid and benefit which bus transportation does afford. . . . I feel that no attorney can expect to go far today in a bus transportation, text book or similar case without forcing a trial on the *facts*. Yet there is a marked disposition on the part of many to treat the question as being one of law or to stipulate to certain basic facts and leave a wealth of probative material out of the case.[47]

Leo Pfeffer has long preached the same doctrine, both in word and in example. Some process of fact discovery, the groups believe, is essential to build a record that fully explores the factual questions on which hinge the central question of the breach of separation. In a case involving aid to religious schools, for instance, those are questions of the nature of the aid, its magnitude, the purpose of the aid, and the intentions of the "aiders," the religious ties and mission of the schools, and the impact of the aid on the schools.

The preferences of the groups notwithstanding, the pressures working against a full and time-consuming discovery are often oppressively heavy. Dockets in most trial courts are crowded, and impatient, often overworked judges frequently take a dim view of the lengthy trial. The following exchange between Judge Bowie Duckett and Melvin Sykes, Baltimore attorney for the plaintiffs, suggests the tensions. It came in the middle of lengthy attempts by the plaintiffs to show the religious ties and commitments of

---

[47] Clausen to Maurice T. Johnson of Fairbanks (date uncertain); copy in AU files, Washington, D.C. The case was *Matthews* v. *Quinton*.

the five colleges that had received aid from the Maryland legislature.

> Duckett: Yes, I think, Mr. Sykes, you are probably overtrying your case. I am not going to decide this case on, by splitting hairs. The only thing I'll decide this case on is broad general principles. I just can't do it any other way. I think the test is pretty well laid down by the Supreme Court and that's what I'm going to follow, and I believe you are overtrying your case. Of course, I don't want to tell you how to do it.

> Sykes: Well the reason that I am trying it in the way I am, if Your Honor please, is that general principles, of course, are applicable only to specific cases and what might be true of one institution might, of course, not be true of another, and what the Court will have to have in order to decide the case is going to have to be a complete factual picture to answer the question of general principle which is what is the essential character of the institution and education.[48]

In fairness to Judge Duckett, it should be noted that the trial was an uncommonly long one of thirteen days. Perhaps that passage also suggests that the jurisprudence and role perception of the trial court judge differ from those of the appellate court judges, for whom the record is intended.

The avoidance of the trial or lengthy discovery of facts may also result from the choices of counsel. The barrenness of the record in *Board of Education* v. *Allen* on which Justice White commented resulted from the decision of the NYCLU cooperating attorney—probably out of inexperience—to seek a summary judgment in the trial court. Unhappily, as it turned out, the court granted it before any record was established. More commonly, lawyers, like judges, are busy. Especially if they are working without fee or with reduced fee—and that is true more often than not in these sixty-seven cases—the temptation is very great to bypass a lengthy trial and get to other professional business. Attorneys may have other reasons for not wanting the lengthy involvement of a trial. In one case that went to decision on the merest suggestion of facts in stipulations, the plaintiff's attorney was a candidate for Congress and eager to get on with the campaign. It was widely

---

[48] From the transcript of the trial in *Horace Mann League* v. *Board of Public Works;* on file in the office of the clerk of Circuit Court of Anne Arundel County, Maryland.

116

thought in the community, indeed, that the defense attorney had maneuvered him into agreeing to the stipulations with the threat of tying him up for weeks in the taking of testimony.

Local groups or litigators may also have their special reasons for deciding against a trial. Trials are expensive, and nothing else escalates the cost of litigation so rapidly. Attorney fees mount, and so also do stenographic and printing costs; there may also be the expenses of expert witnesses or of investigative work outside of the courtroom. There are also the enormous noncash costs of the time of plaintiffs, witnesses, and other participants spent in the courtroom. For a local group of plaintiffs, even for a local ACLU affiliate, the funds simply may not be available to sustain costs of such magnitude. Very simply, a trial may make the difference between a budget of a few thousand dollars and one of more than ten thousand dollars for the case. Furthermore, local separationists may wish to avoid a trial, with all of its attendant publicity, in order to minimize the conflict and turmoil in the setting, and to protect the plaintiffs from the worst kinds of harassment.

Despite the resistance, however, the ACLU, AJC, and AU have persisted. In cases in which they participated as more than an amicus the incidence of a substantial record of fact increased dramatically (Table 5–1). They invariably resisted expediting the case to bypass the trial court stage, and they insisted on full development of facts, either in a trial or in extensive discovery through interrogatories and depositions. The real dichotomy in these cases (and in Table 5–1) is between those cases in which the establish-

TABLE 5-1

Relationship between Participation of Three Groups
and the Fullness of the Trial Court Record

Nature of the Trial Court Record	Cases by Role of Three Groups	
	none or amicus	intermediate or sponsorship
Limited to pleadings and stipulations	20 (76.9%)	17 (41.5%)
Development of legal and factual material	5 (19.2%)	17 (41.5%)
Full record plus expert testimony and/or social science data	1 (3.8%)	7 (17.1%)
Total cases (67)	26	41

117

ment of the facts were restricted to assertions in the complaint, or stipulations agreed to by both sides, and those cases in which the discovery of facts involved additional, adversary methods. It is the latter—with its inevitably richer record—on which the groups insisted. They furthermore agreed that the "facts" developed must, if possible, go beyond the bare statement of the legal facts—that is, beyond a statement of official bodies, their actions, the statutory provisions, the location of the events, the ownership and management of the private institutions, etc. But how far the development of facts goes beyond the legal skeleton, and in what direction, is indeed a point of significant difference among them.

The typical AU fact development is almost predictable, if one remembers that AU participated almost exclusively in cases in which it opposed Catholic interests. These were cases, in other words, in which the AU-supported plaintiffs objected to some form of governmental aid to some kind of Catholic institution—school, university, hospital, or orphanage. (The aid in question may be given, it is true, to other than the Roman Catholic institutions; bus rides to pupils of private schools will also be provided to Lutheran, Reformed, and other religious school systems.) AU attorneys then moved to establish the institution's religious philosophy, its subjection to the decisions and discipline of the Catholic hierarchy, the pervasiveness and supremacy of the religious goals, and above all what AU believes to be the authoritarianism and rigid orthodoxy of the morality and theology that permeate it. In more specific terms, at least in the textbook cases, AU tried to establish precisely the findings that Justice White did not find in the record of *Board* v. *Allen*.

Many of the same documentary sources recurred in AU testimony—the introductions of the same passages from Catholic cannon law, the same quotations from Catholic educational authorities about the primacy of the spiritual mission in the parochial schools, the same references to a small set of books critical of Catholic social and political power. The witnesses generally were either the local diocesan officials or officers of the Catholic institution in question. In general, too, AU testimony reflected an image of monolithic, authoritarian American Catholicism which, if it was ever true, began to seem passé by the 1960s. In similar cases, the AJC and ACLU attorneys pursued a similar development of facts, and in some instances they deferred to AU's collection of documentary materials and professional knowledge about American Catholicism.

118

If there was any way the ACLU and the AJC built the fact record differently from AU, it was in their more frequent use of expert testimony. Of the eight cases employing experts, the ACLU and AJC were each involved in six in either an intermediate or sponsoring role; by contrast, AU was so involved in only one, and none of the three participated in the remaining case. While at least one of the three groups participated above the amicus level in 61.2 percent of all the cases (41 of 67), at least one participated in 87.5 percent (7 of 8) of the cases in which experts gave testimony. The largest single category of the experts comprised local or nearby college professors, with local professionals, largely psychologists and psychiatrists, a second group. The trial court in the Miami case about religious influences in local schools (*Chamberlin* v. *Dade County*) heard from a Miami psychiatrist and from professors of education and psychology at the University of Miami. Dr. Solomon Grayzel, editor of the Jewish Publication Society, testified as a plaintiff witness in the *Schempp* Bible-reading case as an expert on the Bible. The attorneys for the plaintiffs in the case of the cross in Oregon (*Lowe* v. *City of Eugene*) relied on a local psychiatrist, a psychologist with the county health department, a local Rabbi, and professors at the University of Oregon for testimony on the religious and symbolic meaning of the cross and on the psychological and religious impact of the cross on non-Christians.

Leo Pfeffer and the AJC additionally refined the building of records by attempting to introduce social science data and expertise. There is the instance of the Eugene cross case, in which Pfeffer played a prominent part. The AJC had earlier organized an attack on the distribution of the Gideon Bible in the public schools of Rutherford, New Jersey.[49] A central point of contention in the case, as in other similar ones, concerned the issue of "free choice." Since Bibles were given only to children who brought a request form signed by a parent, was it an entirely voluntary distribution system? In dismissing that argument of free choice, the New Jersey Supreme Court cited testimony in the record by two psychologists and an educator that the distribution system created subtle but potent pressures on the children to take the Bibles. In two other instances the AJC encountered unsympathetic trial judges in trying to introduce similar evidence. In the Miami schools case (*Chamberlin* v. *Dade County*), the court allowed testimony showing psychological harm to non-Christian children participating in

[49] *Tudor* v. *Board of Education.*

119

essentially Christian observances, but refused to allow testimony of experts on the issue of coercion and free choice. And in *Zorach* v. *Clauson*—the New York City released-time case—Pfeffer gathered extensive affidavits of students, parents, and former students in the city schools to document both the pressures on children to participate in the released-time program and the intergroup divisiveness that resulted from identifying the children as members (or nonmembers) of various denominations. The New York City trial judge refused, however, to admit any of it.[50]

Finally, Pfeffer and Edgar Fuller of the Horace Mann League carried record-building to its zenith in the League's suit to invalidate Maryland's legislative grants to religious colleges for the construction of buildings. They recognized that colleges and universities with attenuated or nominal religious ties may not be in any operational sense "religious." Since the First and Fourteenth Amendments' separationism (and that of most state constitutions) would apply only to the effectively "religious" schools, they developed a series of indexes for determining whether an institution was or was not religious. The yardstick considered (among others) the following factors: the stated purposes of the institution, the religious ties and affiliations of college personnel, the relationship to religious organizations or denominations, the place of religion in the curriculum, the religious affiliations of students, and religious observances required of students. The introduction of evidence at the trial was, in effect, the first application of the yardstick, and on its basis Pfeffer argued that all four of the defendant colleges were indeed religious. The Maryland Court of Appeals, recognizing the usefulness of the criteria, found that only three of the colleges were religious. Pfeffer later used the same criteria in the unsuccessful attack on federal building grants to four Connecticut colleges.[51]

[50] Pfeffer has reprinted a good deal of this excluded evidence in his *Church, State, and Freedom* (Boston: Beacon Press, 1953). Pfeffer also referred to it in his brief before the U.S. Supreme Court, where the reference caught the eye of Justice William Douglas. The justice alluded to it in a footnote to his *Zorach* opinion.

[51] *Tilton* v. *Richardson*. The only other of these cases in which this empirical test might have been applied was the one about South Carolina's tuition grants to students in the private colleges of the state (*Hartness* v. *Patterson*). The plaintiffs there refused to use it, however; both sides were forced by the politics of their friendly test case to seek an absolute rule on the religious colleges. It would have been politically intolerable to invite a ruling that aid to some was acceptable while aid to others was not.

120

MANAGING THE CONSTITUTIONAL LITIGATION

Once the litigation commences, the plaintiff forces confront an almost infinite range of tactical legal decisions: which precedents to rely on, the possibilities of settlements, the effective use of evidence and witnesses, among many others. They are problems common to all litigation, and they cannot concern us here. But there are some more general strategic problems that recur in litigation aimed at the favorable appellate precedent. They tend to be much more common in planned constitutional litigation of this kind.

The Problem of the Intervenors

The group battle in church-state litigation is most frequently joined when accommodationist interests enter a case with an intervenor-defendant.[52] That status entitles them to participate in the trial and in oral argument before appellate courts, and it gives them the option of appealing a lost case, especially if the original defendants choose not to. The addition of the intervenor with group support thus completes the cast of adversary groups.

The separationist groups almost invariably oppose the entry of intervenors, but they rarely succeed. Local judges will not often say "no" to the intervenor if he can show some tangible interest in the controversy. Most frequently in these cases, for instance, intervenors are parents of children attending religious schools who will lose some benefit if public aids being challenged (such as textbooks or tuition aids) are stopped. In only one of these cases am I aware of any ACLU, AJC, or AU pleasure at the intervention of accommodationists. AU attorneys expressed some glee that representatives of the San Francisco archdiocese wanted to enter their suit against tax exemptions for religious schools in California.[53] The presence of the intervenors opened new lines of testimony and questioning about the mission of the Catholic schools.

The Decision to Appeal

Little needs to be added to the earlier discussion of the problem of whether or not to appeal. There is, however, a related decision on the speed and priority of the appeal—the issue, in other words, of where to stand in the line of emerging church-state cases. In

[52] The role and incidence of the intervenor is more fully discussed in Chapter VIII on the defendants.
[53] *Lundberg* v. *Alameda County.*

some instances organizers of litigation slow down the progress of a case, hoping that an anticipated favorable precedent will be forged in other litigation. More common, at least in this church-state litigation, was the desire to speed up the progress of litigation to catch up with a competing case. The organizers of the case on religious influences in the Miami public schools (*Chamberlin* v. *Dade County*), for instance, hoped to overtake the *Schempp* (Pennsylvania Bible-reading) and *Murray* (Baltimore Lord's Prayer) cases in the U.S. Supreme Court. They did not succeed, and *Chamberlin* was summarily reversed and remanded, an outcome that indicated the wisdom of the attempt to reach the Court earlier. Attorneys in the Horace Mann League's case on Maryland grants for college buildings also wanted very much to get to the state's high court before the challenge to the state's aid for building of religious hospitals.[54] They feared that if the hospital case reached the court first it would, in deciding favorably on that aid, fashion a rule so broad that it could not subsequently decide unfavorably on aid for buildings at religious colleges. In that instance the race was won, and so was the case.

It is the same Maryland case, however, that best illustrates the final irony in the appellate strategies.[55] It is often easier to reach the highest appellate court—the goal of constitutional litigation—if one loses his case. In a manner of speaking, one "loses" one's way to the Supreme Court. The decision to appeal falls to the losing party, and the plaintiff loses initiative in appellate decisions by winning. In the Maryland case the Horace Mann forces won 4–3 in the Maryland Court of Appeals. The state did in this instance appeal, but the U.S. Supreme Court refused certiorari, with a dissent by Justices Harlan and Stewart. Organizers of the case were haunted by the realization that if they had lost there probably would have been a greater chance that the separationist bloc on the Court would have granted certiorari. Had that happened, the separationists would have had before the Supreme Court a stronger case on which to test aid to religious colleges and universities than the one from Connecticut that later became the leading case on the point.[56]

[54] The hospital case is *Truitt* v. *Board of Public Works.*

[55] That is, *Horace Mann League* v. *Board of Public Works.* On the irony (or "paradox") see Joel B. Grossman's "A Model for Judicial Policy Analysis" in Grossman and Tanenhaus, *Frontiers of Judicial Research,* pp. 412–413.

[56] The Connecticut case was *Tilton* v. *Richardson.* The Maryland case

Publicity and Community Relations

Separationist groups are almost uniformly conscious of the tender community relations they strain with suits that challenge the majority religious norms. To protect themselves, their clienteles, and especially the plaintiffs, they work to minimize the community excitement and disharmony. Quiet, respectable plaintiffs are a necessary beginning. Frequently the elimination of formal group ties seems necessary. That stricture falls most frequently on AU, especially in areas with large numbers of Roman Catholics—Maryland, Pennsylvania, and Louisiana, for instance. In fairness to AU, it has at times unfairly been made a whipping boy in this litigation, but that fact only supports the strategy.[57] But if separationist strategy is to move AU underground, the reaction to possible support by atheists' organizations is one of avoidance. The offers to Joseph Lewis and his Freethinkers of America to support the *Chamberlin* case in Miami produced a reaction bordering on panic.

Beyond the desire to calm conflict, there may also be a more generalized desire to keep all groups out of the litigation. In states such as Vermont, attorneys have thought the mere participation of national groups would seem to many locals as the interference of "outsiders." A similar concern about the intervention of "mainlanders" motivated organizers of the Hawaii bus case (*Spears* v. *Honda*) to exclude all groups. Finally, group participation may seem to some older and more traditional members of the legal community, especially in the South, to represent an alien jurisprudence—the "sovietizing" of litigation, in the words of one attorney, or the acceptance of "judicial law-making."

In the same spirit, separationists usually work hard to control publicity about the case, and to present their position in a restrained and dignified way, a way that has no taint of antireligious animus. That strategy, too, begins with the plaintiffs, and with their willingness to remain quiet and passive. Very rare is the attorney who wishes to use a plaintiff to "dramatize" the case or to try it in the public press. Among these sixty-seven cases there was

---

would have been stronger because the religious ties, commitment, and mission of the Maryland colleges were more manifest than those of the Connecticut institutions.

[57] See, for instance, the report of C. Wayne Zunkel, "The Pennsylvania School Bus Fight," *Christian Century* 82 (August 25, 1965), 1036–1037.

only one such instance, and it was a case not sponsored by any of the three leading groups. There are instances, though, in which groups' flair for publicity creeps in; the NYCLU, for instance, delayed bringing its suit challenging the use of the Regents' Prayer in public schools (*Engel* v. *Vitale*) until the newspaper strike in New York City was settled. Such strategies make sense, of course, only when the prevailing religious composition and climate are favorable to separationism.

The Amicus Curiae

The would-be amicus raises with the managers of the litigation—group or individual—the strategic decision whether or not to grant him permission to enter. The policy of the separationist groups has generally been a lenient one. They have even granted permission to groups (especially before the U.S. Supreme Court) that they would have tried to exclude in any other role. The conventions of constitutional litigation are permissive, and it is well understood that the plaintiffs themselves will not bear any responsibility for the lapses or failings of an amicus.

When they themselves participate as amici, the three leading groups all subscribe to the belief that unless the amicus brief "contains material not already before the court, it is an irritating waste of the time of the court or a form of judicial lobbying." They have established a status and a credibility, and they do not want to have either diluted "by merely reiterating, albeit with variations, the main theme of the principal briefs."[58] And yet one cannot say that either the letter or the spirit of those self-denying ordinances has always been met. There have been instances in which the briefs merely parrot—perhaps with more finesse and legal sophistication—the arguments of the parties. And there are instances, too, in which the groups appear as amici, if not to put themselves on record in a discreet bit of "lobbying," then at least for the benefit of members or clienteles who expect them to be there and "counted" at the big decisions. Perhaps one can only say that the general quality of the amici briefs—especially in the case of the AJC—and the degree of self-restraint both rate above the norms for political jurisprudence.

[58] The quotation in this sentence is from Roland Watts, "The Role of the American Civil Liberties Union—In the Courts and Thereafter," mimeographed paper presented at the annual meeting of the American Political Science Association in St. Louis, Mo. (September 6–9, 1961), pp. 8–9. The quotation in the preceding sentence comes from Maslow, "The Legal Defense of Religious Liberty," p. 14.

124

Finally—on the amicus—the myth about the careful orchestration of amici arguments finds little confirmation here. There are tales of the careful use of amici to supplement or complement the arguments of the principal parties, to float constitutional trial balloons, or to provide alternative rationales for reaching the desired results. There are a few instances among these sixty-seven cases in which parties tried precisely that kind of orchestration. Pfeffer, for instance, in the *Tudor* case challenging the distribution of Gideon Bibles, hoped the ACLU as amicus would make the absolutist separationist argument he was prevented from making by reason of originally having a Catholic plaintiff. But such instances are rare. Amici take the positions of their organizations, and not necessarily the position the plaintiff would prefer. When the groups, especially the three leaders, have gone in with different or complementary views, it has usually been because of honest differences rather than strategic arrangements. Basically, however, their positions do not vary greatly, and they generally agree even on the main lines of constitutional rationale. There are, in terms of the leading metaphor, usually no different voices or instruments to orchestrate. They play monophonically and in unison.

THE SUCCESSES OF ACTION AND STRATEGY

The proof of the strategic acuity of the separationist groups ought to be in the record of their litigation. But which record? The most obvious record is the total of wins and losses which the groups have scored in their participation (above the amicus level) in these sixty-seven cases. By that standard the record of the three groups is slightly above the norm for all separationist plaintiffs (Table 5–2). It is, however, largely the exceptional record of the AJC that accounts for that superiority (Table 5–3). The AJC, indeed, scored final victories in two-thirds of the cases in which it participated, against a win record of 48.2 percent for all separationist plaintiffs. (The groups together did not do measurably better than other plaintiffs in trial court decisions, but victory at that level had never been a major goal of constitutional litigation.)

But are simple won-lost box scores as significant in constitutional litigation as they are in professional football or baseball? A case can be made that they are. Groups such as the AJC, which primarily seek constitutional goals, know that in most instances a loss means an unfriendly precedent, one that might decide future cases. But, on the other hand, victories may not mean favorable

TABLE 5-2
Final Outcome in Case According to Aggregate Role
of Three Leading Groups

	None	Amicus Curiae	Intermediate	Sponsorship
Plaintiffs won (27)	4 (33.3%)	3 (50.0%)	10 (55.6%)	10 (50.0%)
Plaintiffs lost (28)	8 (66.7%)	3 (50.0%)	8 (44.4%)	9 (45.0%)
Mixed outcome (1)	—	—	—	1 (5.0%)
Total (56)	12	6	18	20

Note: Represented here are only the 56 cases in which the plaintiffs were separationists; the indications of group participation are therefore somewhat less than in earlier tables, in which all 67 cases are reported. The role noted here is again the role of greatest involvement of any one group.

precedents, and they may block appeals to the United States Supreme Court. Furthermore, the box score treats a victory in the U.S. Supreme Court and one in the New Mexico Supreme Court as equals, and clearly they are not.

Since the United States Supreme Court is the "ultima Thule" of constitutional litigation, success in it must at least be partly measured by success in reaching it. By this standard, the record of the three groups is especially impressive. They sponsored 20 of the 56 cases with separationist plaintiffs, and 8 of the 20 (40 percent) reached the Supreme Court for review; only 2 of the other

TABLE 5-3
Final Outcome in Case According to Roles of Individual Groups

	ACLU		AJC		AU	
	no role	some role	no role	some role	no role	some role
Plaintiff won	13 (44.8%)	14 (51.9%)	14 (38.9%)	13 (65.0%)	15 (51.7%)	12 (44.4%)
Plaintiff lost	16 (55.2%)	12 (44.4%)	22 (61.1%)	6 (30.0%)	13 (44.8%)	15 (55.6%)
Mixed outcome	—	1 (3.7%)	—	1 (5.0%)	1 (3.4%)	—
Total	29	27	36	20	29	27

Note: Represented here are only the 56 cases in which the plaintiffs were separationists; the indications of group participation are therefore slightly less than in earlier tables, in which all 67 cases were reported.

126

36 (5.5 percent) reached the Court. Alternatively, one can look at the "appeal achievement" rate. The three groups succeeded in 47.1 percent (8 of 17) of the cases in which they as sponsors sought U.S. Supreme Court jurisdiction, either by appeal or certiorari. In the remainder of the cases in only 13.3 percent (2 of 15) did the Supreme Court take jurisdiction by appeal or certiorari. (And that despite the fact the groups attempted to take 17 of 20 cases to the Court, while managers of the other 36 with separationist plaintiffs tried to take only 15.) Thus the groups performed above par, and the AJC again excelled.

Regardless of how one measures victory or success in litigation, two conclusions remain constant. First, the three leading groups enjoyed a markedly greater success in the United States Supreme Court than did other plaintiffs. Second, by all measures the American Jewish Congress succeeded to a considerably greater extent than did the ACLU and AU. Those two facts reflect in turn the central importance of the relationship between strategies and success in litigation on the one hand and basic group goals, centralization, and capacities on the other (Table 5–4).

The greater commitment of the AJC to the goals of constitutional litigation—along with the organizational control and capacity for it—leads also to strategies and choices most likely to achieve success in litigation. AU, by contrast, has had other goals to seek, and its litigation style and capability have reflected that fact. One can, therefore, say that the AJC does better in appellate courts because it is more committed to doing so, and has built an ability for doing so. Furthermore—and in the same vein—the groups' collective record may well improve when they reach the U.S. Supreme Court. AU becomes more of a constitutional litigator, and less of an organization builder, when it reaches the Supreme Court, and the national office of the ACLU also exercises control over its more active affiliates as their cases move forward in appeal.

Beyond all of these questions of immediate, case-specific strategy are the questions of overall design or longer-range plans for decisions on priority in litigation. These are the decisions on the level one might call metastrategy or the strategy of strategies. And on this level, too, different goals and capacities lead the three groups to different views and stances. Here the AJC has traditionally stood for a conservative, incremental strategy of the next logical step, of working cautiously for the next orderly increment to-

127

TABLE 5-4

Relationships between Plaintiffs and Goals, Organization,
Capacity, and Strategies in Litigation

	Capacity for Litigation (e.g., skills, information)	Centrali- zation of Litigation	Goals of Litigation	Strategic Caution; Legal Con- servatism	Litigation Success in Appellate Courts
American Jewish Congress	high	high	constitutional	high	high
American Civil Liberties Union	medium high	high and low[a]	mixed[b]	medium high	medium
Americans United	medium	medium	mixed[b]	medium	medium low
Nongroup plaintiffs	low	—	remedy	low	medium

[a] ACLU litigation was highly centralized for at least half of the period covered here; after the granting of litigation initiatives to the affiliates, its organization for litigation became highly decentralized.

[b] Both the ACLU and AU mixed ideological-organizational goals with their constitutional goals, the AU somewhat more than the ACLU and its affiliates.

ward a full-blown constitutional doctrine. AU and the ACLU—and particularly many of the ACLU affiliates—have moved more boldly to seek new breakthroughs and doctrines. They have not always explicitly sought faster constitutional progress, for their litigating strategy is often an unintended byproduct of their pursuit of organizational or ideological goals. But the effect has often been to set the opportunity for a great leap forward in constitutional development. To look at it another way, the AJC has risked less to gain less; the others have often risked more, for whatever reason, and stood to gain more.

The AJC's conservatism in its decisions on priority, its incremental strategy in pursuing constitutional change, is evident in its major decisions on litigation. It preferred to test the surer textbook issue before reexamining the constitutionality of transportation to church schools, and it preferred to take a case involving the Lord's Prayer to the Supreme Court before one testing the nonsectarian and theologically ambiguous prayer of the Regents of the State of New York. Those preferences also reflected the AJC's sophistication in litigation and its desire to provide the courts with the

128

easiest, least controversial test cases in which to stake out new rulings. AU, on the other hand, has litigated with more abandon, and with only one eye on the constitutional goals of litigation. What may appear to be attempted quantum jumps to new constitutional precedent are really grapplings with the deeply felt, incandescent issues that most excite its clientele. Those cases are dramatic and perilous, and even in defeat they have an embattled heroism about them. Whether the decisions of AU (and the more activist ACLU affiliates) are intended to have a constitutional strategy, they do in fact have one, and it is as important for church-state litigation as if it had been intended.

There are, therefore, internal limits to the effectiveness of the three groups in litigation—limits that grow from an interrelated complex of reasons that involves the organization of litigation, the capacity for it, and the goals. The various goals of the groups affect even the selection of issues to litigate, and thus, even when not intended, the priorities they give to the litigation of constitutional questions. Overall, too, the groups are limited in their effectiveness in litigation by the depth of their participation in any case. Unless they sponsor a case and thus control decisions about it, they must share the setting of strategy. And one or more of the three groups sponsored only 20 of the 56 cases with separationist plaintiffs.

In sum, except for the incremental preferences of the AJC, the three leading separationist groups never achieved a strategy of strategies, an overall priority of concerns. And no other litigators were widely enough involved in the church-state cases to have set any such strategy. In the litigating of these sixty-seven cases, there was at most a sometime control of litigation strategies in the individual cases that one or more of the groups influenced. But priorities do emerge, whether or not they are consciously chosen. And in the litigating of church-state relationships, the strategic priorities combined an incrementalist pursuit of legal victories with maximalist, even quixotic, charges down new paths and toward new targets. There resulted a combination of constitutional caution and incaution, a combination of both restraint and activism in litigation. Taken together—and again as an interest group system—the separationist groups covered both sets of long-range strategic options, working both sides of the strategic street, ironically, to the extent to which they were not able to coordinate their priorities.

VI | THE PLAINTIFFS

Iconoclast that she is, Madalyn Murray O'Hair would doubtless be amused to realize that her successful litigation knocks the usual concepts of political power or influence into a cocked hat. Without holding any office or seeking any, without any formal political support or allies, without, indeed, very much support or status of any kind, and with only modest expenditures and a somewhat inexperienced attorney, she ultimately stopped the use of the Lord's Prayer in the schools of Baltimore and the nation. Without, in other words, any of the usual manifestations or concomitants of political power, she fundamentally altered the relationship of religion to the state in American life.

Mrs. O'Hair, for all her celebrity, is not unique among constitutional plaintiffs. Others match her single-mindedness, her willingness to challenge conventional and respectable religiosity, and her success in the appellate courts. Together they make a fascinating, if relatively unknown, group of political activists. They lack the usual signs of political power, and yet by locating access to the judicial process and by entering it at a propitious moment, they alter the course of American constitutional law. Some may, indeed, have the kind of impact on one area of American public policy for which the more experienced and better financed Washington lobbyists would surrender their eyeteeth. All belong to that small subset of political activists who are the constitutional plaintiffs. They frequently play litigation "long shots," and when they win they appear to get more policy impact for the effort than any other group of American political activists. Theirs may, in fact, be the last opportunity in all of the American political process for hitting the policy jackpot with little more than a few nickels' investment.

The plaintiffs in these sixty-seven church-state cases, while they did have their points of dramatic similarity, were in many ways a very diverse group. Only some of them were in fact individuals; a significant portion were private organizations, governmental bodies, or individuals acting in their capacities as public officials.

130

Even the individuals ranged from the boldly assertive to the painfully shy, from the deeply religious to the profoundly antireligious, from the socially apt to the socially inadept, from pillars of the local community to those completely alienated from it. For all their political similarities, constitutional plaintiffs may well be one of the most diverse and heterogeneous groups of American political activists.

A PORTRAIT GALLERY OF PLAINTIFFS

Madalyn Murray O'Hair

If it is true, as she likes to think it is, that Madalyn Murray O'Hair is "the most hated woman in America," she is probably also the most celebrated and publicized constitutional litigant in American history. Lusty, aggressive, and seemingly tireless, a liberated woman long before Women's Liberation, her jousts with organized religion and even her domestic squabbles became instant copy in the newsrooms of America. She has matched wit, quotations, and debater's ploys with William Buckley on television; *Time* has chronicled her crusades, and *Playboy* recorded a justly famous interview with her.[1]

That a fortyish (born in 1919), somewhat matronly, Baltimore divorcée and social worker should have become celebrated in American pop culture is improbable in itself. That it should be constitutional litigation that led her to that fame is even less probable. There certainly were no ingredients of popular fame in her background. She was born in Pittsburgh into a Presbyterian family, the daughter of a contractor. She graduated from Ashland College, a religiously conservative institution in Ohio, enlisted in the WACS in World War II, and one of her assignments was to the staff of General Dwight Eisenhower. After the war she acquired a law degree at the South Texas Law School, and eventually settled into a career in social work while she raised her sons, William and Garth.

While her life seemed to move in fairly conventional ways, her religious and political odyssey did not. She claims to have abandoned Christianity at age thirteen after a weekend bout of reading the Bible. That led to a life of militant atheism, which she capped in 1970 by founding her own atheist "religion," in which she declared herself a bishop and her husband of several years, Richard

---

[1] *Time* (May 15, 1964), pp. 53–54; *Playboy* (October 1965), pp. 61ff.

131

O'Hair, a prophet. Intended at least in part as a tactic in her war against tax exemptions for organized religions, it was called Poor Richard's Universal Life' Church. She later "canonized" Mark Twain as one of its saints. Her political pilgrimage was more circuitous. She early espoused socialism, sampled the available socialist parties (Socialist, Socialist Workers, Socialist Labor), and eventually threw them all over for anarchism.

But it is not so much the views as their very public espousal that made the Madalyn Murray myth. The *Playboy* interview summed up a great deal of her style: the free-swinging, somewhat madcap attack on one sacred topic after another; the brashness and joyous vulgarity; the seeming pleasure in giving offense; the rash articulateness of it all. The interview included among its topics her earthy and explicit views on human sexuality (including her own), and the story of her altercation with the Baltimore police and her subsequent flight to Hawaii, Mexico, and Texas. It also contained a good deal of vintage Madalyn Murray on Christianity and organized religion generally.

On Pope John XXIII: "an amoeba of goodness in a sea of waste"

On the gospels: "Those so-called records were written by devout ecclesiasts who wanted to believe, and who wanted others to believe, in the coming of a Messiah."

On the virgin birth: "The 'Virgin' Mary should get a posthumous medal for telling the biggest goddamn lie that was ever told. Anyone who believes that will believe that the moon is made out of green cheese."

There is no doubt, in other words, that Madalyn Murray O'Hair promotes and even relishes her unpopularity, and that, paradoxically, it is her unpopularity that is at the root of her popularity. As an awed ACLU attorney in Texas, trying to help with her extradition problems, wrote shortly after the interview: "God knows, if I may use the expression, what she will do or say. Any woman who can give the interview she did to *Playboy* doesn't need any help from me. . . . If she stays here another week she will start getting popular and I may quit the practice of law and manage her."[2]

[2] Maury Maverick, Jr., to Irving Murray of the Maryland affiliate of the ACLU (September 30, 1965); copy in ACLU archives, Princeton University Library, Princeton, N.J.

132

In addition to enjoying the shock she gives to others, Mrs. O'Hair appears to enjoy the recitations of her problems after bringing the suits in Baltimore. She suffered mightily, and if there is a bit of the martyr about her, she cultivates not pity but outrage. *Time* magazine's summary of some of the aftermath to her prayer litigation is, if less hair-raising than her own accounts, at least indicative: "The Baltimore public welfare department fired her from her supervisor's job. Various persons—whom she delights in describing as 'My Christian neighbors'—have trampled her flowers, broken her windows, beaten up Bill and his young brother more than 100 times. Flooded with abusive letters, she has received everything from a psychotic document endlessly repeating the word 'kill' to a newspaper picture of herself smeared with excrement."[3] Her accounts of her family's altercation with the Baltimore police are greatly disputed by the police, but whatever may be the truth of her allegations of their brutality, she was accused of assaulting eight police officers, a charge which did little to diminish her mythic reputation.

The reputation of MMO depends on more than public jibes and saucy rhetoric. After her 1961 suit against the saying of the Lord's Prayer, in 1964 she challenged the Maryland tax exemption of religious property.[4] The most widely publicized of her other legal actions came in her opposition to astronaut Frank Borman's reading of the Bible as he orbited the moon. She has also brought various atheists' organizations to life, and at one point even toyed with the possibility of establishing a colony of atheists near Stockton, Kansas, on land given her cause by Carl Brown of Stockton, a former Kansas legislator and ardent atheist. The project apparently died in the legal tangle over the control of the Society of Separationists that followed her flight from Baltimore to Honolulu.

Ellory Schempp

The family of Madalyn Murray and that of Edward Lewis Schempp were irrevocably linked in American constitutional law when the Supreme Court consolidated their separate suits for hearing and decision, thus awarding them the same citation in the U.S.

---

[3] *Time* (May 15, 1964), p. 53. For fuller, somewhat awed accounts of M.M.O., see two articles by Robert A. Wilson: "Most Hated Woman in America" and "The Passion [*sic*!] of Madalyn Murray" both in *Fact* (March-April 1964 and January-February 1965).

[4] These two Murray cases are included in this universe of 67 cases; they are *Murray* v. *Curlett* and *Murray* v. *Comptroller*.

Reports. But the Schempps, authors of the suit challenging the Pennsylvania statute requiring the reading of the Bible in public schools, were constitutional plaintiffs of a different variety. While they shared the depth of conviction of Madalyn Murray, they expressed it in a much more reserved and less flamboyant manner. Perhaps the leading activists in the family were not the elder Schempps but the oldest child, Ellory.

When the events of the case began in 1956, Ellory Schempp was 16. On his own initiative and apparently without consulting his parents, he began to read the Koran while his classmates were hearing the Bible and praying the Lord's Prayer. "My homeroom teacher told me I would have to pay attention," he later recalled. "I replied that in conscience, I didn't think I could."[5] He had at the time been reading Thoreau and Emerson, and through them was exploring questions of conscience and conformity. For the rest of his junior year in high school he went to the school's guidance office during the prayer and Bible-reading period. The next year, his senior year, the school had a new principal who was less tolerant, and who, Ellory recalled, thought him a "rabble rouser." With the pressures on him mounting, he finally capitulated and participated at least to the extent of standing for the Lord's Prayer and listening to the reading of the Bible. But he also wrote the local ACLU affiliate asking for help in bringing litigation; in fact, he wrote a number of times before the Philadelphia affiliate evinced any interest in the case.

To a surprising extent, the litigation was at first Ellory's alone. The Schempps did not apparently at any time register any complaint with school authorities. Yet the family reinforced and supported Ellory in personal terms, and when they went to litigation, it was as a family—"attractive, well-balanced people," in the words of a local CLU official. In fact, it was a family visit to the home of Henry Sawyer, Philadelphia attorney and ACLU affiliate president, that convinced him of their alertness and seriousness. (He himself agreed to handle the case for the ACLU.) Ellory ultimately graduated from high school, and after the case had been mooted by the alteration of the Pennsylvania Bible-reading statute, the case had to be retried, with his younger brother and sister as the family's public school pupils. (It was that second hearing that was eventually consolidated with *Murray* v. *Curlett*.)

[5] Interview by James T. Kaull, *Providence Evening Bulletin* (March 15, 1963).

Ellory remained a social activist, but one with shifting concerns. In 1963, shortly after the successful outcome of the case, he reflected that "This case isn't as important as it appears to be. There are more important things that have to be done, like voter registration in the South or finding out what is the nature of 'peace in our time'."[6] His younger sister, Donna, who had been the family's one original opponent of the litigation, had, however, come to believe that they had done the right thing.

Eleanor Taft Tilton

Mrs. Arthur V. Tilton, as the first listed and most active plaintiff, gave her name to the case in which federal building grants to four Catholic colleges and universities in Connecticut were challenged. The Supreme Court of the United States (in *Tilton v. Richardson*) upheld the grants by a 5–4 vote.

Intelligent, committed, cultivated, and public spirited, Eleanor Tilton typifies in many ways the WASP upper middle class of New England. She speaks in a low, well modulated voice, and she has all the social graces and just a bit of the grande dame manner. Raised an Episcopalian and educated at Vassar, she later became a religious freethinker. Her concerns about church-state relations led her to POAU and to the Connecticut ACLU affiliate (on whose board of directors she served). But her life in Hartford included a wide range of other interests—the chairmanship of the city's Fine Arts Commission and the presidency of its League of Women Voters, to mention two.

What perhaps sets Eleanor Tilton apart from her peers is a highly developed sense of moral outrage and an especially burning set of convictions about Catholicism. In a letter to Leo Pfeffer about another case she wrote, "I personally feel that I am being forced, by the two Acts about which the litigation is being prepared, to do serious damage to certain American children who, as a result of my tax payments, are now attending parochial schools. This violates my conscience as it would if my taxes were used to bind children's feet in the old Chinese manner."[7] In both this sense of outrage and in the tireless expression of it, she has much in common with Madalyn Murray. Mrs. Tilton expresses it, however, in a seemingly endless series of very literate letters—to edi-

[6] *Ibid.*
[7] (November 3, 1967); in files of the AJC, New York, N.Y.

torial columns of newspapers, to public officials, and especially to the officers and functionaries of the ACLU.

It was, in fact, her relentless campaign that finally stirred the national ACLU to active support of the case on aid to higher education. Literally for years Mrs. Tilton had chided and scourged national headquarters for their slowness in responding to the issue. She quickly came to suspect that the ACLU and especially its legal staff had demoted church-state questions to a fairly low position on its list of priorities. ("They always seemed to be rushing off to defend a draft resister in Iowa.") Several trips to New York and conferences with John Pemberton, then executive director of the ACLU, helped spur action. And in her position on the board of the Connecticut affiliate, she was in a position to advance the litigation on the affiliate level by prodding the local attorney to meet the litigation deadlines.

Frederick Walz

It is not often that members of the U.S. Supreme Court inquire about the very existence of a plaintiff in a case being argued before it. On November 19, 1969, however, as the justices heard the challenge of the New York tax exemption for religious property (*Walz* v. *Tax Commission*), Justice Potter Stewart asked for assurances that Mr. Walz really did exist. Walz's attorney, Edward Ennis of New York, assured the Court that he had met Mr. Walz several times and that he would have had him at the counsel's table had Walz not begged off for reasons of health.

Mr. Ennis enjoyed a singular experience, for Walz did not appear in any of the three New York state courts that heard his case, even though he listed himself as his own attorney. Nor have interviewers had any greater success in seeing Walz.[8] He maintains a law office (listed, surprisingly, in the yellow pages) on 42nd Street in mid-Manhattan, but the office is really a secretarial and phone answering service, and he does not respond to messages left there. He lives alone with a number of dogs and cats in a four-room apartment without a phone in a somewhat tacky building in an Irish, working-class area of the Bronx. His neighbors describe him as "quiet, devoted to an undetermined number of dogs and cats he keeps as pets, and a person who never opens

[8] It should go without saying that I have never communicated with Frederick Walz, even though I have tried to by 1) his office phone, 2) personal visits to the 42nd street office, and 3) the U.S. mails.

136

his door. . . . Mr. Walz is frequently seen in the streets in the evening, throwing bits of food under cars for stray cats and dogs. He also is seen feeding pigeons in a small park nearby.[9] For the visual record, there is only a *New York Times* photograph of Walz (*apparently* Walz) withdrawing behind a darkened window, showing only a bit of ear and neck and half a T-shirted torso. A dog and a cat are, however, fully pictured.[10]

Of the personal life of Frederick Walz, understandably, little is known. In the original complaint in the case he described himself as "a Christian and not a member of any religious organization as referred to herein, rejecting them as hostile." He was probably in his early sixties at the time of the origin of the suit in 1968. He appears to have been a member of AU in its early years, but he let his membership lapse. He was admitted to the New York bar in 1929, according to the Martindale-Hubbell directory; but the directory's usual information on date of birth and law school is missing. The rest is unknown.

Of the events surrounding his challenge to the tax exemption there is, again, a mixture of fact and speculation. In 1967 he bought a useless and weed-filled six hundred square feet of Staten Island (about one-fourth the size of a tennis court), apparently expressly for the purpose of establishing standing as a taxpayer (annual tax bill: $5.24). He was the sole originator of the suit, and acted as his own attorney in the lower courts. Furthermore, he apparently sought no help or advice in this single-minded endeavor.

Just what were Walz's motives or his interests in church-state litigation is less clear. According to the *New York Times,* they related to the love of animals that marks his daily existence. He apparently had earlier lobbied extensively for laws ensuring the humane treatment of animals, and became aggrieved in the late 1960s when "he felt that Rabbis and Catholic priests had joined forces to defeat a bill [in the New York legislature] that would have required humane methods of slaughtering cattle in kosher slaughterhouses." The proceeds of his own paperbound tract, *New vs. Old,* are "paid to animal protection agencies." The subtitle of that work also suggests another clue to motive: "The guilt of organized 'religions' in the Decline and Fall of the U.S.A." A very substantial part of its 129 pages are, in fact, devoted to that theme,

[9] Richard Severo article in the *New York Times* (June 20, 1969).
[10] *Ibid.*

137

with special attention given to repetitions of old accusations of Jewish perfidies and conspiracies.[11]

Edwin J. Mangold

Few church-state plaintiffs meet the specifications of the "ideal" separationist plaintiff, but Edwin Mangold of Fairchance, Pennsylvania, did. A devout Roman Catholic, he lived across the street from the town's Catholic church, and taught Saturday morning catechism classes. A civilian clerk-accountant for the U.S. Army in nearby Uniontown, he had also been active in the Army reserve. He had been, as well, a local Boy Scout leader, and the father of two teen-aged boys. He was in his early fifties at the time of his litigation in 1969. And throughout his litigation and his ordeal in it, he maintained a stoical silence, refusing most newspaper interviews and invitations in the community to join battle over the issue.

Approaching the classic specifications for the constitutional plaintiff was no insurance that his way as a litigant would be easy, however. Mangold lived within a school district in Southeastern Pennsylvania's coal country that set out to institute school prayer in defiance of the U.S. Supreme Court's earlier decisions. After he resolved to take that defiance to court, and determined that he couldn't afford to do so by himself, he sought the help of the Western Pennsylvania affiliate of the ACLU. With their help he won his suit (*Mangold* v. *School District*) both in the local federal district court and in the Court of Appeals for the Third Circuit. It was a lonely battle in Fairchance and the rest of Fayette county; few others surfaced with public help or support, and anonymous phone calls threatened his life, the lives of his family, and the bombing of his home.

Mangold explains why he brought the suit with a thoughtful and simple eloquence. In part it was because of a deeply patriotic feeling for the law, the Constitution, and the Supreme Court. "What kind of an example is that for the kids, violating the Constitution and the Supreme Court?" he asks. Convinced that "things" are too slack these days, Mangold believes that adults "need to set a better example." And in the best tradition of Roman Catholic

[11] The *New York Times* article (November 20, 1969) was by Fred P. Graham. The Walz tract was published in 1971 and republished in 1974 in a second edition; the publisher is listed as New and True of New York, N.Y.

138

thought, he reminds one that the Christian has a duty to obey two laws, the law of God and the law of men. In part, too, he acted from a conviction about the wisdom of a separation of church and state—especially the avoidance of social divisiveness. And a pragmatic realism about public religiosity is there, too; it doesn't have much effect, Mangold believes, and it is much more apt to be Protestant than Catholic religiosity.[12]

Stefan Ray Aronow

In mid-1972 Stefan Aronow was modest, even a little ill at ease, in discussing his suit to halt the use of the national motto "In God We Trust." Chunky and with sandy brown hair unfashionably short by the standards of the day, he conveyed a quiet, restless earnestness. By then graduated from the University of California at Davis, he lived with his mother in an attractive, middle-class area of San Carlos, down the peninsula from San Francisco.

At the time of his litigation in 1968 to stop the use of the motto on the coins, stamps, and documents of the United States, Aronow was a twenty-one-year-old history major at Davis. Not especially political, he had, however, been involved in campus protests against the war in Vietnam. Yet he continued to think of himself as an "independent Republican" and, although no admirer of Governor Ronald Reagan, an advocate of an "isolationist" foreign policy in the manner of Senator Robert Taft.

And "his" litigation it was. He neither sought nor received group help. The modest fees and costs he paid himself. Armed with a knowledge of American constitutional law gained in an undergraduate constitutional law course, plus some independent research in the law library, he functioned as his own attorney. There were no stenographic or printing costs; his complaint and brief were written in longhand on ruled notebook paper. (He was, however, coached on the form of the complaint by workers in the office of the clerk of the federal district court.) The suit (*Aronow* v. *United States*) lost both in the district court and in the Court of Appeals for the Ninth Circuit. Aronow himself also decided not to seek certiorari from the Supreme Court because he was persuaded by then that the cause was hopeless. And so modest was the suit and its auspices that it came and went almost unnoticed

---

[12] Most of the materials here result from a personal interview with Mangold. The best newspaper coverage of him and his case can be found in Ben A. Franklin's article in the *New York Times* (November 23, 1969).

139

by the local press. Consequently, Aronow felt no impact or consequences.

And why so singular a suit? By adopting and using the motto, Aronow thought, the government of the United States had taken sides in the religious disagreements of Americans and had thereby demeaned the Constitution and infringed his civil and religious liberties. In his affidavit filed in the case he expanded on those themes:

> My religion is founded on the concept that the universe is the largest entity in existence, that everything is part of the universe, that each thing has a place to play in the universe, and that role is to develop [sic] and act within the natural limits of one's being. My system does not include a transcendental deity which is trinitarian in nature.
>
> I suffer in the minds of most Americans as being un-American because of my religion. I am also being required to pay money to support a religion. I consider the motto 'In God We Trust' as official, government ideology and a slap at my religion.[13]

And yet Aronow had no ties within the national organizations of nonbelievers, and Madalyn Murray O'Hair made no overture to him during the litigation. The chances are that she, too, didn't know of it.

This small gallery of portraits could be extended for many more pages. These few will, however, suggest how very diverse a group these plaintiffs are. They are different personalities, diverse in their separationism, and of very different social statuses. And yet they have a great deal in common. All of them actually originated a church-state case; that is, none of them was a "paper plaintiff," chosen after the origination of the case to serve as a passive plaintiff. Some of them turned the litigation over to groups, others did not. But all put their own stamp on it.

They also have in common either a burning dedication verging on monomania or a moral conviction or outrage of uncommon intensity. They are people of conscience and conviction who are also people of action, even of militance. They are the uncompromising in a pragmatic, accommodative society; they make no bow

---

[13] On file in the office of the Clerk of the U.S. District Court for the Northern District of California in San Francisco.

140

to conventional "going along" or to easy majoritarian social ethics. They are self-contained, inner-directed people by and large. If their opinions seem unnaturally strong or vehement in some cases, it should remind us that it takes some unusually strong views to spur this kind of lonely, often very unpopular action. Men and women with balanced, moderate, tentative beliefs, and who avoid social conflict, do not bring such constitutional litigation.

Above all, these little sketches of the plaintiffs point up the fact that such litigation is one of the few forms of political activity left for the unreconstructed individualist. The loner, the eccentric, the strongly inner-directed, the battler of lost causes, the fiercely independent spirit can still go to the courts in what may seem to the rest of society a quixotic venture. And he may in some improbable, high spirited venture still engage and disable a windmill.

THE 67 PLAINTIFFS: AN AGGREGATE OUTLINE

Plaintiffs in church-state cases come in a number of varieties—some are individuals, some are officials, and some are governmental bodies. The majority are separationists, but some are accommodationists. And while most face the defendants in a genuine adversary relationship, some do not. Before one tries to describe these differences, however, it is necessary to break down the sixty-seven cases into different logical categories:

I.	The Friendly Suits:			9
II.	The Adversary Cases:			
	A.	Accommodationist plaintiffs		5
		1. nongovernmental	4	
		2. governmental	1	
	B.	Separationist plaintiffs		53
		1. nongovernmental	48	
		2. governmental	5	
TOTAL				67

The individuals pictured above—O'Hair, Tilton, Schempp, Walz, Mangold, and Aronow—all fall into the category of the forty-eight private parties who were plaintiffs in adversary cases in which the plaintiffs were separationists (II, B, 1). In addition, all six fall into a single subset of that group not indicated above: the thirty of those forty-eight who had some part in actively organizing the case in which there were plaintiffs.

Nine of the sixty-seven cases were friendly suits into which plaintiffs were recruited in ways and for reasons quite different from those for which plaintiffs participated in the adversary (the "nonfriendly") suits. Since the purpose of the friendly suit was in all nine instances the quick determination of the constitutionality of some law or practice, the suits were in all instances arranged at least in part (and often wholly) by government officials and bodies. In six of the nine, in fact, the original plaintiff was either a government official or agency. As constitutional litigation, the friendly cases are a breed apart, and they will be dealt with separately at greater length.[14]

Of the remaining fifty-eight cases, there were five in which the plaintiffs were accommodationists. They included two suits to force local school districts to provide bus rides to children attending religious schools, and one each to compel a tax exemption for a local Presbyterian retirement home, to compel a local principal to permit prayers in a public school, and to authorize a local special school district to provide auxiliary services (speech therapy, for instance) to children attending religious schools. The plaintiff in one of the five cases was a governmental body: the special school district. Of the four nongovernmental plaintiffs, one was the Presbyterian synod in question. Thus, only three of them were individuals or groups of individuals. In all three cases—the two bus cases and the prayer case—the plaintiffs, not surprisingly, were Roman Catholic.[15] But their number is far too small for much further analysis. Their motives, at least, are obviously the accommodationist ones of maintaining or seeking to establish some cooperation between the church (or its members) and the state.

We have now reduced the total of 67 cases to 53 adversary cases in which the plaintiffs had separationist interests. That number may once again be reduced to 48, when one eliminates the 5 in which the plaintiffs were either government bodies or officials. Those 5 included the 2 school boards who questioned state-mandated aid to religious schools in their districts. The other 3 cases were all instances of state officials trying to make local school districts obey the Supreme Court decisions against prayer in public schools. One was brought by the attorney general and other officials of New Jersey, 1 by the New Jersey State Board of Education,

---

[14] See Chapter XI on the friendly, nonadversary cases.

[15] The five cases in the order referred to in this paragraph are: *Special District* v. *Wheeler, Johnson* v. *Presbyterian Homes, Matthews* v. *Quinton, State ex rel. Hughes* v. *Board of Education,* and *Stein* v. *Oshinsky.*

and 1 by the Massachusetts Commissioner of Education.[16] It is difficult to generalize very much about 5 such plaintiffs, except to emphasize the obvious: that the 5 cases embrace all 3 of the cases among the 67 in which enforcement of compliance is the main goal, and that all 5 come from 3 Eastern seaboard states of very heterogeneous religious populations. One might speculate that in these states church-state conflict had perhaps been institutionalized in the politics of the state or parts of it.

These governmental plaintiffs, separationists though they are, must also be kept apart. For one thing, governmental bodies obviously do not share with individuals characteristics of religion, party, sex, or education—and when, as governmental officials, they do, it is difficult to say what population (other than that of other governmental officials) they might be compared with. They also have different characteristics as plaintiffs. Of their disadvantages we spoke in the last chapter: their decision to enter litigation may be changed in midstream by a shift of opinion in the constituency or a turnover in membership. They have the disadvantage of inconstancy or lack of resoluteness often produced by the political backlash of the initial decision. Governmental bodies or officials, it should also be pointed out, may have certain advantages as plaintiffs. They tend to be more anonymous than individuals; even though the state board of education is made up of individuals, it exists in the public mind as a collectivity. Governmental action also carries with it the status and aura of legitimacy that attaches especially to elected bodies and officials.

Furthermore, governmental bodies and officials have the advantage of being able to act to enforce the law. They may base their action on their oath of office to uphold the laws and constitutions of the state and the United States. Thus they may, if they wish, evade the entire thicket of church-state issues and their own convictions about separation. And it is true that for many the issue is really something else than church-state. In the instances of the three officials or bodies taking action against school districts scheduling prayers in defiance of the Supreme Court, the state and its officials are indeed cast in the role, however uncomfortable, of enforcing the U.S. Constitution. Furthermore, they may be under

---

[16] The five cases mentioned in this paragraph are, in consecutive order: *Board of Education* v. *Allen*, *West Morris Regional Board* v. *Sills*, *Sills* v. *Board of Education*, *State Board* v. *Netcong*, and *Commissioner of Education* v. *Leyden*.

143

considerable pressure from separationist groups to pull the local mutineers into line, or face both private suits and public political opposition. The New Jersey affiliate of the ACLU, for example, threatened suits in both of the prayer cases in that state. Local school boards may, in other words, think they are flinging down the gauntlet to the Supreme Court, but the gauntlet invariably falls at the feet of some state official. Private groups, their own legal staffs, and their own sense of legal responsibility conspire to push attorneys general, state boards of education, or commissioners of education into action.

And now there are 48—the 48 adversary cases in which the plaintiffs were nongovernmental separationists. Of that 48, there were individual plaintiffs—either one or more—in 47. In the 48th the plaintiff was a corporation, the General Finance Corporation of Rhode Island, which brought a suit challenging the state's tax exemption for religious property (*General Finance* v. *Archetto*). Most of these 48 cases had more than one plaintiff, and many were brought on behalf of a mixture of individuals and groups or organizations. In one of them, indeed, most of the adult population of Bradfordsville, Kentucky, and its environs—some 460 in all—served as plaintiffs in what seems to have been the legal incarnation of a community crusade (*Wooley* v. *Spaulding*). To permit analysis of the plaintiffs in all of these cases a composite or "average" plaintiff has been constructed for those cases with more than a single plaintiff. There are, therefore, 48 "plaintiffs" in these 48 cases.[17]

THE 48 PLAINTIFFS

We know a good deal about a number of subsets of American political activists. American voters, party officials, and office-holders have been repeatedly identified and portrayed. The constitutional litigant has not. At least in cases raising church-state issues, the individual separationist plaintiffs both resemble and differ from the classic description of the active minority in American politics.[18]

[17] The specific rules I followed for reducing multiple plaintiffs to one are outlined in Appendix III.

[18] For perceptive observations on "litigants as political participants," however, see Richard Claude, *The Supreme Court and the Electoral Process* (Baltimore: Johns Hopkins Press, 1970), pp. 3–8.

Like the rest of the American political elite, these separationist plaintiffs are predominantly white, male, Protestant, upper middle-class, and well educated (Table 6–1). As a group they are, in fact, even more so, approaching a high status and homogeneity usually identified with groups such as United States senators. If this population is skewed in any way, it is in the usual direction of American political elites—toward more maleness, more whiteness, and higher education. And yet behind the conventional data there are a few surprises and several hidden but important subtleties.

The data on religion indicate, for instance, an unusually high incidence of atheists, agnostics, nonbelievers, and those without religious preference or affiliation—those who are, for various reasons, among the "unchurched." They reflect the special issues of church-state relations with which these cases are involved, for clearly at the root of some of this litigation is a suspicion of or hostility to organized religion. In fact, a significant number of that group fall into the classic stereotype of the nineteenth and early twentieth-century freethinker—readers of Voltaire, glib with the aphorisms of Robert Ingersoll, admirers of Bertrand Russell, and mockingly skeptical of the whole business of organized religion. Joseph Lewis's last biography in *Who's Who in America* is in itself almost a parody of the stereotype:

. . . Responsible for election of Thomas Paine to Hall of Fame, 1946; dedicated Borglum statue of Thomas Paine, Paris, France, 1948 . . . ded. as pub. meml. the house in which Robert Ingersoll was born, 1954; dedicated Thomas Paine statue, Stratford, Eng., 1964 . . .[19]

Among his written works, Mr. Lewis also listed *Voltaire: The Incomparable Infidel* and *Ingersoll the Magnificent*.

The fact that there are very few Roman Catholics among the 48 plaintiffs is not at all surprising, in view of the usually accommodationist views of Catholics. It is, however, surprising how few Jews there are, especially in view of the role of the American Jewish Congress in so many of these cases. (In addition to the three Jews, however, there are also Jews as plaintiffs in five of the seven cases that fell into the "mixed" group.) Finally, among the 24 Protestants, fully 10 of them came from the traditionalist and fundamentalist sects and denominations—

[19] 1970–1971 edition, p. 1358.

145

TABLE 6-1
Characteristics of 48 Nongovernmental Separationist Plaintiffs

	Number	Percentage
I. Sex		
male	37	77.1
female	5	10.4
mixed[a]	5	10.4
inapplicable[b]	1	2.1
	48	100.0
II. Race		
white	45	93.8
Indian	1	2.1
mixed black, white[a]	1	2.1
inapplicable[b]	1	2.1
	48	100.1
III. Religion		
Protestant	24	50.0
Roman Catholic	2	4.2
Jewish	3	6.3
mixed[a]	7	14.6
atheist, nonbeliever, no affiliation	11	22.9
inapplicable[b]	1	2.1
	48	100.1
IV. Occupation		
professional, technical	20	41.7
bus'men, mgr., official	10	20.8
clerical, sales	1	2.1
skilled worker	0	—
semiskilled worker	3	6.3
service worker	0	—
unskilled laborer	0	—
farmer	2	4.2
mixed[a]	6	12.5
unemployed	1	2.1
student	1	2.1
housewife	1	2.1
inapplicable, unknown[b]	3	6.3
	48	100.2
V. Education		
high school grad or less	7	14.6
some college, business or technical school	7	14.6
college graduate	21	43.8
advanced degrees	6	12.5
mixed[a]	1	2.1
inapplicable, unknown[b]	6	12.5
	48	100.1

[a] The mixed categories are instances of multiple plaintiffs whose characteristics were too diverse to be reduced to a single average or modal characteristic.

[b] The "inapplicable" category in all instances refers to the one nonindividual plaintiff: the General Finance Corporation. "Unknown" means exactly that.

146

Baptists, Methodists, Disciples of Christ, Bible Presbyterians, and one member of the Assembly of God. Another 4 were Unitarians, and 2 were Congregationalists. Thus only 6 of the 24 came from the conventional, middle-of-the-road Protestant denominations. Very simply, the special religious composition of the 48 reflects the relationship between separationism and religious affiliation in the United States—the relative absence of it among Catholics, and the zealous commitment to it among both fundamentalist Protestants on the one hand and religious liberals and the unchurched on the other.

There is hidden in the data on the 48 another crucial point, one concerning their occupations. It is obvious, of course, that high-status, generally well-paid occupations predominate. In fact, if one keeps in mind that in all six cases of "mixed" occupations some of the plaintiffs held either professional/technical or business/manager/official occupations, then a total of 36 (75 percent) of the plaintiffs fall into these two categories. In this often unpopular litigation, then, the plaintiffs tended to be drawn from occupations in which they were sheltered from possible economic reprisals. It is precisely this kind of independence that litigating groups prize highly when they set out to find the "ideal" or desirable plaintiff. Furthermore, even within those occupational categories, the plaintiffs often held especially protected positions—medical doctors with the Veterans Administration, independent small businessmen, teachers and college professors, engineers and civil servants in government agencies, and gentlemen farmers, for instance. Few came from the occupations most vulnerable to popular pressures, such as those in sales or personal services.

About two other characteristics, only broader generalizations are possible. Of the 36 on whom there are data about political party preference, 15 were Democrats and 10 were Republicans—a one-and-a-half to one ratio that parallels the distribution of party identifications in the American adult public in the 1950s and 1960s. They had, however, no record of party, election campaign, or office-seeking activity. The plaintiffs also included one Liberal (New York State), one Conservative (that is, the American or Constitutional party), and two socialists (of undetermined particular hue). The remainder had either a "mixed" preference or none at all. Since the age of the plaintiffs was really determined by the necessity of plaintiffs to establish standing, little weight can be given it. The high percentage of school cases resulted

147

in a large number of the litigants being parents of children in the public schools; there is, therefore, a heavy concentration of plaintiffs in their thirties and forties.

On the surface of it, therefore, these appear to be very high-status individuals—their occupations and educations suggest at least that much. But there are repeated signs of a nonconformity that would suggest something to the contrary—that their general socio-economic status is not as high as one might expect from the usual indicators. There is, for one thing, the high percentage of religious skeptics and unchurched, and there is the residuum of third-party adherents. In at least three instances, too, the plaintiffs indicated a political conservatism from the farther reaches of American politics: that is, some distance to the right of the era's conservative benchmark, Senator Barry Goldwater. Philip Carden, organizer and plaintiff in the Tennessee Bible-reading case, for example, was something of a nineteenth-century Jeffersonian libertarian, suspicious of virtually all governmental service, even public education. He and his wife at one point withdrew their children from the public schools and taught them at home. In two other instances the political conservatism was closely tied to nationalism and religious fundamentalism, much in the manner of the Reverends Carl McIntyre and Billy Joe Hargis. The point here is simply that these were not ideological commitments that in the 1950s and 1960s usually bespoke high social status in the community, regardless of the direction in which the conventional status indicators (such as education or occupation) pointed.

To all of that one can only add personal impressions that at least eight of the group of forty-eight were isolated, sometimes alienated, usually maverick members of the community—even more "apart" from the community than ordinary "low status" would indicate. In various ways they had rejected the norms, the conventional social values, even the "society" of the community. Frederick Walz and Madalyn Murray O'Hair typify them. How large a group are they? The characteristics mentioned in this and the previous paragraph obviously cluster to some extent in the same group of individuals. If one takes three characteristics—loyalty to a third party, low SES, or self-description as a nonbeliever or nonmember of a church—17 different plaintiffs display at least one of them, with seven having two or three. Even making allowances for margins of error (especially in attributing low social status), it is evident that this maverick, nonconformist bloc sets

148

off the litigators most dramatically from other political activists of the 1950s and 1960s.[20]

THE PLAINTIFF'S EYE VIEW OF LITIGATION

These plaintiffs, whatever the conventional wisdom might suggest, were usually more than passive, "paper" plaintiffs. In fully 30 of the 48 cases (62.5 percent) plaintiffs originated or participated in the origination of the litigation in which they participated. Another 6 were to some degree active in a general movement to organize the case. Thus in only 12 of the cases were plaintiffs recruited after the decision to bring suit was made. An amazing amount of individual initiative, in other words, coexisted in these cases with a very high level of group activity.

Some of the plaintiff-originators, such as Frederick Walz, proceeded without seeking help or advice of any kind. Others—Edwin Mangold, for example—sought ACLU or other help after deciding to challenge some offending practice. Others formed, often with other leaders and originators, a local ad hoc organization to carry on the legal fight, especially to raise funds and give the cause an organizational substantiality for local publicity. Others, such as Alexander Lincoln, made the origin of church-state litigation something of a personal crusade.

Lincoln, a fighter of many unpopular causes in Meredith, New Hampshire, is a persistent, vastly aggrieved man. He has in his time objected to the religiosity of the magazine of the American Forestry Association (he is a retired tree farmer), to the theological concerns of Harvard University (he is a Harvard B.A. and M.A.), and to the decision of Harry Page, moderator of the Meredith town meeting, to open meetings with a prayer. Lincoln worked at least twelve years to muster support for a challenge to Page's prayer. His letter to Leo Pfeffer asking where he might receive financial help for the litigation drew a brief response saying that he, Pfeffer, knew of no sources and advising him to drop the suit. Lincoln got in touch with the Massachusetts ACLU (New Hampshire had no affiliate then), and then the national ACLU. To Melvin Wulf he wrote, apparently perceiving the priorities: "I admit there are other more important civil rights issues around, but I

---

[20] Claude, in his *The Supreme Court and the Electoral Process,* also notes the incidence of the alienated and the mavericks among litigators of apportionment cases; see pp. 4–5.

am not personally involved in them." Later, contemplating an appeal to the U.S. Supreme Court and still needing assistance, he wrote again to Wulf: "Have you any suggestions as to how I should proceed in this state, what pitfalls to avoid, how to secure whatever minimum knowledge I may need in order to have the case brought in Washington if unsuccessful here?"[21] All the time, however, Lincoln was organizing his own case, filing his own complaint, looking for an attorney. After considerable difficulty he found an attorney and carried his case to the New Hampshire Supreme Court. Looking back on the lonely battle, he wrote to Franklin Salisbury of AU: "But I am distressed that I have had no help at all towards the expenses except for what you and Americans United have given. A few lawyers have shown real interest, but no one else has helped. It is especially bothersome that none of my costs are tax deductible."[22] Lincoln lost his case in New Hampshire, and receiving no offer of help, decided not to seek certiorari in the U.S. Supreme Court. Lincoln's father, incidentally, earlier participated in extensive constitutional litigation on behalf of "wet" and conservative causes.[23] Litigation, like political party activity, may run in families.

Few organizer-plaintiffs write the saga that Lincoln did in starting a constitutional case. And after the litigation commences, they often recede to a less prominent role, for it is at this point that sponsoring or participating groups take over. In fact 22 of the plaintiffs in the 48 cases (45.8 percent) had no role in the decisions during the litigation. A total of 18 (37.5 percent) maintained "some" role, and only 8 (17.7 percent) retained "all" of the decision-making responsibility during the litigation.

If they did not collectively exert a great deal of control over "their" cases, the plaintiffs in these 48 cases did not bear a heavy burden of the costs, either. A full 20 of them (41.7 percent) bore absolutely none of the monetary costs; another 16 (33.3 percent)

[21] Letters of Lincoln to Wulf (January 25 and September 15, 1966); with the ACLU papers at Princeton University Library.

[22] February 3, 1968; letter in AU files, Washington, D.C. Lincoln's case was the only one of these sixty-seven not involving Roman Catholic interests in which AU participated. AU apparently did not contribute a great deal of money to the case; in fact, one in-house memo notes "not much of a suit, but expense is not great." Lincoln subsequently became an active member of AU.

[23] See Clement E. Vose, *Constitutional Change: Amendment Politics and Supreme Court Litigation since 1900* (Lexington, Mass.: D. C. Heath, 1972).

paid only relatively small percentages of the costs, and in all cases less than half. In most of the latter cases the plaintiffs contributed to the general solicitation of funds made either in the community or within the sponsoring organization; they were generally free, therefore, to contribute what they felt they could. When one subtracts 2 cases on which information is missing, there are only 10 in which the plaintiff bore the full costs or a substantial part of them. Three of those cases are the cases of Madalyn Murray and Joseph Lewis, in which one cannot really separate the "national" organizations from the plaintiffs; yet we know that both used those organizations to raise funds for litigation. Within the remaining 7 are the "loners," such as Philip Carden of Nashville, Alexander Lincoln (who bore the entire costs of litigation except for the few hundred dollars he received from AU), Frederick Walz, and Stefan Aronow. In fact, one can really say that of the 7, Lincoln was really the only one who actively sought financial assistance among the separationist groups and was spurned.

"Costs" are of many kinds, however, and for a good share of these plaintiffs the most burdensome "costs" imposed on them were the assorted tribulations that resulted from their participation in patently unpopular litigation. For some the annoyances were minor—perhaps a few frosty neighbors or slights to their children—but for others they approached the trials of Job. The plaintiffs in 28 of the 48 cases reported an "unfavorable" impact or aftermath of the case, but that figure hardly begins to explain their problems. In most cases they challenged some of the cherished values of the community, and the community took its price. As Ellory Schempp reported with a great deal of perceptiveness about the abusive phone callers: "They all found in us an example of some group they had a prejudice against. They'd ask 'What are you—Jews?' or if we were Catholics, Polish, Arabians. Each person saw in us something he hates."[24] Other plaintiffs—at least three—lost jobs as a result of their litigation. Others had employers express concern over their involvement in "controversial" litigation; very probably the business world is less tolerant of such legal shenanigans than it is of candidacy for public office. To such experiences, one can add the harassment of Madalyn Murray and her sons. But none of the other plaintiffs in these cases matched the trials of Harlow Chamberlin, the plaintiff in the ACLU-sponsored suit to end religious influences in the schools of Miami, Florida

[24] Interview in *Providence Evening Bulletin* (March 15, 1963).

(*Chamberlin* v. *Dade County*). Chamberlin, an advertising sales-
man at a local radio station, lost that job within ten days of filing
the suit; a second position in sales also disintegrated as his name
kept appearing in newspaper accounts of the litigation. Harassment
over the phone and by mail persisted, too, and in the words of
one observer the entire Chamberlin family "went through hell."
Mrs. Elsie Thorner, a plaintiff in the same case, recalls being
thrown out of the local bridge club (as "uncongenial"), the phone
ringing incessantly (some calls threatened her and her children),
people shouting "communist!" from cruising cars. Her children
lost playmates, and her two boys began to worry about the next
appearance of her name in the newspaper. The experience, she
thinks, resulted in the boys' later reluctance to become politically
active.

For most of the plaintiffs the unpleasantness involved abrasive
personal encounters, loss of friends, abusive and obscene letters
and phone calls. In the words of another organizer and plaintiff:
"Stacks and stacks of letters. Some encouraging. Some asking for
understanding. Some so downright vindictive and filthy I hardly
wanted to touch them. There were threatening phone calls. . . .
The children were being beat up at school. Stones were thrown
through the windows of the house. One night the telephone
rang all night at 15 minute intervals. I would answer—either there
was no response—or a threat—or just a string of foul language. . . ."[25] The burden falls the most heavily on the most vulnerable, of course—the plaintiffs with insecure jobs, those known
and exposed in a small community, those without a supportive
community or group around them. Majorities in these cases often
seem to have a collective sense of the jugular.

And yet the experience was not as crushing for many as it might
have been. Philip Carden surmises that as "real individualists" a
large number of the plaintiffs suffer less than others might, because
the community has fewer social sanctions over them. They are
accustomed to being unpopular or even pariahs. Furthermore, a
goodly number of plaintiffs also report that while the plaintiff role
may have its trials, it also has its substantial rewards. For many
it brings a sense of social accomplishment they have never had
before, and it opens the way to new friends, new groups, new interests, and a sense of solidarity with fellow activists. For some it
has meant the introduction to a whole new level of community

[25] Harvey Ammerman to Frank Sorauf (undated letter in 1970).

involvement; one plaintiff, for instance, is sure it led eventually to the presidency of the local chapter of the AAUW. Some have even formed a casual guild of church-state plaintiffs in the Pennsylvania area. It appears to center around Edward Schempp, and it involves mail and personal contacts among four or five plaintiffs. Schempp even offered refuge to the Mangold family at the time of their worst troubles in Fairchance.

Considering the potential hurt and the investment of time and ego, and sometimes even of money, perhaps it is just as well that most plaintiff activity happens only once in a lifetime. (That fact in itself may set constitutional litigation apart from all other forms of individual political activity.) At least the plaintiffs in these forty-eight cases had had virtually no experience with earlier church-state litigation. Only Madalyn Murray (in her second of two cases) and Joseph Lewis, among this entire group, had ever before been involved in church-state litigation. In fact, only 9 others had a record of church-state activity (other than litigation) at the time of their plaintiff status. The overwhelming majority (37 of 48; 77.1 percent) of plaintiffs, therefore, came to court without ever having taken public action of any kind to further the cause of separationism. Constitutional litigation—at least on this topic—rises out of little public involvement, and it probably leads only rarely to further litigation. It is a nonrecurring political act, and it is apparently largely unrelated to other political activity. Only very few plaintiffs make a political career in litigation. That role is left to the groups.

PLAINTIFFS AND PLAINTIFFS: THE SUBCATEGORIES

In view of the strategic attention lavished on the selection of plaintiffs, one might expect the plaintiffs in the cases of the ACLU, the AJC, and AU to be somehow different from those in cases carried without benefit of their support. To some extent that is the case. The cases in which the three leading groups played a major role did show a greater instance of high or medium-status plaintiffs. And in religious composition, the plaintiffs in those cases also had the stamp of the groups' preferences—some Jews, more high-status Protestants, and the collections of plaintiffs of mixed religious traditions. So far so good. But the relationships are not especially strong, and the stamp of group preferences is not apparent in other characteristics of the plaintiffs.

153

The fact is that a significant number of plaintiffs chose themselves, even in the cases in which groups were active. Plaintiffs originated (in part, at least) thirty of these forty-eight cases. This litigation accommodated the willful, initiating individual as well as the sophisticated litigating group. The groups came to these cases in most instances after some individual or group of individuals had decided to take action. The plaintiff was frequently already selected, even in many of those instances in which one or more groups took over the sponsorship of the litigation. Not all of the cases sponsored by the groups, therefore, were fully initiated and arranged by them. Conversely, many of the cases originated by strong, dedicated local plaintiffs ended up in the hands of the groups, with the plaintiff-initiator accepting a passive role the rest of the way.

It is the plaintiffs themselves, therefore, who determined in many cases who and what the plaintiffs would be. And thus the most significant differences among plaintiffs are between those who originated their own cases—the self-starters—and those who did not. The latter clearly have been "picked"—often, it is true, merely because of their availability or their volunteering, but often, too, because they fit in some way a strategic "ideal" of the constitutional plaintiff. Therefore they clearly ought to come closer in characteristics to that ideal and they do (Table 6–2). Their experiences as a plaintiff were also different from those of the originators; they paid fewer of the costs and suffered a little less from community outrage.

From all of this there emerge two types of separationist plaintiffs in these forty-eight cases; the originator and the more passive "chosen" plaintiff. In general the chief differences (see Table 6–2) are these:

The Plaintiff-Originator	*The Chosen Plaintiff*
less conventionally religious	more conventionally religious
lower SES; often alienated	higher SES; usually "respectable"
more church-state history	less church-state history
more often a single plaintiff	more often multiple plaintiffs
bears larger share of costs	bears fewer costs
more apt to suffer adverse effects of litigation	less likely to have adverse effects from litigation

They are, in other words, two different kinds of plaintiffs, and they performed different roles in the process of this constitutional litiga-

154

TABLE 6-2
Plaintiffs' Personal Characteristics and Relationships to Church-State
Litigation According to Their Role in Originating Litigation

	Plaintiff-Originators[a]	Chosen Plaintiffs
I. Religion		
low status Protestant and unchurched	16 (55.2%)	5 (27.8%)
others (incl. "mixed")	13 (44.8%)	13 (72.2%)
	29	18
II. Socio-economic status		
high, medium	19 (65.5%)	15 (83.3%)
low, alienated	10 (34.5%)	1 (5.6%)
no information	—	2 (11.1%)
	29	18
III. Church-state and civil liberties history		
none	16 (55.2%)	12 (66.7%)
civil liberties only	3 (10.3%)	2 (11.1%)
church-state activity	10 (34.5%)	1 (5.6%)
no information	—	3 (16.7%)
	29	18
IV. Costs borne by plaintiff		
none	7 (24.1%)	14 (77.8%)
some (less than half)	12 (41.4%)	4 (22.2%)
most or all	9 (31.0%)	—
no information	1 (3.5%)	—
	29	18
V. Impact on plaintiff		
none	4 (13.8%)	3 (16.7%)
favorable or mixed	4 (13.8%)	3 (16.7%)
negative	19 (65.5%)	9 (50.0%)
no information	2 (6.9%)	3 (16.7%)
	29	18
VI. Number of plaintiffs		
one	16 (53.3%)	5 (27.8%)
more than one	14 (46.7%)	13 (72.2%)
	30	18

[a] Where the total in this column is 29 rather than 30 it is because the one corporate plaintiff has been excluded.

155

tion. If the originators are more nonconformist, and lower in SES, that fact may be directly, even causally, related to their willingness to take the often difficult initiatives necessary to bring unpopular litigation of this sort. We might have much less constitutional litigation if it were left to those of higher status and conventional respectability.

IN CONCLUSION

Appellate courts traditionally have offered access to minorities, even to minorities of one. The isolates, the loners, the nonconformists, the dedicated, the fearful, the moralizers, and the independent spirits may invoke the judicial power on much the same terms as majorities might invoke the power of the legislatures. In their ultimate power to shape public policy so boldly, these free spirits turn concepts of power and influence in a democracy on their ear. Many of them indeed appear to shun more conventional electoral or legislative politics; at least few have any record in it. And as a political elite they are oddly deceptive. On the surface they appear to be a conventional, high-status political elite, but beneath that surface they are a much less conventional group. Dogmatic and uncompromising in manner, there also lurks in many a social, political, and religious nonconformity. When most forms of political activity demand organization, cooperation, and accommodation, they have found a refuge and a mechanism for the single-minded individualist.

It is a strange kind of political activity, this litigating constitutional questions. Many of its participants do not really acknowledge that they participate; they seek specific remedies for specific wrongs, and they appear to settle constitutional issues by accident. But even where it is recognized, it is a kind of political gesture that one generally makes but once in a lifetime. (One conjures up metaphors of those insects that are able to sting only once.) Success depends, too, on factors outside of the individual's control. And the costs are as unpredictable as are the chances of success. Costs—both cash and other costs—vary wildly. One case may cost a few hundred and bring no notoriety, while another may cost $10,000 and untold harassment.

Surprisingly, the advent of group-managed and supported litigation has not squeezed out the individual plaintiff. To a considerable extent it is the plaintiff-originator who resolves to undertake litiga-

156

tion. He thus invokes the power of the group in litigation. The group-founded "test" case, with paper plaintiffs from the very beginning, does occur, but it has by no means preempted this area of constitutional litigation. And so they remain in a bizarre alliance: the individual plaintiff, often lonely and without support, and the experienced national organization. It is an improbable alliance, one quite unacknowledged, and yet one peculiarly effective.

VII | THE SEPARATIONIST ATTORNEYS

To a considerable extent the separationist plaintiffs in these church-state cases are a group by definition only. They are grouped together because they took the same action sometime between 1951 and 1971. They did not, with a few exceptions, know each other, and they communicated very little with each other. It is understandable, therefore, that they had little sense of belonging to a group of "plaintiffs." They were, rather, members of a category defined by others than themselves. By contrast, the attorneys representing the separationist plaintiffs had interactions and communications, and even, implicitly at least, a leader. Unlike the plaintiffs, they became expert in the constitutional law of church-state relations, and they often appeared in more than one church-state case. Some, indeed, made a career, a part of a career, or an avocation of these constitutional questions. To some extent, indeed, they formed a "separationist bar."

THE "SEPARATIONIST BAR"

The separationist attorneys in these sixty-seven cases parallel—with one significant exception—the separationist plaintiffs of the last chapter. In other words, one can largely repeat the subtractive arithmetic we indulged in to define the plaintiffs. From the full sixty-seven cases, one subtracts the nine friendly suits for the same reason: their attorneys were chosen in ways and functioned for purposes quite apart from the mainstream of this constitutional litigation. The plaintiff attorneys in these friendly suits were either government attorneys (for example, an assistant attorney general of a state), or they were chosen by or with the help of public officials.

From that reduced total of 58 adversary cases, one again eliminates the 5 with accommodationist plaintiffs, producing the subtotal of 53. At this point the variation on the plaintiff arithmetic occurs. A total of 48 separationist plaintiffs emerged after one deducted the 5 separationist plaintiffs who were either government

158

bodies or government officials. In the case of the plaintiffs' attorneys, however, local ACLU affiliates provided attorneys for 2 of the governmental plaintiffs—the local school boards in *Board* v. *Allen,* and *West Morris Regional Board* v. *Sills.* We include the 2 of them and reach a total here of 50 rather than 48. The case group of 50 separationist attorneys, therefore, is identical with that of the separationist plaintiffs except for the addition of those two cases.[1]

Leo Pfeffer: the Leader of the Bar

By general consensus Leo Pfeffer was the dominant, driving force among separationist attorneys in these cases and in the entire universe of church-state litigation in the 1950s and 1960s. That was the case in part because of the sheer continuity and volume of his involvement: he was an active counsel with the American Jewish Congress for the entire period. In part, too, his position of leadership resulted from his preeminence as a scholar and advocate in the area.

Pfeffer was born in Hungary in 1910 and came to the United States in 1912. He graduated from the City College of New York and won the J.D. from New York University in 1933, after serving for a year as editor of its law review. He joined the legal staff of the American Jewish Congress in 1945, and became the assistant director of its Commission on Law and Social Action in 1947. He served as its director from 1957, until he took the chairmanship of the political science department at the Brooklyn Center of Long Island University in 1964. From 1964 on he remained with the Congress as a special counsel. Throughout this period Pfeffer won for himself a reputation as the leading author and legal authority on church-state questions. Aside from his many essays and journal articles, he published five books on the general topic: *Church, State, and Freedom, The Liberties of an American, Creeds in Competition, This Honorable Court: A History of the United States Supreme Court,* and a one-volume revision and updating of Anson Phelps Stoke's magistral *Church and State in the United States.*[2]

Aside from his scholarly eminence, Pfeffer advised, planned, rehearsed, reviewed, helped, and argued more church-state cases

---

[1] Some rules and conventions were necessary to define and designate a "plaintiff's attorney." They are spelled out in Appendix III.

[2] *Church, State, and Freedom* (Boston: Beacon Press, 1953); *The Liberties of an American* (Boston: Beacon Press, 1956), and a revised edition in 1963; *Creeds in Competition* (New York: Harper, 1958); *This Honor-*

TABLE 7-1
Leo Pfeffer's Trial and Appellate Court Roles in
the 67 Church-State Cases

Nature of Participation	Roles in the 50 Separationist and Adversary Cases	Roles in the Total of 67 Cases
I. Trial court role		
none	30 (60.0%)	44 (65.7%)
advice	7 (14.0%)	8 (11.9%)
helped briefs, argument	3 (6.0%)	4 (6.0%)
active at trial	10 (20.0%)	11 (16.4%)
	50	67
II. Appellate court role		
none	36 (72.0%)	52 (77.6%)
argument (state ct.)	7 (14.0%)	8 (11.9%)
argument (U.S. Sup. Ct.)	2 (4.0%)	2 (3.0%)
amicus curiae	5 (10.0%)	5 (7.5%)
	50	67

Note: The right-hand column reports data from the full universe of 67 cases in this study; the left-hand column reports data from the set of 50 cases employed in this chapter and defined in the text.

than any other attorney of his generation, and by a considerable margin. Most of his activity in the trials and appellate stages of this church-state litigation did indeed take place in the 50 cases we have identified above (see Table 7–1). Remarkably, Pfeffer had some role in the trial stages of 20 of these 50 cases (40 percent) and in 14 (28 percent) of the appellate stages. Pfeffer's work also extended beyond this set of 67 church-state cases. While he argued only two of them before the U.S. Supreme Court (*Tilton v. Richardson* and *DiCenso* v. *Robinson*), he has argued a number of other religion cases there, among them *Torcaso* v. *Watkins,* and *Flast* v. *Cohen.*[3] Pfeffer also prepared and argued the Dade County school case (*Chamberlin* v. *Dade County*) in the Florida courts before it was decided summarily by the U.S. Supreme Court without oral argument. That case was, Pfeffer believes, the most interesting of all the church-state cases in which he was involved.

---

able Court (Boston: Beacon Press, 1965); and, with Anson Phelps Stokes, *Church and State in the United States* (Boston: Beacon Press, 1964), and a revised edition in 1967.

[3] *Torcaso* v. *Watkins,* 367 U.S. 488 (1961); *Flast* v. *Cohen,* 392 U.S. 83 (1968).

Pfeffer's participation in these cases is, in fact, broader even than that of the American Jewish Congress, as Table 7–1 suggests. In some cases in which the American Jewish Congress did not participate because of local Jewish community opposition, Pfeffer either assisted counsel or worked openly with the ACLU. In the *Walz* case over New York tax exemption on religious property, for example, Pfeffer participated in at least one ACLU executive committee meeting to hammer out a policy for the Union, and he later contributed to the ACLU amicus curiae brief before the U.S. Supreme Court. The ten instances of his general advice and strategy and his specific help with briefs and argument often came, too, in cases in which some group other than the AJC was involved in the case.

Indicative of the Pfeffer informal advisory role was his assistance to the Rhode Island CLU in its challenge of the state's law providing textbooks for children attending religious schools (*Bowerman* v. *O'Connor*). Before originating the case, Milton Stanzler, president of the RICLU and one of its attorneys in the case, came to New York to confer with Pfeffer about it. In the complaint he eventually filed to inaugurate the suit, Stanzler drew extensively on the language of Pfeffer's complaint in the Oregon textbook case some years earlier (*Dickman* v. *School District*). They subsequently exchanged letters and phone calls on matters of strategy, with Pfeffer suggesting, inter alia, a full trial to show that the purpose of the legislation was to aid parochial schools. Pfeffer then advised on testimony and depositions, sending questions to Stanzler that he had earlier used. And when Stanzler sent his appellate brief to Melvin Wulf of the national ACLU for comments, Wulf shipped it uptown to Pfeffer with a "what do you think of it?" note attached. Finally, Stanzler invited Pfeffer to participate in argument before the Rhode Island Supreme Court. (Pfeffer did not, for reasons that are not clear.) Granted that this one illustration perhaps involves unusual requests for Pfeffer's help, it nonetheless shows the range in the kinds of assistance he gave in a number of instances.

As these paragraphs also suggest, Pfeffer sat at the center of a network of legal information and communication. His own expertise and experience attracted queries and calls for help. His personal network, plus the AJC's *Litigation Docket,* constituted the major informational network among attorneys working for separationist interests in these church-state cases. Serious conclaves

161

within the ACLU national office on church-state matters often included Pfeffer, and he usually presided over the meetings of the litigation consortium, and over less formal meetings of litigators in related cases or alliances of litigators in a single case. At various times, for instance, ad hoc meetings of litigators of the various parochaid cases were held in New York; again Pfeffer most often presided over them.

Pfeffer's central role was not always easy for others to accept. Some attorneys undoubtedly found it hard to admit their inexperience in the constitutional law of church-state relations, and others were unaccustomed to accepting legal leadership of any kind. Some, more specifically, found Pfeffer's leadership a little demanding. Early in the 1951–1971 period, Pfeffer had some bitter fallings out with representatives of the American Jewish Committee and B'nai B'rith; they were, in part, clashes over the responsibilities of the groups in litigation on behalf of Jewish interests, and in part clashes of strong personalities. Other church-state attorneys found Pfeffer occasionally abrasive and somewhat short with those less learned and experienced than he. In any event, there seems little doubt on at least two points. First, Pfeffer expected recognition of his preeminence in the church-state field. He did not take kindly to suggestions that, despite his preeminence and despite his major role on collective briefs, he should be listed alphabetically among a list of attorneys for assorted organizations. Nor was he anxious to enter cases on equal or subordinate terms with other attorneys—a preference that led a few of them to complain that Pfeffer stole the spotlight. Secondly, it is also true that Pfeffer had and continues to have strong views about the strategy and tactics one ought to use in litigating these cases, and he can be assertive, even unyielding, in advancing them. Above all, Pfeffer is a legal craftsman who does not easily suffer sloppy or mediocre legal work, nor does he easily condone litigation for other than the most serious constitutional reasons. Nonetheless, the tensions attending Pfeffer's central role very probably relate to his leadership in church-state litigation. A less strong personality would probably not have been able to put his imprint on it.

The Other Leaders

It appeared in the 1940s and early 1950s that Kenneth Greenawalt might become for the ACLU's litigation in church-state relations what Pfeffer was for the AJC's. Greenawalt, an active

Congregationalist, had come to his separationism through Congregationalism's religious liberalism and through his commitment to civil liberties, which led him to work as a cooperating attorney for the ACLU. A member of the prestigious Wall Street firm of Davies, Hardy, Loeb, Austin, and Ives, Greenawalt has also represented the Episcopal diocese, and been active in the Religion in Higher Education Fund and the American Friends Service Committee.

Greenawalt prepared the ACLU brief in the earlier *McCollum* released-time case before the U.S. Supreme Court in 1948,[4] and then with Pfeffer he prepared and in 1951 argued the ACLU and AJC's second released-time case, *Zorach* v. *Clauson*. In both cases he participated as an ACLU cooperating attorney. But Greenawalt's involvement in this body of litigation tailed off after *Zorach*. He consulted informally on a few later cases, "almost" taking a later case for the New York Civil Liberties Union (*Board* v. *Allen*), and finally in the late 1960s and early 1970s did some work in preparing new litigation in the New York area for the AU. What happened to Greenawalt's blossoming work in church-state litigation? John Pemberton, who came on the scene as the executive director of the ACLU in 1962 and remained until 1970, had considerable interest in the church-state question, and for at least part of the period he was apparently determined to carry the ACLU away from its absolute separationism. Thus, while Greenawalt remained active in ACLU affairs and on the church-state committee, he found himself in an "absolutist" minority. Furthermore, as the ACLU began to decentralize its litigation to the affiliates, Greenawalt's potential role in New York seemed less important. He was also busy in his own law work, and his inability to meet short deadlines for drafting briefs also cost him opportunities. At the same time, Pfeffer's increasing dominance of the litigation made him the logical person for national ACLU leaders to turn to by the 1960s and seventies.

The legal staff of Americans United never developed expertise and stature to rival Pfeffer's. Glenn Archer, the organization's executive director and a former dean of the Washburn University Law School, was unwilling to surrender direct control of the legal program of AU. In addition, "finding suitable staff counsel has been difficult—the pay is low and many professional persons are reluctant to risk their careers in association with a 'controversial'

[4] *McCollum* v. *Board of Education,* 333 U.S. 203 (1948).

163

interest group."[5] Furthermore, the AU policy of giving control of the litigation to local counsel retained on an ad hoc basis in effect reduced the general counsel to an administrative position. He generally advises local counsel, writes the amicus briefs for AU, and oversees its commitments. The comparatively brief tenures of the general counsels have also worked against development of their stature. Archer was the only lawyer on the staff until 1956; then Paul Blanshard came in to function as a "special counsel." The organization's first general counsel, Edward Felker, was appointed in 1959 and served until his death in 1963, the year in which Blanshard also retired. Franklin Salisbury served as the AU general counsel from 1963 until 1972.

Aside from the overwhelming experience and expertise of Pfeffer, then, the most active attorneys in these separationist causes were local attorneys (Table 7–2). Six of them, in addition to Pfeffer, were involved in two of the sixty-seven church-state cases decided between 1951–1971. In all cases except one (Henry Clausen's affiliation with the separationist defense in *Matthews* v. *Quinton*) they were the major local attorneys of record for separationist plaintiffs. There is certainly no doubt that for all six, their participation in the second case resulted at least in part from their experience in the first. Expertise in the constitutional law of church-state relations thus comes fairly quickly.

Beyond these duplications in the sixty-seven cases, one should also mention that some attorneys, such as Greenawalt and Joseph Lewis's Martin Scheiman, had participated in church-state cases before 1951. (Others were involved in other church-state cases since 1951, either in cases between 1951 and 1971 that didn't meet the criteria for this universe of cases, or in cases that matured after the 1971 cutoff.)

THE ATTORNEYS IN THE 50 CASES

The attorneys in these fifty separationist cases were, not surprisingly, an even more homogeneous group than were the separationist plaintiffs. They were all male, and with the exception of one black (Carl Maxey of Spokane, Washington), they were all white. They were prevailingly Protestant and Democratic, and only in age did they vary greatly (Table 7–3). They attended a wide range

[5] Richard E. Morgan, "Backs to the Wall: A Study in the Contemporary Politics of Church and State," Ph.D. dissertation, Columbia University, 1967, p. 146, quoting an interview with Glenn Archer in 1962.

TABLE 7-2
Separationist Attorneys Appearing in More than One Case, 1951–1971

Name of Attorney	Cases	Dates of Final Disposition[a]	Group Identification
Boyle G. Clark (Columbia, Mo.)	Berghorn v. School Dist. Kintzele v. St. Louis	1953 1961	AU
Henry C. Clausen (San Francisco, Cal.)	Lundberg v. Alameda Matthews v. Quinton	1956 1961	AU
Leonard Kerpelman (Baltimore, Md.)	Murray v. Curlett Murray v. Comptroller	1963 1966	Other Americans, Society of Separationists
Jesse K. Lewis (Lexington, Ky.)	Wooley v. Spaulding Abernathy v. Irvine	1956 1962	AU
Leo Pfeffer (New York, N.Y.)	(see Table 7-1 and text)	1951 to 1971	AJC
Henry W. Sawyer III (Philadelphia, Pa.)	Schempp v. Abington Lemon v. Kurtzman	1963 1971	ACLU
Milton Stanzler (Providence, R.I.)	Bowerman v. O'Connor DiCenso v. Robinson	1968 1971	ACLU

Note: In all instances these attorneys were the attorneys of record for plaintiffs, except for Henry Clausen's role as an attorney for the separationist defense in *Matthews* v. *Quinton*.

[a] This is the year of the final, most important, substantive disposition of the case; it would not reflect, for instance, a later denial of certiorari by the U.S. Supreme Court.

of institutions of higher education, and an equally wide range of law schools, but an inordinately high percentage went to prestigious colleges or law schools. Fully 34 percent, for instance, won their baccalaureate from colleges or universities of the caliber of Harvard, Yale, Princeton, Chicago, Stanford, Oberlin, Swarthmore, or Amherst.[6]

In many ways the picture of these plaintiffs' attorneys approximates the stereotype of the civil rights attorney—good educational credentials, a large number in the younger age groups, prevailingly Democratic (certainly more so than the plaintiffs they represent). Only in religion do these men belie the stereotype, and that, as in the case of the plaintiffs, reflects the nature of the issue under litigation. Roman Catholics are conspicuously underrepresented, and Protestants definitely overrepresented. It is also a group

[6] Appendix III contains the operational definitions for the categories used in Table 7-3.

TABLE 7-3
Characteristics of Plaintiffs' Attorneys in 50 Separationist Suits

	Total (N = 50)	Cases in Which Group Roles Were		
		none or amicus (N = 12)	intermediate (N = 18)	sponsorship (N = 20)
I. Age				
20–29	2 (4.0%)	1 (8.3%)	0	1 (5.0%)
30–39	16 (32.0%)	4 (33.3%)	6 (33.3%)	6 (30.0%)
40–49	14 (28.0%)	1 (8.3%)	4 (22.2%)	9 (45.0%)
50–59	12 (24.0%)	3 (25.0%)	5 (27.8%)	4 (20.0%)
60–69	4 (8.0%)	2 (16.7%)	2 (11.1%)	0
70–79	2 (4.0%)	1 (8.3%)	1 (5.6%)	0
	50 (Med. = 43)	12	18	20
II. Political party				
Democratic	30 (60.0%)	6 (50.0%)	11 (61.1%)	13 (65.0%)
Republican	12 (24.0%)	3 (25.0%)	4 (22.2%)	5 (25.0%)
Ind., none	4 (8.0%)	1 (8.3%)	1 (5.6%)	2 (10.0%)
no info.	4 (8.0%)	2 (16.7%)	2 (11.1%)	0
	50	12	18	20
III. Religion				
Jewish	9 (18.0%)	0	4 (22.2%)	5 (25.0%)
Roman Catholic	3 (6.0%)	1 (8.3%)	0	2 (10.0%)
Liberal Prot.	21 (42.0%)	4 (33.3%)	9 (50.0%)	8 (40.0%)
Conserv. Prot.	8 (16.0%)	2 (16.7%)	4 (22.2%)	2 (10.0%)
none, nonbeliever	8 (16.0%)	5 (41.7%)	0	3 (15.0%)
no info.	1 (2.0%)	0	1 (5.6%)	0
	50	12	18	20
IV. College type				
private, prestige	17 (34.0%)	2 (16.7%)	5 (27.8%)	10 (50.0%)
other private	10 (20.0%)	3 (25.0%)	2 (11.1%)	5 (25.0%)
state, city univ.	15 (30.0%)	4 (33.3%)	6 (33.3%)	5 (25.0%)
state, teachers coll.	2 (4.0%)	1 (8.3%)	1 (5.6%)	0
no degree, no info.	6 (12.0%)	2 (16.7%)	4 (22.2%)	0
	50	12	18	20
V. Law school type				
prestigious	14 (28.0%)	1 (8.3%)	2 (11.1%)	11 (55.0%)
state univ.	14 (28.0%)	4 (33.3%)	9 (50.0%)	1 (5.0%)
local	18 (36.0%)	4 (33.3%)	6 (33.3%)	8 (40.0%)
no law degree	3 (6.0%)	2 (16.7%)	1 (5.6%)	0
no info.	1 (2.0%)	1 (8.3%)	0	0
	50	12	18	20

166

TABLE 7-3 (*Continued*)

	Total (N = 50)	Cases in Which Group Roles Were		
		none or amicus (N = 12)	intermediate (N = 18)	sponsorship (N = 20)
VI. Martindale-Hubbell rating				
none	23 (46.0%)	7 (58.3%)	10 (55.6%)	6 (30.0%)
A	12 (24.0%)	2 (16.7%)	3 (16.7%)	7 (35.0%)
B	10 (20.0%)	0	5 (27.8%)	5 (25.0%)
C	1 (2.0%)	1 (8.3%)	0	0
A for firm	4 (8.0%)	2 (16.7%)	0	2 (10.0%)
	50	12	18	20
VII. Earlier church-state case experience				
none	37 (74.0%)	10 (83.3%)	12 (66.7%)	15 (75.0%)
some	10 (20.0%)	1 (8.3%)	4 (22.2%)	5 (25.0%)
no info.	3 (6.0%)	1 (8.3%)	2 (11.1%)	0
	50	12	18	20

Note: The data of this table reflect the 50 cases identified in the text of this chapter in which nongovernmental attorneys handled the adversary cases with separationist plaintiffs. Attorneys who served as the attorneys of record in two cases are, therefore, counted twice in these data. Their characteristics in the two cases do, however, differ (in their reported age for that case, for instance). For definitions of the main categories, see Appendix III.

heavily involved in other civil liberties questions—much more so, indeed, than the plaintiffs they represented. Only 14 of the attorneys in these cases (28 percent) had no history of involvement in civil liberties causes. Of the other 36, fully 18 (36 percent of the 50) had had previous involvement in church-state issues or other causes, and 10 (20 percent) had earlier participated in church-state litigation.

There are differences among these plaintiffs' attorneys, and the major factor accounting for them appears to be the role played in the case by the ACLU, the AJC, or AU (Table 7–3). Attorneys in which one or more of the three participated beyond the amicus level tend to be a little younger, slightly more Democratic, and much more frequently Jewish. Those differences are undoubtedly a result of the recruitment and self-selection of ACLU and AJC attorneys. More importantly for the litigation of these issues, these data also appear to confirm the widely held belief that the major groups bring higher-quality legal talent to the litigating of constitutional issues.

Quality of legal talent is not easy to measure. The best proof of the quality of the talent, of course, is in its work in the cases themselves. To some extent, the greater likelihood of the development of a full trial record in the cases of the leading groups indicates something about their legal work. And readers of briefs—especially the other attorneys in these cases—generally concur that the quality of the work of AJC and most ACLU attorneys stands at the top of the list. (That judgment, however, may say more about the work of Leo Pfeffer than it does about the work of large numbers of attorneys of record.) Then there are the measures, such as they are, of the qualifications and general reputation of the attorney himself. To a dramatically greater extent, the attorneys in the cases of substantial group participation went to better colleges and universities, graduated from the best law schools, and held the lion's share of Martindale-Hubbell ratings. They also virtually monopolized what prior experience in church-state cases these attorneys had (Table 7–3).

The kinds of inference one draws about graduates of different types of law schools are risky, even dangerous, but they are at least clear. Those of the Martindale-Hubbell system may not be as clear. The M-H volumes are primarily directories of attorneys in the United States published every two years.[7] In addition to listing the names and addresses, dates of birth and admission to the bar, and the college and law school of each attorney, M-H also attempts to rate their legal ability. The basis of the ratings is obscure; they are apparently based on reputational data M-H representatives pick up on their visits to communities. (Say the editors: "We endeavor to reflect a consensus of reliable opinion obtained from various sources deemed to be dependable.") Nor does Martindale-Hubbell vouchsafe how many or what percentage of its listed attorneys (a total of 379,385 in the 1970 volumes) are ranked. Each edition, carries, furthermore, a standard disclaimer in bold type: "Absence of rating characters must not in any case be construed as derogatory to anyone, as we do not undertake to publish ratings of all lawyers." As for criteria:

> No arbitrary rule for determining legal ability can be formulated. Ratings are based upon the standard of ability for the place

[7] For example: *Martindale-Hubbell Law Directory*, 5 vols. (Summit, N.J.: Martindale-Hubbell, 1969).

where the lawyer practices. Age, practical experience, nature and length of practice, and other relevant qualifications are considered.

A lawyer first becomes eligible for the "c" (fair) rating after practicing three years. At least five years of practice is required for the "b" (high) rating and at least ten years of practice is required for the "a" (very high) rating.[8]

My own sampling indicates that 34 percent of the listed attorneys are ranked, with about 12 percent of all those listed receiving the "a" accolade. The "b" rating went to 15 percent, and a final 7 percent were rated "c." David Derge found in 1955 and 1957 that 27 percent of the attorneys from two states were ranked, with the percentages of "a" ratings at 13 and 15.[9] In any event, the fact that 46 percent of the attorneys in these 50 separationist cases were ranked underscores their impressive quality, and the 60 percent (12 of 20) of attorneys in cases sponsored by the three leading groups makes the point again about the superiority of the legal work they command.

Although the numbers are too small to bear a great deal of analysis, one does find significant differences between attorneys selected by AU and those selected by the AJC and ACLU. (Note that not all attorneys in cases in which these groups participated are included; in some instances local plaintiffs, organizers, or groups selected an attorney before the group was summoned into the litigation.) All of the 6 attorneys chosen by AU were Protestants; 6 of the 16 AJC and ACLU attorneys were Jews, and only 6 of them identified as Protestants. Three of the 6 AU attorneys were Republicans, whereas only 1 of the 16 ACLU-AJC counsel was. Some of the expected differences in "quality" are also apparent: only 1 of the 6 AU attorneys, but 9 of the 16 attorneys chosen by ACLU and AJC were graduates of prestige law schools. On the other hand, 5 of the 6 AU attorneys were ranked by M-H as either "a" or "b," but only 8 of the 16 ACLU–AJC attorneys were. That unexpected result reflects in part the inclination of AU to select older, more established attorneys. Many ACLU cooperat-

[8] All of these quotes come from an unnumbered page headed "Confidential Key."

[9] David R. Derge, "The Lawyer as Decision-Maker in the American State Legislature," *Journal of Politics* 21 (August 1959), 408–433. The two states were Illinois and Missouri. My figures are based on a 1 percent sample of all the pages of all the volumes.

ing attorneys are, on the other hand, young and in the early years of a law practice.

The plaintiffs' attorneys in the pursuit of separationism, however, are not so homogeneous a group as to include only high status, M-H paragons. There is another type among them: the free-wheeling, nonconforming pleader of lost and unpopular causes. Jesse K. Lewis, who fought two cases in Kentucky, was a crusading attorney who led legal onslaughts against vice and gambling, litigated "citizens' cases," and accused the state's high court of improperly accepting expense monies. He was also an independent candidate for governor of Kentucky in 1955 on the ticket of the Free Citizen's Party. Aram K. Berberian, originator and attorney in an attack on Rhode Island's tax exemption for religious properties (*General Finance Co.* v. *Archetto*), made a reputation locally as a defender of unpopular causes (the "dirty civil liberties cases the ACLU doesn't handle"). His personal difficulties added to the image of local notoriety: two disbarments, six unsuccessful runs for elective office, and assorted brushes with the law.

Perhaps the freest spirit of them all was Leonard Kerpelman of Baltimore, attorney for Madalyn Murray in her two Maryland suits. It would be more accurate, however, to say that Kerpelman functioned for about one and a half of MMO's suits. Midway in the second she left Baltimore to escape the clutches of the law, and Kerpelman and several other officers of the Freethought Society took over that organization. At that point Mrs. Murray dismissed Kerpelman as her attorney, although he continued to represent the other plaintiffs. Mrs. Murray sought unsuccessfully to have Kerpelman disbarred on assorted grounds relating to these events, and in so doing set some of her correspondence with Kerpelman on the record. Kerpelman's letter to her of July 18, 1964, captured some of the flavor of their deteriorating relationship:

> Dear Amateur Extortionist,
>   Thanks for the letter of July 12. I will use it widely and forcefully.
>   Have they got you in the cuckoo ward yet?
>   As I said before, ahh, go to Hell.
>   Sincerely yours,
>   Leonard[10]

There is also a defter, more subtle, even fey side to Kerpelman. After the turmoil and abuse of the first case with Madalyn Murray,

---

[10] Letter included in the trial court record in *Murray* v. *Comptroller*.

which ended with victory in the U.S. Supreme Court, Kerpelman wrote to the *Washington Post* to respond collectively to all who had written him:

I am Madalyn Murray's attorney. Since nearly all of the persons who have recently troubled to write to me on the subject of the School Prayer Case have done so anonymously, I would appreciate the opportunity to reply through your letters column:

Those whose penmanship made their letters undecipherable: Thank you for what I know were your good wishes.

Those whose letters contained threats of physical violence: Please contact my secretary for an appointment. There is a considerable waiting list.

Those who called me a Communist: It must have been someone who looks like me, whom you met at a cell meeting.

Those whose letters consisted principally of obscenity: I am all innocence and did not get your message.

Those whose letters mixed obscenity with Biblical quotations: Are you all right?

Those who expressed fear for my immortal soul: Don't worry yourselves. I have been a lawyer too long to be eligible for salvation anyway, though when I arrive at the celestial conference on the matter, I think I may be able to talk myself out of whatever difficulties I am in at the time.

Those who sent me envelopes containing only New Testament tracts: And this is seriously said—I am most appreciative of your unquestionably sincere concern for me, a stranger; I am, in fact, quite moved by your pure and Christian act. However, during a lifetime of intermittent consideration of the question, I have never at any time been inclined to change from what I was, and am, religiously, which is an orthodox Jew.

Incidentally, as a Bible fan, may I recommend to all a reading of the latter half of the story of Jonah—the part where the poor, foolhardy, self-centered Jonah laments the passing of a gourd.

Leonard J. Kerpelman[11]

After the first Murray case Kerpelman also acquired something of a local reputation as a tester and connoisseur of civic fountains. That process apparently involved little more than some leg dipping in new fountains in Baltimore at high noon in the presence of a *Baltimore Sun* reporter. On one occasion he was accompanied,

[11] *Washington Post* (July 12, 1963).

if not upstaged, by the somewhat less inhibited dipping of a 23-year-old stripper from the local runways.[12]

ATTORNEY INVOLVEMENT AND ROLE

The attorneys in ACLU, AJC, and AU cases are in some ways a breed apart. The groups have an active role in selecting them. Unlike the plaintiffs, who are often selected—sometimes self-selected—before the groups become active, attorneys are less often retained or involved by the time of group intervention. AU or one of its local chapters retained 6 of the 50, the AJC 3 (one jointly with the Horace Mann League), and the ACLU and its affiliates 13, for a total of 22 (44 percent) of the plaintiffs' attorneys. Of the remaining attorneys, 15 were chosen by the plaintiffs, 12 by local organizers and organizations, and data on 1 are missing. In a few of the last instances, the attorneys were themselves organizers and initiators of the case, but that number probably was no greater than 5 or 6. To a great extent, the attorneys were selected by the sponsors of the cases, whether they were national groups, local groups, or the plaintiffs themselves. Within certain limits of practicality, therefore, those sponsors had the opportunity to enlist or retain the kind of attorney they wanted.

If the sponsors, whoever they may be, clearly recruit the plaintiffs' attorneys, it is less clear with what inducements they do so. More than half of the attorneys in these 50 cases (27 of the 46 on whom there are data, or 58.7 percent) worked for no fees or for partial fees (Table 7–4). The partial fees in many instances barely covered the costs of the attorneys. To put it positively, only 19 (41.3 percent) participated for full fees or regular salary. The overwhelming number of the nonfee cases were those of the ACLU cooperating attorneys, who worked without fees and for only the most direct and case-identifiable out-of-pocket expenses. (ACLU policy is publicly absolute on the matter, but in one instance I am aware of, a local cooperating attorney was paid partial fees, perhaps through the subterfuge of retaining him through a broader consortium of groups.) Table 7–4 suggests, too, that local organizations have some success in recruiting legal talent without money. The AJC, AU, and individual plaintiffs more usually pay. The AJC does not generally reimburse local attorneys, but in one of these

[12] See the *Baltimore Sun* for the mornings of April 13, 1968, and June 27, 1969.

172

TABLE 7-4
Fees for Plaintiff Attorneys According to Method of Recruitment

| | | Recruiter of the Plaintiff's Attorney | | |
Fees	ACLU	AU, AJC, Other Natl. Groups	Individual Plaintiff	Local Organizers
None (17)	12 (92.3%)	0	1 (7.7%)	4 (36.4%)
Partial (10)	1 (7.7%)	1 (11.1%)	5 (38.5%)	3 (27.3%)
Full (19)[a]	0	8 (88.9%)	7 (53.8%)	4 (36.4%)
Total (46)	13	9	13	11

Note: The total number of cases reported here is 46 rather than the conventional 50 of this chapter because of missing data on the fees of attorneys in four cases.
   [a] Includes one on regular salary.

cases Pfeffer participated as the local attorney of record while on AJC salary.

If not by money, how then did the sponsors find their attorneys? By a variety of incentives and rewards. Some of the cooperating attorneys speak of their involvement in the cause itself, their personal convictions about the separation of church and state. Others were more generally attracted to a case involving questions of constitutional law ("I'm hung up on constitutional law.") For many others, constitutional litigation is a refreshing break in the routine of a law practice that either covers the range of civil law, or an intense specialty in corporation law, tax law, or copyrights and patents. A constitutional case lends spice to the daily routines. Others see a church-state case, they frankly report, as a chance (however remote) for an appearance before the Supreme Court or a state appellate court. Still others see some unspecified fatal fascination in the dangers of the litigation; one was even willing to attribute his involvement to "the suicidal urge."

This is not to suggest that other groups and individuals did not rely on ideology or group loyalty as well. In fact, it is too pat to speak of "full" fees—they were open to negotiation, and a group such as AU played on loyalty to the cause of separationism in trying to convince attorneys to accept fees lower than they might otherwise have commanded. In other words, AU offered a mixture of money and involvement in the issues. (Some of the AU attorneys, however, insisted on a strictly professional relationship and their usual fees.) In some instances, indeed, regular fees may not

173

be enough to lure attorneys into a potentially unpopular case; a combination of regular fees and attorney commitment may be necessary. For their part, sponsoring groups or plaintiffs sometimes want a high degree of attorney loyalty or identification with the cause when they pay full and regular fees.

For their efforts in these cases the plaintiffs' attorneys generally came to far less grief than the plaintiffs. Only ten of the fifty reported either a mixed or negative impact of the case on their professional life (Table 7–5). It is interesting that the incidence of unfavorable aftermaths for the attorneys rose steeply as the groups became more involved in the cases. One can assume either that the groups took the "big" cases with explosive potential, or that they inflamed the cases by politicizing and escalating the conflict through their participation. In any event, even of those reporting undesirable effects, almost none matched the hardships and indignities that were endured by the most sorely tried plaintiffs. Several reported instances of tires slashed and office windows broken. ("Some haters will drive two hundred miles to throw a stone.") Several believed they had lost clients. But by and large the attorneys were able to avoid the worst of the unpleasantness, apparently protected by hewing to a strictly professional role in the cases. That the attorneys did, indeed, stay within the traditional lawyerly role is indicated by the fact that only six of the fifty were either plaintiffs in or organizers (or coorganizers) of the cases.

Most of the separationist attorneys, in fact, believed that a quiet professional manner would eliminate most of these problems, especially if it was complemented by a quiet plaintiff and a generally low profile in the conduct of the litigation. It undoubtedly also helped a number of them to be members of firms with the sympa-

TABLE 7-5

Reported Impact of Case on Plaintiffs' Attorneys According
to Role of Three Leading Groups

| | Role of Three Leading Groups | | |
Impact	None or Amicus	Intermediate	Sponsorship
None or favorable	10 (83.3%)	13 (72.2%)	14 (70.0%)
Mixed or unfavorable	1 (8.3%)	3 (16.7%)	6 (30.0%)
No information	1 (8.3%)	2 (11.1%)	0
Total	12	18	20

thy, size, and prestige to protect them. Large urban firms have increasingly become accustomed to the participation of their attorneys in unpopular, or at least unconventional, cases. One successful attorney in these cases reported attempts by the counsel for the defense to reach the senior members of the firm. After the case was concluded, he learned of those interventions when a senior partner of the firm observed that if that same defense attorney "had spent as much time reading constitutional law as he did trying to get you fired, he might have won the case."

Nonmonetary inducements recruited a great deal of the legal skill in these cases, and there were, in fact, many nonmonetary rewards. For most attorneys there were the satisfactions of a job well done in an important task. For others, such as Leonard Kerpelman of Baltimore, there were both an unexpected appearance and a landmark victory before the U.S. Supreme Court. For others there was just the appearance before the Court, no small satisfaction in itself. Others won new clients, made new friends, found new associates. For some it meant subsequent paid appearances at the Americans United conferences on church and state. In other instances it led to additional church-state cases or other civil liberties cases. In several instances it led to almost instant expertise on church-state questions. Melvin Sykes of Baltimore, for instance, was appointed to the Maryland Commission to Study State Aid to Nonpublic Education after his work in *Horace Mann League* v. *Tawes*.

IN CONCLUSION

Lawyers in civil rights litigation often confront a conflict between the interests of their client and the broader constitutional or policy goals they pursue. There is, for example, the dilemma of the ACLU lawyer representing a criminal defendant who finds that he might better serve the interests of his client (that is, the overturning of a guilty verdict) by abandoning the constitutional argument for which he seeks appellate court support. Jonathan D. Casper, in fact, sees the conflict in terms of different types of civil rights lawyers: the advocate who serves the immediate legal interests of his client, and both the group advocate and the civil libertarian, who seek to advance, respectively, the interests of the group he represents and the general libertarian interests of the entire society. Coupled to those role differences, Casper notes, is a

175

divergence in legal philosophy; the advocate sees the law as an instrument for settling conflict and achieving equity for the individual, while the other two types view the law as an instrument of social policy and reform.[13] It is to some extent the difference between the microlegal and the macrolegal view.

These conflicts are at a minimum in these church-state cases for at least two great reasons. In the first place, the nature of church-state conflict is such that the constitutional claimants originate them. They are not defendants accused of a crime, and they suffer few direct adverse effects if they lose (that is, there is no danger of a fine or a prison sentence). The cases, in other words, are all brought for the assertion of a constitutional right, and the range of any divergence of group interest from plaintiff interest is in the small distance between the pursuit of a constitutional right and the establishment of more general constitutional doctrine. Secondly, in church-state litigation the plaintiffs are generally part of a group pursuit of broader constitutional doctrine. They generally recognize, at least, that there is a constitutional principle at stake. Some conflict does, of course, occur—we have already mentioned, for instance, the conflict in some of the AU cases between the group's search for doctrine and the local plaintiffs' quest for remedy and vindication. But compared with the incidence of such conflicts in other bodies of civil rights litigation, it is relatively minor.

Furthermore, some of the more practical professional dilemmas that lawyers face in other civil rights litigation are also less serious here. The problem of abuse and criticism has not been a serious one for church-state lawyers. The litigants they represent are generally respectable in conventional social terms, and they have not been accused of any crime. These cases are, within the broader

[13] *Lawyers before the Warren Court: Civil Liberties and Civil Rights, 1957–66* (Urbana: University of Illinois Press, 1972). Despite my general admiration for this book, I am not persuaded of the distinction between the group advocate and the civil libertarian. The distinction seems to me to depend too much on the specific nature of the civil liberties issue (that is, it seems to depend on the identifiability of the aggrieved group; thus, the interested and affected group in equal protection cases is more identifiable and "apart" than the affected public in church-state cases). It also rests on the organization of the attorney's clientele. On this latter point, a good many civil libertarian attorneys, Casper finds, are ACLU attorneys. While the ACLU does in one sense have a concern for the constitutional rights of all of American society, one cannot overlook the fact that it too has its own specialized clientele, and that its attorneys are in that broader sense also group advocates.

176

universe of civil rights litigation, relatively "clean" ones. In most communities participation in church-state litigation carries a less heavy burden of opprobrium than the representation of accused murderers, draft resisters, drug pushers, or pornographers. The "costs" of participation in church-state cases are thus lower, and the attorney is not so apt to be torn between a desire to participate and the practical, long-run interests of his professional livelihood.

In sum, therefore, even though the separationist attorney represents an unpopular cause in most communities, his activity in most instances brings relatively few of the agonies of choice or community reaction that so often bedevil other civil rights lawyers. Like them, he can find excitement and satisfaction in the involvement, but he works a relatively "clean" civil rights issue, and he also usually enjoys important group support and plaintiffs who are not a public relations liability. He enjoys virtually full freedom and control over the specific legal decisions in the case, even when he works under group auspices. And he is free to restrict his role to the conventionally legal. He does not often organize or manage the litigation or serve in it as a plaintiff. In virtually all of these cases the separationist attorney was a participant without being a combatant. He was free to conform to professional expectations and the lawyerly role.

VIII | THE ACCOMMODATIONIST DEFENDANTS

For every purposeful separationist group or plaintiff in these cases there is at least one surprised, reluctant, even panicky governmental body cast in the role of defendant. The litigation is usually not of its doing, and it finds itself cast without ceremony in the defense of accommodationist interests. It is a role for which it often does not have the experience, the resources, or the stomach.

Constitutional litigation is replete with active participants—groups, plaintiffs, plaintiffs' attorneys—who define their interests and who choose to act to insure them. It is, however, the "unseen hand" of adversary litigation that selects the defendant and defines his role. If others act, he is acted upon (some would say, imposed upon). The structure of this church-state litigation assigns to him the representation of accommodationist interests. It also determines that the defendants will almost invariably be governmental officials or bodies, simply because it is some governmental "coziness" with religion to which the separationist plaintiffs object.

In this strained combat between plaintiff and defense, organized accommodationists themselves are rarely represented. They have taken a few initiatives as plaintiffs, but the major share of their activity has been directed to finding a place and role in these church-state cases, even though others serve as defendants of record. Thus, if the U.S. Catholic Conference, the major representative of Roman Catholic interests in constitutional litigation, moves through these cases as a somewhat shadowy presence, it is less by choice than by the logic of adversary litigation on church-state relations.

ALL OF THE DEFENDANTS

Just as in the identification of separationist plaintiffs and their attorneys, a little reductive and analytical arithmetic is in order. Each of the 67 church-state cases decided between 1951 and 1971 did, of course, have a defendant; most had more than one. But the

178

nine friendly suits must, again, be set aside. Their defendants are only very nominal defendants; in all instances they have helped arrange the litigation, and rarely do they represent even nominally the interests they uphold in the litigation. So, we are once again down to 58 cases.

From those 58 one must again subtract the 5 in which the plaintiffs were accommodationists and the defendants were, by definition, separationists. In 2 instances local school boards were defendants in suits by parents to force them to provide bus rides to children going to private schools. In the other 3 the defendants were county officials in Florida resisting a property tax exemption for a Presbyterian retirement home, a New York City elementary school principal opposed to prayer in his school, and the Missouri state commissioner and department of education, who opposed the decision of a special educational district in suburban St. Louis to give assistance (such as speech therapy) to children attending private and religious schools.[1] With the subtraction of 9 friendly suits and the 5 in which the defendants were "separationists," we are once again down to 53 cases.

At this point, however, we can stop the subtraction, because we have in the fifty-three remaining cases a homogeneous group of accommodationist defendants in adversary cases. There were in all of them governmental officials or administrators of one kind or another, ranging from school principals and local tax assessors to cabinet members heading great departments in the federal administrative establishment. In some instances the defendants were individual officials, in others they were governmental bodies collectively, and often a mixture of the two. Nothing but chance or whim often seemed to determine, for instance, whether the plaintiff's attorney would name a school board or the individual members of a school board as defendants in a specific case. In eight of the fifty-three cases there were also private individuals or groups named as defendants. Roman Catholic nuns served as codefendants in some cases, for instance; private schools receiving aid appeared in others, and a local chamber of commerce even appeared in one case. But, to repeat, there were governmental officials and/or bodies serving as defendants in all fifty-three cases.[2]

[1] The five cases with separationist defendants were (in the order in which they are referred to in this paragraph): *Matthews* v. *Quinton, State ex rel. Hughes* v. *Board of Education, Johnson* v. *Presbyterian Homes, Stein* v. *Oshinsky,* and *Special District* v. *Wheeler.*

[2] The only possible "fudging" in this generalization about governmental

TABLE 8-1

The Defendants in the 53 Adversary Cases with Accommodationist
Defendants

	Number	Percentage
I. Level of government involved as defendant		
national	1	1.9
national and state	1	1.9
state	9	17.0
state and local	8	15.1
local	34	64.2
	53	100.1
II. Incidence of various governmental bodies and positions as defendants[a]		
local school board	28	25.2
state commissioner or supt. of education	10	9.0
local supt. of schools	9	8.1
local govt. unit (e.g., city)	7	6.3
state fiscal official (e.g., treasurer)	6	5.4
state board of education	5	4.5
local mayor or executive	5	4.5
local administrative office, agency	5	4.5
local school principal	4	3.6
state attorney general	3	2.7
others (two appearances or less)	29	26.1
	111	99.9

[a] Two points should be made about the counting in II. First, the total number (111) reflects the fact of multiple defendants in these 53 cases. Second, the individual officials who are defendants are counted collectively by office; thus, five individual members of a local school board would be tallied just as would the presence of the school board as a collective defendant. This part of the table, in other words, obliterates the distinction between governmental body and individual governmental officials.

As one more indication of the way in which school politics have become intertwined with church-state politics, the defense in these cases was dominated by local school boards and officials (Table 8-1). Local boards, superintendents, and administrators made a total of 41 different appearances as defendants; in combining those

bodies and officials occurs in an obscure New Mexico case (*Miller* v. *Cooper*). Local plaintiffs charged the public school with conducting religious exercises in the schools, naming as defendants four teachers, a janitor (!), local and state boards of education, a state educational official, and a local Baptist minister. The New Mexico Supreme Court dismissed all but two of the teachers as defendants.

appearances, one finds that one or more kind of local school func-
tionary appeared as a defendant in 29 of the 53 cases (54.7 percent). It is that dominance that also accounts for the preponder-
ance of local governmental officials as defendants (Table 8–1).
To some extent the repeated presence of local officials suggests
that state and national governmental levels make relatively few
of the policies under attack. But one can be misled on that score.
It is true that relatively few of the policies originate at the national
level, but in instances of challenged state policies it is frequently
the local authorities who become defendants. In a number of the
state bus ride cases, for example, state legislatures had passed laws
requiring local school districts to provide rides to children attending private schools on the same basis as they were providing them
to public school pupils. Even though the state legislature made
the policy, angry plaintiffs brought suits against the local school
boards and officials executing it.

By and large, the defendants in these cases were involved by
the actions of others. They had to assume the defense of accommodationist policies, whether or not the policies were theirs. There
are exceptions—those governmental bodies, for instance, who are
defendants largely because they precipitated the litigation. The
local school boards in Hawthorne and Netcong, New Jersey, and
in Leyden, Massachusetts, must surely have known that their insistence on prayer in the public schools after *Engel* v. *Vitale*—and
especially after they rebuffed the entreaties of state officials to
stop—could only lead to litigation. In several other instances, local
governmental officials, embroiled in a bitter policy conflict, agreed
to make a token appropriation of funds, so that the matter might
be quickly tested in the courts and resolved there rather than in
the legislative processes. A bitter struggle over whether the city
would provide bus rides to the Catholic children of Augusta,
Maine, with its large French Catholic minority, badly divided the
city. Eventually all sides to the controversy, including the city
council, agreed that the council would pass a nominal appropriation for the rides, which would immediately result in a test case.
All sides apparently welcomed the defusing of a local controversy
by allowing the policy questions to be superceded by legal and
constitutional questions.[3]

[3] *Squires* v. *City of Augusta*. The Maine Supreme Court's response was
just as cagey. It held the bus rides illegal (on the absence of a grant of
authority from the state to cities to undertake such programs) rather than
unconstitutional, thus inviting the state legislature to pass enabling legislation. The legislature declined the invitation.

But there were not many other instances in which the ultimate defendants promoted or encouraged the litigation in any active way. Nor were there many instances in which the defendants tried to forestall litigation, such as by abandoning their controversial practices or by reaching out-of-court settlements. In general, the governmental bodies and officials simply accepted the litigation and the prospect of resolution in the courts. The reasons for that acceptance have less to do with law than with politics. When the separationists are only a small minority in the community, the defendant risks a political backlash if it yields to them or compromises with them. When the community is sharply divided, the governmental body will often welcome the chance to "pass the buck" to the courts, as the city council did in the Augusta bus case. If there were cases of governmental bodies defending policies that a solid majority opposed, one could expect them to be willing to avoid litigation or to compromise or settle out of court. But that scenario does not occur. The defendants defend policies and practices that enjoy—at a minimum—very solid community support.

Thus the accommodationist defendants did not, in most cases, respond strongly to the prospect of litigation. They rarely spurred or discouraged it, and they virtually never altered the policy that brought the separationist complaint in the first place. The policy was, in a few instances, altered as a matter of tactic to strengthen the defense position; in several instances in which prayers in schools were challenged, school authorities made them voluntary and initiated procedures by which students might opt out of them.[4] But those were not instances of fundamental policy retreat. Basically, the defendant governmental officials reacted passively, almost hypnotically, to the initiation of this constitutional litigation. Their major input and decisions came later, especially in their decisions whether to carry appeals if they lost the early rounds.

More directly relevant to the way the defendants carry out their accommodationist roles, perhaps, is the way in which they define their own interests in the litigation. In these cases they were thrown into the accommodationist camp, but that position did not always square with their own perceptions of their interests. While it is not easy to determine just how defendants view the litigation in

---

[4] For example, the state of Pennsylvania did exactly that in the first *Schempp* case on Bible-reading in the schools of the state, thus mooting the case before the U.S. Supreme Court and forcing it back to another trial and appellate court cycle.

which they are embroiled, there is reason to think that in at least half a dozen cases the defendants were at best reluctant advocates of the accommodationist position they found themselves defending. One can cite a few examples:

In a number of instances of state-mandated aid to children attending private schools (including religious ones), the state reimbursed local school districts for the expenses, but in some it did not. Thus the local school boards and public school administrators who defended challenges to Oregon's law providing texts and Pennsylvania's law providing bus rides appeared to be quite willing to have the laws declared unconstitutional so that they might spend their scarce resources on items of higher priority.

In the Oklahoma bus case the generous policy was the local board's. But it had been started earlier in response to an informal request, and at its initiation it had not involved a very large number of pupils. But as Catholics moved into the district in greater numbers, the program had "mushroomed" without the board's knowing how to stop it with anything less than a donnybrook. It seems safe to say that by the time of the litigation, it was hoping for a swift end to it in the courts. When the board lost in the trial court, it did not carry an appeal.

One can imagine the feelings of the Alameda County and Oakland, California, officials upon discovering they were defendants in a suit to invalidate the tax exemptions they were forced to grant to religious school property under a recent state-wide law and referendum. Together the two governmental units stood to lose some $45,000 in taxes under the new exemption to Roman Catholic schools alone, and, additionally, the citizens of Alameda County had (unlike much of the rest of the state) voted *against* the exemption in the referendum, 184,341 to 165,083.

The interests of the defendants also diverged in other cases from the interests of the broader universe of accommodationists during the course of the litigation. Consider the South Burlington, Vermont, school board, sued for giving tuition payments to parents of parochial high schoolers. The grants were, in fact, made to all parents of high school students—public and private—to cover the costs of sending their children to high schools elsewhere, since South Burlington had no high school of its own. The board had

183

favored and defended the grants, but shortly after the litigation began, South Burlington began to build its own high school. With the prospective mooting of the whole unhappy issue, it lost much of its appetite for a spirited defense.[5]

Even when the defendants did identify with accommodationist interests, however, they often lacked the expertise and resources for this kind of constitutional litigation. They had public resources at their disposal, it is true, but most, especially school districts, had very limited funds. They also had uses for their monies other than litigation. Furthermore, if they spent tax funds on appeals of any kind, they ran the risk of public criticism for squandering funds on legal will-o'-the-wisps. And although their attorneys had been retained for an expertise in school law, it was an expertise in such matters as liability for student injuries and contracting for supplies, not the constitutional law of church-state separation.

In short, the constitutional defense of public policy and accommodationist interests in these cases often leaned on very slender reeds. And the "real" accommodationists were fully aware of that reality.

THE ACCOMMODATIONIST GROUPS

The three leading separationist groups were, of course, virtually absent from the defense in these cases. There were, however, two exceptions. As an example of the accidents of adversary litigation, AU ended up defending the "accommodationist" position in the New York tax exemption case, arguing in an amicus brief that churches' property used for religious purposes (unlike that used for other purposes) ought not to be taxed; and the ACLU affiliate in Washington State supported the University of Washington against fundamentalist claims that its English course on the Bible as literature breached separation because it purveyed only one theological position on the Bible. But aside from these two constitutional "sports," the accommodationist interests were in the hands of accommodationists.[6]

---

[5] The cases referred to above were (in the first paragraph) *Dickman* v. *School District* and *Rhoades* v. *School District;* those in the second and third paragraphs were *Board of Education* v. *Antone* and *Lundberg* v. *Alameda County*. Finally, the Vermont case was *Swart* v. *South Burlington*.

[6] These two cases were: *Walz* v. *Tax Commission* and *Calvary Bible* v. *Board of Regents*.

The U.S. Catholic Conference

Roman Catholics have traditionally been the major proponents of some degree of accommodationism in American society. That leadership springs in part from Catholicism's traditional values, and its willingness to accept the support of political regimes elsewhere. In part, too, it results from the very pragmatic needs of an organized religion with the separate and costly educational system which American Catholicism developed. But while the leadership of Catholicism seems indisputable, the organizational representatives of Catholicism are less certain. Are they the local bishop and diocesan apparatus, the organizations of the U.S. Catholic Conference and state conferences, local priests and lay people of a parish, political interest groups such as Citizens for Educational Freedom, or fraternal groups such as the Knights of Columbus? Some or all of them? The problem would not exist, of course, if all of them reached and stated the same position on all church-state issues. But assumptions about a monolithic American Catholicism, if they were ever valid, are no longer.

The problem of identifying Catholic action in this litigation is eased to some extent by the fact that the U.S. Catholic Conference and the state Catholic conferences function as the chief spokesmen of American bishops on matters of social and educational policy. (The U.S. Catholic Conference was preceded in time and role by the National Catholic Welfare Conference, which gave way to the USCC in 1968.) Its attorneys described its legal purpose and role in their amicus brief in the *Walz* tax exemption case:

> Among its responsibilities, USCC is authorized to represent the Catholic people of the United States, speaking through their Bishops on matters of public concern. When deemed appropriate, USCC is authorized to offer its views . . . in Federal and State court litigation touching important interests of the Catholic people of the United States, especially in cases involving constitutional issues turning upon the proper construction of the Fourteenth Amendment, . . . as that provision protects the freedoms guaranteed by the religion clauses of the First Amendment.[7]

[7] From the USCC brief of amicus curiae before the U.S. Supreme Court in *Walz* v. *Tax Commission*.

It is indeed the only agency that speaks for the American hierarchy in public matters such as these.

William R. Consedine, general counsel of the USCC, functions at the center of its litigating activities. He came to the old NCWC in 1956 as director of its legal department, and he has in the intervening years built up an impressive set of contacts with attorneys all over the country. Consedine and his staff in Washington are actually the contacts and information clearing center for two rather disparate groups of Catholic attorneys. On the one hand they are in contact with both the diocesan attorneys and the executive directors of the state Catholic conferences (only some of whom are attorneys), sending them information on and analysis of recent church-state litigation, dispensing advice, and periodically meeting with them. On the other hand, they are close to the elite Catholic counsel, especially those in Washington, D.C., referring cases to them, advising and conferring with them on strategy and policy, and generally coordinating their individual cases.

The USCC functions, therefore, as an information, referral, and advisory service for the Catholic hierarchy. Its legal staff does not itself handle the legal work in cases, although it does occasionally draft amicus briefs. Nor does it apparently attempt to set overall "Catholic" strategy in church-state litigation. That is so in part because it is hard to establish priorities when one is on the side of the defense, and thus without the initiatives the plaintiffs enjoy. In part, too, it is because the USCC simply does not control all Catholic litigation or participation in these cases. Separate Catholic groups, bishops, and dioceses are free to act for themselves, and they do so, sometimes to USCC dismay. The monolithic control of the Catholic defense that so many Protestant separationists imagine is simply not there.

The "Catholic bar" of Washington, traditionally so close to the NCWC and the USCC, includes a great many names, but in this single specialty of church-state cases, the list is short. In the 1960s and 1970s the two most active men on the list were Alfred Scanlan, member of the prestigious firm of Shea and Gardner, and Edward Bennett Williams, famous both as a defense attorney and as the owner of the Washington Redskins football team. In the decades before, the list included John Danaher, earlier U.S. Senator from Connecticut; Paul Butler, chairman of the Democratic National Committee from 1952 to 1960; and Charles Fahy, later a federal district court judge in the District of Columbia. Each of these five attorneys appeared for some part of the defense in at least one of these church-state cases.

Two other prominent Catholic attorneys operated more independently of the USCC. Porter R. Chandler has represented the Archdiocese of New York in litigation (he was referred to as the cardinal's lawyer), and while his work was confined to New York State, it was enough to make him a potent figure in church-state litigation. William B. Ball of Harrisburg, on the other hand, became something of an independent Roman Catholic legal authority in his own right. He rose to national attention, in fact, as a liberal Roman Catholic civil libertarian. Ball works from a base as general counsel to the Pennsylvania Catholic Conference, but his writing, speeches, contacts, and legal appearances across the country have made him Catholicism's unofficial legal expert and advocate in church-state matters. Local Catholic attorneys, state Catholic conferences, and bishops contact him directly; aside from the advice they have mined, they have recruited him to argue a rather impressive number of recent cases (he appeared in three of these). His ties with the USCC have been tenuous, apparently because of strained relations with William Consedine. Few referrals to Ball come from the USCC.

The Roman Catholic defense, therefore, is clearly fragmented. Local dioceses and bishops, organizations such as Citizens for Educational Freedom (more on it in a moment), and the Knights of Columbus act independently. So, too, do religious orders, colleges, and other institutions. In church-state litigation between 1951 and 1971, Consedine and the USCC tried only to persuade local Catholic authorities that they needed a sophisticated defense, and then found legal help for them. The Catholic Conference itself took very few initiatives and originated no litigation on its own. Its recommendations on church-state policy were rare. It did, however, prefer the purchase of services to the voucher plan as a way of getting public funds to Catholic schools in the 1960s. But, even then, the USCC's was only one among a number of Catholic voices.

Citizens for Educational Freedom

Founded in 1959, Citizens for Educational Freedom is essentially an organization of parents who send their children to private religious schools. That is to say, it is a coalition of religious accommodationists brought together by the desire to lighten the burden

187

of educating children in religious schools. CEF's grass-roots membership organizations probably enrolled a maximum of between 100,000 and 150,000 members in the late 1960s. A federation of state organizations, it is clearly stronger in some states than in others, and those powerful state organizations operate almost independently of a modest national organization and national headquarters in Washington.

Separationists, especially those of AU persuasion, find around CEF tracks of the Roman Catholic monolith. They are mistaken, and on two counts. While it is true that Roman Catholic leadership and membership has dominated the organization—not surprisingly, since over 90 percent of the religious schools in the United States are Catholic—there are Lutherans, Dutch Reformed, Orthodox Jews, and other non-Catholics in positions of influence within CEF. Second, the Catholics of CEF and the Catholic hierarchy do not enjoy a close, comfortable relationship. The hierarchy is suspicious of its aggressiveness and its grass-roots independence; among other reasons, its thrust towards "parents' power" represents a challenge to the hierarchy's traditional control of Roman Catholic education. Indeed, CEF's basic plan for education—the voucher plan, in which every parent would receive a "voucher" with which he could "pay" for any accredited education, public or private, for his child—is almost as distasteful to the Catholic hierarchy as it is to public school groups. And for many of the same reasons. It would give a powerful weapon of choice to the parents, and it would be an entering wedge into the control of Catholic schools. CEF has at times pursued more easily attainable benefits—bus rides or other forms of aid to religious schools—but the voucher plan remains its ultimate goal.[8]

In general, CEF rose to prominence more for its participation in the legislative processes of the states than for its litigation. Its aggressive pursuit of its goals, its sizeable membership, its militance, and its desire to break so sharply with the status quo all have disposed it to legislative rather than judicial politics. Yet it has done some modest work in church-state litigation. It filed amicus briefs in two of these fifty-three church-state cases, but it did not organize any litigation, nor did it appear or organize

[8] Its entry in the *Encyclopedia of Associations,* 5th ed. (Detroit: Gale Research Co., 1968), p. 444, states in part: "Advocates participation by parents in education tax funds through tuition certificates or scholarships from the government for deposit at the school of their free choice." On the CEF's legislative successes, see *Time* (March 22, 1968), pp. 62–63.

the appearance of intervenors in any of them. In a notable case decided after June 1971, and thus not covered here, it unsuccessfully brought suit in Missouri to compel the state to provide aid to religious schools on the novel constitutional grounds that to provide aid to public school children while denying it to private school children in effect denied their right under the First Amendment to free exercise of religion and equal protection of the laws under the Fourteenth Amendment.[9] The argument and the litigation itself confirmed more traditional Catholic legal opinion about the recklessness of CEF.

National Jewish Commission on Law and Public Affairs

COLPA, as it is called by its members, was, like CEF, a direct response to the crisis many accommodationists perceived in the changing church-state climate of the 1950s and 1960s. Founded in 1965, it represents the divergence of the interests of Orthodox Jewry from those of other American Jews. In church-state issues it represents a parents' interest not unlike that of CEF, for the problems of the Jewish "day schools" have much in common with those of the parochial schools. COLPA itself is, however, not a mass-membership group; it is an elite group made up primarily of young Orthodox attorneys in New York and Washington. (One exception: one of its founders, its president, and its chief spokesman is Marvin Schick, a Ph.D. in political science and in the early 1970s an assistant to Mayor John V. Lindsay of New York.)[10] COLPA serves as a legal arm for Orthodox interests in church-state matters. It also combats the settled separationism of Jewish groups such as the American Jewish Congress. The hostility between COLPA and the AJC (especially Pfeffer) is not concealed.

COLPA functioned only twice as an amicus in these church-state cases. It served in that capacity in the *Walz* tax exemption case and in the Pennsylvania bus controversy.

The accommodationist defense in the period from 1951 to 1971 was thus diverse and fragmented. There was, nevertheless, an "accommodationist bar" to parallel the "separationist bar." Each had

[9] *Brusca* v. *Missouri*, 332 F. Supp. 275 (1971); affirmed summarily by the U.S. Supreme Court at 405 U.S. 1050 (1972).

[10] Schick is also an expert in constitutional law and the judicial process, and the author of *Learned Hand's Court* (Baltimore: Johns Hopkins Press, 1970), a study of the U.S. Court of Appeals for the Second Circuit. See also *Newsweek* of December 28, 1970, for an article on Schick and COLPA.

a leader; William Ball paralleled Leo Pfeffer in his legal preeminence and in the bulk of his activity in church-state litigation. There was, furthermore, communication among the various accommodationist attorneys, communication that often passed through the office of William Consedine. The exchange of briefs and information about litigation was a part of the pattern. There was also some overlapping membership. Reuben Gross of New York, long active in Agudath Israel, a Jewish cultural association, was a founder of COLPA as well as an active leader in CEF. Other CEF leaders had good personal ties with the USCC and with lawyers close to it. It was a "bar" that never attempted, however—much less succeeded in—the kind of coordination that the separationist consortium attempted. And it lacked, too, the kind of personal force for centralization that Leo Pfeffer represented in the separationist camp.

THE ACCOMMODATIONISTS' ROLES

It is in the nature of the defense to defend against the assaults of others. Especially in the judicial process, its initiatives and even its strategic opportunities are sharply limited. There is no role for it at all comparable to the sponsorship role that is available on the plaintiffs' side of the litigation. In the structure of church-state litigation, therefore, the accommodationists have far fewer opportunities to manage constitutional change than do the separationists. Aside from the conventional role of amicus curiae, which differs little if at all from the same role on the plaintiff's side, the accommodationists are reduced to finding ways of representing their interests in litigation in which they are not the main defendants, and in which—worse luck—the defendants may not be willing or able to represent them. They may inject themselves into the defense either by becoming intervenor defendants or by aiding—even taking over—the defense itself. The two roles are not, as we shall see, mutually exclusive. But the crucial point is that while separationists are devising ways to shape constitutional development, the accommodationists are struggling merely to be heard.

Intervening as a Defendant

Individuals not parties to an adversary proceeding may in most American jurisdictions enter the proceeding if they can convince the court that their interests are unrepresented and will be directly affected by the outcome. Once admitted to the case, the intervenor

190

participates in the proceedings by offering evidence, making motions, and generally enjoying the options of a party to the case. The intervenor may also appeal the case, even if the initial defendant chooses not to, and he may in any event participate in oral argument before an appellate court. It is, therefore, a status that permits a degree of involvement far greater than that of the better known amicus curiae.

These church-state cases obviously present almost classic instances of the unwillingness of defendants to protect fully the interests to whose defense they have been assigned. Perhaps the clearest cases were those local school boards that were unenthusiastic about the aid they granted to local religious schools and their pupils, but which granted it either because of local political pressure or because of mandatory state statutes. In the case of the school board of Midwest City, Oklahoma, the school board had begun giving bus rides to a few Catholic school children, and then had seen the program mushroom, become far more expensive, and develop a public support that protected it from termination. Unhappy about the bus ride program and caught in the middle of a bitter controversy, it was a most uneasy defendant. Its attorney admitted as much to the trial court judge, in welcoming the admission of parents of the Catholic students as intervenors:

> As you know, this is a public matter; everybody there is interested. The school board is a public body. It is doing its best to do a good job to satisfy everybody, and we just don't feel like that we should take a strong side for either party in this lawsuit. In other words, we are here to perform the services provided it is proper, but I really think they (the intervenors) are the real interested parties instead of the school board.[11]

When the school board lost in the trial court, it was the intervenors, not the board, who took the appeal to the Oklahoma Supreme Court.

The role of the intervenor, then, is appealing to accommodationist interests for at least three reasons. It enables them to define an interest separate from that of the defendants, should that seem necessary. It also gives them an independent power to appeal an unfavorable decision. And thirdly, it allows them to present issues and arguments where the defendants fail to do so because of lack

[11] Trial court transcript for *Board of Education* v. *Antone,* p. 41; on file in the office of the clerk for the District Court of Oklahoma County, Oklahoma City, Oklahoma.

191

of skills in constitutional litigation, because of political caution, or because of divergent interests in the conflict. Indeed, should the defendants be willing to shed the chief responsibilities of the defense, the intervenors find that their role affords a legitimate and graceful opportunity for taking over the whole burden of the defense.

In 20 of these 53 cases (37.7 percent) there were intervenors. Rarely were there single intervenors, but they could often be viewed as a single "set": a group of parents of parochial school children, for instance, or a group of religious denominations "profiting" from a tax exemption of their properties. Although the parents of children attending Catholic schools constituted the largest single groups of intervenors, the types of intervenors were diverse (Table 8–2). But diverse as they were, the majority of them represented in some way the interests of Roman Catholic accommodationism (Table 8–2). In their diversity they also illustrated the earlier observation about the difficulty of identifying a single, monolithic Roman Catholicism in these cases.

Taking over the Defense

Better organized and experienced accommodationists cringe when they see the defense of their interests fall into the unwilling hands of a small-town district attorney, or a school board attorney whose competence in "school law" extends only very tentatively to constitutional questions. How then to shore up, even take over the defense in these cases? The intervenor role may be one avenue, but it is neither a necessary nor a sufficient condition for dominating the strategies, the resources, or the financing of the defense.

In fifteen of those twenty cases with intervenors, indeed, at least one of the intervenors participated in the defense at some state of the litigation: at the trial, in oral argument before an appellate court, in the making of strategic decisions, in the preparation of briefs. But assistance for the defense was not in these cases limited to intervenors. Nonintervenors in at least eight other cases appear to have had a considerable impact on the conduct of the defense.[12]

[12] The tentative language of this sentence (that is, "at least eight" and "appear to have had") deserves some explanation. It is far more difficult to trace influences on the defense than on the plaintiffs. The defense often is less overt, more diffuse, and less systematic; the relative absence of organized groups also means a paucity of archives and files. Furthermore, when traveling and interviewing at sites of the litigation, I used more of my scarce time developing data on the more important plaintiff interests.

TABLE 8-2
Accommodationist Intervenor Defendants in Adversary Cases

I. Incidence of intervenors	
cases with intervenors	20 (37.7%)
cases with no intervenors	33 (62.3%)
Total	53
II. Nature of 22 intervenors in 20 cases	
A. *Roman Catholic auspices*	
Catholic parents of parochial pupils	8
St. Louis University	1
Catholic Welfare Corporation of the San Francisco archdiocese	1
Ten Pittsburgh area orphanages	1
Louisiana teachers of secular subjects in private schools	1
Total	12
B. *Non-Catholic auspices*	
states (R.I. and Penna.)	2
taxpayers groups	2
parents of public school pupils	1
Penna. private school association	1
Maryland religious bodies receiving tax exemptions	1
Philadelphia school district	1
Gideons International	1
New York City Released Time Coordinating Committee	1
Total	10

Note: The 53 cases here are those described in the text of this chapter. In two cases there were two distinct sets of intervenors; hence the 22 categories in the 20 cases in II. Finally, categories A and B in II should be read as including "primarily" or "predominantly" Catholic or non-Catholic auspices.

In three of the cases local Roman Catholic dioceses, working in two instances with the NCWC or the U.S. Catholic Conference, provided counsel far more expert than local authorities could have provided.[13]

In two other cases local Roman Catholic parents and citizens raised money to provide out-of-town counsel for the defense.

[13] These three cases were: *Berghorn* v. *School District, Zellers* v. *Huff,* and *State ex. rel. Chambers* v. *School District.* In the following paragraph the two referred to are *McVey* v. *Hawkins* and *Squires* v. *City of Augusta.* The Netcong and Leyden cases, two paragraphs hence, and finally the Eugene case were, in order: *State Board* v. *Netcong, Commissioner of Education* v. *Leyden,* and *Lowe* v. *City of Eugene.*

In the bus case in Augusta, Maine, in fact, the special counsel represented Catholic interests in dealings with the city council before the policy, and thus the litigation, ever began.

Two school boards that began prayer in the public schools in defiance of Supreme Court decisions found financial and law-yerly help available to them in their defense. In Netcong, New Jersey, the school board's defense was bolstered by In God We Trust, an organization located in a nearby town. In Leyden, Massachusetts, attorney Ralph Warren Sullivan of Boston came to the aid of the local school board, both in advising it about the form its prayer should take, and then in helping it with its legal defense. Since Sullivan was an old friend and attorney of William Loeb, archconservative publisher of the Manchester (N.H.) *Times Union,* the suspicion that Loeb volunteered the services of Sullivan was widespread.

In the eighth case, a classic illustration of many of the problems of the defense in church-state cases, an ad hoc citizens' group as-sumed the defense burdens that the city of Eugene wanted to set down (see box).

Taking Other Roles

When acccommodationist interests take over the defense, their role is nearly equivalent to the sponsorship role of the separationist plaintiffs. But rarely does their participation engulf the defense as completely as a sponsor does the prosecution of the litigation. As the illustrations have suggested, the two roles of intervenor and surrogate defense are flexible; each can accommodate varying de-grees of involvement. Some intervenors exercise few of the prerog-atives of the status; others exercise most of them. And help with the defense can be merely that: advice and a little help; or it can mean a full replacement of the nominal defendants and their attor-neys, especially in the appellate court appearances.

Aside from these two substantial options open to the accommo-dationists in these cases, there is available only the role of the amicus curiae. That role remains very similar to, and perhaps even identical with, the amicus role for the plaintiffs. In these 53 adver-sary cases with accommodationist defenses, there were amici curiae in 23 (43.4 percent): 1 or 2 in 18 cases, and 3 or more in the other 5. (By contrast, there were plaintiff amici in 22 of these cases.)

194

THE CROSS ON SKINNER'S BUTTE

For many years there has been a series of crosses on Skinner's Butte, a park overlooking Eugene, Oregon. After one fell into disrepair or was vandalized in the 1960s, a service fraternity at the University of Oregon and the Eugene Chamber of Commerce planned as a replacement a lighted concrete cross. They approached the Eugene Sand and Gravel Co. to design and construct it. When their request for a permit to build it was tabled by the City Council, they abandoned their plans. John Alltucker of the Sand and Gravel Co. apparently went ahead on his own (some said in the dead of night), constructed a 51-foot concrete cross, and arranged for its lighting. He then applied for and received, post hoc, a permit for it from the Eugene city fathers.

The appearance of the immense cross high above the city sparked what the local paper, itself opposed to the cross, called "one of the nastiest squabbles ever to blight Eugene" (Eugene *Register Guard,* editorial, January 8, 1967). A local group of citizens organized to bring suit against the mayor, the city, the city council, and the private companies that built, erected, and lit it. As the community divisions became more and more bitter, the city began to waiver in its enthusiasm for the cross. A group of private citizens supporting it sought to enter the case as intervenor defendants, but the trial court judge denied them entry. After the opponents of the cross won the decision in the local trial court, the city and its officials—weary of the controversy, fearful of its costs, and caught between the warring camps—decided not to appeal. At this point, in the absence of intervenors, the private construction companies and their officials took over the defense, working with the ad hoc group (Laymen for the Cross Committee) that had earlier tried to intervene. Despite their fund raising, the provision of an out-of-town attorney, and arrangement for an amicus brief, the "cross" finally lost in the Oregon Supreme Court. The U.S. Supreme Court denied their petition for certiorari.

195

THE PROBLEMS AND DECISIONS OF THE DEFENSE

As governmental officials or bodies, the defendants in these cases always operated within political as well as legal limits. That political status of the defense was, in fact, one of its greatest weaknesses. The single unifying theme that runs through the decisions of the defenses in these cases is that they had to attend to their political constituencies as well as to the favor of the courts deciding the cases. More than one school board accused of permitting religious practices in the schools found that the religious majority in the community would not permit any compromise or negotiated settlement. It was politically easier, in other words, for the school board to run the risk of losing the entire set of practices in the courts than to take the initiative and save part of them in informal negotiation. And local governments thinking of going to an appellate court always had to reckon with the charge—if they lost—of squandering public funds on quixotic legal adventures.

In many regards, however, the legal and strategic decisions of the defense did not differ in kind from those of the plaintiffs. They were directed to the goals of "winning" the case, and thus were often the mirror image of plaintiff tactics. Just as the plaintiffs preferred full trials and the development of a fact record, defense attorneys more often preferred to go to decision on stipulations and the barest outline of the factual circumstances. They, too, tried to find a favorable forum; separationist attorneys in several New York cases accused defense attorneys of diverting cases with procedural motions until the case was assigned to what they thought would be a sympathetic judge (a Roman Catholic judge, for instance). In other cases, defendants or their allies altered practices to moot litigation. One mooting "bought" the state of Pennsylvania three years in the course of the Schempps' assault on Bible-reading in that state. In the Gideon Bible case in Orlando, Florida, the Gideons stopped distributing the offending Bibles in the public schools before the trial began. No party to the case took note of the mooting, however, and the case went all the way to the Florida Supreme Court.[14]

[14] *Brown* v. *Orange County*. The Florida Supreme Court delayed its decision in the case for almost two years, finally deciding "proseparation" (that is, against the distribution of the Bibles in the public schools) in a brief and, clearly, a pained opinion. The court seems not to have realized that the controversy had been mooted, and that it therefore had a "way out" for its accommodationist preferences.

196

One defense strategy that recurred in these cases was so ironic, and yet so puzzling, as to deserve greater mention. It was the inclination on the part of defenses to take a "this is not religion" tack in defending the challenged practices. For example:

In the Eugene, Oregon, controversy over the cross on the butte, defense attorneys at the trial noted that the tapered modern cross could have many meanings, among them patriotism and the end of the winter solstice, and the city attorney argued that it was erected, maintained, and lit at Xmas and Easter times to "encourage trade." (The trial court observed that the latter claim was "an egregious insult to many Christians.")[15]

In at least three prayer cases (*DeSpain* v. *DeKalb, Mangold* v. *Gallatin,* and *Murray* v. *Curlett*) the defense argued that a main purpose of the prayer was to calm the school children or to teach them social graces or good manners. Francis Burch, city solicitor of Baltimore and later a national leader for a constitutional amendment authorizing prayer in the schools, argued before the U.S. Supreme Court in *Murray* that the prayer had a sobering effect. Justice Potter Stewart queried whether tranquilizers might not be more effective.

There is, of course, a disingenuousness, even whimsy, in some of those arguments. And yet one wonders how they could be made acceptable to the communities of deeply committed and often fundamentalist Christians supporting the general position of the defense.

The most substantial decision facing the defense in these cases, the one recurring strategic problem, came after a loss in court: should the defense carry an appeal, and how far? This was the single set of decisions that most clearly affected the securing of appellate decisions in constitutional litigation. The defense carried one or more appeals in only 24 of these 53 cases. The defense carried a single appeal in 19 cases and 2 in another 5, making a total of 29 separate appeals or petitions for certiorari in the 24 cases. Who made those 29 appellate decisions? Intervenors carried 7 of those appeals, private party defendants carried 2 (both in the Eugene cross case), and in 6 more (all involving local prayer

---

[15] Opinion in the trial court decision in *Lowe* v. *City of Eugene;* reprinted in the record of the case before the Oregon Supreme Court, and on file in the clerk's office.

in local schools), an ad hoc group or a financial angel assisted a local school board with the appeal. That makes 15 appellate decisions. Thus in only 14 of the total of 29 appeals (48.3 percent) did the regular governmental defendants carry the appeal without substantial aid.

The considerable extent of assistance with appeals of the defense stems from the financial vulnerability of governmental officials and bodies who are the defendants. They do not often have large sums budgeted for costly constitutional litigation, and even if they can muster the funds, they do not want to risk citizen displeasure over the expenditure of taxpayers' money in hopeless appeals.

Almost invariably, the governmental defendants will handle the expense of the trial court hearing, although local governmental units often defer to state officials when both have been named in the same case. When there are both governmental and private parties as defendants, the governmental units may defer to the private parties. In the Horace Mann League's challenge of Maryland aid to its religious colleges, and in the challenge to federal aid to construction on religious college and university campuses (*Tilton* v. *Richardson*), the defense in both cases was carried substantially by the colleges and universities. In *Tilton,* indeed, the colleges were convinced—in part by the Bishop of Hartford and in part by the U.S. Catholic Conference and William Consedine—to retain a single attorney for a strong, concerted defense. They retained Edward Bennett Williams of Washington, D.C.

At each successive appellate stage—especially if the defense had the option of moving to the new appellate stage—the monetary constraints become more severe. It is at this point that governmental defendants may withdraw from the field and leave the appeals to intervenors or private defendants. Alternatively, they may seek outside aid or accept that which is volunteered. Of the latter course only one remarkable coincidence remains to be pointed out. In only five of the cases were unusual and unexpected sources of funds available to the governmental defendants, and all five involved community testing or defiance of the Supreme Court's rulings on prayer in the public schools.

In DeKalb, Illinois, local citizens, led by prominent bankers and businessmen in town, raised funds to carry on the fight and retain a classy Chicago lawyer. Local counsel for the school board recommended against an appeal to the U.S. Supreme Court, but the donors wanted to go, and the board obliged. Certiorari was denied.

Similarly, in Hawthorne, New Jersey, a special account in a local bank received about $2,000 to carry the litigation as far as the New Jersey Supreme Court.

In Leyden, Massachusetts, not only was attorney Ralph Warren Sullivan volunteered (presumably by publisher William Loeb), but the beleaguered board received contributions from all over the country. The board's secretary, Mrs. Edith Snow, also reported: "Some man called me from Texas—I forgot his name, but I have it put away—and said for us to go all the way, and he'll pay the costs and keep the Leyden schools open, too, if state aid is cut off."[16] Once again the Supreme Court denied certiorari.

The Netcong, New Jersey, school board had voted 6 to 3 not to appeal the case from a trial court loss, but it reversed itself when Warren Abraham and his organization, In God We Trust, came forward with money for fees and costs. From there on it was appeal all the way; the case was lost in the New Jersey Supreme Court, and the U.S. Supreme Court again denied certiorari.

An ad hoc local group set up the Albert Gallatin Area Prayer and Bible Reading Fund to assist that school district in its battles in the federal courts. William Duffield, leader of the group, functioned as cocounsel in the case, an effort that observers thought assisted him shortly thereafter in winning a state senate seat. Most of the funds were raised locally in the time-honored ways of small-town America: plate-passing in the local churches, bake sales and rummage sales, among others. With some $3,000 in the hopper, they too went to the U.S. Supreme Court. Certiorari again denied.[17]

So, the lessons are numerous. Freed from financial constraints, governmental defendants apparently lose their inhibitions about long-shot appeals; five of the six carried their defiance all the way for a denial of certiorari by the Supreme Court. It would also ap-

[16] Boston, *Herald Traveller* (March 29, 1970).
[17] These five cases were, in order: *DeSpain* v. *DeKalb County, Sills* v. *Board of Education, Commissioner of Education* v. *Leyden, State Board* v. *Netcong,* and *Mangold* v. *School District.*

pear that funding for constitutional defenses is available in some but not all instances; perhaps only in those cases of the most publicized defense, the most emotional issue, the most committed community.[18] One might even conclude that defense funds are most easily available in the most hopeless causes—or at least that their availability has no relationship to the legal promise of the defense position. But whatever the moral or morals of the tale, they are not particularly encouraging for the process of sophisticated constitutional litigation.

IN SUMMARY: THE AIDS FOR ACCOMMODATIONIST DEFENSE

The politics of the defense in these church-state cases is far more diffuse than those of the plaintiffs. There are no national groups such as the ACLU, the AJC, or AU to give it a shape or focus. It is not easy to apply any concept of "group" or "organization" even to the main set of actors or articulators of their interests, the Roman Catholics. So diverse are the centers of Catholic decision-making in these cases, one is finally reduced to lumping them into one literally categorical group that includes William Ball, local bishops, the USCC, the Knights of Columbus, St. Louis University, and a set of Catholic orphanages in and near Pittsburgh. If that is some sort of "scholarly fiction," the justification will have to be that it is simply useful as a shorthand summation for the characteristics of institutions and groups that share some common interests in church-state matters.

The strength of separationist group management perhaps leads one to expect it in the accommodationist defense as well. It is not so in church-state cases. The central fact remains the relative absence of surrogate defendants or aids to the nominal defendants. In 21 of the 53 cases here—virtually 40 percent—the defense went unaided by anything more than an amicus curiae—no intervenors, no noted counsel, no group help with the defense, not even informal, nongroup help with costs. Much of the defense in these cases, therefore, was of necessity local, inexperienced, unaided, and out of any touch with broader patterns of church-state litigation.

[18] It may be, of course, that such financing was available in other defenses, and that the aid was public knowledge only in these five cases because of the celebrity of the issue. I can only say that I have no evidence that this is the case, even though I have looked for it.

200

Clearly these defendants were mismatched against the far better organized and mobilized forces of the plaintiffs.

Of the remaining cases in which help was made available to the defense, the major forms of aid occurred within the same cases (Table 8–3). That is, there were 19 cases (35.8 percent of the 53) in which the accommodationist battle seems to have been concentrated, for in those 19 cases were enlisted all but 1 of the intervenors, all but 6 instances of group activity for the defense, and 9 of the 13 appearances by the nationally known accommodationist counsel. Furthermore, the support in those cases was usually under the auspices of one or another Catholic group or institution. That much is clear simply from the facts that the intervenors were chiefly Roman Catholic (see Table 8–2), the group support was heavily Catholic (in 15 of the 25 cases with group activity it is wholly or predominantly Roman Catholic), and all of the accommodationist attorneys (see Table 8–3) except Charles Tuttle were Roman Catholics (see box). In sum, in 14 of those 19 cases, the main auspices were Roman Catholic.

The mobilization of Roman Catholic support appears to depend on the presence or absence of Roman Catholic interests in the case (Table 8–4). Catholic assistance seems unrelated to the nature of the defendants or to any other variable. Catholics enter cases when some form of aid to one of their institutions seems threatened. It is as simple as that. In its way, that singularity of purpose

TABLE 8-3
Assistance to the Accommodationist Defense

Kinds of Aid to Accommodationist Defense	Total Cases	Cases with Appearance of Noted Counsel[a]
None	21	1
Intervenor only	1	0
Group(s) only	6	3
Nongroup aid	6	0
Intervenor(s) and group(s)	19	9
Total	53	13

[a] Noted counsel and the number of their appearances were: William Ball (3), Porter Chandler (2), Alfred Scanlan (2), Edward Bennett Williams (2), and Paul Butler, John Danaher, Charles Fahy, and Charles Tuttle (1 each).

201

ROMAN CATHOLIC INTERVENORS AND ATTORNEYS FOR THE DEFENSE

The marriage of the various sources of Catholic assistance to the defense in church-state cases produces briefs like the one illustrated here. In the Louisiana parochaid case intervenors Maurice Williams and other teachers of secular subjects in the Louisiana religious schools sought (and were eventually denied) certiorari in the U.S. Supreme Court. On the brief for the intervenors was Alfred Scanlan and a colleague at Shea and Gardner. Three of the Louisiana Archdiocese's most trusted attorneys were also recorded: Hebert, Hebert, and Gravel. William Consedine and George E. Reed of the U.S. Catholic Conference were also "of counsel."

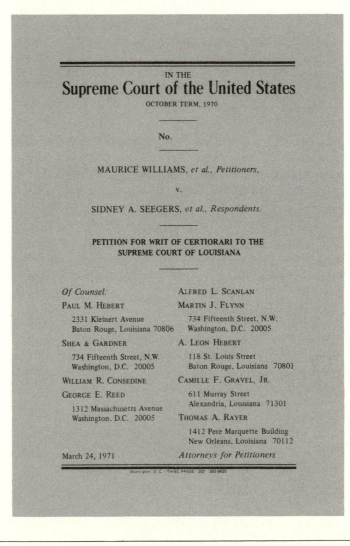

IN THE

Supreme Court of the United States

OCTOBER TERM, 1970

No.

MAURICE WILLIAMS, *et al., Petitioners,*

v.

SIDNEY A. SEEGERS, *et al., Respondents.*

**PETITION FOR WRIT OF CERTIORARI TO THE
SUPREME COURT OF LOUISIANA**

Of Counsel:

PAUL M. HEBERT

    2331 Kleinert Avenue
    Baton Rouge, Louisiana 70806

SHEA & GARDNER

    734 Fifteenth Street, N.W.
    Washington, D.C. 20005

WILLIAM R. CONSEDINE

GEORGE E. REED

    1312 Massachusetts Avenue
    Washington, D.C. 20005

ALFRED L. SCANLAN

MARTIN J. FLYNN

    734 Fifteenth Street, N.W.
    Washington, D.C. 20005

A. LEON HEBERT

    118 St. Louis Street
    Baton Rouge, Louisiana 70801

CAMILLE F. GRAVEL, JR.

    611 Murray Street
    Alexandria, Louisiana 71301

THOMAS A. RAYER

    1412 Pere Marquette Building
    New Orleans, Louisiana 70112

March 24, 1971

Attorneys for Petitioners

Washington, D.C. THIEL PRESS 202 393-0625

TABLE 8-4

Group Support for Accommodationist Defense According
to Presence of Catholic Interests in Case

	Nature of Group Support for Defense		
	None	*Catholic group*	*Non-Catholic group*
In facts of case, Catholic interests:			
present	13 (46.4%)	14 (93.3%)	4 (40.0%)
not present	15 (53.6%)	1 (6.7%)	6 (60.0%)
total	28	15	10

appears to be the direct obverse of AU's limited concern. But there are differences—the difference between plaintiff action and the more limited scope of the defense, and the difference between an organization claiming a broader commitment to separationist principle and one that makes no parallel claim.

When the forces assisting the defense were not Roman Catholic, they were of the most diverse sort. In some half-dozen instances the group was a local ad hoc group of the kind that supported the cross in Eugene, Oregon, or public school prayers in New Jersey or Pennsylvania. In the *Zorach* released-time case, a local Protestant interdenominational group arranging for released-time classes came to the defense of the New York City Board of Education. In another case the Gideons supported a school district distributing their Bibles, and in several tax exemption cases the religious bodies directly affected came to the aid of the governmental defendants. And in the one strange suit at the University of Washington, a local ACLU affiliate found itself an "accommodationist for a day." There were other non-Catholic auspices supporting the defenses, but these specifics make the general point: aside from the Catholic support they received, the defenses relied on the most various kind of group support. And in these non-Catholic quarters only one attorney of stature emerged: Charles H. Tuttle of New York, long a counsel for the National Council of Churches and other Protestant groups.

In sum, therefore, two conclusions stand out. First, the diffuseness of the Roman Catholic support and the absence of any other accommodationist organization or nucleus seriously hampered the defense in these cases. There was little or no coordinated plan of defense, no agreed-on set of litigation priorities, no efficient allocation of resources for the defense. Secondly, where no Roman Catholic interests were apparent, the collective support for accommodationism broke down. Its interests were then far less well organized than those of separationism. In general there was nothing approaching the interest group division of effort—the "system"— one could find in the separationist camp. As a result of all of this, the battle over church-state issues in American courts was a very unequal one.

IX | THE JUDGES

The first myth of the old jurisprudence to fall before the scrutiny of political jurisprudence was the myth of the judge as a detached, completely impersonal "finder" and expounder of the law. The old vision of the judge who discerned the true path of the law with a combination of legal learning and intuitive insight—uncorrupted, of course, by personal preference or world view—could not stand against the understandings and knowledge of social science, philosophical relativism, and the new legal realism. A change of verbs symbolized the change in view; judges ceased to find, expound, uncover, reveal, or announce the law; they made it. The parent of the law replaced its midwife.

But old myths have a way of yielding to new ones. To replace the view of the judge as oracle we devised, among others, a visceral vision that, in its parodied form, argued that the judicial decision resulted from the state of the judge's digestion. Other less physical myths seemed to propose a simplistic social determinism that saw the judicial decision as the result of a lifetime of experiences and loyalties the judge had accumulated. And yet for all the variety and simplism, we have come to agree on a central premise: judges do have choices and options in their decision making, and their perceptions, values, and cognitions do affect the directions in which they choose.

It is not with the premise of judicial law making that one quarrels, but with its simplistic explanation. No single background characteristic—not even the religious affiliation of judges in church-state cases—will explain the decision of large numbers of judges. Nor, indeed, will all the characteristics (that is, experiences) and values about which we can collect information. Judges also take cues from the facts of the case, even from the parties, the groups, and the attorneys; and they are doubtless also affected by the quality of the legal argument. They may, as well—especially the trial court judges—be affected by the community setting and reaction to the litigation. But the list of influences is endless, at least in

205

logic. The point is a simple one: that there are no quick, cheap, or simple explanations of judicial behavior, even in a relatively homogeneous universe of constitutional cases.

THE JUDGES THEMSELVES

Even by the standards of American political elites, the elite of the American judges is an exceptionally homogeneous one. This is, in part, by definition; they all belong to the single occupation of lawyer, and have gone through its conventional professional preparation. In part, their homogeneity derives from the political and social "prerequisites" for any political advancement. The judges who sat on these 67 church-state cases share that quality of homogeneity (Table 9–1). They are a heavily Protestant group of well-educated, white, middle-aged males. (It is not easy in the printed biographies to identify nonwhites. I am aware of only 7 of them among the 351 individual judges—3 blacks and 4 of oriental backgrounds. I also believe there are only 2 women.)

The judges who sit in decision on any body of constitutional law are not, however, necessarily typical of the universe of judges, much less of their age cohorts in the general population. In these cases, for example, they came disproportionately from the northeastern and border states, simply because the cases were litigated in disproportionate numbers in those states. For the same reason, they came also disproportionately from urban areas rather than rural. Until the mid-1960s, at least, they came almost exclusively from the state courts; since then they have come in increasing numbers from the federal courts. And since it is the nature of the cases to recur in certain state high courts and in the U.S. Supreme Court, some judges appear more than once as deciders in these sixty-seven cases. Justices Hugo Black and William Douglas of the U.S. Supreme Court, in fact, each appear in ten.[1]

[1] In the descriptive materials of Tables 9–1 and 9–2 the universe will be the 351 individuals who decided one or more of the 67 cases. In the other tables and analysis of this chapter the universe will be the 599 judicial decision makers rather than the 351 individual judges; that is, judges who make decisions in five cases will appear five times. (Their characteristics will not always be constant, of course; age will change, and in a few instances, so will the nature of the judicial selection change.) That scholarly convention of turning 351 individual judges into 599 decision makers is necessary for and limited to an analysis of judicial decisions (rather than the judges themselves). Obviously, too, if one judge participates in or makes five decisions, his own characteristics (for instance, religious commitments) weigh more heavily in the total set of decisions than those of a judge who decides only one case.

The universe of judges controlling the development of a specific area of constitutional law is, in other words, unique to that area of the law. It is defined by the parameters of the litigation in that area, by the mix of jurisdictions, by the federal-state court balance, by the mix between trial courts and various appellate courts involved in the decisions. In part, of course, the characteristics of

TABLE 9-1
Personal Characteristics of Judges

	Total (N = 351)	Trial Judges (N = 62)	Appellate Judges (N = 289)
I. Age			
median	61 years	56 years	62 years
% under 55 years	21.7%	41.9%	17.3%
II. College			
prestige	76 (21.7%)	19 (30.6%)	57 (19.7%)
state U	68 (19.4%)	11 (17.7%)	57 (19.7%)
other college or U	55 (15.7%)	10 (16.1%)	45 (15.6%)
no college degree listed	138 (39.3%)	18 (29.0%)	120 (41.5%)
no information	14 (4.0%)	4 (6.5%)	10 (3.5%)
	351	62	289
III. Religion			
Roman Catholic	63 (17.9%)	9 (14.5%)	54 (18.7%)
Protestant	223 (63.5%)	39 (62.9%)	184 (63.7%)
Jewish	30 (8.5%)	7 (11.3%)	23 (8.0%)
other, no affiliation, no information	35 (10.0%)	7 (11.3%)	28 (9.7%)
	351	62	289
IV. Political party			
Democratic	195 (55.6%)	35 (56.5%)	160 (55.4%)
Republican	114 (32.5%)	18 (29.0%)	96 (33.2%)
other, no information	42 (12.0%)	9 (14.5%)	33 (11.4%)
	351	62	289
V. Law school type			
natl. prestige	106 (30.2%)	22 (35.5%)	84 (29.1%)
state university	91 (25.9%)	14 (22.6%)	77 (26.6%)
other law school	115 (32.8%)	19 (30.6%)	96 (33.2%)
none, no information	39 (11.1%)	7 (11.3%)	32 (11.1%)
	351	62	289

Note: These 351 judges are the total number of individual judges who decided at least one of these church-state cases; many decided more than one. Appendix III contains definitions of the specific terms, indexes, and measures.

207

the judicial decision-makers may be defined by the plaintiffs and the organizations supporting them. If they decide that certain judges in certain jurisdictions will be more sympathetic to separationism, if they angle for the judge with no religious commitments, if they opt for federal courts because they believe them more separationist, or if they decide to take all lost cases to a receptive U.S. Supreme Court, they participate in defining the universe of judges before whom they argue.

It is the mix of courts and jurisdictions, then, that chiefly defined the universe of judges deciding these church-state cases. Within that universe, too, somewhat different subpopulations decided different subsets of cases. While it is difficult to see marked differences between trial and appellate court judges (Table 9–1), there are important differences between judges grouped by region (Table 9–2). The heavy weighting of judges in the Northeast (New Eng-

TABLE 9-2
Religion, Party, and Mode of Selection of Judges by Region

	Northeast	North Central	South	West
I. Religion				
Roman Catholic	41 (28.3%)	8 (18.2%)	7 (7.8%)	7 (9.7%)
Protestant	70 (48.3%)	31 (70.5%)	73 (81.1%)	49 (68.1%)
Jewish	23 (15.9%)	2 (4.5%)	4 (4.4%)	1 (1.4%)
other, none, no info.	11 (7.5%)	3 (6.8%)	6 (6.6%)	15 (20.8%)
	145	44	90	72
II. Party				
Democrat	60 (41.4%)	28 (63.6%)	79 (87.8%)	28 (38.9%)
Republican	75 (51.7%)	14 (31.8%)	5 (5.6%)	20 (27.8%)
other, no info.	10 (6.9%)	2 (4.5%)	6 (6.6%)	24 (33.3%)
	145	44	90	72
III. Selection				
election	56 (38.6%)	27 (61.4%)	77 (85.6%)	51 (70.8%)
appointment	89 (61.4%)	4 (9.1%)	9 (10.0%)	7 (9.7%)
Missouri plan	—	13 (29.5%)	3 (3.3%)	11 (15.3%)
no information	—	—	1 (1.1%)	3 (4.2%)
	145	44	90	72

Note: These 351 judges are the total number of individual judges who decided at least one of these church-state cases; many decided more than one. Appendix III contains definitions of the specific terms, indexes, and measures.

land plus New York, New Jersey, and Pennsylvania) most significantly resulted in a greater representation of Jews and Roman Catholics. The regional imbalance also altered the distribution of judges chosen under the three main methods of selection. To the extent that religious affiliation and mode of selection turn out to be related to the judges' decisions in church-state cases—and we shall soon see they are related—any such distributions are crucially important.[2]

THE SELF-DEFINED JUDICIARY

Celebrated and notorious cases are said to make bad law. They also seem to make reluctant judges. For whatever reasons—heightened ethical sensibilities, political prudence, delicate health, or challenges to their detachment—trial court judges in significant numbers depart church-state cases in their jurisdictions, leaving the trial duties to special judges. In other instances (see box) judicial defections in an urban area with a large number of judges in the local court only barely stop short of the need for substitution. It is, in any event, an important way in which the judges themselves shape the population of the men and women who will decide the church-state cases.

In seven of the fifty-two adversary cases with separationist plaintiffs, the local trial court judge bowed out, leaving the trial to a special judge brought in for the case. But, one suspects, that figure doesn't begin to measure the full extent of the problem. It does not take into account the kind of fast shuffle that took place in Honolulu, and which probably occurred in other jurisdictions with a number of judges; since "replacement" judges come from the same bench, they are not noted in the records of the case. Furthermore, the figure of seven does not consider the few instances in which the bowing out of a local trial court judge motivated the parties to the case to bypass the entire trial court process. In the Louisiana parochaid case, for example, the first trial judge in Baton Rouge recused himself on the grounds that his children attended Roman Catholic schools. The second was about to do the same on the grounds that he was a Mason, and other local judges

---

[2] Interestingly enough, there were few significant differences between the state and federal judges among the 351. The only one of importance was in law school training. Of the federal court judges, 55.6 percent attended nationally prestigious law schools; the comparable percentage for the state court judges was 26.9.

"WHY THEY REFUSED BUS SUBSIDY CASE"

Under this headline, the Honolulu *Star Bulletin* of August 21, 1967, reported more fully than usual the flight of local trial court judges when a controversial church-state case appeared on the docket:

> Seven out of 10 Circuit Court judges were either unavailable or disqualified themselves from hearing trial arguments in the school bus subsidy case.
>
> Why?
>
> Judges Thomas Okino and Thomas Ogata were out of the State and therefore unavailable for the assignment.
>
> But five other Circuit Court judges admitted frankly they would not accept the case for trial. Here are their reasons:
>
> Samuel P. King said his Family Court calendar was full, so he withdrew from the bus case.
>
> Acting assignment Judge Allen R. Hawkins said he eliminated himself because of lodge affiliations and other reasons.
>
> William Z. Fairbanks said, "I have a fixed opinion on the case. I have a fixed opinion as to the law and to the justice of it. It's not an ordinary case. It's a case on which a good many people have a fixed opinion, and I happen to be one of them."
>
> Newly-appointed Judge Alfred Laureta said "I have a direct interest in the outcome. I have a child in the Waialae Catholic Center so I thought I'd better stay out of it."
>
> Judge Masato Doi said he felt he should not try the case because he had been involved in the bus subsidy controversy while a member of the City Council.
>
> "I had taken a position," he said.
>
> Judge Yasutaka Fukushima, a former Republican legislator, said he had no comment on what he would have done if assigned the case. Family Court Judge Gerald R. Corbett said he was not asked, but did not think disqualification would have been a question with him.
>
> Judge Herman T. F. Lum was assigned finally. A former U.S. District Attorney here, Lum was nominated to the bench this spring by Gov. John A. Burns.

210

were reportedly hinting that they were going to pass the case, too. At this point the parties, anxious to settle the issue before plans for the approaching school year were set, shifted the case to the original jurisdiction of the Louisiana Supreme Court.[3]

Nor do replacement figures include the judges who offer to disqualify themselves, but whose offers are rejected by the parties in the case. Judge Fred B. Perkins of the Superior Court for Providence and Bristol Counties, Rhode Island, explained such an offer in his trial court opinion in the state's tax exemption case:

At the trial the Court indicated to counsel that it felt it was disqualified to act upon this petition involving the challenged constitutionality of tax exemptions for churches, professors of Brown University, cemeteries, and veterans, among others. The justice constituting this Court is the president of a church possessing tax exemption, is one of the four charter officers of Brown University, the tax exemption of the professors of which is challenged, is a veteran himself enjoying tax exemption, and while not in a cemetery enjoying the same, even though having closely approached that status a year ago, is nevertheless upon the Board of Trustees of such a cemetery. The Court indicated that it was confident no one would be more disqualified to act. Counsel for the petitioner, however, stated that one justice of the court had already disqualified himself and that he was confident that there was no one upon the Court who would not be disqualified in some of the aspects of the case and accordingly urged the Court to accept the case both by consent of the petitioner and as a matter of necessity. Under those circumstances and those circumstances only has the Court consented to hear the case, with the consent of both parties thereto.[4]

Similar cases may have occurred in these church-state cases without being so clearly or wittily set upon the public record.

So, leaving out all speculation about instances of which we know nothing, there were seven instances in separationist suits of the replacement of the trial court judge. The reasons varied.

[3] The case was *Seegers* v. *Parker*. The verb "to recuse," notes *Webster's New International Dictionary,* 2nd ed., is obsolete except in civil and canon law. "Recuse" (v.t.) is thus defined: "to refuse or reject; esp. to challenge or except to a judge or judges as interested or otherwise incompetent."

[4] *General Finance* v. *Archetto*. Judge Perkins' opinion is on file with the clerk of the court.

211

In Irvine, Kentucky, the local judge disqualified himself without stating a reason; local opinion believed it was because of the politically sensitive nature of the case.

Claiming that he had a "fixed opinion on the merits of the case," a rural Missouri judge yielded up a case on Roman Catholic domination of local schools.

In both Oklahoma City and Seattle some number of judges "passed" the assignment of cases, presumably because of their sensitivity. (Such passing of an assignment without reason is possible in multijudge courts in many cities.)

In another Oklahoma case the defense petitioned the Oklahoma Supreme Court successfully for the disqualification of the local judge on the grounds that he was "biased and prejudiced against the defendants" and that he had "pre-judged" the case. Conversely, in a New Mexico case it was the plaintiffs who had the local judge disqualified because they thought he could not "preside over said cause with impartiality."

Finally, in a Montana case the official court records were silent, but the local paper attributed replacement to the "illness" of the local judge. Local attorneys, however, thought that the judge's health was robust at the time.[5]

So the reasons were mixed, but there were unquestionably pressures of plaintiff challenge and judicial avoidance at work here. Both pressures reflect the involvement of the judiciary in sensitive and exacerbated local conflicts. Perhaps, too, their incidence among these sixty-seven cases has something to do with the fact that all seven instances happened in a fairly homogeneous set of cases. All were in state cases and in adversary cases; there were no friendly or federal cases. Furthermore, all came from states outside the Northeast—Kentucky, Missouri, Oklahoma, Montana, New Mexico, and Washington—(although the Northeast was the area of the largest number of cases). Their locations suggest a judicial culture and a politics of the judiciary that encourage this kind of avoidance of local conflict by the local judge. It is also significant that all occurred in states with an elective judiciary.

[5] The seven cases in the order taken up here were: *Abernathy* v. *City of Irvine, Berghorn* v. *School District, Board of Education* v. *Antone, Calvary Bible* v. *Board of Regents, State* v. *Williamson, Zellers* v. *Huff,* and *State ex rel. Chambers* v. *School District.* The quotations in the text were in all instances from trial court records on file with the clerks of the courts.

212

Those substitutions are little more than interesting and isolated events—piquant details in the broader picture of this litigation—unless they have some broader significance. They certainly alter the trial forum, and introduce an element of uncertainty in it for the parties and attorneys. To the extent that substitution reduces the effects of known localism and friendships, it neutralizes the "home" advantage for the defense, especially in relation to national or outside groups or counsel. It is true that the substitutions occur in only 7 identifiable cases. But if one eliminates the federal cases and the friendly units—which as categories of litigation seem to be completely immune from the phenomenon—and if one subtracts the cases that bypassed the trial court stage altogether, we have not 67 cases, but 45. The 7 of those are a not insubstantial 15.6 percent. And that figure does not reckon with 3 or 4 instances in which judges avoided cases in urban, multijudge courts.

The ultimate consequence, of course, is the effect of the substitutions on the decision of the cases. Since we have no idea of how the local judges might have decided the cases, that is a consequence we cannot assess. Yet it is suggestive to note that 4 of the 7 were decided in favor of separationism (57.1 percent), when the total universe of trial judges decided proseparation in only 22 of 72 instances (30.6 percent). Perhaps the trial judge was freed from the pressures and constraints of local feelings in instances of substitution. It may not be that simple, however. It may be a case of a judge with one constituency replacing a judge with a quite different one, such as a judge from a rural Bible Belt area replacing one from a county with a sizeable Roman Catholic population.

These judicial substitutions occur much less frequently in the appellate courts, and account for a negligible percentage of decision-makers at the appellate levels. There are isolated cases, such as Justice Bernard H. Levinson of the Hawaii Supreme Court, who disqualified himself from the Hawaii bus case "for the reason that prior to his appointment to the bench, he consulted with some of the plaintiffs and their attorney concerning this case."[6] There are not very many other recorded instances of such disqualification. When the appellate courts are below strength for a particular church-state case, it usually is for reasons of vacancy or the illness of a member. Furthermore, the replacement of one appellate judge means only the replacement of from one-third to one-ninth of the

[6] *Spears* v. *Honda.*

213

decision-making complement. The replacement of the trial court judge represents in most instances a one hundred percent turnover.

A much more common form of "self-definition" in appellate courts happens through the ad hoc filling of vacancies. In five cases in state supreme courts, special judges—usually lower court judges in the state system—were added to the court for the disposition of a church-state case. (In one instance it was to replace two disqualified judges, in three cases it was for the filling of vacancies, and in one it was divided, one temporary judge to replace a disqualified judge and one to fill a vacancy.) But in three of the five instances, the special judge made the margin, voting with the majority in three separate 4–3 decisions.[7] Of these three, the Oregon case involving the cross above the city of Eugene presents perhaps the most striking and complex instance of the impact of a justice pro tem. With a special judge sitting on the court, it decided against the separationists of Eugene, 4–3. Some months later, however, the court granted a rehearing, and in a second decision reversed itself and took the separationist position, 5–2. The shift was accomplished by a change of vote by one justice and by the separationist vote of a justice who had returned from a leave of absence. (That decision was, incidentally, the only reversal on rehearing in the entire set of sixty-seven cases.)

To summarize, there were 7 instances of replaced trial judges, all in one-man trial courts, and thus all replacements of significance to the decision. There were also 3 more instances of significant additions of pro tem judges in high state appellate courts. All 10 of them took place in the 50 state cases that were not friendly suits; that is, in 20 percent of the adversary cases a move within the judiciary significantly affected the composition of the judging contingent. The state supreme court or its chief justice—the usual agents for making temporary judicial assignments—thus have perhaps a greater capacity for affecting the direction of constitutional decision than we have ordinarily suspected.

THE JUDGES ON THE WALL OF SEPARATION

In any study of the judicial process and of judicial decision making, there is always one consideration that is grandly and conspicuously missing: the feelings of the judges about the issues under consider-

[7] The three cases were: *Horace Mann League* v. *Board of Public Works, Lowe* v. *City of Eugene,* and *Murray* v. *Curlett.* In the *Horace Mann League* case there were, indeed, two special judges with the majority in the 4–3 separationist decision.

ation. Much of scholarship on judicial behavior is little more than a marshalling of subtle strategies for inferring or imputing those unknown judicial views or values. Short of asking the judges directly or presenting them with a questionnaire on their attitudes, there is no alternative to the inferential strategies. We look for hints and clues in the judge's personal life—his own religious background and affiliation if the issue is in church-state relations—and in his written opinions, his offhand utterances, and his general judicial demeanor. The prevailing and very powerful judicial norms do not make it easy to read the mind of a judge.

On the bench the judges, whatever may be their personal feelings, would appear to be models of circumspection. Their written opinions and their reported verbal comments mask their own personal feelings. In very few instances can one cite examples of personal emotionalism on the church-state issue. The main exception to that generalization might well be the opinion of Judge J. Gilbert Prendergast of the Superior Court of Baltimore in one of the most inflamed church-state cases of them all, Madalyn Murray's assault on prayer in the Baltimore schools. Judge Prendergast's opinion records perhaps the low-water mark both of understanding of the constitutional issue and of the ability to separate personal values from issues of law:

> If religion, pure and undefiled in every form, were removed from the classrooms, there would remain only atheism. While the present petitioners clamour for religious freedom, their ultimate objective is religious suppression. . . . Our government is founded on the proposition that people should respect the religious views of others, not destroy them. . . . It is abundantly clear that petitioners' real objective is to drive every concept of religion out of the public school system. . . . Thus, the beliefs of virtually all the pupils would be subordinated to those of Madalyn Murray and her son.[8]

Paralleling those observations, perhaps, was the questioning of plaintiff's counsel in which Justice Michael Musmanno of the Pennsylvania Supreme Court indulged in the course of that state's bus transportation case. The justice repeatedly interrupted and harassed the plaintiff's attorneys (sample comment: "medieval thinking"). At the point at which the attorney mentioned the extra expenses that the school districts had to incur in order to provide

---

[8] *Murray* v. *Curlett;* Judge Prendergast's opinion was in the trial court, the Superior Court for Baltimore.

bus rides for parochial students, Musmanno interrupted. "Do you realize the prohibitive costs if there were no parochial schools? The Pennsylvania school system would go to smash. Parents of parochial school children are taking the burden from the backs of the taxpayer. Current expenditures would be nothing to compare if you abolish parochial schools." Another member of the high court apologized to the attorney, saying that he was "sorry that you have not had the opportunity to present your case without intrusion."[9]

Special pleading, impassioned irrelevancies, parades of horrible possibilities, and ad hominem remarks do creep into the records of judicial demeanor in these cases. But illustrative cases, however titillating and shocking, do not indicate a trend or a broader, widespread condition. The important thing is not the sensational details but the fact that one cannot multiply them into any significant magnitude. It is certainly not news to document one more time the well-known passions of a judge such as Michael Musmanno. One hopes also that it is not news that there is no explicit evidence of widely held prejudicial commitments.

On the operational level of the actual judicial decisions, most of these courts and judges seemed willing to accept and apply the church-state precedents of the United States Supreme Court, even when they disagreed with them. Wrote the trial court judge in the Oregon textbook case (in upholding the statute mandating local school districts to provide the texts to students in religious schools): "I . . . emphatically dissent from this decision which I am required to make as a result of the majority opinion of the United States Supreme Court."[10] (It is less than clear, however, why the judge was "required" to follow *Everson* and its "child benefit" rationale. He might have decided the case under separation clauses of the Oregon constitution, as the Supreme Court of the state eventually did.) Some judges have been more discretely unhappy with the separationist thrust of Supreme Court opinions: "It may be elucidating and inspirational to have Bible readings and prayer recitations in school, and it may well be what an overwhelming majority of pupils and parents in the school district desire. It may even be that I agree that it would be most beneficial to the students to have these exercises, but I can do nothing more

[9] *Rhoades* v. *School District*. The report on Musmanno comes from the McKeesport, Pa., *Daily News* (April 28, 1966).

[10] *Dickman* v. *School District*. The opinion of Judge Ralph Holman is on file with the clerk of the Circuit Court for Clackamas County, Oregon.

than observe the dictates of our law as interpreted by our Courts."[11] In the end these judges applied the decisions and interpretations of the higher court. And these courts, especially the appellate courts, dealt sternly with local school boards that skirted the rulings of the Supreme Court. In both the Hawthorne and the Netcong cases, attorneys for the local boards reported a frosty reception before the New Jersey Supreme Court. In both of the cases the court also filed very brief, terse per curiam decisions, perhaps a judgment in itself on the merit of the constitutional assertions of the boards.[12]

In the entire universe of sixty-seven church-state cases, in fact, one can find only a single instance of judicial defiance or heel-dragging in the face of uncongenial precedent. It is, however, something of a classic. The action centered on the Florida Supreme Court and on the Dade County case brought to oppose a package of religious practices in the Miami schools: prayer, Bible-reading, baccalaureate services, religious pageants, and a religious census of pupils, among others. After a decision in the trial court that permitted some of the practices and prohibited others, the Florida Supreme Court in June of 1962 (a few days before *Engel* v. *Vitale*) affirmed the decision. After its decision a year later in the *Schempp* and *Murray* cases, the U.S. Supreme Court vacated the Florida decision and remanded the case to the Florida Supreme Court for further consideration in light of those two decisions. The Florida high court refused to knuckle under: "We have, without avail, endeavored to find, in the diverse views of the several justices of the United States Supreme Court who participated in these decisions, a clear course for us to follow. It seems, therefore, more fitting that the responsibility for any enlargement [of those precedents] be left to that Court. We affirm our judgment as expressed in the original opinion herein." In June of 1964 the U.S. Supreme Court accepted the invitation and reversed the Florida courts summarily.[13]

[11] Opinion of Judge Louis Rosenberg in *Mangold* v. *School District,* 307 F. Supp. 637, 641.

[12] The cases: *Sills* v. *Board of Education* and *State Board* v. *Netcong.*

[13] *Chamberlin* v. *Dade County.* Curiously, the Florida Supreme Court was dallying over another church-state case at the same time: *Brown* v. *Orange County,* a case involving the distribution of Gideon Bibles in Orlando. An intermediate appellate court had overruled the trial court and held the distribution unconstitutional. The Florida Supreme Court heard oral argument in October 1961, and then held off its decision for almost two years; in July of 1963 it affirmed the lower appellate court with a tight-lipped reference to *Schempp* and *Chamberlin.*

Apart from issues of personal attitude and commitment, there is another side to the cognitive baggage of the judges: their legal understanding of the constitutional issues of church-state separation. It is an article of faith of some of the plaintiffs' attorneys in these cases that the state trial courts, especially, lack experience in and even grasp of the constitutional questions. One can again point to specific cases that would support that generalization. Some we have mentioned in earlier paragraphs, and to them can be added the artless definition of a Florida judge in deciding the constitutionality of a local school board's allowing a Catholic congregation to use a school auditorium for Sunday mass: "The separation of Church and State, the well recognized and basic law that no particular religious faith shall be taught to our children in our public schools, are matters not even remotely connected with the case at bar."[14] But it is easier to document misunderstanding than understanding, and isolated instances remain just that. The separationist groups would be the first to admit, in any event, that it is not the trial court decision that concerns them. Whether or not that trial court judge will let them develop a full trial record is considerably more important than the direction of his decision.

THE ROOTS OF JUDICIAL DECISION

The American political experience has been an ambiguous one on the problem of assuring judicial "independence." Article III of the U.S. Constitution, with its guarantee of life term and undiminished salary, indicates one way of protecting the judge from assertive presidents and congresses, and from powerful private and highly placed interests. It is, in effect, the concept of a fortress judiciary isolated from the usual disturbing forces of politics. On the other hand, a populist democratic faith was later embodied in many of the state constitutions that looked to the watchfulness of an electorate as a guarantee of the responsiveness of the judiciary. We have vacillated, in other words, between assumptions that judges ought to be above the currents of opinion and assumptions that they should not, between a desire to isolate them from politics and a desire to subject them to political controls. The American political culture appears to consider the judges Delphic oracles, detached high priests of the law, and at the same time

---

[14] Judge A. W. Grassle, Jr., in his order of December 15, 1958, in deciding *Southside Estates Baptist* v. *Board of Trustees*.

218

spokesmen for the values and aspirations of the electorate. They are to be guided both by a rational legal calculus and by the mores and values of the community.

And yet there is always and has always been a third influence on the judge. It is the whole system of socially-acquired perceptions, values, and attitudes the judge himself holds. "The great tides and currents which engulf the rest of men," wrote Cardozo, "do not turn aside in their course, and pass the judges by."[15] The same assumption surely lies behind the care with which presidents sift through possible appointees to the Supreme Court to find men congenial to their views. But men we have known as political creatures, we have hesitated to acknowledge as judicial philosophers. It was not until the advent of the new jurisprudence that we came openly to recognize the power of the judges' cognitions on the way they perceived, organized, and made judicial decisions. Both the great tides which engulf the rest of men and specific personal loyalties must weigh upon the judge who has a choice between legitimate legal options.

The problem of mapping the cognitive territory of judges is a formidable one. Presidents conduct talent searches that probe for indications of ideology, and senators joust and parry at hearings for indications of the appointee's views on the great issues of the moment. Scholars of judicial behavior have their own complex of strategies for probing the cognitive world of the judges. Except for the few direct assaults on the problem—questionnaires sent to judges, and, more surprisingly, received from them—the assaults are indirect. Chief among those indirect strategies has always been the examination of background characteristics. The former corporation lawyer has been supposed to be more sympathetic on the bench to corporate interests, the Southern judge less sympathetic to blacks and other racial minorities, the small-town fundamentalist less tolerant of "big city" vice and commercial sex.[16]

[15] Benjamin Nathan Cardozo, *The Nature of the Judicial Process* (New Haven: Yale University Press, 1921), p. 168.

[16] For the "direct assault," see Theodore L. Becker, *Political Behavioralism and Modern Jurisprudence: A Working Theory and Study in Judicial Decision-Making* (Chicago: Rand McNally, 1964). The indirect approaches are typified by John R. Schmidhauser, *The Supreme Court: Its Politics, Personalities, and Procedures* (New York: Holt, Rinehart and Winston, 1960) and Glendon A. Schubert's, *The Judicial Mind: The Attitudes and Ideologies of Supreme Court Justices, 1946–1963* (Evanston, Ill.: Northwestern University Press, 1965) and *Quantitative Analysis of Judicial Behavior* (Glencoe, Ill.: Free Press, 1960).

Behind the elegant simplicity of the studies of judicial back-grounds lies a welter of unclear and complicated assumptions. Do we assume that the prebench experiences of the judges set within him a pattern of values and loyalties that endures forever? Do his values never change; is it a case of the child *being* the man rather than his father? Or do his values foster dispositions that are later reinforced and triggered by the events of the case? Are we talking of direct loyalties and sympathies that result from the experiences of life, or of deep-seated values shaped by them? And why should some experiences set these loyalties and not others? At bottom, however, it is clear that we take the judge's personal characteristics as evidence of some social experience or conditioning, and from it we infer the implanting and survival of some values and disposi-tions. We know that in the controversies over church-state separa-tion in the United States, organized Roman Catholicism and a large number of individual Catholics take the accommodationist position, that organized and individual Jews (with a few notable exceptions) take the separationist view, and that Protestants tend to be in diverse array. It is therefore easy to suppose that Catholic, Jewish, and Protestant judges behave the same way in church-state cases. The logic is easy, familiar, and unsophisticated.

The logic and suppositions are indeed simple, but they work. Simplicity can, indeed, be more confounding than complexity or obscurity. Nothing explains the behavior of the judges in these church-state cases as frequently as do their own personal religious histories and affiliations. Jewish judges vote heavily separationist, Catholics vote heavily accommodationist, and Protestants divide (Table 9–3). That relationship is evident primarily in the nonunan-imous cases decided in the appellate courts, but there are even signs of it in the total group of appellate decisions, unanimous and nonunanimous. (The unanimous decisions are heavily padded with cases that are by definition the "easy" ones; considerable con-sensus exists on them, and the judges very probably decide them on the logic of a constitutional provision or an earlier judicial pre-cedent.) The decisions of the trial courts are another matter. They are, as a group, more accommodationist than the appellate deci-sions; but even so, the same pattern is discernible: Jewish judges are the most separationist, Catholics the most accommodationist.

One can hardly claim that this relationship between church-state decision and the religious affiliation of the judge is a total surprise. It is in part heralded by a number of studies finding Jews—both

TABLE 9-3
Votes of Judges in Church-State Cases by Their Religious Affiliation

| | | Religious Affiliation of Judge | | |
Judges and Votes	Jewish	conservative Protestant	other Protestant[a]	Roman Catholic
I. Appellate judges in nonunanimous cases[b]				
separationist	14 (82.4%)	23 (56.1%)	55 (48.7%)	5 (15.6%)
accommodationist	3 (17.6%)	18 (43.9%)	58 (51.3%)	27 (84.4%)
total (N = 203)[c]	17	41	113	32
II. Appellate judges in all cases				
separationist	23 (57.5%)	53 (48.2%)	106 (46.1%)	18 (22.0%)
accommodationist	17 (42.5%)	57 (51.8%)	124 (53.9%)	64 (78.0%)
total (N = 462)[d]	40	110	230	82
III. Trial court judges in all cases				
separationist	3 (37.5%)	2 (22.2%)	13 (37.1%)	1 (11.1%)
accommodationist	5 (62.5%)	7 (77.8%)	22 (62.9%)	8 (88.9%)
total (N = 61)[e]	8	9	35	9

[a] This category combines those judges of the mainline, high-status Protestant bodies with those describing themselves simply as "protestant."

[b] If one constructs a two by two table of the votes in I for Jews and Catholics, the phi test of association is .65.

[c] The N here of 203 is out of a maximum of 233; two of the judges were Buddhists (both in Hawaii), there was no information on the religious preferences of 14, and another 14 cast votes in the cases that were either ambiguous or on other than church-state grounds.

[d] The N of 462 here is out of a total of 527; there were no religious data on 37, and another 28 cast votes on other grounds.

[e] The N of 61 here is out of a total of 72; there were no religious data on 8, and 3 cast votes on other grounds.

on the bench and in American society generally—more sympathetic to the civil liberties of individuals and minorities than are Catholics and Protestants. In another test of religious differences, the Vines study of federal judicial decisions in equal protection cases in the South also found Catholic judges far more integrationist than the Protestant judges. In these and other instances, it is apparent that different general social values associated with the three major religious traditions lead individuals to different positions on policy issues, even when they are judges rather than legislators. In these church-state cases we can sense not only those different social values, but also a more specific religious self-interest. For in the church-state issues, as in no other, the religious affiliation of the judge relates in the judicial decision to the direct and immediate interests of his religious group as well as to the social values derived from the religious tradition and its belief system.[17]

What is convincing in the aggregate totals is, of course, particularly striking in individual instances. In the New York state courts, a total of 13 judges heard the 1951 released-time case from the city of New York—1 trial judge, 5 in the Appellate Division of the Supreme Court, and finally 7 in the state's Court of Appeals. Among the 13, the 5 Roman Catholics voted for the program (accommodationist), the 2 Jews voted against it, and the 6 Protestants divided, 5 for it and 1 opposed. The single Protestant separationist vote was cast by a Congregationalist. Those positions, incidentally, were exactly the positions those denominations were taking in the state on the released-time issue and on questions of separation generally. Similarly, the Alaska Supreme Court divided 2–1 on a bus case, with the two Protestants voting against the one Catholic.[18]

Among the cases in which appellate courts split along religious lines, however, none was quite as dramatic as the Louisiana case, *Seegers* v. *Parker*. Set in a state divided roughly between the Bible Belt Protestantism of the north and the Creole and Cajun Catholicism of the south, the decision in the Louisiana Supreme Court mirrored all of the religious tensions and divisions of the state. In its 4 to 3 decision holding the state's parochaid program unconstitutional, the court divided, with the four Protestants invalidating the legislation and the three Catholics voting to uphold it. Furthermore, since Louisiana is one of the few states in the country to elect its supreme court justices from separate and individual judicial districts, each justice had a separate constituency. Two of the Protestant justices in Louisiana represented heavily Protestant districts in the north, two of the Catholics were from heavily Catholic districts in the south, one Protestant came from a balanced district around Baton Rouge, and a Protestant and a Catholic came from the two-judge district in and around New Orleans.

---

[17] The relationship between Jewish judges and decisions in favor of individuals in civil liberties cases can be found, for instance, in Don R. Bowen, "The Explanation of Judicial Voting Behavior from Sociological Characteristics of Judges," (Ph.D. dissertation, Yale University, 1965). The study by Kenneth N. Vines, "Federal District Judges and Race Relations Cases in the South," can be found in the *Journal of Politics* 26 (May 1964), 337–357.

[18] *Zorach* v. *Clauson* and *Matthews* v. *Quinton*.

The judges' religious affiliation clearly does not explain all of their behavior in nonunanimous cases, however. Especially unclear are the other variables that impel the Protestants to come down on one side or the other. Their view of separation—if indeed it is that view or value that operates—is clearly more complex or selective. Alternatively, it may be less strong and dominant, and thus more frequently subordinate to other desiderata. One suspects that the church-state dimension as something approaching a clear and absolute issue is especially salient for the Roman Catholics and the Jews; that much they share, even though they cling to opposite sides on the question. But the issue is apparently less salient for the Protestants. Other more demanding considerations mediate and deflect the force of their separationist-accommodationist feelings.

And yet it is not easy to find other relationships that would suggest more salient attitudes or values among the Protestant judges. Their ages, their educational differences, their party preferences, their prior political and governmental experience, their region of birth do not suggest important relationships. There is a slight tendency for Democrats to be more separationist, but that in turn seems to reflect little more than the concentration of Democratic judges in the federal courts and in the northeast section of the country generally. And while there is no difference between the decisions of Masons and non-Masons when one controls for religion, judges who are members of the Shrine or the Scottish Rite are, indeed, heavily separationist. The 28 judges who were members of one or the other cast 21 of their 28 votes in appellate, nonunanimous cases (75 percent) on the separationist side, a degree of separationism approaching that of the Jewish judges. (All 28 were, incidentally, Protestants.) While the relationship illuminates the decisions of these judges, there were not enough of them to account for the major share of Protestant choices. Nonetheless, it remains interesting that the more involved and committed Masons apparently still carry the traditional Masonic separationist values. In a way, too, that relationship brings full circle the relationship between Masonry, especially the Scottish Rite Masonry of the Southern Jurisdiction, and the organization of separationist litigation, especially by Americans United.

The basic issues that divide Protestant judges become more evident when one breaks the church-state cases into subgroups. They voted more heavily separationist in cases in which Roman Catholic

223

interests were involved and in which the controversies centered on the elementary and secondary schools, either private or public (Table 9–4).[19] But while the fundamentalists and the other Protestants shift together from separationism where the schools are involved to accommodation where they are not, their behavior diverges in the cases in which Roman Catholic interests are at stake. The presence of those Catholic interests apparently discriminates between the kind of separationism of the fundamentalist sects, heavily influenced by its fear of Romanism and "popery," and the "mainline" separationism of traditional and liberal Protestantism. Those "Catholic" cases tend to indicate the reasons for the greater general separationism of the fundamentalists; the "school" cases, on the other hand, give a clue to the main consideration that determines whether the Protestant judge generally will vote separationist or accommodationist.

One set of church-state cases triggers different cues or stimuli than do other sets, especially for the Protestant judge and his understanding of separation. The presence of Roman Catholic interests in a case appears to activate the particular brand of separationism we have come to associate—correctly it seems—with the conservative and fundamentalist Protestant denominations. The nature of the "school" cue is less obvious. Perhaps to some judges it suggests a threat to the ideal of the secular, universal, public school as the transmitter of democratic values and the cradle of a pluralist culture. There is in that ideal a goodly dose of philosophical separationism—hence the name of the Horace Mann League—as well as a desire to protect the public schools against the loss of their monopoly of public funding. It may even constitute a separate and even more salient value than separationism. For other judges the school cue may suggest the impressionable young, the possibilities of implicit coercion whenever the very young are confronted with religion in the schools. The distinction between the religious indoctrination of children and the religious study of the college student is, indeed, one that the Supreme Court ob-

---

[19] The cases in which elementary and secondary schools are involved include two chief types of cases: 1) cases in which religious exercises or influences in the public schools are alleged, and 2) cases in which aids of some kind to private religious schools and/or their pupils are alleged. The cases in which Roman Catholic interests are involved overlap that second category almost completely, and, additionally, include cases involving aid to Roman Catholic hospitals, orphanages, and colleges and universities.

TABLE 9-4

Votes by Religion of Judges in Nonunanimous Appellate Cases by Presence or Absence of Roman Catholic and School Interests in Cases

Votes in Non-unanimous Appellate Cases	Roman Catholic Interests Present				Roman Catholic Interests Not Present			
	Jewish	conservative Protestant	other Protestant	Roman Catholic	Jewish	conservative Protestant	other Protestant	Roman Catholic
Schools Involved								
Separationist	10 (76.9%)	16 (61.5%)	32 (44.4%)	2 (8.3%)	4 (100%)	7 (46.7%)	23 (56.1%)	3 (37.5%)
Accommodationist	3 (23.1%)	10 (38.5%)	40 (55.6%)	22 (91.7%)	0	8 (53.3%)	18 (43.9%)	5 (62.5%)
Total (N = 203):	13	26	72	24	4	15	41	8
No Schools Involved								
Separationist	13 (86.7%)	20 (74.1%)	44 (56.4%)	4 (14.3%)	1 (50.0%)	3 (21.4%)	11 (31.4%)	1 (25.0%)
Accommodationist	2 (13.3%)	7 (25.9%)	34 (43.6%)	24 (85.7%)	1 (50.0%)	11 (78.6%)	24 (68.6%)	3 (75.0%)
Total (N = 203):	15	27	78	28	2	14	35	4

Note: The universe of 203 cases is the same one for nonunanimous decisions in appellate courts that is explained in the note in Table 9-3. In addition, the reader will note the striking relative scarcity of Jewish and Catholic judges in the cases in which no schools were involved; it is a reflection of the fact that school cases have been most common in those states and regions (such as the Northeast) in which there are other than Protestant judges in appreciable numbers.

served.[20] But whatever the issues the "school" triggers, it is clearly an elaboration or modification of the separationist-accommodationist continuum, and it appears to influence the decisions of the Protestant judges.

EXTERNAL PRESSURES ON THE JUDICIAL DECISION

When we interpret the judge's vote in terms of values—whether they be those indicated by religious affiliation or those somehow stimulated by the presence of Catholic or educational interests—we are basing our explanations on the judge's internal values and perceptions. Alternatively, however, the judge's vote on issues of separation might well be influenced by external pressures—by some widely held views in the community or the state that might, if they were ignored, support sanctions on the offending court or individual judges. Might elected judges facing close decisions in very sensitive church-state cases anticipate and be influenced by the possibility that an unhappy electorate might turn against them in their next election?

About the transmittal of social and political pressures to the judges one can suggest two logical hypotheses. First, one would assume that elected judges would be more sensitive to those pressures than appointed ones, and, additionally, that partisan judges would be more sensitive than those elected in nonpartisan elections. Those assumptions would reflect the major premise that judicial selection systems differ in the extent to which they protect the judge from the sanctions of the party and the electorate. And, indeed, all of this turns out to be true of the judicial decisions in these church-state cases (Table 9–5). Those judges who need to be concerned about party and electoral support do in fact seem to be more majoritarian in outlook, more deferential to the views of the community, and less activist in their decisions. The data may also suggest that states with partisan judicial elections are states in which judicial politics are not isolated from the battles over public policy. In any event, these states, either by the selection process for judges, or by reason of the general political milieu, do not encourage judges to decide for unpopular minorities.

Secondly, it seems reasonable to suppose that federal judges will

[20] See Chief Justice Warren Burger in *Tilton* v. *Richardson*. For example: "There is substance to the contention that college students are less impressionable and less susceptible to religious indoctrination," p. 686.

TABLE 9-5

Appellate Court Judges' Votes in Nonunanimous Cases by the
Method of Their Selection

Judge's Vote	partisan election	Selection by nonpartisan election	appointment or Missouri plan
Separationist	19 (28.8%)	28 (58.3%)	55 (55.6%)
Accommodationist	47 (71.2%)	20 (41.7%)	44 (44.4%)
Total (N = 213)	66	48	99

Note: The universe of 213 is 20 short of the total of 233; there were 6 special judges chosen in ways other than the way for the court with which they were sitting, and 14 whose vote in the case was either ambiguous or on grounds other than those of church-state relations. Control for religion in no significant way alters the relationships shown here.

be more willing to overturn public policy—and thus to be more separationist—because of their selection by appointment, and because of their "distance" from the origin of the policy. Since the public policy objected to is in almost all instances the product of the states or their civil subdivisions, state courts, by the same reasoning, will be more supportive of that policy and thus more accommodationist. That hypothesis, too, is confirmed by the data of these cases (Table 9–6). And this, too, shows the wisdom of the separationist groups' preference for the federal courts.

Finally, there appears to be another relationship that may offer a clue to judicial decisions in these cases. Judges with no prior judicial experience surprisingly—and contrary to the conclusions of other studies—are substantially more separationist than the judges who have held other and earlier judicial posts. Protestant judges with no judicial experience, for example, voted separationist 39 of 62 times (62.9 percent), but those with earlier judgeships were proseparation in only 38 of 90 decisions (42.2 percent). Is it possible that the judges without experience on another court are more innovative, less bound by the traditional tolerance of public religion—more activist, in short? Since the public policy they deal with is overwhelmingly accommodationist, these are the judges who are more willing to overturn policy and thus be less deferential to the elected policy-making institutions. Is it indeed possible that there is some truth in the American Bar Association's conventional wisdom about greater judicial restraint resulting from "prior judicial experience"? Or might it be the case that having

TABLE 9-6
Votes of Judges in State and Federal Courts

	Judges in	
	state	*federal*
Votes	*courts*	*courts*
I. Nonunanimous appellate court decisions		
separationist	59 (41.0%)	43 (59.7%)
accommodationist	85 (59.0%)	29 (40.3%)
total	144	72
II. All appellate court decisions		
separationist	140 (35.9%)	75 (70.1%)
accommodationist	250 (64.1%)	32 (29.9%)
total	390	107
III. All decisions		
separationist	154 (34.9%)	82 (66.1%)
accommodationist	287 (65.1%)	42 (33.9%)
total	441	124

Note: All judicial votes not clearly on the substance of the church-state issue have been eliminated.

the prior judicial experience merely reflects a political aptitude (perhaps the same one that marks a judge for success in partisan elections) by which judges move up career ladders from one position to another?[21]

IN SUMMARY

Once again, despite all of the related issues, the key question concerns consequences and results—the direction of the judicial decision. Among the influences on it is the nature of the judge himself. This, in turn, is affected by two chief kinds of influence: one set that defines who the judges will be, and another that determines how the judges will decide. In these church-state cases the "selection" of the judges rests, as always, on a series of factors that de-

---

[21] In any event, the age of the judges is not the factor that explains the relationship. There are 211 appellate court judges deciding nonunanimous cases on whom we have data on age, and whose decision was unambiguously on church-state grounds. Of those under age 60, 32 of 73 voted separationist (43.8 percent), while 68 of 138 (49.3 percent) age 60 and over voted separationist.

fine in what courts the legal actions will be brought; not the least of those factors is the litigating intelligence of the separationist groups. But, to a striking extent, substitutions and replacements also define the universe of judges in church-state cases, with, again, some possible advantage to the separationists.

As for the influences on the judges' decisions, they are, first of all, less apparent in the trial than in the appellate courts. Trial court judges are less inclined to disturb public policy. Perhaps that is so because they are more closely bound by precedent and because they do not see themselves as constitutional courts. Perhaps it is also because they are more attentive to community and majority values. They are certainly closer to an identifiable community than appellate judges, and it is often the preferences of its majority that they must approve or disapprove. In this body of cases, for instance, trial court judges voted separationist in only 30.9 percent of the decisions (21 of 68), while appellate judges in all cases were separationists 43.3 percent of the time (215 of 497), and those in nonunanimous cases decided at a 47.2 percent rate (102 of 216) for the separationist side. It is a finding that parallels Peltason's discovery that federal trial court judges in the South were less integrationist than judges on the Court of Appeals.[22] Trial court judges also decide the fairly noncontroversial cases, the cases with only one plausible route to decision, which later become the unanimous cases in appellate courts. For all of these reasons, the relationships for trial court judges between their decision and either personal characteristics or judicial selection are attenuated. It seems fair to speculate that dispositions to uphold public policy and to avoid constitutional innovation or activism to a great extent override their personal values or constitutional world views.

The decisional world of the appellate court judge is far more open and expansive. He works amid cases that, by the time they come to him, have acquired policy overtones, and he decides much more consciously in an environment of conflicting social and public values. The appellate court judge can be sensitive to the widest range of both legal and policy considerations. In the face of such a welter of competing influences—not the least of which are the

[22] Again, the totals in these categories are a little below the maximum possible because of ambiguous votes or votes cast on other than church-state grounds. For the parallel finding in equal protection cases, see Jack W. Peltason, *Fifty-Eight Lonely Men* (New York: Harcourt, Brace, and World, 1961).

demands of the system of law for consistency, symmetry, and equity—one does not expect easy or clearcut explanations of the judicial choice. That there is such a relatively simple explanation in the instances of the Roman Catholic and Jewish judges is remarkable.

The decisions of the Protestant appellate judges take one back to the expected complexity of explanation. Without the overriding influence of a view of church-state relations somehow caught up in religious loyalties, they are open to a whole passel of diverse and even unrelated influences. A set of issues related to fear of Roman Catholicism appears to animate some fundamentalists, and the most involved Masons seem to have their own lights. For some members of the traditional, high-status Protestant churches, the church-state issue seems to intersect an even more salient value dimension that has to do with elementary and secondary education, perhaps even with the ideology of the American public school. For the Catholics and Jews the issues of these sixty-seven cases fall easily along a single overriding policy dimension. It is not that simple for many of the Protestants, just as it is not that simple for their churches and denominations.

And yet is it really the values and preferences, even the firmly set religious commitments, of the judges that primarily determine the outcomes in these cases? The temptation is great to create, at least implicitly, a judge-centered explanation of the judicial decision, for the external influences on the judicial decision are not at all as obvious as they are on the legislative, executive, or even administrative decision. The temptation is all the greater because the religious affiliations of Roman Catholic and Jewish judges, at least, explain more of the variance in these church-state decisions than personal characteristics of judges have in other studies.[23] Nonetheless, a good deal of the influence on these decisions remains unexplained, and for that explanation one must turn to factors external to the judge: the legal logic or imperatives, the nature of the public policies and controversies in the cases, the participants and groups involved in the case, for example. The next two chapters introduce those considerations more fully.

[23] Bowen, "The Explanation of Judicial Voting Behavior," p. 201, reports that his multivariate analysis of characteristics explains between 15 and 43 percent of variance in decisions. The single variable of religious affiliation here in the cases of Roman Catholics and Jews will explain 42 percent of the variance; see the phi coefficient in the note in Table 9–3 of this chapter.

X | THE ADVERSARY CASES:
INCIDENCE AND OUTCOME

It is not the judges, the plaintiffs, the attorneys, the defendants, or even the powerful national groups, who mark the change or development of American constitutional law. It is the cases themselves and the decisions in them. It is the decisions in specific factual contexts and the rationale for them that move constitutional doctrine in one direction or another. The initiatives, choices, and activities of actors in these cases have meanings in and of themselves. But for all the emphasis on the politics of the judicial process, one ought to remember that it is not the politics but the effect or consequence of the politics on the product of appellate courts that counts.

The problem can be approached in another manner. It is, to use a cliché, the problem of the forest and the trees. Analytical concentration on particular actors or parts of the judicial process may take the eye away from its entirety. We need to capture something of the "macrojudicial" perspective: the aggregate movement of church-state litigation through the American appellate courts. The sixty-seven cases on which this study is founded, in other words, have a reality and a motion of their own, quite apart from the activity of the people involved in them. It is to that level of analysis, the level of the sixty-seven cases themselves, that this and the following chapter are devoted. This chapter examines the aggregate histories of the fifty-eight adversary cases, and the following chapter deals with the special world of the nine friendly suits.

THE UNKNOWN ICEBERG

Putting together a picture of the whole is, however, easier promised than accomplished. The whole, while it is perhaps a semantic absolute, is at the same time a very relative matter. The whole under consideration here is sixty-seven church-state cases decided in high state courts or federal appellate courts between 1951 and 1971.[1]

---

[1] A full discussion of the universe of cases that are the data of this study can be found in Appendix I.

But that "universe" is itself merely the visible tip of an iceberg of all litigation on church-state matters. Those sixty-seven cases clearly represent the final reduction of a larger number of cases. Between the trial courts and the high appellate courts, there has been a winnowing of cases, a separation of the constitutional wheat from the chaff. We clearly ought to know what percentage of cases survives the weeding-out processes, and what special kinds of cases they are. But we do not. It is still unhappily true (to return to a cliché) that while we know the visible tip, we have not taken the measure of the iceberg itself. Indeed, we do not have any easy way of measuring it; that is the problem itself.

State trial court cases—unlike the decisions of high state courts—go generally unreported, and by no means all of the cases decided in U.S. district courts are reported in the *Federal Supplement*. Private attempts to catalogue church-state cases have had mixed successes. The *Civil Liberties Docket,* established in the 1950s by the Alexander Meiklejohn Institute at Berkeley, California, attempted to list all civil liberties litigation in American courts. Its reports on church-state litigation were, however, notably incomplete, even in their reporting of appellate cases indexed in the usual legal sources. Its listings would also appear to be fuller for the western states, an indication perhaps that its information system and contacts are stronger in its home region. The listings of the American Jewish Congress's *Litigation Docket,* begun in January of 1966, have been much more nearly complete. But even the sedulous efforts of the AJC do not unearth all cases, nor are they always able to elicit responses from parties to cases they do unearth. Furthermore, the AJC *Docket* is intended for the use of the church-state bar, not as a complete historical record, and fast-moving cases that are concluded before they can be listed do not appear. Understandably, also, the AJC's contacts are best among the separationist organizations; it is generally the local case without national sponsorship that goes un-*Docket*ed. Yet for all those reservations, the AJC *Docket* is surprisingly complete for the period from 1966 to 1971, and its listings provide the major basis for estimating the bulk of all church-state litigation in all American courts.[2]

[2] The *Civil Liberties Docket,* edited by Ann Fagan Ginger, appeared ten times a year; it appears to have ceased publication in the late 1960s. The AJC's *Litigation Docket,* under the general editorship of Joseph Robison, is published semiannually. The former covers civil liberties and civil rights issues generally; the latter is limited to church-state and religious freedom litigation.

Between 1966 and 1971 the AJC *Litigation Docket* reported a total of 113 separate church-state cases. Of that number, 42 were listed by the *Docket*'s editors as not "closed" (that is, still in litigation). Thus, 71 of the listed church-state cases had completed their trip through the courts. Of that 71:

31 (43.7 percent) never got beyond a state or federal trial court;

6 (8.5 percent) were decided finally in a state intermediate appellate court;

25 (35.2 percent) reached and were decided in the highest appellate court of the state;

4 (5.6 percent) received final decision in a U.S. Court of Appeals;

5 (7.0 percent) were finally settled in the U.S. Supreme Court.[3]

Of the 71 cases, therefore, fully 34 (the last three categories tallied above), or 47.9 percent, were eligible for inclusion in the universe of cases that make up the data of this book. Since the *Docket* does miss some church-state cases, and since the "misses" are probably largely trial court cases, one might well introduce a 10 percent correction and bring the base total from 71 to 78. Even so, the 34 would still represent 43.6 percent.[4] One may approach the same question another way. Between the beginning of 1966 and late June of 1971—a period which both this study and the *Docket* include—33 of the cases in this study reached high appellate court decision, while 68 of the *Docket*'s list reached decision in some trial court. With the 10 percent correction again, the "tip" of the iceberg is by this computation 44 percent (33 of 75). Thus, something close to 45 percent of church-state cases were by the late 1960s entering that body of well-recorded opinions and decisions that make up the constitutional precedents on the separation of church and state.

[3] These cases in the U.S. Supreme Court are: *Board* v. *Allen, DiCenso* v. *Robinson, Lemon* v. *Kurtzman, Tilton* v. *Richardson,* and *Walz* v. *Tax Commission.*

[4] The reader may wonder how, if I do not know of all church-state litigation, I can say that the *Docket* does not list all church-state cases. I have my own litigation list made up from group files, newspaper accounts, local reports, reported cases, as well as the *Docket,* and the *Docket* has not reported all cases on my list. I fully acknowledge that my own list is also incomplete, and that it owes a great deal to the *Docket.* It should also be clear that since the *Docket* has also missed some cases that have reached appellate levels, the introduction of a 10 percent correction on the base total may be closer to a gross correction in total cases of closer to 15 percent.

Since the "tip" amounts to almost half of the iceberg, we have here a body of constitutional law with an astounding ratio of high appellate court decisions. All evidence would suggest that other areas of public law litigation do not approach it.[5] It is, in fact, so large a "tip" that one uses the iceberg metaphor somewhat uneasily. But three caveats should be kept in mind. We speak here only of actual cases that reached some maturity and decision in an American court; the *Docket* does not usually record the threatened, the withdrawn, and the otherwise aborted litigation. Second, the data are for the late 1960s and early 1970s; they may not be representative of the years before. Finally, all of these calculations depend on the exhaustiveness of the listings in the *Litigation Docket*. Working in favor of that exhaustiveness, however, is the flow of information centering generally on the litigating separationist groups and on the AJC in particular. Especially since this litigation flows from public and well-publicized policy disputes, it does not seem likely that the information channels failed badly. Even if we expand our calculation of error, however, we still have a most impressive ratio of appellate decision.

More important than the question of the size of the iceberg's tip is the question of its composition. That is, are the cases that reach high appellate courts similar to the aggregate of all the cases? Are they a reasonable sample of the totality? To a very surprising degree they are (Table 10–1). It is hard, in fact, to find any important characteristic by which the 33 cases of this study from 1966 to mid-1971 differ from the 68 in the *Docket* decided in the same period. They are alike even where one might have expected differences, such as in the incidence of sponsorship by the three leading separationist groups.[6] There are small differences here and there, to be sure. For example, more federal cases appear in the *Docket* group, suggesting, perhaps, that it is easier to appeal cases in the

[5] For example, J. Woodford Howard reports the appeal of 29.4 percent of trial court decisions in the three circuits under study in "Litigation Flow in Three United States Courts of Appeals," *Law and Society Review* 8 (1973), 33–53. Kenneth M. Dolbeare in *Trial Courts in Urban Politics* (New York: Wiley, 1967) finds that about 7 percent of the trial court public law cases (except zoning cases) he studied went to New York's highest appellate court, the Court of Appeals.

[6] In determining "sponsorship" for the 68 *Docket* cases, I could only accept the editors' listings. I suspect—with some reason—that their criteria were less rigorous than mine for the cases in the study, and probably close to a combination of my "sponsor" and "intermediate role" categories. If I adopted that definition here, I would show 18 of the 33 (54.5 percent) so sponsored.

TABLE 10-1

A Comparison of the 68 Docket Cases and the 33 Cases from
This Study Decided from 1966 to Mid-1971

	Docket Cases (N = 68)	Cases from This Study (N = 33)
I. Region		
Northeast	27 (39.7%)	14 (42.4%)
North Central	15 (22.1%)	4 (12.1%)
South	19 (27.9%)	9 (27.3%)
West	7 (10.3%)	6 (18.2%)
total	68	33
II. Plaintiff interest		
separationist	54 (79.4%)	25 (75.8%)
accommodationist	14 (20.6%)	7 (21.2%)
ambiguous	0	1 (3.0%)
total	68	33
III. Sponsorship[a]		
by one or more of leading three	28 (41.2%)	12 (36.4%)
none or by others	40 (58.8%)	21 (63.6%)
total	68	33
IV. Facts in case[b]		
bus rides	13 (19.1%)	5 (15.2%)
aid to religious schools	10 (14.7%)	5 (15.2%)
tax exemptions	6 (8.8%)	3 (9.1%)
religion in public schools	9 (13.2%)	5 (15.2%)
texts, auxiliary services for religious schools	9 (13.2%)	3 (9.1%)
V. Roman Catholic interests		
present	42 (61.8%)	19 (57.6%)
not present	26 (38.2%)	14 (42.4%)
total	68	33
VI. School interests		
present	41 (60.3%)	17 (51.5%)
not present	27 (39.7%)	16 (48.5%)
total	68	33
VII. Courts of origin		
state	47 (69.1%)	27 (81.8%)
federal	21 (30.9%)	6 (18.2%)
total	68	33

[a] See footnote 6 of this chapter.

[b] These fact categories, obviously, do not account for all of these cases; they are, however, the largest ones.

235

state court systems. But the overall similarity of the two groups is astounding. One cannot, therefore, escape the conclusion that the appellate processes in state and federal courts do not materially alter the nature and kind of church-state cases by reducing their numbers.

THE ORIGINS OF THE ADVERSARY CASES

Thirty-seven of the 58 adversary cases decided between 1951 and 1971 originated under at least partial auspices of some national or local group—20 by at least one of the three separationist leaders, and another 17 by some local or other national group.[7] But to be present at the origin of a case is not to determine its site, its actors, its local setting, its factual context. There is much in the basic components of these cases that even the most watchful and thorough litigating group cannot manage or control. To a considerable extent, the events and the conflict of the litigation were there before the groups were. Groups to a great extent seize (or are invited to seize) ready-made or emerging opportunities. Each one of these cases has its own history of conflict and disagreement, and in many of them the history is a long one even before litigation commences. That history often determines why it is this case and controversy rather than tens or hundreds of others that becomes the grist for constitutional mills.

To a very great extent the origin of the case is related to the nature of the public policy at issue. Take, for example, the four cases involving some form of prayer in public schools after *Engel* v. *Vitale* and *Schempp-Murray*—the cases in Netcong and Hawthorne, New Jersey; Leyden, Massachusetts; and Fayette County, Pennsylvania. In only one of the four—the Pennsylvania case—did a local resident bring suit to halt the religious exercises; in the other three cases state officials brought the actions. No local conflict or disagreement, in other words, sparked three of these cases. It was rather the nature of the communities that led them into the course of defiance of *Engel* in the first place. None of the locales was in a larger city or metropolitan area. All mixed their desire for prayer with a social conservatism that saw prayer as something more than religious devotion: as a bulwark of the tradi-

[7] For this section of the chapter we shift from the 67 cases to the 58 of them that were adversary. The nine friendly suits will be the subject of the next chapter.

236

tional social and ethical values against the winds of contemporary change—student demonstrations, black militancy, the new sexual morality, rejection of traditional patriotism, crime in the streets, and the drug culture. In three of the four communities local informants believed there to be considerable support for George Wallace.

Or take the example of the parochaid cases. Within the short span of a year, state supreme courts or the U.S. Supreme Court decided four cases involving statewide programs of aid in Pennsylvania, Rhode Island, and Louisiana, and a local aid program in Montana. Policy in all cases originated in states or localities of high Roman Catholic population and many Roman Catholic schools, an observation that would seem to be little more than a truism. The subsequent litigation in the statewide cases, in fact, had no really identifiable locales within the states. Attempts to explain the origin of litigation, therefore, come hard against the fact that it is often not the litigation but the public policy under challenge that is the operative consideration.

Indeed, as these difficulties suggest, the distinction between policy disputes in the other branches and those in the judiciary are not in fact very great. A significant percentage of these 58 cases were really little more than uninterrupted extensions of policy disputes in other arenas of the political process. Virtually one-third of the cases merely transferred the policy dispute from another arena to the judiciary (19 of the 58; 32.9 percent). Three of those cases were extensions of local referenda, 10 of state legislative battles, and 6 of local council or school-board fights. The coalition of educational and religious groups fighting parochaid in Pennsylvania and Rhode Island, for instance, were amply on record during the legislative debates and hearings with statements about the bills' probable unconstitutionality and their own intention of initiating suits immediately if they passed.

Of the remaining two-thirds of the cases, more than one-third (22) came from cases in which settled or established local policy was challenged only after repeated complaints or after attempts (in 18 of the 22) to negotiate or modify the offending practices. The Orange County case challenging the distribution of Gideon Bibles in the public schools came some years after the policy had been set, and after earnest attempts to persuade the school board to discontinue the practice. Of the remaining cases—fewer than a third of them—it can only be said that the litigation came

237

THE TOWN THAT WENT TO COURT

The acme of community conflict as litigation among these church-state cases was reached in Bradfordsville, Kentucky, a conservative little Protestant (and Republican) town set in the middle of a larger Roman Catholic area near Lebanon, the county seat of Marion County. In resistance to what they believed was religious discrimination against a Protestant minority in the closing of Bradfordsville High School, 460 adults—virtually all in Bradfordsville—signed on as plaintiffs in the litigation (*Wooley* v. *Spaulding*).

So broad and numerous were the concerns of Bradfordsville that at times the church-state issue was totally obscured. The county school board, the majority of whose members was Roman Catholic, closed the Bradfordsville High School when it fell below the minimum enrollment of 100 required normally for state accreditation—this despite the fact that the state was apparently ready to make an exception to the minimum. It also assigned the high schoolers to the Lebanon high school, some eight miles away by bus over narrow, twisting roads. The Bradfordsville people countered that the county board had driven the high school enrollment down by permitting students from the Roman Catholic areas around the town to transfer out of the school and to another high school that was, while public, heavily Catholic in its students and even in its religious influences. They feared that the closing of the Bradfordsville High School would deprive the town of its main institution and activities. They also resisted the busing of local children to Lebanon, not only for the usual reasons of inconvenience and deprivation of extracurricular opportunities, but also because Lebanon was reputed by Bradfordsville standards to be a "wide open" town whose young people "ran wild." They sued, therefore, to compel the continuance of the high school in Bradfordsville.

Early in the litigation the town leadership enlisted the support and modest help of POAU, which in the course of litigation formed a local chapter in Lexington. That unit helped, too, but the main financial burdens in the case were carried by the locals, especially by several well-to-do families. The mass community conflict expanded in the courts when 302 parents from the predominantly Catholic areas outside of town (near Gravel Switch) intervened on the side of the defense to express their happiness with the abolition of Bradfordsville High School. (Some ten years before they had rebelled against going to the school and had actually staged an attendance strike. Then in 1954–1955, shortly after the closing of Bradfordsville High, the Bradfordsville citizens staged their own strike, keeping their children out of school rather than send them to Lebanon.) After a long trial, which produced stenographic transcripts about eighteen inches thick, the litigation stretched into an almost endless series of inconclusive decisions as it bounced back and forth among Kentucky courts. Eventually, the morale of the plaintiffs and their supporters broken, the high school at Bradfordsville was closed and the town's youngsters sent to Lebanon. Bradfordsville's life and population dwindled, and by the 1970s its one short main street was pocked with empty and fire-gutted stores.

in the form of attacks on more or less settled policy without prior attempts to reach some accommodation by persuasion or negotiation.

Beyond the fact of the policy dispute and the influence of the groups as explanations of the origin of litigation, a third factor is also important in a number of cases: community conflict. A large proportion of these cases features an aroused community—among them the battle in Eugene, Oregon, over the cross on the hill, and the four communities defying the Supreme Court decisions on prayer in the public schools. At the trial stages, at least, these cases are more pitched battle than legal proceeding, with all segments of the community choosing one side or the other. These cases growing out of community conflicts have a number of characteristics in common:

With some exceptions, they are the small-town cases among these fifty-eight adversary cases; the parties and issues are known to a large percentage of the local population (see box).

They tend to be locally initiated as a result of a wider policy dispute, with some substantial segments of the community on each side.

The cases tend to become foci for the fears of large numbers of people about the decline of religiosity and traditional values, or they become battles against the outsider, the deviant, or distant governmental authority.

They are, indeed, community crusades, and their concerns are as much moral as legal. They become crusades for the right of majorities in localities to preserve their values and life styles without some distant voice—even a remote Supreme Court or a constitution—interfering with them.

The influence of policy in shaping constitutional litigation is a constant, but the influences of group management and community conflict tend to be mutually exclusive. From their interaction, one can construct a grand dichotomy of the church-state cases: those that grow out of deeply-felt community conflict, and those that begin primarily as constitutional test cases. We have just described the cases that originate as local community conflict. The constitutional test cases, on the other hand, often are plunked down on a surprised locale, it usually being the hope of the sponsoring group to avoid a superheated community. (If they test a statewide policy they may have no identifiable locale at all.) Group roles are much stronger in the test cases. There also tend to be more federal and state policies at stake in them, and more county, city, and school board policies under question in the cases arising from conflict situations. If there is any subset of these adversary cases that does not fit easily into one or the other of these categories, it is the "lonely crusade," the one-person crusade of Madalyn Murray in Baltimore, Lyle DeSpain in DeKalb, and Joseph Lewis in New York. They do produce community conflict of a sort, but it is the outrage of the community at the individual who challenges its consensus. Separationist litigating groups and the indigenous community conflict thus are chief instigators of this constitutional litigation. To the extent the groups expand their role, it is at the expense of the "home grown" conflict.

If it is parsimony we seek in explaining the rise of constitutional litigation, however, then let it be noted that constitutional litigation seems to spawn more constitutional litigation. In even so small a universe of cases as this, litigation comes in pairs. There is, for instance, a considerable tendency for more than one church-state case to develop in the same locale. The pairs are actually of several kinds. The purest form is of pairs that actually develop from precisely the same locales:

The two Madalyn Murray cases came from Baltimore (both with the same attorney, as well), one challenging prayer in the schools, and the other tax exemptions for religious property.

The *Rawlings* and *Wooley* cases from Marion County, Kentucky, dealt first with nuns and religiosity in the public schools, and second (when in stipulations in the first case this issue was carved out for separate litigation) with allegations that a Catholic-dominated county school board discriminated against a Protestant community's high school.

Abington Township, Pennsylvania, served as the locale and its school board the defendants in two cases, the *Schempp* attack on Bible-reading in the schools and the *Rhoades* test of bus rides to religious schools. Direct links between the two cases, however, are not easy to establish. (One could also pair the *Schempp* and the *Lemon* parochaid cases, both brought in Federal district court in Philadelphia, both supported by the local ACLU, and both argued by Henry Sawyer of Philadelphia.)

New York City provided the locale for three cases: the *Zorach* released-time case, the *Walz* tax exemption case, and *Stein* v. *Oshinsky,* an accommodationist suit seeking to reinstate prayers in a local school. Connections are not easy to establish, but some of the parent organizers and plaintiffs in the *Stein* case were aware of, and perhaps encouraged by, earlier church-state litigation in the New York area.

Nassau County, New York, site of *Engel* v. *Vitale,* the first of the Supreme Court prayer cases, also provided the second plaintiff school board in the New York textbook case (*Board* v. *Allen*). Members of that board had followed the nearby *Engel* litigation some years earlier.

There are other pairs among this church-state litigation which, while they do not occur in the same place, do occur in the same states, at about the same time, and with connections or ties of some sort in strategy or personnel.

The *Horace Mann League* and *Truitt* cases both came from Maryland at about the same time. The former's attack on aid to religious colleges cast doubt on the constitutionality of state bond support for religious hospitals, and led to *Truitt*.

The *Berghorn* (nuns in public schools) and *McVey* (bus rides) cases originated in Missouri at the same time; they were, in fact, decided on the same day by the state supreme court. The Missouri Association for the Public Schools and its officers were active in both.

Just after the *Zellers* case (nuns in public schools) was decided in New Mexico, a case was brought in one of the same counties in the state charging several teachers with bringing Protestant religion into the public schools. One Santa Fe attorney was involved in the defense in both cases.

Rhode Island served as the locale for challenges both to the state's textbook aid and to more direct parochaid to religious schools; the state ACLU affiliate and the same attorney led both.

The resolutions adopted by the local school boards in Leyden, Massachusetts, and Netcong, New Jersey, setting up programs of prayer in their schools (*after* the Supreme Court decisions of 1962 and 1963) were identical.

Two cases—both of them friendly suits—also emerged from South Carolina within months of each other, one to test the constitutionality of the state's tuition grant program to private college students, and the other to test its bonding support for building on private college campuses.

One can find other pairs composed of a case in this group of sixty-seven and a case either before or after the 1951–1971 time span. Hawthorne, N.J., site of a post-*Engel* prayer case, was also the earlier site of the *Doremus* Bible-reading case.[8] Miami also had a spate of litigation after the *Chamberlin* cases,[9] and the same attorney who argued the *Antone* bus case in Oklahoma later brought suit to remove religious symbols from the Oklahoma state fair grounds.[10]

Cases tend to spring up, therefore, in well-prepared soil. In part it is a result of the experience and confidence of plaintiffs and attorneys; success especially creates an appetite for more combat. Experience in one case also seems to make an expert of an attorney. In others of the pairs, the tie is legal or constitutional; the first case has created a need for attempted clarification by the second. It may even be that the two are aspects of the same conflict. In other cases the pair is a part of the same commitment, drive,

[8] *Doremus* v. *Board of Education*, 342 U.S. 429 (1952).
[9] *Paul* v. *Dade County*, 419 F.2d 10 (1969).
[10] The attorney was Jack P. Trezise of Midwest City, Oklahoma; the second case, *Meyer* v. *Oklahoma City*, 496 P.2d 789 (1972).

or strategy of the same group. All of these things are identifiable. What is less tangible, less verifiable, is the possibility of some sort of constitutional "suggestibility." A constitutional case, especially one that is well publicized, may suggest other constitutional litigation. It may make obvious a form of political action not otherwise apparent. It may suggest that such recourse is more and more conventional, more and more respectable, both in the courts and with the public. And a case won by a separationist may also suggest that the chance of success (especially for the separationists) is greater than had been imagined. Whatever the specifics, however, the sheer incidence suggests that a case having once been litigated in a locale may well be the single most important factor (or complex of factors) determining the development of another case.

There is another plausible, common-sense expectation about the origin of church-state litigation: that it will be directly related to the religious composition of the locale. This assumes that there is a relationship between the interests of groups of people—best indicated here by their religious affiliations—and the policy conflicts giving rise to litigation. The relationship is, unhappily, a good deal more complicated than that. The central assumption implies not one but two kinds of population mix: a mix (that is, religious composition) of the right kind to achieve the public policy in the first place, and a population mix that is likely to produce a challenge to its constitutionality. Moreover, the mixes that produce one kind of policy dispute and litigation may differ from those that produce another. One would not logically expect to find a challenge to a parochaid statute (or even the statute itself) in the same kind of locale as a "captive schools" controversy. But whatever the mix may be, the crucial point is, perhaps, that the argument suggests that there must *be* a mix, that it is the religiously heterogeneous locale that spawns church-state litigation.

The "locale," moreover, has characteristics beyond the religious composition of its population. The greater incidence of group activity in urban centers suggests that urban locales provide the interactions, the associations, the expertise in litigation, perhaps even the veils of impersonality, needed for constitutional litigation. Urban centers, we may reasonably expect, would also have greater concentrations of two classic groups of separationists: Jews and the nonchurched. A locale, too, may be prepared for constitutional litigation by earlier constitutional litigation. The incidence of pairs of cases among these sixty-seven suggests that one case "sensitizes"

243

the groups and individuals in a locale to the possibilities of the judicial process, while at the same time creating the experience to manage it.

Even if one cannot, therefore, assume a grand relationship between locale and constitutional litigation, some general associations are evident. This body of litigation came to a great extent from urban areas and from the religiously diverse states. Of the 67 cases, 64 originated in the 48 states (the present 50 minus Alaska and Hawaii) for which data on religious memberships in 1956 are available. Only 9 of the 64 cases (14.1 percent) originated in the 16 most heavily Protestant states; 23 (35.9 percent) were located in the middle 16 states; 32 (50 percent) came from the 16 least Protestant states. A plotting of the cases on a map would show a concentration on the coasts, in the border states, and in a few states of the upper Midwest. The states of the Deep South, the plains, the prairies, and the mountains are underrepresented. Furthermore, these 67 cases also came from the urban centers. Of the 56 with identifiable locales—as opposed to a statewide site— 37 (66.1 percent) were brought in a county within a census-defined standard metropolitan statistical area (SMSA). Only 310 of the country's 3043 counties (10.2 percent) were in SMSAs.[11]

To go beyond these generalizations in defining the relationship between locale and litigation, one must begin to deal with legal and judicial variables and with subtypes of cases. There are identifiable reasons, for example, for the origin of some cases outside of the SMSAs. These were the cases that arose out of an aggravated community conflict, often without group sponsorship or auspices. These cases, too, reflected specific kinds of policy issues. The "captive school" issues, for example, were by their nature nonurban; they occurred only in isolated, heavily Catholic commu-

[11] The religious data in this paragraph come from the 1956 survey of church membership in the United States compiled by the National Council of the Churches of Christ. (Because of its date the study included no data on memberships in Alaska and Hawaii.) The reports are entitled *Churches and Church Membership in the United States: An Enumeration and Analysis by Counties, States, and Regions.* The reader of this paragraph may also suspect (correctly) that corrections for population would negate the reported relationships. For example, 63 percent of the American population in 1960 lived in SMSAs (compared with 66 percent of the church-state cases from them). But both as makers of public policy and as sites of litigation, governmental units by themselves do promote litigation, regardless of population. To conclude that these relationships have no significance, one would have to conclude that the incidence of litigation is solely a function of population.

nities. Similarly, the parochaid cases came entirely from states of relatively large Roman Catholic populations. Once again, therefore, one comes back to the central fact that locale as an explanation of the origin of litigation must be joined to the nature of the policy dispute and to the presence or absence of the necessary actors: plaintiffs, attorneys, and groups.

THE TIP OF THE TIP OF THE ICEBERG

The step-by-step elimination of cases culminates in the entry of a small number of cases to the U.S. Supreme Court for decision. Ten of the 67 cases that are the data of this book were ultimately decided by the Court.[12] All 10 of them were drawn from the 58 adversary cases, a remarkable 17.2 percent of them, or 14.9 percent of the whole 67. And if the 1966–1971 case projections for all American courts are applicable to the 1951–1971 period in the same ratio as the cases of this study, we project a total of 152 total church-state cases decided in any American court.[13] The 10 Supreme Court cases would be a small but very impressive 6.6 percent of that total. Such percentages, again, range well above those in other bodies of litigation, and they certainly mark this period as one of exceptional attention to church-state issues by the Supreme Court.[14]

The 10 cases in some ways do resemble the 67, and in some they do not. The resemblance is strongest in the kinds of policies challenged (Table 10–2). It is almost as if the Supreme Court were guided by some poll of preferred litigation. It is true that the most frequent issue in the 67—that of transporting pupils to religious

[12] This total does not count the remandings by the Supreme Court of *Clayton* v. *Kervick* and *Hunt* v. *McNair*. Judgment in both cases was vacated, and the cases were returned to the two state supreme courts, an outcome that does not seem to me to be a substantive decision by the Court.

[13] The estimate of 152 is reached this way. The 33 cases decided from 1966 to 1971 are 49.3 percent of the 67 cases in this study decided in appellate courts from 1951–1971. In the same 1966–1971 years, 68 of the cases in the *Litigation Docket* reached decision in a trial court. Projecting that 68 to the full 20-year period, one estimates 138 cases ($138 \times .493 = 68$); then adding the 10 percent correction pushes that estimate to 152, the number of cases decided in trial and appellate courts between 1951 and 1971.

[14] Howard, in his article, "Litigation Flow in Three United States Courts of Appeals," finds that only 100 of 13,406 trial court cases within three federal circuits (about three-fourths of one percent) reached the U.S. Supreme Court.

245

TABLE 10-2

Frequency of Policies at Issue in the 67 Church-State Cases
and in 10 That Reached the Supreme Court

Policy Categories	Number in 67 Cases	Number in Supreme Court
Bus rides for pupils of religious schools	12	0
Prayer or Bible reading in public schools	10	3
Aid to religious schools	6	2
Aid for buildings of religious colleges	6	1
Tax exemption of religious property	5	1
Religious influences in public schools (baccalaureates, pageants, etc.)	5	1
Control of public schools by religious group ("captive schools")	5	0
Textbooks, other auxiliary services for pupils in religious schools	4	1
Aid to religious hospitals	3	0
Released-time program	2	1
Distribution of Bibles in public schools	2	0
Others (no more than one per category)	16	0
	76[a]	10[b]

[a] The total of 76 reflects the fact that nine of the cases raised two distinct factual issues.

[b] The 10 Supreme Court decisions listed here are, beginning at the top of the column with the three: *Engel* v. *Vitale, Murray* v. *Curlett,* and *Schempp* v. *School District; Lemon* v. *Kurtzman* and *DiCenso* v. *Robinson; Tilton* v. *Richardson; Walz* v. *Tax Commission; Chamberlin* v. *Dade County; Board of Education* v. *Allen;* and *Zorach* v. *Clauson.*

schools—did not receive Supreme Court attention in the period, but the Court had shortly before decided the issue in the historic *Everson* case.[15] The *Zorach* case, the Court's single sortie into a less salient issue, can be explained as a follow-up and clarification of the *McCollum* case of a few years earlier.[16] But otherwise the Supreme Court's agenda appears almost to be a sample of the litigation reaching all appellate courts.

Two other categories of fact—religious domination of the schools and aid to religious hospitals—each merit a short comment, because the Supreme Court did not take a case from either one. None of the three cases involving religious hospitals had spon-

[15] *Everson* v. *Board of Education,* 330 U.S. 1 (1947).
[16] *McCollum* v. *Board of Education,* 333 U.S. 203 (1948).

sorship by the three separationist groups, and in only one of them did the losing separationists seek certiorari. The U.S. Supreme Court may also have considered its ancient precedent in a Washington, D.C., hospital case to be lively.[17]

As for the religious domination of public schools—the so-called "captive schools" issue—the fault for the failure hardly falls to the Supreme Court. No one sought either certiorari or appellate jurisdiction in any of the five cases. Catholic authorities lost three and were hardly anxious to bring the issue to the Court. For their parts, the separationists never managed to fashion a strong test case. The cases, all AU-supported, were marred by hazy definition of the issues and by generally inadequate trial court records. Furthermore, the three groups differed among themselves on the central question: the hiring of nuns to teach in the public schools. On the issue the AJC supported their right to public employment so long as they did not wear religious garb, while both AU and the ACLU vacillated on the question, local activists in each favoring an absolute ban on employing the sisters. Finally, the practice of merging the Catholic and public schools, always restricted as it was to isolated small towns, never really achieved any national visibility despite the best efforts of AU. And so the "captive schools" issue never reached the U.S. Supreme Court; that failure made it the major "nonissue" in the constitutional law of church-state relations.

The cases that reached the Supreme Court, therefore, were a good cross section of church-state issues under litigation in the American courts. By largely ignoring the less common issues, the Court concentrated on cases in which the schools were in some way involved, but that emphasis flowed naturally from a concentration on the most common issues. In some other ways, however, the ten cases reaching the Supreme Court were hardly typical of the full sixty-seven (Table 10–3). Most strikingly, they were largely from the Northeast, and sponsored by one or more of the three separationist groups. The incidence of the group sponsorship is not surprising; their success in reaching the Supreme Court is the culmination of their strategies and the final testimony to their skills. Since their efforts are concentrated in the Northeast, the regional concentration is to some extent related to group sponsorship, but not entirely.

The ten cases, indeed, all came from eastern states—eight from

[17] *Bradfield* v. *Roberts,* 175 U.S. 291 (1899).

TABLE 10-3
Comparison of Characteristics in 67 Church-State Cases
and in 10 That Reached the Supreme Court

	All 67 Cases	Cases in Supreme Court
I. Sponsorship		
one of three sep. groups	20 (29.9%)	8 (80.0%)
none, or other groups	47 (70.1%)	2 (20.0%)
	67	10
II. Roman Catholic interests		
present	39 (58.2%)	5 (50.0%)
not present	28 (41.8%)	5 (50.0%)
	67	10
III. School interests		
present	43 (64.2%)	8 (80.0%)
not present	24 (35.8%)	2 (20.0%)
	67	10
IV. Court of origin		
state	59 (88.1%)	6 (60.0%)
federal	8 (11.9%)	4 (40.0%)
	67	10
V. Region		
Northeast	26 (38.8%)	8 (80.0%)
others	41 (61.2%)	2 (20.0%)
	67	10

the Northeast and one each from Baltimore and Miami. All also came from metropolitan centers and areas: New York, Philadelphia, Baltimore, Miami, Providence, suburban Long Island, Hartford, and Albany. That geographical concentration appears to reflect a number of causes. One is the incidence of group activity in the area. The greater frequency of federal court cases is another; all of the cases before three-judge panels were in the Northeast. The locales of the cases were also the religiously diverse areas; each one had a relatively high percentage of either Catholics or Jews. Perhaps, too, there was some "celebrity" factor at work. Some of the cases grew out of heralded public policy disputes— such as those in state legislatures over parochaid bills—and others featured long and bitter trials. These were also the cases made famous even before they reached the Supreme Court by the coverage of such eastern newspapers as the *New York Times* and the *Washington Post*. One is reminded of the lament of professional athletes who, after a career in Milwaukee, Oakland, or Kansas City, regret that the reporters and columnists of the eastern press never heralded their accomplishments. Celebrated cases, like celebrated quarterbacks and outfielders, seem to blossom in the eastern metropolises.

GOING TO THE U.S. SUPREME COURT

The relatively high incidence of church-state cases ultimately decided in the Supreme Court of the United States bears some testimony to the determination of the parties in the cases to seek those final decisions. Some party in 34 of the 58 adversary cases (58.6 percent) sought entry to the Supreme Court. Their efforts came out this way:

No attempt to go to Supreme Court:	24	cases	(41.4%)
Certiorari sought and denied:	18	"	(31.0%)
Appellate jurisdiction sought, denied:	2	"	(3.4%)
Both certiorari and appeal sought, denied:	4	"	(6.9%)
Appellate jurisdiction granted:	9	"	(15.5%)
Certiorari granted:	1	"	(1.7%)
Total:	58		

Nine of the 10 cases the Supreme Court decided arrived in the Court's mandatory appellate jurisdiction. The Court appears to have been saying that it will decide only the church-state cases that it believes it must decide, the cases that fall within its mandatory jurisdiction. (Since the Court is also the judge of what is mandatory, it is free to engage in tautologies on the point.) In any event, it exercised its certiorari discretion only once in 19 requests. The success of the appellate route, to the practical exclusion of certiorari, may well reflect also the experience of attorneys taking these cases to the Court. The attorneys in the nine cases that succeeded on the appellate route were all either experienced church-state or Supreme Court attorneys, or they had ready access to that experience. The single case to make it to the Court on certiorari was Madalyn Murray's attack on prayer in the Baltimore schools, a case brought by the 1 attorney in all of the 10 without access to that expertise or experience. (One might add that it was joined to and decided with the *Schempp* case.)

The willingness of parties to go to the Supreme Court—and the willingness of the Supreme Court to accept them—increased steadily within the period between 1951 and 1971. By seven-year periods, the record of attempts to get into the Supreme Court is as follows:

> 1951–1957: 3 of 11 cases sought entry (27.3 percent)
> 1958–1964: 12 of 21 cases sought entry (57.1 percent)
> 1965–1971: 19 of 26 cases sought entry (73.1 percent).

That sharp increase over time is also undoubtedly related to the Supreme Court's performance. In those same three seven-year periods, the Court decided 1, 4, and 5 cases, respectively; furthermore, 9 of the 10 were decided in the second half of the 1951–1971 span. In thinking of the Supreme Court's encouragement to parties to seek access, it is also well to remember that the Court's decisions were separationist in 6 of those last 9 cases.

More predictably, perhaps, cases sponsored by one or more of the three leading separationist groups enjoyed the easiest access to the Supreme Court (Table 10–4). Eight of the 10 cases decided in the Supreme Court had the full sponsorship of at least one of the groups, a ninth (*Murray* v. *Curlett*) had a lesser degree of group support, and the tenth (*Walz*) had the amicus support of the ACLU. That last case did, nonetheless, enjoy the services of Edward Ennis, an experienced civil liberties attorney and at the time one of the general counsel of the national ACLU. If, as other scholarship has suggested, the Court is guided by the cues of major

TABLE 10-4

Entry of the 58 Adversary Cases to the U.S. Supreme Court According to Role of Three Separationist Groups

Supreme Court Jurisdiction	No Role	Amicus Curiae	Inter- mediate	Sponsor- ship
Not sought	8 (72.7%)	2 (25.0%)	11 (57.9%)	3 (15.0%)
Appeal or certiorari denied	3 (27.3%)	5 (62.5%)	7 (36.8%)	9 (45.0%)
Appeal or certiorari granted	0	1 (12.5%)	1 (5.3%)	8 (40.0%)
Total	11	8	19	20

Note: In those cases in which more than one group has participated in a case and at different levels of involvement, the role recorded here is the role of greatest involvement.

250

group participation in a case, it could easily have spotted those cues in 9 of the 10 cases it accepted for decision.[18] To look at the question another way, the three major separationist groups sought access to the Supreme Court in fully 17 of the 20 cases they sponsored. It is, apparently, no exaggeration on their parts when they say they are prepared to go all the way if they enter a case. And while other cases were enjoying an acceptance rate of 13.3 percent (2 of 15), the three separationist groups reached the Court in 47.1 percent of their tries (8 of 17).

The question of why the Court takes this or that case and not another is almost purely one for speculation. In part it is a matter of legal logic and the public importance of issues. In part the reason or reasons may also lie in the realm of strategy or tactic. Why indeed did the Supreme Court take the *Walz* case after refusing certiorari to two earlier tax exemption cases, both of which offered a fuller record, or at least a fuller set of facts?[19] Some observers of the Court have speculated that in the late 1960s it might have wanted an occasion for an "accommodationist" decision after the separation decisions that had antagonized powerful segments of American society. The strategy would have been, therefore, to give organized religion a "victory" for fence-mending purposes. Alternatively, the Court may have realized that its recent separationist decisions in other church-state areas had clouded this issue, too, and as a result it may have felt the need to eliminate the doubt. Perhaps, too, it might have noted the incidence of tax exemption cases—there were others under way besides *Walz*—and the growth of serious debate about the practice of tax exemption, even in church circles themselves.

[18] For a full examination of cues in a somewhat different context, see Joseph Tanenhaus, Marvin Schick, Matthew Muraskin, and Daniel Rosen, "The Supreme Court's Certiorari Jurisdiction: Cue Theory," in Glendon Schubert (ed.), *Judicial Decision-Making* (New York: Free Press, 1963), pp. 111–132. The authors hypothesized (p. 118) that "some method exists for separating the certiorari petitions requiring serious attention from those that are so frivolous as to be unworthy of careful study. We further hypothesized that a group of readily identifiable cues exists to serve this purpose. The presence of any one of these cues would warn a justice that a petition deserved scrutiny. If no cue were present, on the other hand, a justice could safely discard a petition without further expenditure of time and energy." They go on to note that among the possible cues that occurred to them were the parties seeking review. Their study, however, tests that possibility only in the instance of the United States as a party.

[19] The cases were *Lundberg* v. *Alameda County* and *General Finance* v. *Archetto*. In both cases there were dissents from the refusal of certiorari, Justice Hugo Black in both, and Justice Felix Frankfurter in the former.

But, on the other hand, some of the Court's decisions to take cases seem tied to the group appearances and sponsorship of cases. It is hard to ignore the figures of Table 10–4. One can only speculate that the Court does take some cues from the sponsorship of the cases in granting jurisdiction. To some extent, too, these are the nationally celebrated cases. They are certainly the cases with major coalitions of interests behind them; aside from the main separationist support, other national groups supported the plaintiffs in five of the eight cases. Perhaps, too, the Court has confidence that the group-sponsored cases are the more substantial and plausible cases, that they have better records, and that they will be better briefed and argued. Perhaps, too, the justices use that kind of group sponsorship as a test of the ripeness of a constitutional question.

Those are only the most insubstantial speculations, and speculation they must remain so long as the Court gives no reasons for its decisions on the granting or denial of jurisdiction. All we know positively is that the Court suffered through an uncommon degree of division on whether or not to accept these cases. Of the 24 cases rejected (among the 58 adversary cases) one or more members of the Court dissented from the rejection in 10 of them (one justice in 5, and two justices in 5). The dissenters were Douglas (five times), Stewart (three), Black and Frankfurter (two), and Harlan, Marshall, and White (once apiece). There are, indeed, patterns to the dissents; four of Douglas's five were in bus cases, two of Stewart's three were in prayer cases, both of Black's were in tax exemption cases. But the single dominant conclusion in examining the dissents is that justices dissent only when the position they favor has lost in the court below. The implication seems clear that they want to overrule rather than merely to consider the merits of the case. More generally, it is one more challenge to the humbug that the denial of certiorari says nothing about the substance of the issue.

THE OUTCOMES: WINNERS AND LOSERS

In 29, or exactly half, of the 58 adversary cases, the final decision favored the separationist interests. Accommodationists won 28, and the outcome in the final one was evenly divided between opposing interests. It is true that not all appellate court victories are of equal importance, of course, and the fact that the separa-

TABLE 10-5

Outcome of Adversary Cases According to Presence
or Absence of Elementary or Secondary Schools
in Facts of Case

Final Outcome of Case	Schools Present	Schools not Present
Separationist	27 (65.9%)	2 (11.8%)
Accommodationist	13 (31.7%)	15 (88.2%)
Mixed	1 (2.4%)	0
Total	41	17

tionists won 6 of 10 cases before the U.S. Supreme Court is of
no little significance. But however one looks at it, the separationists
built a substantial record of success in American appellate courts
between 1951 and 1971, especially when one considers that decisions in their favor had to go against public policy. It is also a
record of success related to the ongoing nature of litigation on
the subject. For it is very likely that considerable prospect of success must be present to encourage plaintiffs, and especially the
national interest groups, to continue the litigation. Success in the
courts creates an expectation of further success, and thus tips the
strategic balances in favor of further activity in the judicial process
rather than in some other policy arenas.

The 29 separationist victories, however, came almost exclusively
in cases in which elementary or secondary schools were involved
(Table 10–5). Those "schools" cases were generally of two kinds:
those touching religious influences, such as prayer or Bible-reading
in the public schools, and those in which the issue focused on aid
to private religious schools or their pupils. To put the point the
other way, in the two decades of this study the separationists
scored only two wins in cases not concerned in some way with
the schools: the Oregon case about the cross on the bluff above
Eugene, and the Maryland case invalidating the state's aid to its
religious colleges.[20] Both decisions, incidentally, were by the closest
of margins. The Oregon case was won only on rehearing and full
consideration by the Oregon Supreme Court, and the Maryland
decision carried in a 4–3 split of that state's Court of Appeals.

[20] The cases were: *Lowe* v. *City of Eugene* and *Horace Mann League*
v. *Board of Public Works.*

253

TABLE 10-6

Origin of Litigation in Policy Disputes According to Presence
or Absence of Elementary or Secondary Schools
in Facts of Case

Origin of Litigation in Policy Dispute	Schools Present	Schools not Present
None apparent	25 (61.0%)	14 (82.4%)
Outgrowth of referendum	3 (7.3%)	0
Outgrowth of legislative conflict	9 (22.0%)	1 (5.9%)
Outgrowth of local policy conflict	4 (9.8%)	2 (11.8%)
Total	41	17

The school cases, it is no exaggeration to say, constitute the most important subset of church-state cases. They attract considerably more extensive and intense group activity than do the others, and they also attract greater numbers of amici curiae (see Chapter IV). With Catholic and Jewish judges firmly on one side or the other of the church-state division, these are the cases that draw out the separationism in many of the Protestants. And these, too, are the cases that grow more directly out of the policy disputes in the states and localities (Table 10–6). In short, the cases entangled with the future of the schools tend to be the most salient and the most "politicized" of the cases. The school cases, that is, appear to touch separationist interests and concerns more profoundly than the other cases. They threaten religious minorities who fear the implicit coercion on their children of the religiosity of the majority in the public schools. They also alarm all separationists and public education interests who see any alliance between religion and public schools, and between public treasuries and religious schools, as a threat to the ideal of the secular, pluralistic public school. In short, these are the cases that appear to marry the interests of separationism and public education; the marriage, if one is to judge by the decisions of American courts, is a very fruitful one.[21]

[21] Compare the special characteristics of these school cases with a similar finding in Kenneth N. Vines, "Federal District Judges and Race Relations Cases in the South," *Journal of Politics* 26 (1964), 337–357. Vines found in his cases that only in the subset of cases on education did blacks win more than half of the cases decided in federal district courts in the South. That outcome he attributed in part to the large number of cases litigated on racial equality in education. The suggestion that success rates vary with the size of the subset of cases would apply also to these church-state cases.

The final outcomes in these fifty-eight adversary cases do not, however, appear to be related to the nature of the parties and participants. The presence or absence of major litigating groups, of amici curiae on either side, or of intervenors is not particularly related to the direction of the final decision. The groups' record in the U.S. Supreme Court is, of course, a winning one, and those successes have an importance that offsets the groups' less productive record in the other appellate courts. (It should also be remembered that the won-lost record of the AJC and the ACLU is somewhat better than that of AU.) Even more impressive than the record in the Supreme Court is the groups' record in getting cases into that Court. That, rather than any won-lost percentage, was their major accomplishment in the 1950s and 1960s. Nonetheless, it appears to be the facts of the cases, and the varieties of issues and interests involved, that make the major differences in the outcomes in these cases. Individuals and groups move for advantage within those broader limits.

Trial court decisions in these cases offer some dramatic contrasts to the pattern of appellate court disposals. Since 5 of the adversary cases were not heard in a trial court—because of the certification of issues, for example—there were only 53 trial court decisions. In only 18 of them (34.0 percent) did the trial court judge or judges decide for the separationist side. They were more separationist in the school cases (40.5 percent; 15 of 37), but markedly less so than the appellate courts. Moreover, trial courts were more apt to react to the nature of the parties, especially the plaintiffs. In not one instance did they decide for an atheist or agnostic (there were 11 of them), or for the alienated, "outsider" plaintiff (8 of them, although 4 overlapped the "ungodly" category). All in all, trial courts appeared less innovative and activist in the law, and more attentive to local pressures and conventionalities.

The gap between the patterns of trial court and final decisions meant inevitably a considerable overruling of the trial courts or the intermediate appellate courts that upheld them. In 22 of these 58 cases (37.9 percent), in fact, the trial court decision was eventually reversed—16 accommodationist decisions made separationist, and 6 decisions reversed in the other direction. That in itself indicates a substantial degree of activism in the final courts' disposal of these cases. There were in these cases, in other words, a good many appellate court judges asserting their understanding of a constitution by rejecting public policies hammered out in the democratic political processes.

TABLE 10-7

Final Outcome in Adversary Cases According to Level
of Government Making Policy under Challenge

Final Outcome	National	State	County, City	Local Schools
Separationist	0	10 (33.3%)	4 (26.7%)	21 (77.8%)
Accommodationist	3 (100.0%)	20 (66.7%)	11 (73.3%)	6 (22.2%)
Total	3	30	15	27

Note: This table excludes the one case of the 58 adversaries with a mixed outcome; there are therefore 57 cases. The total of 75 levels of government in the table results from the involvement of more than one governmental body in the policies at issue in a single case. The most common instance is the permissive state statute, in which state law says, for instance, that local school districts *may* provide bus rides for pupils attending religious schools. Local board action then follows, inaugurating the rides.

The judicial activism in these church-state cases was not, however, directed evenhandedly at all policy makers. Separationist decisions occurred much more frequently in instances of school-district policy than in those involving other governmental levels (Table 10–7). In part that reflects the dominance of school policy on the courts' agendas, and especially their inclination to decide them in favor of separationism. But the greater overruling of local school boards and officials remains true even if one separates out the forty-one school cases and thus holds that factor constant.[22] The differences in treating the policy of different governments can be explained in one (or both) of two ways. The courts may simply have been paying greater deference to state legislatures in particular, and more generally to governmental policy makers of broader scope and legitimacy. Alternatively, it may have been the case that local governmental units—out of either ignorance or brashness— were more often torturing or fudging constitutional clauses.

IN SUMMARY

Constitutional litigation over church-state issues originates in ways and places that do not fall easily into explanatory patterns. In con-

[22] Thus in the 41 school cases (with a total of 54 governmental policy makers), the final decisions were separationist in 9 of 22 cases of state policy (40.9 percent), in 3 of 5 local policies (60.0 percent), and in 19 of 27 instances of school district policy (70.4 percent).

siderable part that is so because the origins vary so greatly with the kinds of public policies challenged. Different policies originate in different locales and disturb different values and interests. But three generalizations can be made about the origins of church-state cases. They are more common in the metropolitan areas and in the least Protestant states. Second, they originate in two general ways: they grow out of intense community conflict, or they result from the desire of litigating groups to begin a test case. Finally, there is a marked tendency for one church-state case to spawn another.

Once begun, the church-state cases of 1951 to 1971 became constitutional precedents in unusual numbers. Something more than 40 percent of all cases probably reached high state or federal appellate courts—and thus the kind of recorded status that brought them into constitutional use. Ten of the 58 adversary cases in those appellate courts (17.2 percent of them) reached the U.S. Supreme Court. Such exceptional appellate rates are perhaps the best indication that litigation over church-state questions was at floodtide in these decades. They perhaps also explain the fact that the reduction in number of cases still produced an accurate sample of the issues of the entire set of cases. The larger the sample, the smaller the distortions in it.

In the 58 adversary cases to reach high appellate courts, the separationist interests recorded final victories in half. They also won 6 of 10 cases in the U.S. Supreme Court. The appellate courts were, in fact, considerably more separationist than the trial courts, and because of their willingness to overturn public policy, considerably more activist. The separationist score in appellate courts was even higher in the school cases, a subset of church-state cases that in so many ways seems to have been special in the whole universe of cases.

Two facts predominate in this chapter: the high percentage of cases carried to appellate courts, and the high percentage of separationist (plaintiff) victories in those courts. One can reasonably speculate that the two conclusions are related. The hope of ultimate victory must certainly have encouraged the litigation of the separationist groups and plaintiffs, even through their losses in trial courts. It is, indeed, hard to imagine a sustained strategy of litigation without substantial prospects of access to and victory in the appellate courts.

XI | THE FRIENDLY CASES

Amid the turmoil and controversy surrounding so much of constitutional litigation over church-state relations, there is a small island of quiet, almost isolated litigation: the nine friendly suits brought to the courts by plaintiffs and defendants agreed on the necessity of a quick, definitive settling of the constitutional question. They often slip through the courts quickly and almost unnoticed, free of the notoriety and tumult that surrounds so much of the adversary litigation in the field. And yet they weigh as heavily as constitutional precedent as do the decisions in the most openly contested and most celebrated of the adversary cases.

Precisely because they are not truly adversary cases, the friendly cases have a process and dynamic of their own. Their plaintiffs, for instance, do not usually share with the plaintiffs in adversary cases great convictions about issues of separation. Nor do the plaintiffs here share the role in originating or organizing the litigation. They are passive, in fact, as virtually all actors in the friendly cases are passive—committed not to one side in the church-state conflict but rather to the conflict's speedy settlement.

A PROFILE OF THE NINE

The friendly cases introduce new sets of actors and mechanisms of litigation to our account. Improbable as it might seem, they reveal the nationally known and well-connected bond attorneys of New York and Chicago as considerable forces in church-state litigation. Five of the nine friendly suits (see box) were staged to determine the constitutionality of state bond issues, the proceeds of which were eventually intended to assist the construction of buildings at hospitals or colleges under the direction of various religious orders or denominations. It was the bonding attorneys who ordered the litigation so that they could certify the legality and constitutionality of the bond issues. Without that certification, of course, a bond issue will not sell. The bonding attorneys not

258

only dictate the need for constitutional clarification, but they dictate as well the extent of clarification necessary. They often provide local counsel with lists of the constitutional questions they consider unsettled, and it is usually their advice that determines whether an appeal from the high state court to the U.S. Supreme Court is called for.[1]

The remaining four cases defy categorization. One of them, the Michigan test of a state constitutional amendment, raises some of the most interesting questions of all—including questions about the line between adversary and friendly proceedings. But these four share with the five bond cases the common attribute of being friendly cases; at bottom the interests of both parties in bringing the litigation are similar or identical. In addition, they share a number of secondary characteristics.

The nine friendly cases are, first of all, all state cases; the rule of "case or controversy" in the federal courts would prohibit their origin in the federal courts. The history of their attempts to get to the U.S. Supreme Court has been a checkered one. The Michigan case had been granted certiorari by the U.S. Supreme Court, but the accommodationists appealing it withdrew their appeal after the Court's decision in the parochaid cases of 1971. Both the New Jersey and South Carolina bond cases were accepted by the Court, and, after their earlier decisions were vacated summarily on June 28, 1971, they were remanded to their respective state supreme courts for decisions in the light of the Court's historic decisions of that same day. The only other case to approach the portals of the Court, the Vermont bond case, was withdrawn while the Court was weighing the jurisdictional question. The reasons are not altogether clear, but one of the religious colleges that would have been helped under the bonding program rejected the state bonding assistance. Apparently the managers of the case thought that the Court might not look with special favor on a "made" case contesting a moot issue.[2]

Furthermore, the nine friendly suits all involved statewide

[1] The firm of John Mitchell, better known for his service as attorney general and in the elections of Richard M. Nixon, served as the bond attorneys advising both Vermont and New Jersey in these cases.

[2] As this paragraph suggests, the insistence of the federal courts on cases presenting a "case or controversy" does not prevent the Supreme Court's accepting cases of dubious adversary origins from the state courts. It should also be added that after the 1971 cutoff date of this study, the case of *Hunt* v. *McNair* returned to the U.S. Supreme Court for final disposition.

NINE FRIENDLY ENCOUNTERS

The nine friendly cases can be divided into two groups: the five testing the validity of state bonding programs, and the four miscellaneous cases.

The Bond Cases

Truitt v. *Board of Public Works,* a suit testing loans to religious hospitals under the Maryland Hospital Construction Loan Act of 1964, the dollars for the loans to be raised by state bonds.

Vermont Buildings Agency v. *Mann,* a test of the plan whereby the Educational Buildings Financing Agency of the state floated bonds to build buildings for private colleges and then leased them to the colleges with title to pass to the colleges at the termination of the lease.

Hunt v. *McNair,* a test of a South Carolina bonding program similar to Vermont's, the purpose again being the indirect use of the state's ability to issue tax-free (and therefore lower interest) bonds as a way of lowering finance charges for the colleges.

Clayton v. *Kervick,* a test of the New Jersey bonding plan, very similar to those of Vermont and South Carolina, to underwrite building at private colleges and universities.

Nohrr v. *Brevard County,* challenge of the Florida law permitting the creation of county bonding authorities to function very similarly to the statewide agencies in Vermont, South Carolina, and New Jersey.

The Other Cases

State v. *Nusbaum,* a case involving the Wisconsin law requiring some school boards to bus pupils of private schools to the nearest public school; arranged by two state officials.

Community Council v. *Jordan,* a test of the payment of state funds to the Salvation Army, a religious social service organization, as the agency to handle emergency relief cases in Maricopa County, Arizona.

260

> *Hartness* v. *Patterson,* a suit questioning the constitution-
> ality of a South Carolina program of tuition grants to
> students attending the private colleges of the state.
>
> *In Re Proposal C,* a complex testing of the range and
> application of a recently passed amendment to the Michi-
> gan constitution, which in general terms prohibited state
> aid to religious education.

policy: only in the Florida bonding case was there even a mixture
of local with state policy making. None of them except the Florida
case really had an identifiable site in a local community. But even
though all involved church-state questions of aid to religions—
rather than issues of religion in public life—only 2 of the 9 (con-
trasted with 41 of 58 adversary cases) concerned the elementary
and secondary schools. In view of that fact, the decisions are predictably far less separationist than those in the adversary cases.
In only two of them was the outcome separationist; there were
six accommodationist outcomes, and one very mixed and ambiguous outcome—the decision in that mysteriously complex Michigan
case.

Two more characteristics should complete this short profile of
the friendly cases. They have gained rapidly in popularity after
a late advent in this area of constitutional litigation. Eight of the
nine fall in the period between 1965 and 1971. Only *State* v. *Nusbaum* precedes it. And second, none of them enjoyed group sponsorship. The groups did enter them in other roles, however; in
2 of the 9, one of the three separationist leaders played an intermediate role, and in 2 more, several of them entered as amici.
In the 9 cases generally, the incidence of amici and intervenors
was almost as great as it was in the 58 adversary cases.

THE BORDERLINE: WHO'S FRIENDS AND WHEN

The line between adversary and friendly suit is not always easy
to discover. The friendly suit does have an artificial, a "made"
aspect about it; but so does some adversary litigation. For example, the *Squires* case from Augusta, Maine, originated when both
sides in a bitterly fought local dispute over bus rides to parochial
school pupils agreed to a strategy by which the council would ap-

propriate a token sum for the busses and the opponents would bring a test case. The most basic element of the friendly suit would appear to be the lack of strongly opposed interests; at least one of the parties is only nominally upholding a position or set of interests. The litigation is "friendly" in the sense that plaintiffs and defendants arrange it jointly and amicably.

All of the ambiguities—and many of the shortcomings—of the friendly suit are very obvious in the celebrated Michigan case. It was set in a policy context of almost Byzantine complexity. The Michigan legislature passed a $22 million program of aid to non-public schools, most of them Catholic parochial schools. At the legislature's request, the state's supreme court considered the program's constitutionality and affirmed it, 4–3, in an advisory opinion. Opponents then circulated petitions to place a constitutional amendment (Proposal C) on the November 1970 ballot, declaring programs of such aid to religious schools unconstitutional. Even though the proposal had the requisite number of signatures, it quickly became enmeshed in political controversy. The attorney general ruled it was an invalid proposal because of its ambiguity, and the state Board of Canvassers initially excluded it from the ballot. Only a decision (5–2) of the Michigan Supreme Court put it back.

The amendment touched almost all aspects of the November election. The attorney general, Frank Kelley, opposed it, and so did the incumbent governor, William Millikin; both were candidates for reelection. Millikin's Democratic opponent, after some initial fence-straddling, finally supported the amendment. The politics of the amendment itself were in the hands of two statewide ad hoc groups: Citizens Against Parochaid, headed by Erwin Ellmann, president of the state ACLU affiliate and drafter of the amendment; and Citizens Against Proposal C, headed by Stuart Hubbell, a national leader of Citizens for Educational Freedom. Much of the debate over Proposal C hinged on its scope, Kelley charging that it was cast so broadly as to threaten tax exemptions on religious school properties and a number of programs of federal aid to Michigan schools, and Ellmann labelling these sweeping explications so much "poppycock."[3] On November 3rd, the

[3] Proposal "C," a proposed amendment to Article 8, section 2 of the Michigan Constitution of 1963, reads: "No public monies or property shall be appropriated or paid or any public credit utilized, by the legislature or any other political subdivision or agency of the state directly or indirectly to aid or maintain any private, denominational or other nonpublic, pre-

262

amendment carried with about sixty percent of the vote, while both Millikin and Kelley won reelection. On the same day two liberal Democrats and former governors of the state, G. Mennen Williams and John Swainson, were elected to the Michigan Supreme Court.

The victory of "C" settled nothing. In a postelection opinion the attorney general interpreted it to stop a large range of programs, including shared-time programs and auxiliary services— reiterating generally his preelection position. The proponents, including Ellmann, repeated their arguments that it was never intended to do so. The state Board of Education received the attorney general's opinion at its November meeting, and acted on its basis. Ellmann, refused even a hearing by the board, charged that the old opponents of the amendment were intentionally interpreting it in such a way as to threaten its constitutionality under the U.S. Constitution. In the middle of the continuing controversy, both sides began to plan court action. Ellmann and the remnants of Citizens Against Parochaid were anxious and willing to support a challenge to the attorney general's opinion. The governor and his advisors were meeting over their strategy, especially since the amendment was scheduled to go into force on the 18th of December. In their planning they were in contact with Hubbell, who had grown up with Millikin in Traverse City, and Hubbell, in turn, was in touch with Washington attorneys and the staff of the U.S. Catholic Conference.

Into this supercharged legal atmosphere stepped Harry Running, long-time attorney for the Traverse City schools. At his suggestion the Traverse City School Board voted at its November 10th meeting to bring a suit for a declaratory judgment of the rights of the school district under the new amendment to continue its shared-time program, under which it admitted students of Catholic schools for certain classes in the public schools. The Traverse City locale raised a good many suspicions that the suit was merely a stalking horse for the bigger things Millikin and Hubbell had planned, but all parties denied it. Running indeed opposed Hubbell's later intervention in the case, and for his part, Hubbell tried to dissuade

---

elementary, elementary, or secondary school. No payment, credit, tax benefit, exemption or deduction, tuition voucher, subsidy, grant or loan of public monies or property shall be provided, directly or indirectly, to support the attendance of any student or the employment of any person at any such nonpublic school or at any location or institution where instruction is offered in whole or in part to such nonpublic school students. The legislature may provide for the transportation of students to and from any school."

Running, arguing that the suit was too narrow in scope and misplaced in locale. But Running persisted and the case moved to trial in the local court.

Apparently at this point the governor and the accommodationists decided to move into the framework of Running's modest suit. The attorney general, a defendant in Running's suit, responded with a counterclaim for a declaration of rights on a range of topics suggested by the new amendment but never even intimated by Running. At the same time Hubbell organized a group of defendant intervenors representing the schools, parents, and teachers whose aid was threatened. Hubbell's counterclaim was even broader than Kelley's; it charged that the amendment had been unconstitutionally adopted and that it violated assorted sections of the U.S. Constitution. While these participants negotiated the stipulation of facts in the case—not very substantial by any measure—Ellmann and his forces tried unsuccessfully to intervene as plaintiff intervenors. They succeeded later, but not in time to affect the stipulations.

With the case expanding far beyond Running's initial purposes, on December 4, 1970, the governor reached for a little-used rule of the Michigan Supreme Court under which it could direct a lower court to certify to it for decision certain questions in a case before it.[4] In his executive message the governor noted the passage of the amendment, its imminent enforcement, and the expanded Traverse City litigation. "This matter," he told the justices, "now raises controlling questions of public law which are of such public moment as to require early determination. Dependent upon the resolution of these questions is the immediate administration and operation of the entire elementary and secondary educational program and structure, public and nonpublic, of the State of Michigan." He concluded by suggesting to the court seven questions for certification, and urging it to use its power to direct their certification by the court below.[5] The Supreme Court did so three days later, adopting the governor's seven questions verbatim and adding to them one of its own on the propriety of the process by which the amendment was submitted to and adopted by the voters.

[4] Rule 797 of the Michigan general court rules of 1963.

[5] Executive Message of William G. Milliken, Governor, to the Chief Justice and Associate Justices of the Michigan Supreme Court, December 4, 1970.

Pressed by the considerations of time, the Michigan Supreme Court set December 30th as the deadline for the filing of all briefs and arranged oral argument for the 5th of January, 1971, less than one month from the time it directed certification. It was a timetable that brought the sharpest possible comment from Ellmann:

> Normally, in the adversary appellate proceedings before this Court, an appellant has the obligation to present by brief his reasons why the judgment of the lower tribunal should be reversed. The appellee is then permitted to respond by brief. In this proceeding there is no judgment or order from any inferior tribunal which is being reviewed and all participants are invited to submit 'briefs' simultaneously. No one can do more than conjecture what any other participant may comment, what authorities may be cited, what arguments may be raised. Instead of an adversary proceeding, various Hindu blind men are separately set to evaluating an elephant. Intervening plaintiffs are particularly handicapped since they are not privy to the inner councils of Traverse City or Lansing; they are burdened to defend their interests against accusations not yet known. While this may be congenial to the inquisitorial system of the Continent, it is not sanctioned by the usages of Anglo-American law.[6]

On March 31st the court decided, 4 to 3, in favor of the "constitutionality" of the amendment and in favor of an interpretation closer to the Ellmann position than to that of the attorney general. The two new justices, former governors Williams and Swainson, hearing their first case on the court, voted with the majority.

It is, in short, an incredible and troubling case—perhaps the most troubling of all the sixty-seven. What started as an adversary proceeding was transmuted into a very friendly case lacking even the pretense of an adversary argument. So lacking was it in the adversary quality, indeed, that in the end one cannot say who were the plaintiffs and defendants or which parties won or lost. Running, Hubble, and the attorney general—all accommodationists to some degree—stipulated the facts without the participation of even a nominal defender of separationism. The defendants and intervening defendants filed counterclaims that had nothing to do with Running's little case. Ellmann and his plaintiff intervenors were

[6] Pp. 16–17 of Ellmann's brief for the intervening plaintiffs before the Michigan Supreme Court.

admitted late to the proceeding, and in the Christmas mail rush he received notice of the deadline for briefs less than forty-eight hours before the deadline fell. It is, in sum, hard not to agree with Ellmann's conclusion that the case was "no bona fide lawsuit but a contrivance for shortcutting the normal judicial function."[7]

In its transmutation the original Traverse City case disappeared. What eventuated was really a judicial refighting of the whole controversy over Proposal C—and with virtually the same leading personnel. At the same time it was a friendly suit verging on an advisory opinion. It combined much of the nonadversary form and the abstract issues of an advisory opinion with the binding, precedent-yielding quality of a friendly suit. A case can be made that it thus combined the worst of both worlds. What is especially unsettling is that great and complex issues of constitutional law should be settled in such a process.

It would be reassuring to be able to say that the Michigan case was some sort of judicial freak. But there is another instance among these nine cases of a similar carelessness with the expectations of constitutional litigation. In the Florida bond case the authority of Brevard County was poised to support the financing of a dormitory for the Florida Institute of Technology in the city of Melbourne. The F.I.T.—a locally used abbreviation—had no religious ties whatsoever. Bonding attorneys apparently wanted all conceivable issues clarified, and the church-state issue was litigated and settled in the Florida Supreme Court without any apparent question about its relationship to the facts of the case. It is ironic to note that the state supreme court was so troubled by the complexity of an unrelated bonding issue in the case that it asked for additional briefing and oral argument on the issue, and then appointed an experienced bonding attorney to file an amicus curiae brief on the question. Such scrupulousness unhappily did not prevent the court from deciding a church-state question that had no basis in fact whatsoever in the litigation.[8]

So some friendly cases are more amicable than others. The great majority do follow the traditional forms and norms of adversary litigation even if, indeed, they are not truly adversary cases. At least two of these nine do not, however. That ratio is perhaps just

---

[7] *Ibid.,* p. 4.

[8] One supposes that this is the reason (or a reason) why in this case alone of the five bond cases the attorneys made no attempt to go to the United States Supreme Court.

large enough to confirm the deep distrust and suspicions that attend these cases and their equivalents in other areas of the law.

ORIGIN AND BIRTH

The Michigan case—extraordinary as it is in most respects—shares with the eight other friendly cases a justification that is primarily temporal. Interested parties resorted to the friendly suit because a deadline demanded speedy resolution of the issues. In the bond cases it was the need to clear up the constitutional questions before the bonds could be sold. Reliance on a true case or controversy rests on the assumption that policy can apply and be in effect so long as it is not challenged. That assumption does not reckon with the market mechanism, for the sale of bonds simply does not proceed without the settlement of the constitutional uncertainty. The argument for speed looms large in the other friendly cases as well. In the Wisconsin bus controversy, for instance, a whole year's set of contracts with the bus operators were about to be signed by various school districts.

And speed there is in friendly litigation. In Brevard County, Florida, for instance, the county educational buildings authority was formed on February 11, 1970, and the friendly suit had a trial court decision by May of the same year and a final resolution in the Florida Supreme Court by April of the next. Among the fifty-eight adversary cases the median number of months between the date of the trial or the hearing in the case and the final substantive decision was 18 months; in these nine cases it was 5 months.[9] (That figure of 5 months is so low partly because three of these cases were originally heard and decided by state supreme courts.)

The decision to initiate a friendly suit in several other of these cases was conceived and sealed as the policy passed through the legislative process. In the Wisconsin bus case the state legislature debated the constitutional issue at length, the state Senate even asking for an opinion from Attorney General John Reynolds. Reynolds opined that the issue was doubtful, that he was uncertain, and that "possibly the Wisconsin Supreme Court would hold that the transportation of parochial school pupils violates the Wisconsin Constitution." When Governor Gaylord Nelson signed the mea-

[9] The median number of months for the nine friendly cases includes the remanding of two back to state supreme courts by the U.S. Supreme Court after the June, 1971, cutoff date for this study.

267

sure, he did so "with the request that the attorney general seek
to bring the issue before the supreme court for adjudication at
an early date."[10] Similarly, the South Carolina legislature agonized
over the constitutional issue as it considered tuition grants for college students. "The constitutionality of the legislation is in question," wrote one newspaper report, "and a test case seems inevitable once the bill has been signed into law by Gov. McNair. Only
$5,000 was appropriated to underwrite the expected test case."[11]
What the observer after the fact cannot know, of course, is the
extent to which those constitutional objections masked more specific policy opposition and the extent to which, therefore, elected
officials passed the policy "buck" to the courts in the guise of a
constitutional issue.

It appears easier, however, to conceive a friendly suit than to
give birth to it. In some cases there has been considerable planning
and arranging of the occasion, the "conflict," in the litigation. But
there also appear to be traditions for handling such matters in
some states—ways or mechanisms that have been used in the past,
and more importantly, to which the courts of the state have not
objected. There appear to be, in other words, traditional clothings
or veilings for friendly suits, and in many instances they appear
to have developed because of the jurisdictional rules or traditions
of the state courts.

Two general routes or mechanisms account for six of the nine
friendly cases. Three of the cases "began" when some state fiscal
official held up the funds intended for the program under suspicion.
A New Jersey state treasurer refused to release funds to the agency
charged with issuing bonds for financing new buildings at private
colleges. The agency was forced to sue him. In Arizona the state
auditor refused to approve a check intended for reimbursement
of the Salvation Army. In the Wisconsin case the mechanism was
more complicated, but basically the same; the secretary of administration (Nusbaum) refused a voucher (for $23.71) of the Superin-
tendant of Public Instruction for forms and materials with which
to begin to administer the busing program, forcing the attorney
general to seek a declaratory judgment on the question of constitutionality and a writ of mandamus compelling the secretary of ad-

[10] Reynolds in an opinion of the attorney general of August 1, 1961;
Nelson quoted in the *Milwaukee Journal* of January 26, 1962. One could
argue that the governor's request did not necessarily imply a friendly suit,
but in reality it is hard to see what role the attorney general would play
in any other litigation.
[11] Kent Krell in *The State* of Columbia, South Carolina (April 24, 1970).

ministration to approve the voucher.[12] In another trio of cases state officials and/or private interests arranged for taxpayer suits challenging the state policy. Apparently in such instances the plaintiff's attorney is recruited first, and then—often with his help—the plaintiff. Except for the fact that the challengers may not have the same depth of feeling for the separationist position as genuine adversaries might, this variety of friendly litigation most closely approximates the adversary constitutional test case.[13]

The other three of the nine began in more idiosyncratic, even bizarre, fashions. Of the transmogrification of the Traverse City case into an inquiry about Proposal C we have already spoken. The origin of the test of the Vermont bonding program is recounted in the court records. The Vermont Educational Buildings Financing Agency passed two resolutions authorizing the execution of leases with two Vermont colleges for buildings to be underwritten by the agency's bonding authority. The chairman of the agency refused to sign the leases, explaining:

> As chairman of the Agency, I have conferred with bond counsel in New York and personal counsel here in Vermont concerning certain constitutional problems they see connected with the sale of bonds of the Agency necessary to finance the foregoing projects. Counsel have informed me that there could well be constitutional problems which could affect the marketability until the Vermont Supreme Court rules that the issuance of our bonds is constitutional. I am further advised that it would be well to proceed to that end before we do anything else.
>
> Because of possible constitutional objections pointed out by counsel, which will be stated further along in this letter, it has been recommended by them that I refuse to take action described above until a final judicial determination can be obtained, whether in the form of a declaratory judgment or otherwise, which would resolve any possible constitutional objections. Therefore, I am following the advice of counsel and respectfully refuse to sign the Leases and Subleases as directed by the resolutions dated January 10, 1967, until there is judicial determination relating thereto.[14]

---

[12] The three cases in the order discussed were: *Clayton* v. *Kervick, State* v. *Nusbaum,* and *Community Council* v. *Jordan.*

[13] These three cases were *Truitt* v. *Board of Public Works, Hartness* v. *Patterson,* and *Hunt* v. *McNair.*

[14] P. 143 of the printed record of the case; on file with the Clerk of the Vermont Supreme Court. The specific document is a memorandum to the agency board by Daulton Mann (August 30, 1967).

Mann concluded his memo by requesting appropriate legal action to clarify the issue. The agency's board obliged by bringing suit to compel him to sign and execute the leases.

Finally, the ninth case, the Florida bond case from Brevard County, developed according to provisions of Florida law for testing bonding authority. State statutes envision the agency's suing the state for a declaratory judgment of its rights under the state statutes and constitution; they also invite any private parties who object to come forward and join as intervenors in the proceedings.[15] The Brevard County authority brought the suit and arranged for a local attorney who would intervene and raise all of the constitutional objections the Chicago bonding attorney outlined, and who would (and did) carry the appeal to the Florida Supreme Court.

THE ISSUE OF THE FRIENDLY SUIT

In one long rhetorical question, Erwin Ellmann asked the Michigan Supreme Court in the assault on Proposal C:

> May this Court, at the instance of the Governor, undertake to determine issues under both federal and state constitutions involving the hypothetical application of the Michigan Constitution, as amended, to various educational activities in the State, in the absence of necessary and indispensible parties having vital interests therein, without any evidentiary record following adversary hearing, and in proceedings in which genuinely adverse parties have either been barred from intervening or given inadequate opportunity to protect their interests?[16]

The question invites its own answer, and while it is a statement on the proceedings in one case, it also makes the main case against friendly suits of all kinds in all jurisdictions. It reflects the widely held belief that the adversary clash of interests, evidence, and argument in disagreements rooted in reality gives the appellate court the best and fullest materials for its deliberation. And in these days after the Supreme Court's statement in the *Button* case, the Ellman question suggests another argument: that courts should not, any

---

[15] Section 75.08 of the *Florida Statutes Annotated.*
[16] P. ix of the brief of the plaintiff intervenors before the Michigan Supreme Court in the case *In Re Proposal C.*

more than legislatures, exclude any concerned interests from representation in the process of fashioning great declarations of constitutional policy.

The participants and the states often struggle to take the curse
off the friendly case. In *Hunt* v. *McNair,* for example, the bonding
attorneys in Charleston, South Carolina, advertised the case to invite the intervention of interested parties, hoping to attract as
broad a range of interests and views as possible. (The Florida law
under which the Brevard County case developed in effect extends
the same invitation to interested parties.) The State of New Jersey
turned over the defense of the state treasurer in its bond case to
a private law firm of stature in order to avoid having the attorney
general's office represent both parties in the case. In a more general
way, everyone hopes that the ethical and professional standards
of the bar will guarantee the vigor of the argument regardless of
the parties' preferences, and that they will work against collusion
between the parties. The hope persists that adversary debate and
argument is possible without adversary parties.

And yet the concern remains about these cases as vehicles for
constitutional interpretation. Attorneys often have feelings of un-
ease or guilt about participating in them. The attorney general of
one of the states involved in these cases continues to be "somewhat
concerned about the ethical considerations involved in this procedure and somewhat dubious about the value of the procedure in
that it does not always produce an honestly litigated case."[17] And
there are, indeed, causes for concern in these nine friendly cases:

> The entire Michigan case on Proposal C can be read as an object
> lesson on the dangers of friendly cases.

> The Florida Supreme Court in its bond case decided a com-
> pletely fictitious church-state question.

> In both of the South Carolina cases the private accommodation-
> ist interests had to organize the separationist challenge to state
> policy; that is, they recruited the attorneys who challenged their
> own interests.

> The same assistant attorney general worked on the briefs for
> both sides in the Arizona Salvation Army case.

[17] A letter to the author. I have granted the writer's request for anonymity
for obvious reasons; it should be clear, however, that the expression of
skepticism applies generally to friendly test cases rather than to this particular church-state litigation.

Except for the New Jersey bond case—in which the American Jewish Congress intervened—separationist interests really went unrepresented in these friendly suits. If there was to be a genuine and effective adversary argument in these cases, therefore, it would have to depend on the quality and standards of counsel rather than on the clash of opposing groups.

The important operational question thus comes down to the quality of the argument and record that counsel presented appellate courts in these cases. While that is not an easy question to answer, consider these relevant data:

> Plaintiff attorneys attended prestige law schools somewhat less frequently than did plaintiff attorneys in the adversary cases (22.2 versus 27.6 percent).

> But six of the nine had either an "a" or "b" rating with Martindale-Hubbell, an incidence greater than the 41.4 percent among the adversary lawyers.

> None of the nine attorneys, however, had any history of involvement in church-state causes or litigation.

> Only one of the nine (11.1 percent) went to trial to develop any kind of a factual record, a percentage in marked contrast to the 41.4 percent of the adversary attorneys.

The conclusions are apparent, and they are supported as well by personal observation and judgment. The plaintiffs' attorneys in these nine cases were well-connected, well-regarded, conscientious members of the local bar. Their work certainly never fell below the high level of competence one might expect. For a number of reasons—the pressures of time and their own church-state (and general civil liberties) inexperience among them—they limited their "cases" largely to well-researched briefs and oral argument. By no stretch of the imagination could one say that the separationist interests were represented at the level of effectiveness the ACLU, AJC, or AU achieved during the same years in the cases they sponsored.

The friendly cases persisted, and still persist, because constitutional questions often cannot go unresolved. At least their resolution often cannot await the more or less fortuitous combination of actors and events that will resolve them in the normal course of adversary litigation. The friendly suit is a reflection of various needs to know, or, conversely, of various needs to avoid constitutional uncertainty—the bond market's inability to accept uncertainty, the public official's unwillingness to accept uncertainty about his constitutional responsibility, even the legislature's or executive's inability to resolve constitutional uncertainty with their own judgments. If it is true, as the old saw says, that it is often more important that an issue be settled than that it be settled correctly, one may have all the justification he needs for the friendly suit.[18]

A NOTE ON THE ADVISORY OPINIONS

There are at least eleven states that permit, even require, their high state courts to give advisory opinions.[19] Those opinions are even further removed from the standards of adversary proceedings than are the friendly suits. A legislature or a governor usually poses a legal question or set of questions for the judges' opinion. The questions anticipate rather than reflect real controversies, and in the format there is not even the semblance or fiction of adversary parties. The judges do not have the advantage of adversary argument unless they order it. For all of these reasons the courts that grant them have "sharply restricted the precedential effect of their adversary opinions."[20] Since they are not either adjudications or precedents in any real sense, the advisory opinions have been excluded from the universe of cases in this study.

For all of their precedential infirmities, advisory opinions did have considerable impact on the constitutional politics of church-state relations between 1951 and 1971. There were nine of them in the period: three each from Massachusetts and New Hampshire, and one each from Delaware, Maine, and Michigan (Table 11–1). The first of them, and the least typical, came from New Hampshire in 1955, and concerned the constitutionality of state aid to religious hospitals for nurses' training. (The New Hampshire Supreme Court gave its blessing.) The other eight opinions were all given between 1966 and 1970, and all eight involved proposed legislation to aid religious education in some way or another. Six con-

[18] For an excellent survey of both judicial practice and basic issues, see the editors' note, "Judicial Determinations in Nonadversary Proceedings," *Harvard Law Review* 72 (1959), 723–737.

[19] They are Alabama, Colorado, Delaware, Florida, Maine, Massachusetts, Michigan, New Hampshire, North Carolina, Rhode Island, and South Dakota. All but Michigan are mentioned in the note, "Advisory Opinions on the Constitutionality of Statutes," *Harvard Law Review* 69 (1956), 1302–1313. Michigan added the practice in its 1963 constitution.

[20] "Judicial Determinations in Nonadversary Proceedings," p. 732.

TABLE 11-1

Nine Advisory Opinions on Church-State Constitutional
Issues, 1951–1971

State and Year	Source of Request	Policy in Doubt	Opinion, Division of Court	Church-State Decision
1. New Hampshire 1955	House of Representatives	aid to religious hospitals	approve 5–0	accommoda-tionist
2. Delaware 1966	Governor	bus rides to religious schools	disapprove 3–0	separationist
3. New Hampshire 1967	Governor	aid to religious schools	disapprove 4–1	separationist
4. Massachusetts 1968	Senate	bonds for buildings of colleges	disapprove 7–0	separationist
5. New Hampshire 1969	Senate	aid to religious schools	split 5–0	part accomm., part separa-tionist
6. Maine 1970	House of Representatives	aid to religious schools	disapprove 4–2	separationist
7. Michigan 1970	Legislature (both houses)	aid to religious schools	approve 4–2	accommoda-tionist
8. Massachusetts 1970	Senate	aid to religious schools	disapprove 7–0	separationist
9. Massachusetts 1970	Senate	voucher plan for parent's choice of school	disapprove 7–0	separationist

CITATIONS: 1, 113 A2d 114; 2, 216 A2d 668; 3, 233 A2d 832; 4, 236 NE2d 523;
5, 258 A2d 343; 6, 261 A2d 58; 7, 180 NW2d 265; 8, 258 NE2d 779; 9, 259
NE2d 564.

cerned some form of aid to parochial schools, and one each involved bus rides for pupils in religious schools and state financing for buildings of religious colleges and universities.

As Table 11–1 also suggests, the request for the advisory opinion most often came from one or both houses of the state legislature. The opinions were overwhelmingly separationist—more so than the degree of separationism of the U.S. Supreme Court, and often in advance of that court's rulings. These opinions also had an advantage in speed, even over the friendly suits. The median time for decision in the nine was exactly thirty-two days after the posing of the questions, and the longest wait was less than three months.

In view of the speed of the process, it is surprising how many interested parties did manage to file briefs before the courts. In fact, there appear to have been no briefs in only one of the nine considerations (the one from Maine). At least one of the three leading separationist groups had a role in five of the nine. The usual role was that of an amicus, but in at least one the ACLU helped shape the questions posed, and in another the AU assisted a special counsel appointed by the Delaware Supreme Court to represent separationist interests. Given the speed with which these high courts moved toward giving their advice, however, it is problematic how effective those speedy representations were.

How important or definitive are the advisory opinions as constitutional statements? Even though the state courts may in some instances not consider them to have the force of precedent, state legislatures act as if they do. Compliance with these nine opinions was one hundred percent. By their nature, of course, the advisory opinions add little to the fabric of constitutional interpretation in more general terms; courts outside of the state of their origin do not often cite them. Their major impact is as an authoritative statement of constitutional limits in the policy-making processes of one state. More specifically, they shaped the policy battle over aid to parochial schools in several states just as surely as decisions in adversary litigation would have.

IN CONCLUSION

There were nine friendly cases and nine advisory opinions on church-state questions in the two decades before 1971. To an amazing degree their histories are parallel. Sixteen of the 18—8 of the 9 in each group—fell between 1965 and 1971, the final one-third of the period. Furthermore, fully 7 of 9 friendly cases and 8 of 9 advisory opinions—15 of the total of 18—concerned some form of aid to religious educational institutions or their pupils. The increasing importance of nonadversary settlement of church-state issues is thus closely tied to the crisis in religious education in the 1960s and 1970s, and the attempts of many states to do something about it.

One can only speculate about the reasons for this trend to nonadversary resolution of constitutional issues. It may be that state courts and public officials are becoming more tolerant of speedy nonadversary resolutions of constitutional uncertainty. On the other hand, the explanation may be in a combination of two related factors. The fact that the public policy involved here is state policy, rather than local policy, makes a significant difference. In the entire period between 1951 and 1971, the push for parochaid in the late 1960s resulted in the first real involvement of state governments in church-state issues. The structure of the issue and the statewide "site" of the policy, in other words, make these nonadversary tactics more likely. Secondly, although it is a point hard to document, one suspects that behind this rush to constitutional certitude is a good deal of old-fashioned buckpassing. Legislatures, finding these to be inflamed questions, moved the debate from the policy level to the constitutional level in the hope that the courts could resolve the policy conflict in their own special ways.

Regardless of cause or origin, however, the fact remains that in the period between 1951 and 1971 a very substantial portion of authoritative judicial statements on the constitutional law of church and state was made in nonadversary proceedings in which the well-organized interests were but fitfully represented. (One need only remember that the kind of sponsorship role at which the ACLU, AJC, and AU had become so adept was completely absent in these proceedings.) It was, in brief, a relatively unnoticed but portentous development in the politics of this constitutional litigation.

XII | THE IMMEDIATE IMPACTS

In the days before the onset of "political jurisprudence," a constitutional decision was considered to have one chief "impact" or consequence. It became a binding precedent by which similar issues would be settled in the future. Under the rule of stare decisis, the decision itself became a rule, and individual decisions added together formed more general rules or "doctrines." With the understanding of the political and governmental nature of the judicial process, perspectives on "impact" have shifted from the decision to the entire case. Now—conceptually at least—those impacts embrace all conceivable consequences of the events and decisions of a case for any other actor or process in the political system, if not, indeed, in the society itself. One has troubling visions of standing in a room of mirrors and seeing images reflecting into infinity.[1]

The new jurisprudence has also shifted the time perspectives on impact. The earlier, formal view of the judicial process considered as "impact" only a linear sequence of events after the final appellate court decision was handed down. In a somewhat physical sense, the final decision in the case stamped its own impact on the body of precedents that would guide future courts. Now, however, we realize that the impact of the case may well commence even before it comes to trial. The early impact of litigation may in some instances even affect the outcome itself. Community furor may, for example, affect the ability of a beleaguered school board to reach a compromise settlement in a case or to appeal an unfavorable decision. A constitutional case and decision thus produce a series of successive impacts, perhaps beginning as early as the first plans to initiate it.

In such an expanded view of impact there is virtually no limit to the types and kinds of impacts a constitutional case may have.

[1] A note on definitions and vocabulary is necessary. The term "aftermath" is used very similarly to the term "impact" as I have used it: a generic term that includes all consequences or results. The terms "compliance" and "enforcement" refer to one variety of impact, that concerned with the application and self-application of judicial decisions to further behavior.

277

The litigation may distort, even change, the lives of the participants. It may shock and scar the community in which it takes place. It affects the courts that must decide it—the effects on the Supreme Court of its unpopular decisions in the prayer cases began to subside only some ten years after the decision in the first of them. Constitutional decisions, moreover, alter the public policy debate either by affirming or by overturning public policy. They may spur new political activity or negate the old. For confirmation of the reality of the "political jurisprudence" lies precisely in the fact that what happens in the court affects the rest of the political system; that when, for instance, the Supreme Court invalidates some form of state aid to parochial schools, it sets off a search for other forms of aid that may be constitutional, and it touches the very survival of religious schools in American society.

THE INITIAL IMPACTS

The impact of the litigation per se is of a kind quite different from the legally binding impact of the decision or outcome of the case. The initial shock of the litigation generally strikes both the local community and some or all of the principal actors in the case. Especially in cases such as these, in which a minority of separationists are asserting constitutional guarantees against the wishes of the majority, the heaviest impact hits the individual or a small number of individuals whom the majority views as the instigators of the litigation.

If there is to be an impact on the individual participant, there must be an outraged community with a large number of aroused, angered, and active citizens. They are, by and large, not uncommon in these cases. Almost invariably in the adversary cases the plaintiffs challenged the majority on matters of the greatest emotional intensity: matters of organized religion, religious worship, and ultimate morality. The constitutional questions were easily transmuted into questions of believer versus nonbeliever, God versus anti-God, and (especially in the fifties and sixties) God-fearing "Americanism" versus "atheistic, godless Communism." Furthermore, in the nature of the controversy these issues were often cast in contexts having to do with the education and moral upbringing of the young. Small wonder, then, that they were calculated to explode into full-blown community *causes célèbres*.

Often the reaction—the impact—on the separationist plaintiff

TABLE 12-1

Impact of Case on Community According to the
Relationship between the Site of the Case
and the Policy Challenged

Community Reaction to Case	Litigation Site Same as Policy Site	Litigation Site Smaller than Policy Site
None or little	7 (20.6%)	15 (71.4%)
Some or great	27 (79.4%)	6 (28.6%)
Total	34	21

Note: The universe here is the 58 adversary cases
minus three on which data are missing; thus, a total
of 55 adversary cases.

resulted as the majority focused its outrage on him. Often, too,
the manner and the rhetoric of the litigants contributed to the esca-
lation of the conflict; the trials of Madalyn Murray come to mind.
In other communities, however, the separationist plaintiffs felt the
most severe impact of their litigation even though they did not
engage in that kind of rhetoric. The trials of Harlow Chamberlin
in Miami (see box) are a case in point. The Chamberlin case also
illustrates in one form the fairly complicated mechanics of the impact of a church-state case on a metropolitan area, especially in
the way it creates subissues with subimpacts that reinforce the
main impact.

The immediate impact of litigation actually depends on its relationship to the origin of the policy in dispute. The likelihood of
a community outcry is far greater when the litigation site is the
policy site than it is when the policy locale is broader (Table
12–1).[2] In a test of religious practices in the local schools, separationists challenge public policy made in the community. Other litigation may take place in a jurisdiction narrower than the scope
of the policy. Stefan Aronow's attack on the use of the motto "In
God We Trust" could have taken place anywhere in the United
States. Furthermore, it grew out of no events, no controversy, no

[2] The assessment of community impact reported here and in Table 12–1
needs some explanation. I have assigned cases to categories of community
impact on the basis of impressions gained from interviews and newspaper
accounts of the litigation. Needless to say, these are somewhat crude judgments, and even at that, often not easy to make, especially when the litigation took place some fifteen years or more before my investigations.

CHURCH AND STATE IN DADE COUNTY

Experienced ACLU officials in Miami tried to warn and prepare Harlow Chamberlin for the impact of his suit to halt religious practices in the public schools of Dade County. But even they were taken aback at the virulence of the community reaction. Chamberlin—a self-described "nonatheistic humanist"—lost his job in radio advertising within ten days after the case, and he and his family suffered a storm of harassment, threats, and obscenities by phone and mail. The plaintiffs in the companion suit organized later by the AJC fared no better. Mrs. Elsie Thorner's bridge club suddenly found her "uncongenial," and asked her to resign. The Thorners' children lost playmates, their phone rang at all hours, and people in cruising cars shouted "communist" at the Thorner home.

Unhappiness with religious influences in the Dade County schools had smoldered for some years before the origin of the Chamberlin case in 1959. The ACLU and American Jewish Committee, among others, had sought in 1956 to end the Gideons' distribution of their Bibles in the schools. The school board refused, with only Mrs. Anna B. Meyers, a Jew, voting against distribution. It was a decision in keeping with the prevailing "Bible Belt" fundamentalism of the area. The Bible as divinely inspired writ and true history held a central place in the religious life of many Miamians. Shortly after the initiation of the *Chamberlin* case, indeed, the Greater Miami Council of Churches gathered over 30,000 signatures on "pro-Bible" petitions at 179 churches in the area. The same leadership organized a group of intervenor defendants in the case. As the trial approached, groups and governmental bodies such as the Junior Chamber of Commerce and the Dade County Metropolitan Commission passed resolutions in support of Bible-reading and other religiosity in the public schools.

The trial itself lasted six days. Supporters of Bible-reading were first in line every day before the trial commenced, and so a phalanx of white-shirted, blue-trousered, Bible-toting young men occupied the front two rows of the spectators' sections. Lines of waiting spectators snaked through the corridors outside the courtroom. Inside the attorneys battled: Leo Pfeffer for the consolidated ACLU-AJC forces, and for the school board its attorney, E. F. Brigham, a colorful, stentorian barrister of the old, old school. Brigham played skillfully to the sympathetic crowds in a performance some journalists—inevitably perhaps—likened to that of William Jennings Bryan at the Scopes trial. The Miami *Herald* reported the trial fully and with a good deal of reportorial fairness, but nonetheless with five-column headlines on the front page.

In the summer of 1960, the time of the trial, the religion-in-the-schools issue also permeated the contest for a seat on the school board between Arthur Atkinson, an Episcopalian, and Jack D. Gordon, a Jew. Atkinson ran on a conservative, Bible-reading platform and enjoyed the support of both the Miami Ministerial Association and the Greater Miami Council of Churches. (Atkinson on Gordon: "I don't accuse my opponent of being a Communist. But if something has feathers like a duck, walks like a duck, quacks like a duck, and looks like a duck, it might be a duck." Miami *News* of October 12, 1960.) Gordon, a Democrat and a director of the local ACLU affiliate, had the endorsement of the Miami *Herald,* and won by a small margin.

All of these events happened before the trial court's decision in April of 1961. Under such circumstances a separationist plaintiff's lot is clearly not a happy one.

clash of interests in the San Francisco area. The case went to court there solely because it was the place of Aronow's residence.

Instances in which the litigation site is the policy site—and thus cases more likely to have intense community reaction—are more often those with origins in a particular controversy with involved plaintiffs; they are less likely, that is, to be simply test cases with passive plaintiffs. They are also more apt to be cases involving the elementary and secondary schools. These "local cases" are the ones more likely to be separationist victories, and are most likely to result in the overturn of public policy and thus of majority preferences. Finally, they are more apt to be cases in which the defense really holds the position of the defense. In other cases—say the group-sponsored challenge to a statewide mandatory busing pro-

TABLE 12-2

Impact of Case on Community According to
Presence of Litigation Site in Standard
Metropolitan Statistical Area

Community Reaction to Case	Location of Litigation Site	
	in SMSA	not in SMSA
None or little	17 (48.6%)	3 (17.6%)
Some or great	18 (51.4%)	14 (82.4%)
Total	35	17

Note: The universe of cases here begins with the 58 adversary cases; six are then subtracted either because they have no identifiable site or because of missing data, giving a total of 52.

gram—the particular locale may have been chosen precisely because the sponsors thought the local school boards would not fight too hard, or because they thought community reaction would be less excited than it might be elsewhere in the state.

Furthermore, community reaction differs with the nature of the community. The cases arising outside of metropolitan areas have a far higher incidence of strong community reaction (see Table 12–2). These are the cases in which litigation is often no more than an eruption of old community antagonisms or cleavages, and in which the events of the litigation often divide friends and families. That appears to have been the fate of Commerce, Missouri, a little river town on the banks of the Mississippi below Cape Girardeau, in a 1951 dispute over the use of public funds to bus children to Roman Catholic schools (*McVey* v. *Hawkins*). In the delicate understatement of a small-town paper, "Feeling ran high and a record crowd was at Benton [the county seat] the day the case was heard. . . . This case has been followed with high interest throughout Missouri and the nation."[3] Behind those laconic lines was a history of conflict between Catholics and Protestants in the area, often culminating in school board elections contested on the bus issue and along religious lines. The case, probably organized by members of the local Masonic lodge, polarized the community, set former friend against former friend ("it split this town

[3] Illmo, *Jimplicute* (September 20, 1951).

right down the middle"), and dug wounds that even the passage of years did not heal. Twenty years later the bitterness lingered.

In the larger cities and metropolitan areas the key to the reaction is in the reporting of the daily newspaper or newspapers. But newspaper coverage is always a slippery matter—it both records and makes the event. Take the case of Aronow's suit in opposition to the motto, "In God We Trust," the case that could have happened anywhere in the United States. Aronow himself was not a resident of the San Francisco area at the time, being a student at the University of California at Davis, some seventy-five miles away. There was no controversy or confrontation that led to the litigation, no group activities, no press conferences, no celebrity or notoriety surrounding the case—and nothing but one brief three-inch report in the San Francisco *Chronicle*. Front page reports, on the other hand, whether they make or record the event, appear to generate a substantial impact. The impact of a church-state case on the community is thus directly related to the amount of newspaper coverage (Table 12–3).

The controversy over the course in the Bible as literature at the University of Washington in Seattle became an exemplary exercise in Hearst puffery and sensationalism. Two fundamentalist churches sued to stop the teaching of the course on the ground that in presenting one view of the Bible—and excluding other views, including that of the plaintiff churches—the university had engaged in a form of sectarian teaching. The plaintiffs eventually lost, but the litigation featured a week-long trial before a crowded courtroom with large numbers of spectators displaying open Bibles. The Rev. Carl McIntyre, a national figure in fundamentalist

TABLE 12-3

Impact of Case on Community According to Extent of
Newspaper Coverage

Community Reaction to Case	Extent of Newspaper Coverage		
	front page spreads	limited front page coverage	back page or no coverage
None or little	3 (18.8%)	6 (33.3%)	9 (69.2%)
Some or great	13 (81.3%)	12 (66.7%)	4 (30.8%)
Total	16	18	13

Note: The universe of 47 cases here begins with the 58 adversary cases; 11 are then subtracted for missing data in one or both of the variables.

Protestantism and founder of the Bible Presbyterian Church, came to Seattle to testify, and other local theologians, Biblical scholars, and academics also appeared. To all of this the local Hearst paper, the Seattle *Post-Intelligencer,* responded with six-column, front-page coverage for several days. Their political cartoonist attended, drawing sketches of the principle figures, and reporters drew the inevitable parallels ("the case has been likened to the celebrated 1925 Scopes trial. . . ."[4] In the ecstasy of its front-page coverage the *Post-Intelligencer* overlooked the fact that the case seemed to have neither a Darrow nor a Bryan). The coverage was also less than favorable to the Bible Presbyterians. Under such circumstances, the emotional drain on the plaintiffs and the general tension attending the case were considerable.

Aside from the small-town cases in which virtually the entire community is involved, there is considerable variation in the size and number of waves the urban church-state cases make. Some slip by almost unnoticed, others plunge the actors and much of the community into a factious turmoil. What accounts for the difference?

The nature of newspaper coverage and communication, for one. And that in turn depends on local newspaper policy (one has the impression, for instance, that the Salt Lake City papers do not report challenges to the local Mormon dominance), on the degree of local conflict and "interest," and on the following factors.

The presence or absence of a trial. Newspapers must have an event to report, and the trial is an event. Almost all of the searing consequences in these cases have come from publicity accompanying trials. Of the cases in which there was no trial on the facts, 47.1 percent had "some or great" impact on the community, but of the cases with trials, 81.8 percent had a similar impact. The litigation groups are aware of that relationship, and it creates a great dilemma for them; they are attracted to a trial for legal reasons, but for political and human reasons they would like to avoid the consequences of one.

The nature of the plaintiffs. The free-wheeling performance of a plaintiff such as Madalyn Murray O'Hair inevitably "heats up" a case by increasing its visibility and salience, by threatening

[4] *Post-Intelligencer* (June 14, 1966). The case was *Calvary Bible* v. *Board of Regents.*

the majority values in the community, and by bringing an element of the sensational to otherwise placid litigation. Even more sedate plaintiffs who espouse unpopular causes or religious (and irreligious) preferences inject a predictable element of controversy into church-state litigation.

A number of other factors serve in a smaller way to push litigation into public controversy. Flamboyant local organizers and counter-organizers have that effect. So, too, do church-state issues that bring to mind other related and sensitive social issues, especially those of morality and life styles. The "prayer in public schools" cases had exactly those overtones. In view of other associations in this study, it is interesting that the intensity of the controversy does not seem to be related to the likelihood of public involvement. Cases that do not involve the schools can as easily convulse a community as those that do. It is the connection with the locale and not the substance of the dispute the matters. Cases not rooted in the policy or events of the locale of the litigation have little capacity for spurring major reactions.

These generalizations can best be summarized by a church-state case of little impact and visibility: the suit led by the Horace Mann League against an appropriation of the Maryland legislature to assist the building plans of religious colleges within the state. The very presence of a group plaintiff, by whose name the case was generally referred, shielded the individual parties who served as plaintiffs with the League. Many news stories in the Baltimore and Washington newspapers, in fact, did not even mention them. There was, moreover, no local community site for the case. The policy under challenge was statewide, and the plaintiffs and defendant colleges were located in various sectors of the state. The individual plaintiffs were also of high status, well educated, generally religious, and content to stay in the background of the case. Most of them were economically independent—doctors, government employees, and teachers, for instance. And there were also thirteen of them (including a number of married couples). So, despite the earlier inflammations of Madalyn Murray in the state, the role of the individual plaintiffs in this case passed without major attention.

COMPLIANCE: THE FIRST AFTERMATH

Once the litigation stops and some appellate court has made a final substantive decision, do the parties abide by that decision?

285

In 34 of these 67 cases there was no question of compliance. The public policy was affirmed, the status quo remained undisturbed, and the plaintiff had no alternative but to accept the decision. But in the 33 instances in which courts overturned a public policy—that is, declared the status quo to be in some way an impermissible breach of the wall of separation—there could have been compliance issues.

In all of the cases in this group, however, there was a history of evasion or avoidance in only one: the Eugene, Oregon, case over the concrete cross on Skinner's Butte. There was some foot-dragging in several other cases. In at least one case involving religious influences in the schools (*Miller* v. *Cooper*), threats from the county school board and the persuasion of its attorney nudged the teachers to compliance. And in another instance—the one involving the 460 plaintiffs seeking to keep the high school in Bradfordsville, Kentucky—the defendant school board was slow because of what it said was financial inability to comply with the court order to build a new, centrally located high school. (Those reasons were ultimately recognized in subsequent court decisions.) It is, indeed, only the Eugene case among the thirty-three in which one finds a sustained, clearly evasive noncompliance with a court decision.

After the second decision of the Oregon Supreme Court, reversing itself in October of 1969 and ruling against the cross, the Eugene Sand and Gravel Company sought certiorari in the United States Supreme Court. At the same time the procross forces began a campaign to convert the cross into a war memorial, hoping to draw the city under the protection of an Oregon statute permitting a city to have a veterans memorial in a city park. The Supreme Court denied certiorari in April, and in a public referendum in May the voters of Eugene approved the necessary charter amendment to convert the cross to a memorial by a vote of 16,680 to 5,871. (The original plaintiffs in the case argued that a cross was a cross whether it was a war memorial or not.) The Supreme Court denied rehearing on its denial of certiorari less than a week after the referendum, and more than five years after the initiation of the suit. Within the month the local county court directed the Eugene Sand and Gravel Company to remove the cross, adding that if it were not removed in ten days that the city should tear it down, and that if that failed, the county sheriff was to take it down. At that point the Sand and Gravel Company went to court to suspend the decree on the ground that the referendum had altered the nature of the controversy and thus the enforcement decree. After desultory legal sparring, that action still had not come to trial by May of 1972, and after seven years of litigation the plaintiffs were exhausted and demoralized. Having won their case, they were not sure that the cross would ever come down, and not sure even that they had won a symbolic victory.

The record of general compliance in all other of these cases extends even to the cases that themselves grew out of noncompliance (the prayer cases from Netcong and Hawthorne, New Jersey; Leyden, Massachusetts; and Fayette County, Pennsylvania). In all of these communities school boards had pressed on with some form of prayer in the schools, more or less in defiance of *Engel, Schempp,* and *Murray.* (So also, we know, had thousands of other school districts across the country, especially in the South.)[5] They were in the appellate courts because (in three of the four instances) state officials had invoked the power of the state to force compliance, and because the local boards and communities persisted long enough to force the confrontations into the courts. But even the local boards finally "knuckled under"—to use their favorite phrase—after a little hesitation. What, then, is it that produces such a high degree of compliance with these separationist decisions, even in these deeply-felt, "second generation" compliance cases?

Some general considerations work toward compliance in any area of litigation. For one, the specific litigants find it much harder not to comply than those who were not parties to the litigation. Their dispute has been under litigation, their policy a matter of public record; their legal options are fewer, and they do not have a cover of anonymity. Furthermore, the decision of the appellate court often comes well after the deep feelings in the community have subsided. There is a certain usefulness, therefore, to the deliberate pace of appellate litigation. Resignation and fatigue have set in. The litigants have lost their "fight," and the possibly inflammatory decision falls on dying (or dead) embers. Finally, compliance in these and other constitutional cases is very much facilitated simply by the deep-seated values of most of the principal defendants and policy-makers. Local attorneys to school boards and

[5] For example, see H. Frank Way, Jr., "Survey Research on Judicial Decisions: The Prayer and Bible Reading Cases," *Western Political Quarterly* 21 (June 1968), 189–205.

other defendants repeatedly urge compliance with the law, and the commitment among professional schoolmen to constitutionalism and the orderly resolution of legal questions is also high.[6]

Compliance in these cases also results from reasons that have to do with their specific nature. The first and unquestionably the most important of them is the authority of county and/or state educational authorities to compel the compliance of local school authorities; they may, for instance, threaten to cut off state aid to recalcitrant local school districts. State departments and boards of education are generally strong supporters of the free, secular public school, and these cases are replete with instances of their insistence on that ideal. In three instances, of course, they brought suits to force compliance with earlier Supreme Court decisions— the cases involving Leyden, Massachusetts; and Hawthorne and Netcong, New Jersey. In other instances local districts considering the possibility of evasion or noncompliance understood the financial danger they ran. In some cases, the cutoff of funds for a challenged program was automatic; when the busing of children to nonpublic schools was invalidated in some states, the state reimbursement checks to local districts for busing immediately reflected the drop in number of children bused. And in New Mexico, after the decision in the case of the Catholic nuns, the state Board of Education issued stern guidelines for compliance to the districts of the state. Regardless of the form of the pressure for compliance, it clearly results from the centralization of state public school finances.

Furthermore, some of the "pressure" for compliance in these thirty-three cases merely expresses the interests of the defendants. In some cases, which we have already described, the defendants only reluctantly accepted the accommodationist interest. They may have been pleased to lose the case, and thus only too willing to comply. The hard-pressed school district forced by state law to provide bus rides, texts, or auxiliary services to nonpublic school pupils will find no difficulty in cutting back those unwanted obligations. Or the local authorities who have gone to court as a way of resolving a public policy dispute too emotional for political resolution may also be more than happy to comply. On some occasions the accommodationist interests may retire from the lists even be-

[6] For a fuller description of the role of one complying schoolman, see Richard M. Johnson, *The Dynamics of Compliance: Supreme Court Decision-Making from a New Perspective* (Evanston, Ill.: Northwestern University Press, 1967).

fore the final decision; the Gideons in Orlando stopped their distribution of Bibles before the final decision, mooting the entire question of compliance.

Quite another circumstance prevails to promote compliance in the voiding of a statewide policy—the invalidation of Maryland's grants for buildings at religious colleges; Pennsylvania, Louisiana, and Rhode Island's parochaid statutes; college tuition grants in South Carolina; and busing programs in Hawaii and Wisconsin. In these cases there were not even stirrings or motions toward defiance. The state policy was centralized and universal within the state; one blow, and it was invalidated. Both the political and the legal pressures for compliance are also greater on state officials than they are on isolated local officials whose inclinations to defiance may be encouraged by homogeneous local constituencies. If the state were not to comply, the strategy of counteraction in the courts would be swift and easy; one court action would, again, suffice. And the nature of these statewide controversies is such that they all involve the appropriation of funds. The court action voids the appropriations, the money stops flowing, and the program is over. Local school districts or communities do not even have the opportunity not to comply.

In sum, therefore, the high order of compliance in these thirty-three cases that invalidated public policies has very much to do with the facts and realities of public education, especially with the centralization of authority within the states, and with the separationist values of the men and women who wield that authority. It is striking and significant, indeed, that the only instance of noncompliance among the thirty-three—that of the cross in Eugene—came in the only local, nonschool case among them. It is not only the unusual fact of noncompliance in Eugene that sets it apart, but the very difference of its postdecisional politics. Finally, one should note that with such built-in pressures for compliance in these cases, little responsibility was left to the original plaintiffs and their supporting groups. There are instances in which they prodded or took a vigilant stance, but compliance did not hinge on their willingness to go another round in the courts.

THE BROADER COMPLIANCE

Much as a stone striking still water, the decision that voids a public policy sends waves out from the point of impact, each successive one weaker and less distinct. The rule of stare decisis mandates

289

that there be waves of some force beyond the initial and central impact. The decision in a case becomes a precedent that governs similar practices and policies in the jurisdiction of law invoked in the decision. The compliance of the original plaintiffs and defendants is expected, but so, too, is the compliance of parties and interests similarly situated.

The dimensions of the problem of compliance beyond the original litigation are, however, vastly complex. Take, as an example, these thirty-three church-state cases in which public policies were struck down. Six were decided in the United States Supreme Court, and thus raise issues of nationwide compliance; they will be considered later in the chapter. Of the twenty-seven remaining cases:

> Statewide policy was invalidated in 8. The issue of compliance was therefore one of encouraging or forcing compliance in other similar circumstances within that same state.

> Local policy was invalidated in 19, and local school policy in 18 of those 19. The compliance issue here, therefore, is the extension of the precedent both to other circumstances and to other policies in other parts of the jurisdiction. (The "jurisdiction" is, in all but two instances, a state, since the decision was that of a state supreme court. Two of the decisions were by U.S. Courts of Appeals.)

These twenty-seven cases—the invalidations of both state and local policies—deserve a closer look, if only to suggest that the broader compliance issues are not as extensive as they might seem.

Consider those eight instances of the invalidation of state policy by state supreme courts. The Michigan tussle over Proposition C, the new constitutional amendment, hinged on an interpretation of the new amendment, more or less abstracted from issues of real policy. The policy it overturned was merely a collection of advisory and administrative interpretations of the state's attorney general and board of education; in other words, it established no "precedent" growing out of a justiciable conflict. Three other cases involved appropriations of state funds: for college tuition grants in South Carolina, parochaid in Louisiana, and college buildings in Maryland. Once the courts invalidated the appropriations, the matter was ended. That leaves four cases in which textbooks for and bus rides to religious schools were at issue:[7]

[7] The four cases discussed earlier in this paragraph were: *In Re Proposal C, Hartness* v. *Patterson, Seegers* v. *Parker,* and *Horace Mann League*

In the Hawaii bus case, since the state has a state school system with no local districts, compliance at the single, statewide school level settled the issue. There was, therefore, no issue of parallel compliance.

In the Wisconsin case, the voiding of the state's bus law was followed by the elimination of state reimbursement funds. Some local districts continued the rides out of their locally-raised funds, but the state soon amended its constitution to permit the bus rides, thus mooting the compliance question beyond the short run. Again, because of the amendment, no real issue of parallel compliance persisted.

In the Oregon and Alaska cases state laws authorizing textbooks and bus rides, respectively, were struck down. Since neither had carried reimbursement of funds, the possibility of local noncompliance was greater. While state officials in Oregon were slow in applying the decision, it was eventually enforced, and general evidence, however sketchy, indicates that there was little or no noncompliance by the school districts of the states.

Thus, compliance was not a problem when subsequent "follow-up" decisions were not required, or when they were required at the statewide level. Noncompliance became a real possibility only when the compliance decisions were decentralized to the localities of the state. The legal and financial structure of the policy disputes under litigation, in other words, sharply limited the number of instances in which noncompliance was even a logical possibility. In these eight cases it was a real possibility in only two.

To shift now to those nineteen instances in which local policy, usually school policy, was knocked down in either a state supreme court or a U.S. Court of Appeals, one again finds an overall pattern of compliance. In ten of the nineteen, compliance was uniform across the state, usually in part because of the willingness of state officials to enforce. In three cases that originated in noncompliance with the prayer decisions—those from New Jersey and Massachusetts—state officials had indicated similar willingness by originating the litigation. (In at least one of the three cases, in fact, the state official acted precisely for the purpose of centralizing the enforce-

---

v. *Board of Public Works.* The four taken up in the following sentences were: *Spears* v. *Honda, State* v. *Nusbaum, Dickman* v. *School District,* and *Matthews* v. *Quinton.*

ment rather than wait for the decentralized confusion of enforcement by private suits.) In most of the remaining instances, state attorneys general or superintendents of public instruction, or both, had issued orders, guidelines, or explanations that communicated word of the decision across the state, also suggesting their intention to enforce it. In five other cases there was no real issue of parallel compliance because the practices struck down were unique, or at least very rare, in the state. The special educational district in St. Louis was the only one in the state; and so, too, was the cross above Eugene, Oregon, unique in that state. Kanawa County, West Virginia, alone among the counties of the state refused to grant bus rides to parochial school students, and the program of local aid to a religious school in Anaconda, Montana, was also without parallel. The same was also true of the troubled relationship between Bradfordsville, Kentucky, and the county school board.[8] In only four of the nineteen cases, therefore, were there demonstrable compliance problems outside of the site of the litigation.

In these four instances of noncompliance, the specific school district involved in the litigation did comply with the final appellate decision in the case, no matter how painful or distasteful it might have been. But other school districts in the area did not.[9]

> The school board in Midwest City, Oklahoma, did stop bus rides to children attending the local Catholic school, but some other districts in the state did not. The practice was not widespread in Oklahoma, however, if only because of the small number of Catholic schools. In one of the few instances in these cases of plaintiff follow-up, the Antones and their attorney threatened to organize court action to stop the bus rides in at least one other district.

> In Orlando, Florida, the Gideons stopped distributing their Bibles even before their case was finally lost, but the Bible distribution continued in other parts of Florida as a part of a broader pattern of religiosity in the public schools of the state. There is no evidence whatsoever that state officials tried to force compliance with the decision in the case.

[8] These cases with unique local policies were: *Special District* v. *Wheeler, Lowe* v. *City of Eugene, State ex rel. Hughes* v. *Board of Education, State ex rel. Chambers* v. *School District,* and *Wooley* v. *Spalding.*

[9] The four cases of noncompliance were, in the order discussed here: *Board of Education* v. *Antone, Brown* v. *Orange County, DeSpain* v. *DeKalb County,* and *Mangold* v. *School District.*

292

The Illinois ACLU affiliate won the case of the "cookie break" prayer in the kindergarten of DeKalb, Illinois. The same ACLU officials knew of other instances of prayer in the state and would presumably have assisted a willing plaintiff.

Another ACLU affiliate, this one in Pittsburgh, helped Edwin Mangold end school prayer in a school district south and east of Pittsburgh. The ACLU affiliate advertised its plea for a plaintiff in nearby areas without success, both before and after the Mangold case. None came forward, and the prayers went on in the other communities.[10]

Four instances do not afford a great deal of opportunity for analysis, but they do suggest some observations. Among the four are the only two in which local practices were invalidated by a U.S. Court of Appeals. Those two cases, when added to the compliance problems of the U.S. Supreme Court, reinforce the suspicion that state officials do a better job of enforcing decisions of their state courts than they do with those of the federal courts. Secondly, three of these four instances involved religion in the public schools, generally the most troublesome church-state questions for the courts. In fact, of these nineteen cases in which local policy was invalidated, a total of eight involved essentially non-Catholic religious practices in the public schools. (That is, they did not include the cases of alleged Catholic "capture" or domination of public schools.) Of those eight, three began as noncompliance cases, three are included in the four above, and in two instances there was broad compliance.

COMPLIANCE WITH THE U.S. SUPREME COURT

On only four occasions (involving six different cases) between 1951 and 1971 did the U.S. Supreme Court invalidate state or local policy on separationist grounds. In June of 1971 it struck down the Pennsylvania and Rhode Island parochaid statutes, decisions that met with compliance, but also with frenzied attempts in a number of states to devise alternative policies that might pass the Court's tests of constitutionality. The other four decisions, from the period of June 1962 to June 1963, all touched on prayer

[10] See, for example, the *New York Times* reports of prayer in Clairton, Pennsylvania, on March 26 and December 19, 1969.

293

or Bible-reading in the public schools.[11] These decisions sparked an outpouring of noncompliance and evasion, which for persistence has perhaps been matched recently only by the aftermath of the desegregation cases. The Court had clearly struck a very sensitive public nerve, indeed the same nerve that the lower appellate courts had found. Despite all the variety of church-state issues represented in these sixty-seven cases, noncompliance with and defiance of appellate court decisions was very largely restricted to questions of religion in the public schools. Only the events in Eugene, Oregon, and some sporadic evasion of bus ride decisions stand as exceptions.

Defiance of the decisions of the federal courts has long been a troublesome issue in American federalism. The federal courts, especially the Supreme Court, often attempt to generalize compliance with decisions in cases that arose in conflicts a continent away. Often the group and individual opposition to policy that gave rise to the litigation does not exist in other sections or states in the country. There is, in other words, little organized support for compliance. Local public officials and the general public also resent the interference of a distant authority with the values and traditions of the locality. Nor do public officials feel the same loyalty to and protectiveness of federal judges that they do for state judges. When one mixes those attitudes with the emotional issue of religion in the education of the young, and adds the opportunities for avoidance and evasion in the decentralized world of public education, conditions are more than merely "ripe" for major noncompliance.

Initial reaction to the Supreme Court's first prayer decision, that in *Engel* v. *Vitale* in June of 1962, probably exceeded even the worst fears and expectations of a Court grown accustomed to public unhappiness with its decisions.[12] Congressmen and Senators vied with each other in their condemnation of the Court, and both Protestant and Catholic leaders joined them. It is interesting, especially in view of the prevailingly Protestant character of the obser-

[11] The two parochaid cases were: *Lemon* v. *Kurtzman* and *DiCenso* v. *Robinson*. Those on prayer and Bible-reading were: *Engel* v. *Vitale*, *Schempp* v. *School District*, *Murray* v. *Curlett*, and *Chamberlin* v. *Dade County*.

[12] Justice Tom Clark, in a San Francisco speech a month after the *Engel* ruling, noted that "the Court had received a greater outpouring of criticism through telegrams and the mails than at any time in recent history." Quoted in Johnson, *The Dynamics of Compliance*, p. 69.

294

vances in the schools, that it was the Catholic spokesmen who appeared most united in their opposition. Many of them, indeed, reacted to it in terms of their residual anticommunism. Richard Cardinal Cushing of Boston thought that "the Communists are enjoying the day," and Cardinal McIntyre of Los Angeles allowed as how the decision "can only mean that our American heritage of philosophy, of religion, and of freedom, are being abandoned in imitation of Soviet philosophy, of Soviet materialism, and of Soviet regimented liberty."[13] Protestant leaders were somewhat more cautious, many of them urging compliance, but many of them bitterly criticizing the decision.

Few of the religious leaders counselled noncompliance, but many local political leaders and officeholders were not so restrained. Governor George Wallace of Alabama, by then accustomed to standing in the schoolhouse door, pledged to continue Bible-reading in the schools of his state even if he had to do the reading himself. Indeed, the Alabama law requiring daily Bible-reading in the public schools was not ended until a 1971 action in a federal district court brought by the Alabama Civil Liberties Union. Innumerable local city councils and school boards vowed to continue prayers and Bible-reading. In general, few among the political and governmental elite counselled compliance. The one conspicuous exception was the president of the United States. At a press conference shortly after the decision in *Engel,* John F. Kennedy responded to a question with the observation that:

the Supreme Court has made its judgment and a good many people obviously will disagree with it. Others will agree with it. But I think that it is important for us if we are going to maintain our constitutional principle that we support the Supreme Court decisions even when we may not agree with them.

In addition, we have in this case a very easy remedy and that is to pray ourselves. And I would think that it would be a welcome reminder to every American family that we can pray a good deal more at home, we can attend our churches with a good deal more fidelity, and we can make the true meaning of prayer much more important in the lives of all of our children. That power is very much open to us. And I would hope that as a result of this decision that all American parents will

[13] Quoted in Ellis Katz, "Patterns of Compliance with the Schempp Decision," *Journal of Public Law* 14 (Fall 1965), 398.

intensify their efforts at home, and the rest of us will support the Constitution and the responsibility of the Supreme Court in interpreting it, which is theirs, and given to them by the Constitution.[14]

The presidential advice was either not heard or not taken. And perhaps understandably, in view of the deluge of counsel to the contrary and the weakness of voices and groups favoring acceptance and compliance. Certainly local teachers, school administrators, and school boards could find ample support for a policy of noncompliance or evasion.

Even though the Supreme Court had left a summer in which reaction to its *Engel* decision might subside, schools opened in the fall of 1962 with reports of prayer and Bible-reading in most parts of the country.[15] (The Supreme Court may have hoped that reactions to its "church-school" decisions would soften or dissipate over the summer vacation; all six of its decisions invalidating public policy involved the schools, and all six were handed down in June.) In some states the authorities tried to encourage or force compliance, but in others they supported the rebellion. The Alabama State Board of Education, for example, openly reaffirmed its regulation that Bible-reading be a part of every school's curriculum. Other officials—the Governors' Conference of July, 1962, for instance—limited themselves to criticism of the decision and a call for a constitutional amendment permitting prayer in the schools. And if noncompliance did diminish or quiet down during the 1962–1963 school year, the Court's decisions in the *Schempp* and *Murray* cases in June of 1963 reawakened it. The shock and reaction to those decisions were certainly more muted than to *Engel,* but they nonetheless refueled the entire controversy over religion in the public schools.

Specific instances of defiance, no matter how well publicized the events or how celebrated the individuals, do not make a national pattern. Several attempts to survey nationwide compliance do sketch such a pattern, and their sketches are reassuringly similar. The Dierenfield surveys of samples of the country's school systems (in forty-eight states) in 1960 and again in 1966 showed both dramatic changes and equally dramatic absence of change

[14] Quoted in the foreword to William O. Douglas, *The Bible and the Schools* (Boston: Little, Brown, 1966).

[15] See, for example, *Time* (September 21, 1962), p. 69.

TABLE 12-4

Comparison of Religious Practices in American Public
Schools, 1960 and 1966

| Type of Practice | Percentage of Schools Reporting Practices | |
	1960	1966
Regular devotional services	33.2	8.0
Devotional Bible reading	41.8	12.9
Distribution of Bibles	42.7	37.4
Baccalaureate services	86.8	84.0

SOURCE: data from R. B. Dierenfield, "The Impact of the Supreme
Court Decisions on Religion in Public Schools," *Religious Education*
62 (September-October 1967).

in public school religion (Table 12-4).[16] A national survey of elementary school teachers taken in 1964–1965 by H. Frank Way,
Jr., reported data not at all at odds with that of Dierenfield. Way
reported, for instance, that 48 percent of his respondents recol-
lected reading the Bible in class before 1962, but that the percentage still reading the Bible in the school year 1964–1965 had
dropped to 22 percent.[17] Both also found the incidence of noncompliance far higher in the South than in any other part of the country (Table 12–5). Way, indeed, in trying to account for variation
in religious practices in the schools in 1964–1965, concluded that

TABLE 12-5

Variations in Incidence of Bible Reading in Public
Schools by Region, 1960 and 1966

| Region | Percentage of Schools Reporting Bible Reading | |
	1960	1966
East	67.6	4.3
Midwest	18.3	5.2
South	76.8	49.5
West	11.0	2.3

SOURCE: data from Dierenfield, "The Impact of the
Supreme Court Decisions on Religion in Public Schools."

[16] R. B. Dierenfield, "The Impact of the Supreme Court Decisions on
Religion in Public Schools," *Religious Education* 62 (September–October
1967), 444–451. The earlier materials of 1960 are reported in *Religious
Education* 56 (May–June 1961), 173–179, and in Dierenfield's *Religion in
American Public Schools* (Washington, D.C.: Public Affairs Press, 1962).
[17] Way, "Survey Research on Judicial Decisions."

297

region accounted for more variance than any of the independent variables he adduced, more even than the personal views and religiosity of the teacher.

Whether compliance continued to grow after the soundings of the Dierenfield and Way studies is not easy to say. There is, however, some evidence to suggest a resurgence of religious practices in the late 1960s. For one thing, the issues of a constitutional amendment came alive again in 1971 and 1973 after several years of dormancy.[18] In the late 1960s one also sees the resurgence of community resistance of the sort that led to the cases in Hawthorne and Netcong, New Jersey, in Leyden, Massachusetts, and in Fayette County, Pennsylvania. To put the evidence the other way, there is no reported evidence to suggest that the great number of noncompliers reported in 1966—which was, after all, some three or four years after the first of the decisions—had capitulated or modified their policies. And Dolbeare and Hammond found in one Midwestern state reason to think that surveys had indeed overestimated the degree of compliance.[19]

The compliance data suggest a number of specific comments and conclusions. One is struck, first of all, by the narrowness of the compliance with *Engel, Schempp,* and *Murray.* Aside from the Southern schools, the great majority of American school systems seem to have backed away from prayer and Bible-reading in the schools. That is, they stopped the practices specifically litigated in the leading cases. But very few of them have been willing to extend the logic of doctrines of those cases to issues not litigated before the Court. And so, baccalaureate services before the high school graduation and the distribution of Gideon Bibles went on virtually unaffected by the words and decisions of the Court. A case can very well be constructed that those decisions left the Gideons and baccalaureate services in an ambiguous twilight of constitutionality. If so, the ambiguity appears to have been resolved almost universally on the side of retaining the practice. Thus the precise facts of the precedent rather than any more general logic or doctrine appear to have governed compliance. Compliance, and indeed the effect of the principle of stare decisis, was confined to the barest minimum.

[18] The question of constitutional amendment to permit aid to religious institutions or religious practices in public institutions will be considered in the next chapter.

[19] Kenneth M. Dolbeare and Phillip E. Hammond, *The School Prayer Decisions* (Chicago: University of Chicago Press, 1971).

The fact of the South's major defiance also stands out. At first blush one might "excuse" it on the assumption that since the South had more deeply set and widespread religious practices, its task of compliance was of a magnitude not faced by other regions. The same argument has, of course, marked the assessment of Southern noncompliance with the Court's desegregation decisions. But the assumption is faulty in this case. The East (see Table 12–5) had virtually the same incidence of Bible-reading as the South before the decisions. Way's data even suggest that the New England states may have topped the South in pre-1962 morning prayers.[20] In degree of compliance measured as percentage change in the practice, therefore, the East easily outstrips the South. Explanations for the Southern noncompliance are not hard to adduce—the conservative Protestant homogeneity, the general traditionalism of values, the reinforcement of noncompliance in other areas of constitutional decision, indeed the whole complicated web of the Southern culture that relates religion to other social values and institutions.

Finally, one must keep this record of noncompliance in some perspective. It is restricted largely to one type of issue, religious practice in the public schools; it is not endemic to the entire question of separation. Why then should one find noncompliance so concentrated in one type of church-state conflict? It springs in part from the fervor of the convictions and the reactions involved. It touches the education of children, and more, the guarding of basic social values and traditions, for prayer and Bible-reading in the schools become weapons against the disintegration of traditional morality. For the truly devout, moreover, such religious practices involved the individual's religious obligations both to worship his God and to study the word of God. But it is not especially instructive or novel to note such an explanation. On one level it is obvious, as obvious here as it is in the explanations of noncompliance with the Supreme Court's assorted desegregation decisions. And it is also circular if the only or major evidence we have of the passion surrounding the issue is the degree of noncompliance itself.

Noncompliance in issues such as religion in the schools also results from the structure of the issue and responses to it. Passion, depth of feeling, there must certainly be. But additionally there must be opportunities for noncompliance, and it is the very structure of the policy issue that defines those opportunities. Religion in the schools results from highly decentralized decisions. Initia-

[20] Way, "Survey Research on Judicial Decisions," p. 199.

tives rest with every teacher in the country, and policy on such issues resides ultimately in the nation's eighteen thousand school districts.[21] Furthermore, no appropriation or funding is a necessary or integral part of the policy. Enforcement by court order would have to be literally on a school-district-by-school-district basis, assuming the availability of plaintiffs willing to come forward against the pressure of the community. By contrast, compliance with the parochaid decisions benefitted from the centralized nature of the policy and its dependence on state appropriations. The fact that parochaid policy was statewide permitted a single attack on any possible noncompliance. The statewide scope of the issue also brought it into a more diverse statewide political arena, in which opposition might more easily be expressed and felt.

There is another important, though less tangible, fact behind the noncompliance in the prayer and Bible-reading decisions: the unavailability of acceptable policy substitutes. As an alternative to religious practices in the schools, public educators proposed teaching "about" religion in a scholarly, uncommitted way. But their proposal generated little enthusiasm—and small wonder. It must have seemed terribly clinical and detached to the devout believer who clearly had no "objective" study of various religions and theologies in mind. Nor was the alternative of forming private religious schools a realistic one for most parents disappointed with *Engel, Schempp,* and *Murray.* There remained, then, little recourse but transparent evasions—the last verse of "America," or readings from the Congressional Record that include the daily invocation—or outright defiance. Either that, or a surrender of religious worship and indoctrination as a part of their children's formal schooling. In the instance of parochaid—to return to that example—there did remain in the early 1970s policy alternatives that had not yet been explored, especially tuition grants and tax credit systems. The process of exploring and exhausting policy alternatives remained before any potential resort to noncompliance.

THE GROUPS AND COMPLIANCE

Of the major litigating groups, it can safely be said that they are far more effective in the bringing of cases than they are in the enforcement of the separationist decisions they have won. The

---

[21] Dolbeare and Hammond also document the decentralized nature of enforcement and compliance in the school prayer conflict.

chief goal of the national litigating groups remains the establishment of the initial precedent. Whether or not they care to admit it, skirmishing over compliance problems adds little to the constitutional edifice they seek to build. They have limited resources and other causes in which to invest them. They therefore largely leave the legal "mop-ups"—the constitutionally less important and rewarding enforcement actions—to the uncertain zeal and resources of local groups and parties.

The lingering litigation over the cross in Eugene, Oregon, illustrates the problems that those local groups and individuals have in securing compliance. The subsequent, follow-up litigation and its expenses fell to the original plaintiffs and to their attorney and ad hoc organization. Plaintiffs and their local supporters in cases such as these quickly loose their enthusiasm after the initial flush of the crusade. As evasion or noncompliance appears to rob them of their victory they are quickly demoralized; they also find it hard to raise funds with which to carry on the struggle for additional months and even years. Indeed, as a church-state case drags on, all advantages appear to be with the defense. It is a governmental body, and it has a budget and legal talent for a long battle in the judicial trenches. Its commitment to litigation is institutionalized, and it thus does not depend on the enthusiasm, morale, or resources of involved individuals.

The major use and effectiveness of local parties and groups in these cases seems to be of a somewhat different sort. Consider again that in most instances local compliance on the site of the litigation is good, if occasionally grudging. In these cases, and even in some instances in which the separationist plaintiffs have lost the case, the plaintiffs and their supporting groups use the litigation to keep local church-state practices under scrutiny. The very act of litigation—whether successful or not—warns local school authorities, for instance, that there is a militant minority in the community that is prepared to challenge breaches of the separation in local schools. Separationist plaintiffs in many parts of the country remain convinced that their very litigation produced a new level of compliance with current constitutional norms of church-state relations in practices beyond those litigated. Although Philip Carden lost his suit against school prayer and Bible-reading in Nashville, the little punishments for failing to attend Sunday schools that some teachers imposed were eliminated by administrative order. And while the nuns were not driven from the local

301

hospital in Ketchikan, Alaska, the plaintiffs noted that the exterior cross came down and that there were no more prayers over the hospital's loudspeaker system. In short, the classic mechanism of political pluralism seems to be at work. Once opposing individuals and groups make their influence felt, local public policy will reflect that influence and threat of action. New "costs," including even the possibility of extensive litigation, attach to policy decisions that ignore constitutional strictures.

Noncompliance with decisions of the U.S. Supreme Court presents the national litigating groups with an entirely different challenge. Through the 1950s the groups did little; indeed, they had little to do. Occasionally they tried to extend compliance with a favorable state court decision. The American Jewish Congress, for instance, sent copies of the New Jersey decision barring the distribution of Gideon Bibles (*Tudor* v. *Board of Education*) to all state attorneys general and prepared a summary of it for the June 1954 issue of *The School Administrator*. But by and large, the groups left the advertising of favorable decisions to local leaders and to chance. And since the Supreme Court did not make a separationist decision between 1951 and 1962, there was really no national issue of compliance to attend to. Certainly they were unprepared for the defiance that greeted the first of the Court's prayer decisions (*Engel* v. *Vitale*) in June of 1962.

Having been surprised and shocked by reaction to *Engel,* a number of national separationist groups were better prepared for *Schempp* and *Murray* a year later. The preparations in anticipation of those decisions were formidable. The United Presbyterian Church, in general assembly in late May of 1963 (less than a month before the forthcoming decisions), issued a general statement on church-state relations that opposed devotional observances in the public schools as tending to "indoctrination or meaningless ritual." The statement also favored a political order "in which no church will dominate the civil authorities or be dominated by them."[22] In May of 1963 the American Association of School Administrators also issued a background memo to its members that outlined the major constitutional issues and questions that would be raised if the Court were to make separationist decisions. And on June 7, 1963, the general board of the National Council of Churches published a resolution on *Churches and the Public Schools*. The resolution, passed by a vote of 65 to 1, opposed the holding of religious observances or the saying of prayers

[22] *New York Times* (May 22, 1963).

in the public schools. Meanwhile, the religious leaders in the separationist camp were lining up Protestant and Jewish spokesmen who could be counted on for supportive public statements if the Court went separationist.

In all the anticipatory preparations, none was more complete than those of the Joint Advisory Committee (JAC) of the Synagogue Council of America and the National Jewish Community Relations Advisory Council. Its executive secretary, Phil Jacobson, distributed a memo in March of 1963 entitled "Preparation and Planning in Advance of Supreme Court Decisions in Schempp and Murray Cases." The memo, which had earlier been reviewed in draft by AJC officials (among others), described itself as an aid in preventing "community hysteria from developing in the event that the United States Supreme Court should strike down Bible reading and prayer recitation in the public schools." The memo advised a number of courses of action—study sessions on separation within the Jewish community, broader community seminars designed to familiarize community leaders with the issues in the cases, the recruitment of religious and political leaders who would be available to speak out right after the Court decisions, and a similar recruitment of school administrators in areas without prayer or Bible-reading, who would attest that the moral values of their pupils had nonetheless not deteriorated. And in May of 1963 the JAC circulated a statement that it suggested its local contacts might use for their own comments in the eventuality of a separationist outcome in the two cases. It is hard to assess the effect of efforts such as these, but the fact remains that public reaction to *Schempp* and *Murray* was not as hostile as it was to *Engel*.

COMPLIANCE: FINAL THOUGHTS

The problem of noncompliance runs unevenly through the church-state litigation after 1951. It was a possible problem, of course, only in the approximately half of the decisions in which a public policy was declared unconstitutional. Within the set of thirty-three cases that actually led to the decisions, compliance was the rule. The controversy over the cross in Oregon stands as the only substantial exception. The pressures of the litigation itself, the publicity surrounding it, and the immediate applicability of the ruling all apparently work toward compliance with even very unpopular decisions in the site of the litigation.

Compliance with the precedent in locations not under litigation

303

is a far more complex problem. Here, too, noncompliance is un-evenly spread over the universe of issues and jurisdictions. Despite the widely publicized instances of defying the Supreme Court's prayer decisions, compliance with other appellate court precedents has generally been acceptable. The major set of factors making for compliance are those structuring the dispute itself, and thus determining the possibility and feasibility of noncompliance. A great number of precedents raise no issue of compliance because they confirm public policy, because they involve uncommon or unique practices, because they eliminate the appropriated public funds supporting the practices, or because enforcement is easy. Ease of enforcement is greater when policy is centralized, when there are willing enforcers, and when enforcers have sanctions with which to act. The logic and structure of the particular church-state policy dispute, more than anything else, thus set the major limits to noncompliance. Instances of religious practice in the decentral-ized schools of the country, not surprisingly, present a far greater compliance and enforcement problem than do decisions invalidat-ing centralized, statewide appropriations to the religious schools.

The scholarly literature on compliance with unpopular appellate decisions suggests that the compliance elites and leadership within them also greatly affect the rate of compliance. In some local com-munities that were the subjects of intensive study, a lawyer member of the local school board and a local superintendent of schools led their respective school systems to compliance with the much-criticized prayer decisions.[23] Indeed, in considering the whole uni-verse of church-state litigation, one may well conclude that the only systematic, across-the-country pressure for compliance among the actors in church-state affairs comes from the public education "establishment." In state office its members have been willing to enforce compliance, and locally they have counselled compliance in many communities. Their commitment to a secular public school system and their opposition to public support of private education is deeply engrained in their educational philosophy. In the absence of an enforcement commitment by the major separationist litigat-ing groups, American public school leadership most nearly ap-proached an enforcement group in this church-state litigation.

And what of the general public in issues of compliance? It is

[23] William K. Muir, Jr., *Prayer in the Public Schools* (Chicago: University of Chicago Press, 1967); and Johnson, *The Dynamics of Compliance*. But note Dolbeare and Hammond to the contrary.

a truism to say that its inclination to noncompliance reflects, all other things being equal, the depth or passion of its feelings. Most people are indeed willing to comply with decisions they think are of no importance. Beyond the popular perception of the issue and the decision, popular attitudes toward the court making the decision also apparently affect compliance. The special vulnerability to noncompliance of the United States Supreme Court in these cases illustrates that point. It is surely significant that the massive noncompliance with the Supreme Court's prayer decisions of 1962 and 1963 came at the crest of mounting criticism of the Court for its decisions in civil rights cases in the 1950s and after.[24] Beyond public disapproval of the decisions of the Supreme Court, there probably lies a growing awareness of the politicality of the Court. It is widely thought now to "make" law and to engineer constitutional innovation (if not revolution). Its legitimacy as a conventional court of law making Delphic decisions therefore becomes suspect. For what more and more Americans see as political decisions, the more conventional political response seems appropriate. If the judges are no longer godlike, the faithful are less inclined to be reverent.

And so what begins as a centralized, group-dominated litigation of church-state issues ends in a decentralized, almost chaotic judicial politics of compliance. In beginning the litigation, the plaintiffs control the options. But it is the defendants, and the majorities for whom they often speak, who control the initiatives in compliance. What results is a politics of constitutional compliance almost completely different and quite separable from the politics of constitutional litigation.[25] Major litigating groups dominate the litigation because they seek a precedent, a constitutional statement that will affect later cases. Their finite energies and resources do not permit their involvement in the decentralized, precarious politics of en-

[24] See Walter F. Murphy and Joseph Tanenhaus, "Public Opinion and Supreme Court: The Goldwater Campaign," *Public Opinion Quarterly* 32 (Spring 1968), 31–50.

[25] There is evidence, indeed, that the efforts of the groups in bringing the litigation are virtually unknown to compliance elites. Ellis Katz found that none of the state educational officers responding to his inquiry could identify the group "supporters" of the *Schempp* and *Murray* decisions. He thus concludes that "this would indicate that either state-wide educational officials are not keyed to the demands of groups like the ACLU and the American Jewish Congress, or that these groups, once they obtained the decision that they desired from the Court, did not follow up the case and try to influence public opinion or see to the enforcement of the decision." "Patterns of Compliance with the Schempp Decision," p. 405.

forcement. Often, therefore, a victory in the future is won at the expense of the immediate enforcement of a victory in hand. If noncompliance were the rule rather than the exception, the litigators' later victories would always be overcome by the present failure in enforcement. But compliance is common, and that fact makes sensible, even rational, the long-range strategy of the litigating groups. If they attend to the long-run considerations, it is indeed the case that the short run will take care of itself most of the time.

XIII | THE IMPACT ON POLICY

When an appellate court strikes down a public policy on constitutional grounds, it leaves a policy problem at least temporarily without solution or resolution. By taking away a politically acceptable solution, it also affects the bargaining and the political power of the major interests in the policy process. At the very least, such a voiding of public policy sets off a scramble among policy-makers in the executive and legislative branches to find a substitute policy in which they can attend to the interests and concerns involved. When the Supreme Court of the United States holds, within the span of twenty years, that prayer, Bible-reading, and some forms of released time religious education are forbidden in the public schools, it drastically alters the public policy debate over the moral and spiritual education of the young. It also forces proponents to seek alternative means to old and cherished goals, and it probably even alters the education of American children in some significant way.

Confronted with the voiding of their policy on constitutional grounds, legislatures and executives find themselves with three broad options. The brouhaha following the Supreme Court's prayer and Bible-reading decisions of 1962 and 1963 illustrates all three. The politically responsible officials may choose, first of all, not to comply with the decision; they may, in a word, choose to defy the decision and the authority of the Court. That was what George Wallace proposed to do, and that is what numerous school boards and officials across the country did. That, too, is what the Illinois state legislature proposed to do in 1963 when it passed a bill permitting teachers in public schools to lead a daily recitation of the national anthem, especially that verse reading "And this be our motto, 'In God is our Trust'." (Governor Otto Kerner vetoed the bill, noting that the purpose of the bill was defiance of the United States Supreme Court.) Secondly, the legislature may, with the necessary popular concurrence, overturn the decision by amending the appropriate constitution. That was the intention of those in Congress who proposed prayer amendments after 1962. Thirdly and finally, executive and legislature may embark on a search for alternative public policies which will both meet the tests of constitutionality and solve the policy problem. After the Court's prayer and Bible-reading decisions, educators began to talk about introducing into public school curricula a course or courses "about religion"—more or less "objective" studies of the history, theology, and sociology of the world's major religions. That such courses would be constitutional could safely be assumed; the Supreme Court's dicta in *Schempp* insured as much. Whether they would meet the special goals in religious education about which the critics of *Engel, Schempp,* and *Murray* were so concerned was quite another question.

As the Supreme Court of the United States and the state courts weigh the constitutionality of public policy, they are inevitably caught up in the policy-making process. The making of policy shuttles back and forth across the gulfs that separate the three branches of government. A judicial decision on the legality or constitutionality of a public policy spurs additional action in the legislature. Even the anticipation of judicial consideration may indeed alter the nature of legislative decision. For their parts, the courts are not anxious to encourage either defiance or overruling in the legislature, and anticipation or expectation of such an aftermath may affect their considerations. Very simply, decisions in both the legislature and the judiciary have consequences for each other's work. This feedback, or even its anticipation, occurs constantly and reciprocally. Aside from the immediate issues of compliance, it is the most important form of impact from a decision of an appellate court.

RECOURSE TO STATE CONSTITUTIONAL AMENDMENT

Constitutions only sometimes mean what the judges say they do. Constitutions may also clearly mean what the constituent power wants them to mean, and a constitutional amendment passed with the explicit intention of reversing a court's interpretation of the constitution quickly asserts that final and supreme control of the constitution. While they are hardly common, constitutional amendments passed to reverse judicial interpretations are not unknown in American practice. Of the sixteen amendments to the U.S. Constitution passed after the initial ten, four were passed explicitly to overturn a constitutional interpretation of the Supreme Court: the Eleventh prohibiting suits against a state by citizens of another state or country, the first sentence of the Fourteenth conferring citizenship on all persons born in the United States, the Sixteenth authorizing a progressive tax on incomes, and the Twenty-sixth granting the suffrage to eighteen-year-olds.

In all of the instances here in which a state high court struck down state policy on state constitutional grounds, only twice was that decision overturned with an amendment to the state's constitution. The Wisconsin Supreme Court in 1962 held (in *State* v. *Nusbaum*) that the state's constitution forbade the granting of public transportation to children attending religious schools. Five years later the state adopted a constitutional amendment providing that "nothing in this constitution shall prohibit the legislature from providing for the safety and welfare of children by providing for the transportation of children to and from any parochial or private school or institution of learning" (Art. I, section 23). And in 1972 the citizens of South Carolina amended their constitution to replace a specific prohibition of all direct and indirect aids to religious institutions with a less definite one outlawing direct aid. The object was, in part, to bypass the 1971 ruling of the state supreme court (in *Hartness* v. *Patterson*) forbidding tuition grants to students in religious colleges.

The Wisconsin amendment did not come easily, and its history, in fact, predated the 1962 decision. The constitutionality of bus rides for children attending religious schools had long been considered uncertain under the Wisconsin constitution, and the first attempt to amend it to make them constitutional failed in 1946 by a vote of 437,817 in favor to 545,475 opposed. The second attempt at amendment began immediately after the 1962 decision, led primarily by a new and vigorous Citizens for Educational Freedom. The state legislature passed the proposed amendment in 1963, but errors in the form in which it was printed negated the approval. The legislature then passed it correctly in 1965 and 1967—successive legislative actions being required before submission to the vote of the people of the state—and put it on the ballot of the April election in 1967. In a somewhat desultory battle, CEF led the proponents, and AU and its associate director, C. Stanley Lowell, led the opposition. The amendment carried by a vote of 461,354 to 355,782. In just two decades the separationist opposition had shrunk from 55.5 percent to 43.5 percent. At the same election the incumbent chief justice of the Wisconsin Supreme Court, George Currie, who had also written the decision in the bus case in 1962, was defeated by a candidate who enjoyed the support of the Knights of Columbus. Observers were inclined to attribute part—though certainly not all—of Currie's defeat to the six-year fight to provide transportation for parochial school pupils.

The best-chronicled attempt to alter state constitutional strictures on church and state, however, was not the result of a separationist decision. It arose out of New York's attempt to rewrite its constitution in the 1960s. The constitutional convention proposed to eliminate from the new constitution the clause prohibiting state aid, either direct or indirect, to religious schools.[1] The proposed repeal went down with the entire new constitution of 1967 in a referendum in November of that year. Subsequently a separate repealer of the old clause was passed by both houses of the state legislature in early 1970. An amendment in New York, however, requires two passages by the legislature, and in 1971 supporters of the amendment abandoned the effort, apparently more hopeful of lenient judicial interpretations of the clause than of the passage of the repealer in a popular referendum. Despite the great flurry of state constitutional conventions in the 1960s, in only one other state did church-state relations assume the proportions of a major issue. A proposal for a clause permitting public aid for religious schools was defeated in the New Mexico convention in 1969.

But if one looks at state constitutional amendments as a response to judicial decisions striking down public policy, there remain only the two successful attempts among these cases: the Wisconsin transportation amendment of 1967 and the South Carolina amendment in 1972. Why were there no more such responses? For one thing, amending an American constitution is no simple matter; the procedures are beset with procedural pitfalls and the need for extraordinary majorities. Furthermore, in a number of instances the state high court relied on the U.S. Constitution as well as the state's, making state amendment by itself a dubious

[1] Article XI, sec. 3 reads: "Neither the state nor any subdivision thereof shall use its property or credit or any public money, or authorize or permit either to be used, directly or indirectly, in aid or maintenance, other than for examination or inspection, of any school or institution of learning wholly or in part under the control or direction of any religious denomination, or in which any denominational tenet or doctrine is taught." It is among the most clearly prohibitive among such state constitutional clauses, and it has been so interpreted by the New York Court of Appeals.

remedy. But a somewhat less obvious explanation becomes clear if one looks at the instances among these sixty-seven cases in which amendment might have been a useful response.

In only 12 of the 33 instances in which public policy was struck down on constitutional grounds was the policy a statewide policy. But of those 12, one case involved the interpretation of a state constitution itself (*In Re Proposal C*) and four others were decided by the U.S. Supreme Court on grounds exclusively growing out of the U.S. Constitution (*Lemon, DiCenso, Engel,* and *Schempp*). There remain, then, only seven cases in which state constitutional amendment might have been an effective countermove:

one involving textbooks (*Dickman* in Oregon),

two involving aid to religious colleges (*Horace Mann* and *Hartness*),

three involving transportation (*Nusbaum, Spears,* and *Matthews*), and

one involving statewide parochaid (*Seegers*).

Amendment did follow two of the decisions: those in *Nusbaum* and *Hartness*. And in one of the seven, the *Horace Mann* case from Maryland, the state supreme court rested the case for unconstitutionality as much on the U.S. Constitution as on the state's. Thus the amending process was employed in two of the six instances in which it might logically have been expected. Again it is the nature of the public policy and the dispute itself that structures the logic and likelihood of political responses in the judicial process.

There is an additional fascinating constitutional issue here. By rejecting bus rides under their constitutions, a number of states tried to maintain a higher wall of separation than that erected by the U.S. Supreme Court. The Wisconsin decision, along with those in Alaska, Hawaii, Missouri, and Oklahoma, in effect rejected the thrust of the *Everson* case, and more importantly perhaps, rejected the rationale of the "child benefit" theory.[2] One would suppose

[2] *Everson* v. *Board of Education,* 330 U.S. 1 (1947). The four other cases from Alaska, Hawaii, Missouri, and Oklahoma were, respectively, *Matthews* v. *Quinton, Spears* v. *Honda, Board of Education* v. *Antone,* and *McVey* v. *Hawkins.* See also from Delaware, *State ex rel. Traub* v. *Brown,* 172 A. 835 (1934), and from Washington, *Visser* v. *Nooksack Valley School District,* 207 P.2d 198 (1949).

that it is not easy for a state court to reject the example and the logic of the U.S. Supreme Court; at the least to do so would probably leave the state decision more open to criticism, and perhaps more vulnerable to reversal by amendment. Wisconsin did amend its constitution, but how was it that the other states, having initially found the political support for a state-adopted policy, did not attempt to reassert the policy by constitutional amendment? In part the answer may lie in the newness of the Alaska and Hawaii constitutions—the framers were on hand in both instances to argue what their intentions had been—and the denial, therefore, of the assertion that the state high court had misinterpreted the intended and "true" meaning of the document. Perhaps, too, the answer lies in the lack of effective political support for an amendment. While Wisconsin in 1968–1969 had 25.7 percent of its children attending nonpublic elementary schools, the percentages in Alaska, Hawaii, Missouri, and Oklahoma were only 2.2, 15.6, 18.1, and 2.7 respectively.

NATIONAL AMENDMENT POLITICS

The First Amendment's "no establishment" clause stood without formal change, and virtually without judicial elaboration, from its adoption to the years of World War II. Only once had a major attempt to alter it been mounted. In 1876 a proposed amendment, advocated most vocally by James G. Blaine—eight years later the Republican presidential candidate who lost to Grover Cleveland—passed the House and fell short of Senate approval by only two votes. It would have permanently denied tax support of any nature to church-related private schools.[3] The amendment grew out of resurgent anti-Catholicism, and would have elevated to constitutional principle the marriage of Protestantism and public education in the United States. With its failure, the "no establishment" clause lay dormant until the judicial interpretations of the years after World War II.

Within hours after the Supreme Court's 1962 decision in *Engel* v. *Vitale,* public outrage was transmuted into proposals for constitutional amendments. The hoppers of the two houses of Congress accumulated some 147 different resolutions before the first consid-

---

[3] The amendment also prohibited the teaching of religion in publicly supported schools. Blaine's original amendment contained no such provision, and some of the amendment's early supporters opposed the addition.

eration of an amendment in 1964. A total of 75 Senators and Representatives introduced amendments in response to *Engel*. The operative clause of that year's chief proposal read: "Nothing in this Constitution shall be deemed to prohibit the offering, reading from, or listening to prayers or Biblical scriptures, if participation therein is on a voluntary basis, in any Government or public school, institution, or public place."[4] This was the proposal advocated by the most tireless of the supporters, Representative Frank Becker of New York. In part because of some accomplished heel-dragging in the House Judiciary Committee by its chairman, Representative Emmanuel Cellar, also of New York, neither house voted on any of the proposals in 1964. By 1966 Senator Everett McKinley Dirksen, the Republican floor leader, had made the cause his own. What had been known as the Becker amendment became in somewhat altered form the Dirksen amendment. It came to a vote in the Senate in 1966, and fell short of the needed two-thirds vote when 49 Senators supported it and 37 opposed it. Five years later, and somewhat unexpectedly, the issue returned to the Congress, promoted this time more by external group pressures rather than internal leadership. On November 9th of 1971 the House took up consideration of the proposal in new form: "Nothing contained in this Constitution shall abridge the right of persons lawfully assembled, in any public building which is supported in whole or in part through the expenditure of public funds, to participate in voluntary prayer or meditation."[5] Again the vote, while in the affirmative (240 to 162), failed for want of the two-thirds majority. And so ended—apparently—one of the most persistent attempts to amend the Bill of Rights.

Over the seven years of its controversy, the amendment's supporters changed far less than its opponents. The early controversy of 1964 saw the Reverend Billy Graham, Bishop James Pike of the Episcopal church, and Francis Cardinal Spellman supporting the amendment; in 1971 it continued to enjoy Billy Graham's support, and added that of Bishop Fulton J. Sheen. In addition to the support of the popularizers of religion, there was continuing support from groups such as the Knights of Columbus, the American Legion, the Veterans of Foreign Wars, the Junior Chamber of Commerce, and a bevy of right-wing organizations. A number of ad hoc organizations also lent their weight, among them Project

[4] House Joint Resolution 693 (1964).
[5] House Joint Resolution 191 (1971).

313

Prayer, which featured Hollywood luminaries such as Pat Boone and John Wayne. In the Congress the pattern of support could roughly be described as Republican and Southern, with additional strength in the House from some of the urban Democrats. For example, in the 1966 vote in the Senate on the Dirksen proposal the vote went this way:

	Democrats	Republicans
in favor	22 (39.3%)	27 (90%)
opposed	34 (60.7%)	3 (10%)
	56	30

The three Republican opponents were Jacob Javits (New York), Clifford Case (New Jersey), and Thomas Kuchel (California). From the Southern states only Senators J. William Fulbright (Arkansas) and Sam Ervin (North Carolina) voted against it.[6]

Opposition in the country as a whole was slow to build up. Throughout the entire consideration the main separationist groups—AU, AJC, and the ACLU—fought against it and appeared repeatedly at Congressional committee hearings. So, too, did the National Council of Churches, even though in the early years some of its board members favored the amendment. But by 1971 the opposition had forged a coalition that included the main spokesmen for a wide range of American organized religion. The breadth of that opposition was certainly indicated by the formal opposition in 1971 of both the United States Catholic Conference and the Southern Baptist Convention. What had begun in 1964 as not much more than the separationist coalition that functioned in the judicial process, by 1971 broadened into a new separationist coalition that embraced much of organized religion in America. It was in many ways a classic illustration of the fact that the coalition that functions satisfactorily in the judicial process may not suffice in the legislative process. The negligible minority needed to organize constitutional litigation is not the substantial minority needed to block constitutional amendments.

But while coalitions must perforce change as issues move out

[6] For something of the flavor of the support, see Robert S. Gallagher, "God's Little Helpers," *The Reporter* (June 4, 1964), pp. 24–26.

of the judicial process, the leading actors do not. The knowledge and experience—not to mention publicity and visibility—gained in litigation is often the sort of expertise that legislative committees seek. The 1966 hearings before Senator Birch Bayh's Subcommittee on Constitutional Amendments featured a cast of witnesses right out of the rolls of church-state litigation. Leo Pfeffer, John Pemberton, and Stanley Lowell—of AJC, ACLU, and AU—were there. So, too, were the accommodationist attorneys for Vitale and the other members of the Roslyn School Board (Bernard Daiker), and the attorney for Stein and the other members of PRAY in their suit to restore prayer in Flushing (Edward Bazarian). And throughout the 1964 hearings, a major figure among the proponents of amendment was the city solicitor of Baltimore (and later Maryland attorney general), Francis B. Burch. Burch, who defended the city of Baltimore in Madalyn Murray's suit, appeared as the national chairman of Constitutional Prayer Foundation, a group he organized shortly after his defeat in *Murray* v. *Curlett*.

THE SEARCH FOR POLICY ALTERNATIVES

Short of attempts to restore the status quo by constitutional amendment, legislatures search for more clearly constitutional policies to replace the ones struck down. If the state constitution prohibits grants to religious colleges for new buildings, for example, perhaps it will permit loans or governmental guarantees of private loans. The search for the constitutional alternative must, of course, take into consideration more than just the question of constitutionality. There are also questions of political consent and policy efficacy to be considered. Loans for college buildings do not constitute as much aid as grants, and as public policy they may do too little to alleviate the financial crisis of the recipients.

In this search for the constitutional alternative it is not always easy to separate the true search from the act of defiance. In part it is a matter of motive—of the collective attitude of the legislators toward the court, and of their intention in asserting a new policy. (Often, indeed, one must infer motive from the degree of variation, the distance of the new policy from the old, unconstitutional one.) But even with the best will in the world, the legislature may not be able to perceive the elements of the old policy that made it unconstitutional, especially when faced with a vague or obscure judicial opinion. If, on the other hand, the appellate court has gone

315

out of its way to point explicitly to constitutional alternatives, there is no problem. That kind of judicial guidance for legislative action is indeed one of the chief and most useful purposes of judicial obiter dicta.

Take the state legislative responses to the Supreme Court's decision in *Engel, Schempp,* and *Murray* as an example of the problem. The Illinois bill of 1963 to permit teachers to lead recitations of the national anthem was judged by the governor of the state to have been more defiance than alternative. Similarly, the New Jersey legislature in 1968, 1969, and 1971 passed and sent to the governor bills permitting brief periods of silent prayer and meditation at the beginning of the school day. (Governor Richard J. Hughes vetoed the first two, and his successor, William T. Cahill, vetoed the third.) The Massachusetts House passed a bill in April of 1970 to permit voluntary prayer in public schools, providing that the teachers took no part in it. Both legislatures acted during the course of litigation by administrative officials in their states to stop defiance of the Supreme Court prayer decisions by schools in Netcong, New Jersey, and Leyden, Massachusetts. Certainly the high courts of Massachusetts and New Jersey could reasonably have read the bills as "votes" on pending or subsequent litigation, especially since, in effect, they wrote into law the practices under challenge. At the least the two legislatures were testing the constitutional waters with the smallest possible degree of policy change from the earlier, unconstitutional practices.

In other instances the search for the constitutional "variant" goes on without hint or suspicion of defiance. Something approaching a classic form of that search happened after the Supreme Court's decision in 1948 in the *McCollum* case. In it the Court struck down the released-time religious education program in the cities of Champaign and Urbana, Illinois, because they drew too directly and heavily on the resources of the public schools. The classes were held in the public schools, teachers were certified by the schools, and most of the administrative details were handled by public school personnel. But what, then, of released-time programs conducted off public school grounds and run exclusively by volunteer personnel? It was a type of released-time program that did in fact exist at the time of the *McCollum* litigation, and thanks probably to the attention of Charles Tuttle's amicus brief, four of the justices inserted a discussion of the various "released-time" plans and the differential impact of the majority decision

316

on them in a concurrence.[7] Programs of that sort were validated three years later in the decision in *Zorach* v. *Clauson*. Communities across the country had the constitutional alternative they had been seeking. Some communities, however, sought no alternative, preferring defiance and unconstitutionality in maintaining released-time classes within the public school structure.

In other instances the search for constitutional policy finds "alternatives" that are perhaps more truly alternatives than merely variants of the invalidated policy. Shortly after the Supreme Court's prayer and Bible-reading decisions (1962 and 1963), a number of educationists began to promote the introduction into public school curricula of courses teaching "about" religion. Indeed, the Supreme Court's dicta in the 1963 case again invited the alternative: "it might well be said that one's education is not complete without a study of comparative religion or the history of religion and its relationship to the advancement of civilization. . . . Nothing we have said here indicates that such study of the Bible or of religion, when presented objectively as part of a secular program of education, may not be effected consistently with the First Amendment."[8] Early explorations in courses "about" religion centered on the study of the Bible in literature, on the fuller study of religious influences in history, literature, and art, and ultimately on the development of new courses on religious history and comparative religious systems. In 1967 Pennsylvania began a pilot course in Western religious literature in several dozen schools of the commonwealth; the materials were to be introduced into eleventh or twelfth-grade English courses. And in early 1968 the National Council of Churches formed a special task force to work with educational groups and teacher-training institutions to develop both teachers and materials for similar courses.

And yet the courses "about" religion were slow to catch hold. They had the weight of customary curricula against them. Nor were there trained teachers to teach them. (The teachers in the Pennsylvania pilot project went through a four-week summer institute to prepare themselves.) Public educators and religious groups were also frankly skeptical of the ability of many teachers to maintain the stance of detachment and "objectivity" that such courses

[7] *McCollum* v. *Board of Education,* 333 U.S. 203 (1948), beginning at p. 225. Tuttle, who later filed the brief in *Zorach* v. *Clauson* for the agency overseeing the New York City released-time program, filed this one for the Protestant Council of New York City.

[8] *Schempp* v. *School District,* 374 U.S. 203 (1963), p. 225.

presumed. Others doubted the readiness of high school students—especially in their understanding of their own religious commitment—to undertake a course in comparative religions. But more fundamentally, the proponents of prayer and Bible-reading in the schools, especially the more conservative and traditional Catholics and Protestants, had in mind something less "objective," less clinical, than merely teaching "about" religion. They advocated religious commitment, devotion, and observance within a specific religious system, and in many cases even religious teaching and indoctrination. The best mark of the shortcoming of courses "about" religion as an alternative to prayer and Bible-reading rests in the observation that after 1964 there were not even remotely as many school systems with programs of teaching "about" religion as there were with religious practices directly in defiance of the Supreme Court's decisions.

In the search for constitutional alternatives one may, instead of adopting new policies, learn to live "constitutionally" within the old. One may, in other words, change the activity or actors rather than the policy. In the responses to this church-state litigation it is apparent as a strategy in only one instance: the attempts of religious colleges and universities to become less obviously "religious," both in their governance and in their teaching. When programs of aid to religious colleges and universities are prohibited for separationist reasons, this specific answer is to make them less religious, and thus to alter not the terms of the aid but the nature of the recipient.

It was the suit of the Horace Mann League in 1965 to invalidate the Maryland grants to four colleges with religious ties that first stimulated the adaptive reactions. In the final 4–3 decision, the Maryland Court of Appeals invalidated the appropriations to three of the colleges, two Catholic colleges and the Methodist-affiliated Western Maryland College, on the grounds that they were in fact religious institutions. Aid to the fourth—Hood College, a school with attenuated ties to the United Church of Christ—was upheld on the Court's judgment that Hood was not in fact religious. In reaching its decision, the Maryland court was aided by a series of criteria drawn up by Edgar Fuller of the Horace Mann League for determining the extent of religious control or domination. In the lengthy trial the plaintiffs applied the criteria by exploring a wide range of questions about the operation of the colleges: the religious composition of their faculties, the nature of their aca-

318

demic mission, requirements that students take religious courses or make religious observances, the nature of the curricula generally and of individual courses within them, the religious composition of the student bodies, and the nature of the colleges' financing. (In applying their own criteria, the plaintiffs agreed that Hood College was the least religious of the four, although they believed aid to it did breach the separation.) In late 1966 the United States Supreme Court declined to grant certiorari, over the dissents of Justices Stewart and Harlan.

The success and yet the final failure to reach the Supreme Court in the *Horace Mann* case spurred subsequent litigation in the fall of 1968 to challenge federal aid for buildings at four Catholic colleges in Connecticut. Leo Pfeffer, who had been deeply involved in the Maryland case, assumed the leadership in the Connecticut case on behalf of the major separationist groups. Again the Fuller criteria provided the basis for a lengthy record-building effort by Pfeffer and his colleagues. They brought to the stand the presidents of the defendant colleges and introduced over a hundred exhibits, among them the constitutions of the colleges, their advertising and public relations materials, faculty handbooks, and student newspapers and yearbooks. The three-judge federal court ruled unanimously in favor of the constitutionality of the grants—and thus of the Higher Education Facilities Act of 1963—and in June of 1971 the U.S. Supreme Court upheld that decision, 5–4.[9]

From the Maryland decision in 1966 through the final decision in *Tilton* almost exactly five years later, a number of private colleges and universities set about reducing their "religiousness." The major activity came in New York State, as religious schools attempted to qualify for state grants under the state's strict constitutional limitations. The U.S. and New York Catholic Conferences hosted conferences for their officials and officers of Catholic colleges and universities on the problems of qualifying for the grants. William Buckley, in fact, publicly accused at least one of the Catholic colleges of divesting itself of its Catholic identity in order to qualify.[10] Fordham University commissioned a study by two distinguished scholars of constitutional law at Columbia University,

[9] The case was *Tilton* v. *Richardson*.

[10] See Buckley's article, "Cruising Speed," in the *New Yorker* of August 21, 1971. The president of the "accused" college replied and rebutted the Buckley charges in the *New Yorker* of December 18, 1971. An unconvinced and apparently unrepentant Buckley replied at the foot of the rebuttal letter: "Radix omnium malorum cupiditas est" [the root of all evil is greed].

319

Walter Gellhorn and Kent Greenawalt, to tell it what had to be done. At least enough was done for the New York state commission to certify that Fordham was a nonsectarian institution of higher learning, and thus eligible for state aid.[11]

Even in the *Tilton* case itself there were signs that the attorney for the four defendant colleges, Edward Bennett Williams of Washington, put them through some process of "secularization" as he prepared for that case. Apparently crucifixes were removed from the walls of classrooms, for example. The changes in Catholic higher education continued long past the litigation, it should be added. Indeed, the claims of nonreligious control made by the defendants in the *Tilton* case were authenticated less than half a year after its decision in the Supreme Court. The board of trustees of Fairfield University, a majority of whom were laymen, and some of whom were not Roman Catholic, overruled the president's attempt to dismiss a faculty member who had left both the Jesuit order and the Roman Catholic faith.[12]

The changes afoot in religious higher education in this period clearly reflected much more than these few appellate court cases, or even the more general debate over the constitutionality of public aid to them. The liberalization of Catholicism generally, and changes within the orders and religious communities that have long run many Catholic institutions, were clearly at work. To separate out the impact of the constitutional challenges and precedents would be impossible. That they had some impact, altered some directions of change, perhaps even accelerated it, seems, however, impossible to deny. The timing of the change, and the repeated references to the criteria of the *Horace Mann* case, all point to that conclusion.

THE CASE OF PAROCHAID

Politically, educationally, and constitutionally the most important fact about alternatives to public education in the United States is that they are largely Roman Catholic. As the data of Table 13–1 suggest, it is not much of an exaggeration to say that the debate

[11] The study was published; see Walter Gellhorn and R. Kent Greenawalt, *The Sectarian College and the Public Purse* (Dobbs Ferry, N.Y.: Oceana, 1970).

[12] See the *New York Times* (December 12, 1971), p. 49. Opponents of the dismissal cited the testimony on faculty freedom given by the president, the Rev. William McInnes, at the trial in *Tilton*.

TABLE 13-1
Students Enrolled in Nonpublic Schools in 1965–1966

	Elementary School Enrollment	Secondary School Enrollment
Total in nonpublic schools	4,928,682 (100.0%)	1,376,090 (100.0%)
Total in church-related schools	4,747,060 (96.3%)	1,216,442 (88.4%)
Total in Roman Catholic schools	4,370,277 (88.7%)	1,111,048 (80.7%)

SOURCE: U.S. Office of Education, *Statistics of Non-Public Elementary and Secondary Schools, 1965-66* (Washington, D.C.: Government Printing Office, 1968).

over public support for private education in the United States is in fact debate over aid to Catholic schools. Against the total of 5,481,325 students in Roman Catholic elementary and secondary schools (86.9 percent of the total of 6,304,772 in all nonpublic schools), the next largest share of the total among the religious denominations is the Lutherans' 188,521 (3.0 percent of the total). Furthermore, in 1965–1966 the growth curves were gently upward. After the greater growth of all nonpublic education in the 1950s, including Catholic education, the growth curve was levelling off in the 1960s, as it was for all American education. Catholic elementary enrollment, for example, increased only from 4,233,451 to 4,370,377 (a 3.2 percent increase) in the years from 1961–1962 to 1965–1966.

The school year of 1965–1966 is not chosen arbitrarily. While there had been distant signs of trouble for some time, 1965–1966 was perhaps the last year of prosperity undisturbed by crisis for the parochial schools of America. In the next year a wave of closings hit the Catholic schools. They reached a peak in 1968–1969, a year in which some 445 Roman Catholic elementary and secondary schools across the nation were lost. And that figure does not in any way measure the retrenchments in programs of other schools. At the same time a number of Catholic dioceses began to report steeply rising deficits. Individual parishes reported parallel financial problems. Whereas the parish school had consumed only a third or so of parish revenues some years before, it began to account for fifty or sixty percent of the outlays in many parish budgets. The time of troubles also began to be apparent in enrollment figures, especially by the end of the decade. While Catholic

321

elementary schools had enrolled 4.4 million students in 1966, they counted only 3.7 million in 1970. Even the Catholic secondary school enrollment, which had held up throughout the late sixties, began to dip by 1970.

The time of troubles for Catholic parochial schools developed for an intricately woven fabric of reasons. It is possible to capsulize the explanation as a problem in rising costs and lagging revenues, but to do so begs a great many questions. The problem of explanation is also confounded by serious data problems. Data on parochial schools systems, especially the Catholic schools, are not easy to come by. Individual religious orders and individual parishes and dioceses often guard information (and their autonomy), and often, too, they collect data less than systematically. Only recently have many of them felt the pressures for a public accounting of the administration of their schools.[13]

With all of these caveats, however, one can suggest four brief explanations for the crisis. First, the recruitment of young sisters and brothers into the religious orders declined to such an extent that lay teachers were actually in the majority among the teachers in Catholic schools by 1969. Their salaries were far higher than those paid to the religious teachers, and they were more militant, too. Second, Catholics increasingly left the center cities for the suburbs, often leaving the center city parishes with property and physical plants that were either unused or outdated, or both. Third, middle-class Catholic parents increasingly begin to prefer for their children what they saw as the better facilities, more varied programs, and greater pluralism of the public schools. Those preferences, too, were doubtless signs of the new mobility of young Catholics, and of their rebellion against religious orthodoxy and discipline. And finally, parish revenues by the late 1960s were barely keeping up with inflation; Sunday church attendance and giving fell off in Catholic churches, as they did in the churches of many Protestant denominations. Many parochial schools, therefore, were forced to institute or raise tuitions, thus shifting the costs of parochial education to young parents. All of this, furthermore, is not to mention the factors raising costs of all education in the United States, both public and private. General inflation in the economy, higher salary levels for teachers, and new expecta-

[13] There are exceptions, of course. See the 1969 report of the findings of the special committee on education in the Roman Catholic Archdiocese of New York. The *New York Times* (June 18, 1969).

tions for education all also raised the costs of maintaining the religious school systems.

These problems in parochial education emerged in the middle 1960s in a constitutional atmosphere that could best be called ambiguously unfriendly. There was a vast uncertainty about how courts might rule, but all specific signs pointed to an uneasy time for any program of public aid to shore up the troubled religious schools. The Supreme Court's constitutional law on the subject was dominated by the *Everson* decision, both by its "child benefit" rationale, and its rhetoric of an explicitly absolute separation. The more direct and more substantial the aid to parochial schools, the less likely was it that the logic of the "child benefit" doctrine would apply. Nor was the accommodationist victory of *Zorach* much consolation. While its rhetoric was less absolutely separationist, it extended only to a limited range of programs, and it left standing (if somewhat "distinguished") the Court's broader ruling on released time in the earlier *McCollum* case. Few state appellate courts had faced issues of direct aid to religious schools, but a good number (New York, for example) had been so restrictive in applying state constitutions in instances of limited aid that no one imagined an easy road in the states. Some, indeed, promised a higher wall of separation—as in the earlier instance of bus rides after *Everson*—than the U.S. Supreme Court might erect.

In anticipation of the constitutional climate, perhaps, the friends of parochial schools first sought less drastic and direct forms of aid. For the years of the early 1960s a good deal of the search for policy responses centered on "shared-time" programs. Shared-time programs—or "dual enrollment," as it is also called—have in common the part-time attendance at public schools by students in parochial schools. The students remain as enrollees in the religious school, but move for some part of the school day (or school week) to the public school for classes in the less value-laden subjects, perhaps in mathematics, the physical sciences, vocational programs, or remedial reading and speech classes. The parochial school students thus satisfy the state's compulsory educational requirement by a mixture of public and parochial school courses.[14]

Shared-time programs had existed for years in somewhat

---

[14] "Shared time" (or dual enrollment) is not to be confused with "released time." The latter programs involve only religious instruction, are taught privately and away from the public school, and are not a part of the student's regular school curriculum.

limited, sporadic, even ad hoc forms in some states. The onset of the crisis in the parochial schools gave them new impetus in the 1960s. By 1963–1964, there were by the count of the National Educational Association some 280 school systems in the country with shared-time programs. The concentration was heavily in the Midwest; there were 42 such school systems in Michigan, 36 in Ohio, 31 in Pennsylvania, 27 in Illinois, and 25 in Wisconsin. In practice the parochial students in the programs took more vocationally oriented subjects—mechanical drawing, metal shop, agriculture, home economics, typing, bookkeeping—than anything else. Enthusiasm for shared time peaked sometime in the middle sixties. By then it had become important enough for the American Civil Liberties Union to react to it, and in 1965 the ACLU issued a policy statement opposing it on separationist grounds.[15] Even in their heyday, however, the shared-time programs had a very limited impact. HEW estimated that in 1965 they touched only some 65,000 pupils in religious schools.

As their problems worsened in the late 1960s, Catholic educators moved from shared time to a commitment to more substantial forms of aid. Many had never considered shared time an adequate answer to their financial problems. They had seen it, indeed, merely as a way of enriching the curricula of the Catholic schools. Shared-time programs were both too limited and too limiting. For one thing, their very nature made them inapplicable to the single-teacher class and thus to the great, troubled universe of Catholic elementary education. There were also practical problems: the logistical problems in moving students to public schools, the joint scheduling and record keeping, the lack of congruence between parochial and public school attendance zones, and the coolness of public school administrators on both practical and separationist grounds. But, more fundamentally, many Catholic educators became concerned on basic tactical and philosophical grounds. It was the nature of shared-time programs to give away the enveloping environment of religious education, to secularize a part of the parochial education, and to accept at least in part the validity of public school education. They worried, too, that even where shared-time programs went smoothly, too many people would interpret such a limited remedy as an answer to all the problems of the parochial schools. They feared, that is, that such programs would create the illusion of aid without really offering much aid.

[15] See the ACLU's *Civil Liberties* for June 1965.

Coincident in time to the flirtation with shared time was the emerging advocacy of voucher plans as an answer to the problem of the parochial schools. The voucher plan proposed to give all parents in the community a voucher for a fixed sum with which they could pay for the education of their children, either in the public schools or in privately run alternatives. Vouchers attracted an improbably broad spectrum of both support and opposition. Among the supporters, conservatives such as Milton Friedman supported it for maximizing individual choice, blacks such as Kenneth Clark supported it for opening alternatives to the ghetto public schools, general critics of public education (Christopher Jencks, for instance) supported it as providing needed competition for the public school establishment, and Catholics saw it as a way of supporting their schools. Citizens for Educational Freedom began primarily as a group committed to the enactment of the voucher system, a plan proposed by one of its founding fathers, Father Virgil Blum.[16] But the opposition was impressive, too. The public school leadership vigorously opposed the voucher plan, and so, too, did the separationists and some blacks, who saw it as a way out of integrated schools for some middle-class whites. More surprisingly, perhaps, and surely more crucial for CEF at least, was the coolness of many Catholic bishops and educators. Some thought it too unlikely to spend time on, and others saw it creating a new and troublesome form of "parent power" for parochial schools. For all these reasons and probably more, the voucher plan was never a viable solution to a mounting problem. Ironically, the alternative with the least constitutional vulnerability was politically the most improbable.

In the early 1960s, with storm clouds darkening, the private schools and their advocates began both to press on with the logic of the child benefit theory and to talk of a radical new program of direct aid to the private religious schools. Pursuing the logic of the child benefit theory meant extending those auxiliary aids and services that courts, in cases such as *Everson*, had thought to be aids to the children rather than to the religious schools. They clearly included the provision to parochial school pupils of transportation, textbooks, and lunches in the schools. Some thought the category could constitutionally include more—guidance and counselling programs, for instance, or the loan of educational

[16] See Virgil C. Blum, *Freedom in Education: Federal Aid for all Children* (Garden City, New York: Doubleday, 1965).

325

equipment, programs for speech and learning disabilities, and remedial reading programs. In the 1960s a number of states either beefed up old programs of auxiliary services or inaugurated new ones. In 1963 Rhode Island legislated to permit local school districts to furnish textbooks to students attending private schools; in 1965 New York passed a textbook statute, and Michigan began to provide a series of auxiliary services. Between 1966 and June of 1971 Connecticut, Delaware, Hawaii, Idaho, Illinois, Iowa, Minnesota, Nebraska, New Hampshire, North Dakota, Ohio, and Vermont all extended some service or another—most often texts or transportation—to children attending religious schools.[17]

Separationists in Michigan, New York, Ohio, and Rhode Island all brought suits to challenge the constitutionality of the extended programs of aid to children in religious schools. It was the New York case from East Greenbush that first reached the Supreme Court as *Board of Education* v. *Allen*. In its decision of June 1968, the Court reaffirmed the rationale of the child benefit theory and gave its constitutional cachet to the new auxiliary aids. The attempts of the separationists to halt the logic of *Everson* at transportation had failed. The Court stepped over the boundary to accept aids to the education per se of the child. But *Board* v. *Allen* had far less impact than one might have supposed; it was already overtaken by events. The crisis of the parochial schools had worsened so seriously even before the decision that their supporters had increasingly begun to press for more direct and substantial aid to parochial schools. Pennsylvania had, in fact, passed the first state "parochaid" statute in the spring of 1968.

Like many terms that began as political epithets, "parochaid" quickly entered more or less common discourse. In some use—especially in separationist circles—it came to mean virtually any form of direct or indirect public aid to religious schools. The term will be used a bit more narrowly here to include only those forms of more substantial assistance to religious schools (and parents

[17] Not all of the legislation fared well in the courts. Hawaii's transportation bill was voided by the state's high court in 1968 (*Spears* v. *Honda*), and so was Idaho's in September of 1971. The Illinois auxiliary and remedial services program was invalidated by the Illinois Supreme Court on procedural grounds. The 1971 bill of the Vermont legislature provided for the lending of teachers as well as texts; that part of the Vermont law was invalidated by a three-judge federal court in March of 1972. It can perhaps more properly be thought of as "parochaid."

of their pupils) devised in the 1960s. The most common forms were:

"purchase of services" plans, in which public funds purchased from the religious schools the nonreligious courses and services that they offered, by which their pupils met the state's public instruction laws.

provision of teachers to the religious schools by one of a number of means (for instance, by paying the salaries of those teaching nonreligious subjects, or by "lending" public school teachers to them).

payment of tuition plans, whether by prior grants or vouchers given "pre hoc" to parents, or by some form of reimbursement "post hoc."

tax credits, by which parents would be permitted to deduct some specified maximum of the sums paid in religious school tuition from their income tax liability.

Of all of the state "parochaid" plans, only those of New York moved substantially outside of these four options. The special, even somewhat incredible, history of that state's efforts on behalf of its parochial schools will shortly receive special treatment.

Pennsylvania began the march to parochaid with a "purchase of services" plan in 1968, and Connecticut, Ohio, and Rhode Island followed in 1969 with either purchases of services or teacher salary payments or a combination. Their early initiatives set the direction of parochaid consideration in other states. The 1970 parochaid legislation in Louisiana, Michigan, New Jersey, and New York all followed some form of the "purchase of services" model, the Pennsylvania plan as some called it. The early innovators also became the sites of the major challenges to the constitutionality of parochaid. The AJC, ACLU, and AU in various combinations brought suits in all four states; two of them eventuated in the historic decisions of June 27, 1971, *Lemon* v. *Kurtzman* from Pennsylvania and *DiCenso* v. *Robinson* from Rhode Island.[18] They dealt a swift and fatal blow to the purchase of services, and the

---

[18] The Ohio case never reached the U.S. Supreme Court. The Connecticut case lagged a bit behind *Lemon* and *DiCenso*, and the Supreme Court decided it summarily a few days later on the basis of those two decisions. See *Johnson* v. *Sanders*, 403 U.S. 955 (1971).

rhetoric of the Court in the majority opinions threatened alternative programs as well.

THE AFTERMATH: SUMMER OF 1971

The immediate reactions to the decisions in *Lemon* and *DiCenso* were predictable. In statements tinged with despair, Catholic leaders predicted accelerated school closings. The crescendo of criticism peaked in mid-August, as Terrence Cardinal Cooke of New York called the decisions unreasonable and discriminatory. His audience at a Knights of Columbus dinner included the president of the United States, who contributed an impromptu pledge that "You can count on my support."[19]

In the state legislatures, the historic decisions turned supporters of parochaid to the untested alternatives of tax credits and tuition grants or reimbursements. Both of them had the advantage of being unscathed by judicial decision. At least on the surface, moreover, both involved aid to parents rather than directly to the schools. They appeared to be the most likely candidates for inclusion under the Court's "child benefit" theory. The turn to tuition reimbursements and tax credits had, in fact, begun before the decisions in *Lemon* and *DiCenso*. In the first half of 1971 two states ventured into these types of parochaid—Illinois with tuition grants for lower-income families, and Minnesota with tax credits for parents sending children to private schools.

It may be very well that the legislation of Illinois and Minnesota marked an anticipation of constitutional difficulties with purchase of service programs. In 1970 the Minnesota Supreme Court, in approving the transportation of parochial school pupils, had opined that that program carried the legislature to "the verge of constitutional power."[20] Furthermore, by early 1971 the Louisiana Supreme Court (*Seegers* v. *Parker*) and a federal district court had already held unconstitutional the parochaid programs of Louisiana and Rhode Island. But if the turn toward tuition reimbursement and tax credits had begun before June 1971, it was clearly accelerated under the spur of the decisions that month. Pennsylvania enacted a tuition reimbursement program in August of 1971, and Ohio was only a few months later with a similar

[19] *New York Times* (August 19, 1971).
[20] *Americans United* v. *School District,* a case included in this universe of 67 cases: the quotation is at 179 N.W. 2d 146 (1970), p. 149.

program. Maryland also passed a tuition voucher plan; petitions forced it to a referendum, however, and it was defeated at the polls in November 1972. Connecticut, Louisiana, and New York all enacted similar statutes in the early months of 1972.

The legal-judicial attack on these "second generation" parochaid programs began immediately. Again the main organizers of the litigation were the AJC, ACLU, and AU. The tuition reimbursement plans of Ohio fell first, a lower federal court ruling being affirmed in one brief sentence by the U.S. Supreme Court in October of 1972. Then in another of its late June parting shots—this one in 1973—the Court struck down two New York statutes that contained, among other features, a program of tax credits, and the Pennsylvania reimbursement program. To all intents and purposes the federal courts thus closed the ring of constitutional options, leaving the proponents of aid for religious schools with no other option than an extensive voucher plan that would apply to all children and all parents. It was of all the options the one most threatening to the public school interests, and it was therefore the most vulnerable politically.[21]

At the same time that they cast about for new forms of aid, supporters of parochaid also sought a new source of aid: the United States government. Pressures on the Congress for some program of assistance had begun earlier, but the 1972 presidential campaign undoubtedly gave them the major impetus. It began with President Nixon's words of encouragement to Cardinal Cooke before the assembled Knights of Columbus in the summer of 1971. About the same time, the President's Commission on School Finance, headed by Neil H. McElroy, a secretary of defense in the Eisenhower administration, was deliberating on the issue. In March of 1972 it recommended prompt and serious consideration of tax credits and tuition reimbursement by the Congress, although in more general terms than some accommodationists had hoped for. The president reaffirmed his commitments in April of 1972 in a speech in Philadelphia before the National Catholic Education

---

[21] The 1972 case was *Essex* v. *Wolman,* 409 U.S. 808, and those of 1973 were: *PEARL* v. *Nyquist,* 413 U.S. 756; *Levitt* v. *PEARL,* 413 U.S. 472; and *Sloan* v. *Lemon,* 413 U.S. 825. In addition in the 1972 case of *Brusca* v. *State Board of Education,* 405 U.S. 1050, the Supreme Court closed off a far broader accommodationist argument. The plaintiffs had argued that their religious freedom under the First Amendment and their equal protection under the Fourteenth had been impaired by the refusal of the state of Missouri to assist them in the education of their children in the manner it assisted parents of children attending the public schools.

329

Association (and before John Cardinal Krol of Philadelphia): "I am irrevocably committed to these propositions: America needs her nonpublic schools; that those nonpublic schools need help; that therefore we must and will find ways to provide that help."[22] The president repeated that theme at various points in his campaign for reelection, and George McGovern also moved to offer help to the parochial schools. McGovern apparently had tax credits or reimbursement in mind when he spoke of aid to families rather than directly to the religious schools. Tax credit bills were introduced into the Congress in the spring and summer of 1972, and hearings before the House Ways and Means Committee in August and September featured support by the Nixon administration in the persons of the secretaries of the treasury and of health, education, and welfare, George Schultz and Elliot Richardson.

It is in the nature of politics that happenstance, even "fortune," plays an unpredictably large role. Having suffered the ill fortune of the Supreme Court's decision, it was the good fortune of the parochaid supporters to find themselves in the middle of a presidential campaign in which an incumbent president was trying to detach them from their traditional loyalties to the Democratic party. They had become, at least for the 1972 elections and probably well into the 1970s, a relatively mobile part of the normally Democratic coalition. And at the same time, it also became clear that the cause of parochaid would be aided in the Congress by another fortuitous conjunction of interests. Southerners, many of them from districts hard pressed to maintain largely white private schools, saw general aid to nonpublic schools of all kinds as a potent issue in their states and constituencies.

At the same time as the push to tuition reimbursement and tax credits was taking place, however, less dramatic policy adjustments occurred in other states. Some states settled for new or more expensive programs of auxiliary services or shared time—settled, that is, for constitutionally well established routes. It was in fact a trend that had started before the decisions of June 1971. Connecticut, Delaware, Idaho, Illinois, Iowa, Minnesota, Nebraska, New Hampshire, Ohio, Washington, and Vermont added or increased some form of auxiliary aid after 1965. After the June 1971 decisions, California provided state-paid texts and some funds for dual enrollment programs. Ohio augmented its auxiliary services program right after the decisions, and Missouri began a textbook purchase

[22] *New York Times* (April 7, 1972).

program in 1972. But the greatest reliance on this route to aid was perhaps New Jersey's. When its $9.5 million parochaid program fell in 1971 with Pennsylvania's and Rhode Island's, it immediately undertook a massive program of lending texts and other materials, and providing auxiliary and remedial services—with the same price tag of $9.5 million.

PAROCHAID IN NEW YORK

The game of constitutional hide-and-seek took a more manic form in New York. The New York legislature was one of the first to respond with a parochaid measure in 1968. The governor vetoed it on constitutional grounds. It had only been in November of 1967 that the citizens of the state had voted down the proposed new constitution with its repealer of the stern clause against direct or indirect aid to religious schools, and the governor favored a constitutional amendment removing the clause. Plans for that amendment went on apace, the legislature even passing the amendment the first of the required two times. In April of 1970 the legislature also passed a $28 million program of grants to private schools in recompense for performing "mandated services" for the state (for instance, data and record-keeping and testing). This the governor signed, apparently confident it would meet the state's constitutional strictures.

In early 1971, however, parochial school forces decided to abandon the amendment to the state's constitution; it was never brought for second legislative approval. Instead they united for an immediate push for some form of more direct, immediate, and substantial aid, preferably some form of tuition grants or reimbursement. The governor was initially opposed. In February of 1971 he opined that a major parochaid measure would be the "first step to undermine, if not destroy, the public schools system"[23] and that he would veto a proposal for tuition grants. But half a year later, and on the very day the Court handed down its decision in *Lemon,* the governor signed a bill providing for a massive purchase of services. That bill was the first of New York's to be tested in the courts. A three-judge panel struck it down half a year later, in January of 1972, in a case brought by the Committee for Public Education and Religious Liberty (PEARL), and argued by Leo Pfeffer. The unanimous court noted that the New York program

[23] *New York Times* (February 9, 1971).

331

differed in no significant way from the Pennsylvania program the Supreme Court had struck down in *Lemon*. Following that decision, the governor, now apparently in the parochaid camp, vowed to press on in the search for an "appropriate" vehicle for aid to the embattled religious schools. In February, however, the governor's own commission surveying the quality and financing of education in the state—called the Fleishmann commission after its chairman, Manley Fleishmann, a Buffalo attorney—recommended against further parochaid programs by a vote of 13 to 5.

The progress of parochaid in New York continued, nonetheless, with a major step a month. In March the governor, undeterred by his commission, proposed a program of reimbursement to parochial schools for their maintenance and repair costs. Such aid, he argued, could be justified in terms of the health and safety of the pupils. Other parochaid activists stayed loyal to tuition grants and tax credits. In April of 1972 another three-judge federal district court invalidated the old 1970 "mandated services" aid program. PEARL had again brought the suit. In May the state legislature passed an omnibus measure to aid religious schools which included *both* maintenance-repair grants and a combination of tax credits and tuition grants for low income families. Finally, in the summer of 1972 yet another three-judge panel in a series of decisions struck down all of the May 1972 law except the tax-credit portion. PEARL had once again gone to court. Final disposition came with the Supreme Court's spate of decisions in June of 1973.[24]

And so it ended. New York had enacted more parochaid legislation and undergone more parochaid litigation in that hectic five-year period than had any other state. And it was New York alone of the states that refused to abandon its purchase of services programs (or programs closely resembling them), and that insisted on its own redundant days in court after the U.S. Supreme Court decisions of June 1971. Why? It is New York of all the states that is the cockpit of American church-state politics. Its unique three-way religious division among Catholics, Protestants, and Jews, especially when married to the two-party competitiveness and the ethnic politics of so many sections of the state, translates church-state relations into a major political issue. Then, too, it is the state of separationist organizations, of their home bases, and their leading advocates. Perhaps, too, the manic quality of the search for viable parochaid measures springs from the desperate

[24] See note 21.

plight of parochial schools—Jewish as well as Catholic—in the New York City metropolitan area.

But whatever the reason, the New York search for relief for religious schools is most notable for the fairly clear and surprisingly early abandonment of constitutional niceties. Very early in 1971 the proponents of parochaid and the governor apparently abandoned the attempt to repeal the "Blaine" amendment from the New York constitution. Apparently abandoned also was the sense of restriction on legislative options growing from the clause, and the generations of strict applications the New York courts had given it. The signing of the purchase of services bill on the very day the U.S. Supreme Court voided a very similar Pennsylvania act perhaps indicates the attitude. Add to that the unwillingness of the state to abandon programs of the most dubious constitutionality until forced to do so by specific court action. It was, in short, an illustration of the inability of American legislative and executive branches to deal with constitutional issues so long as there is another agency of government charged with the final constitutional responsibility. It may well have been New York that the officers of the American Civil Liberties Union had in mind when they wrote in their annual report for 1971–1972: "ACLU lobbying to defeat such measures in legislative bodies is generally not very successful. The issue is dealt with by legislators with extraordinary cynicism. Knowing that the courts will strike down aid measures, legislators vote for them anyway in order not to offend constituents to whom the issue is important."[25] One may have here, in other words, not only an ignoring of constitutional limits to legislative action, but also a reliance on their ultimate imposition by courts. If so, it is both a legislative invitation to judicial activism and constitutional buck-passing in its purest form.

CONSTITUTIONAL CONSTRAINTS AND PUBLIC POLICY

It is very easy to overestimate the impact of a constitutional decision on the policy-making process. The constitutional decision enters the policy process largely as a constraint, as a limit to the range of policy options that legislative and executive branches may consider. At the most, it forces the search for a public policy solution to move in different directions. But the new directions may not be those of the most obvious or clear constitutionality. More-

[25] *Civil Liberties* (December, 1972), p. 10.

over, when a court says that the challenged policy is constitutional, it does not necessarily push the development of policy into that clearly constitutional route. The direction and extent of policy development is determined politically, not constitutionally. Political perceptions of the problem and political support for a solution determine the movement of policy decisions. The policy processes have a political rather than a constitutional dynamic.

To put in perspective the impact of constitutional decisions on the policy processes, one need only look to their effect on policy agendas. The Supreme Court reaffirmed and broadened the constitutionality of auxiliary aids to religious schools and to their pupils in 1968 (*Board of Education* v. *Allen*). At that very time, however, the imperatives of the parochial school crises were pushing legislators to more direct and substantial forms of aid to religious schools. Political and policy realities, as it were, forced the state legislatures to leap-frog over the new precedent to new solutions for worsening problems. At other times, the policy process moved on to new issues before the major constitutional issues of the time were settled. Take, as an example, the controversy over Roman Catholic nuns as public school teachers. In the 1950s, at least three American state high courts confronted the issue with inconclusive results. But the issue soon slipped out of attention as nuns became less and less available to staff the Catholic schools, much less public ones. The decline in the number of teaching nuns that mooted that issue, indeed, led directly to the placing of parochaid at the top of the church-state policy agenda.

The cycle of policy considerations in church-state relations from 1950 to 1971 followed very closely the fortunes of organized religion in America. (Political agendas appear to shape the constitutional agenda; the reverse relationship is much less likely.) The 1950s was a time of confidence in religious values and institutions, and a time of their great influence in public life. The constitutional issues before the U.S. Supreme Court in the 1950s and the early 1960s were therefore those of growing religious influence in public life: released-time religious education, and prayer and Bible-reading in the public schools. By the late 1960s the agenda of policy issues in church-state matters had turned to assisting the educational institutions of hard-pressed religious denominations with new auxiliary aids, and with direct forms of aid. From the issues of religious ascendency we shifted to the issues of religious dependency. The policy agenda and then the constitutional agenda re-

334

flected the change in religious fortunes very directly. In the entire period, only the Supreme Court decision on tax exemptions for religious property in the late 1960s seems to be independent of the policy agendas of church-state issues.

The limited nature of the constitutional impact on policy options can also be surmised by looking at state legislation in support of religious schools both before and after the June 1971 decisions. The initial adoption of programs of aid relates very strongly to the percentage of elementary school children attending Roman Catholic schools in 1968–1969 (Table 13–2). Both direct aid and auxiliary aids came in states with the greatest percentage of pupils in Catholic schools, and the more direct forms of aid came in the quartile of states with the highest percentage. After the decisions of June 1971, two broad strategies were available to the states: the search for constitutionally uncertain forms of direct aid, or a retreat back to the constitutionally proven option of indirect aid.

TABLE 13-2

State Assistance to Parochial Schools before and after June 1971, by Percentage of Elementary School Pupils Attending Roman Catholic Schools

States Ranked by Percentage of School Pupils in Catholic Schools	1965 through June 1971 States Enacting		June 1971 through 1972 States Enacting	
	direct aid	indirect aid	direct aid	indirect aid
I. First quartile 13 states (25.3 to 14.5 percent)	8	6	5	3
II. Second quartile 12 states (14.2 to 8.3 percent)	3	6	1	0
III. Third quartile 13 states (7.8 to 4.0 percent)	0	2	0	1
IV. Fourth quartile 12 states (4.0 to 1.3 percent)	0	0	0	0
Total	11	14	6	4

Note: See Appendix III for a full listing of the states in rank order. The distinction in the headings between "direct" and "indirect" aid is the distinction between parochaid and some form of auxiliary aid.

335

But the choices appear not to have been made on strategic terms. The postdecision responses of whatever sort came in the states of greatest Catholic school population, and indeed a greater number of these later cases (6 of 10) were in the constitutionally fragile category of direct aid than there were before the decisions of June 1971. Constitutional strategy clearly appears not to have dominated the policy decisions.[26]

Legislatures and executives basically sought policy outcomes rather than constitutional purity or orthodoxy. They wanted the "best," the most useful, and most politic policy solution, even if it meant opting for questionable forms of parochaid over the constitutionally certain forms of indirect aid. The movement for new policy options for helping the troubled parochial schools thus followed the route of greatest potential advantage and the closest match between the magnitude of the problem and the amount of the aid. In the end, of course, if all else failed, states could fall back on the less useful policy programs of settled constitutionality. In the interim they would have given—as some states did in this instance—some three to five years of substantial aid to parochial schools while the plans were under litigation. All of the incentives in such instances, therefore, are on the side of constitutional adventurism. Those who play it safe in constitutional terms probably do so for political reasons—because majorities will support or demand no more than that.

Constitutional policy making has its major impact on the judiciary, especially in the traditional impact of a precedent under the rule of stare decisis. The incentives for the observance of constitu-

[26] There is also a strong alternative regional relationship to explain the incidence of parochaid legislation. Of the nine states of the Northeast, all either passed parochaid legislation before June 1971, or were explicitly prevented from doing so by advisory opinions in the states' highest courts. Parochaid passed in six: Connecticut, New Jersey, New York, Pennsylvania, Rhode Island, and Vermont. Adverse advisory opinions in Maine, Massachusetts, and New Hampshire blocked proposed legislation. Nonetheless, the main point remains: decisions appear not to have been guided by any view of constitutional options or priorities. As for explanation of the regional phenomenon, one can suggest three possibilities:

a) Within a concentrated region there is the power of example, one of the major determinants of the spread of policy innovation.
b) Catholics and other proprietors of religious schools in those states may benefit from their ethnic-religious block politics.
c) There may be within the region an identifiable set of different church-state outlooks, perhaps reflected in what are generally considered the less restrictive church-state provisions in the constitutions of those states.

tional norms and rules are far greater in the judiciary than they are in the legislative or executive arenas. Moreover, constitutional policy making in the courts has its own rhythm and dynamic. Constitutional policy grows slowly and incrementally, by tentative, short steps along an uncertain constitutional frontier. In the tumult of the real world the imperatives of specific and exigent problems force policy innovation by greater strides, and by extraconstitutional considerations.

XIV | THE CHANGING SHAPE OF CONSTITUTIONAL LITIGATION

We have bravely dispelled the old myths of mechanistic, apolitical jurisprudence, and we are no longer shocked by the proposition that political conflicts and the political processes reach into the judiciary. Constitutional questions come to appellate courts inseparably bound up with great issues of public policy, and judges in those courts, often enjoying choices and options in their decision, may shape the law and at least indirectly settle great issues of policy. But to dispel a myth is not to reconstruct reality. We banish myths more easily—and with a lower level of knowledge—than we build new realities and new explanations.

The constitutional litigation on church-state relations between 1951 and 1971 enlisted an extensive roster of actors and interests. Interest groups, attorneys, individual parties, governmental bodies and officials, courts, and judges all figured prominently. But what marked the litigation above all was the relatively orderly, purposeful way in which the issues were litigated by groups and individuals whose chief goal it was to develop or clarify some body of constitutional law. Constitutional questions of church and state came less often to the high courts of the nation as byproducts of some individual's seeking redress for wrongs. They came instead as constitutional questions, and they were brought with skill, persistence, and strategic sophistication.

While the process of constitutional litigation doubtless varies from one area of constitutional law to another, it seems clear that the sheer amount of purposeful constitutional litigation increased—especially in a number of civil liberties areas—over the past twenty-five years. Litigation over church-state relations is one very conspicuous example. Nonetheless, it becomes increasingly clear that great variations mark the processes of constitutional litigation. There is no one mode of political jurisprudence. Even within the brief span of the two decades between 1951 and 1971, the pace and profile of constitutional litigation on church and state changed clearly and revealingly.

338

CHURCH-STATE ISSUES FROM 1951 THROUGH 1971

Even the most casual headline readers would not be surprised to learn that the quantity of litigation on church-state issues increased significantly between 1951 and 1971 (Table 14-1). As the pace of litigation accelerated, its characteristics also changed. The incidence of litigation in the federal courts rose sharply during the two decades, the frequency of friendly suits in the state courts increased, and so too did the frequency with which cases were expedited to appellate courts by certification, removal, or some other unusual procedure (Table 14-1).[1] Taken together, these changes marked in their various ways a shift to more explicitly constitutional litigation moving more rapidly and efficiently to ultimate resolution in high appellate courts, especially the United States Supreme Court. Furthermore, since the friendly and expedited cases were all state cases, and since they overlapped in only two instances, these trends marked a total of 22 (64.7 percent) of the 34 church-state cases decided between 1965 and 1971. And so the political and constitutional nature of this litigation was sharpened by taking the cases out of the ordinary processes of litigation.

That acceleration and change in constitutional litigation on church-state questions was accompanied by changes in the activities of the litigating groups. The three leading separationist groups—the American Civil Liberties Union, the American Jewish Congress, and Americans United for Separation of Church and

TABLE 14-1

Total Incidence of Church-State Cases, and the Incidence of Federal, Friendly, and Expedited Cases by Seven-Year Periods, 1951–1971

| | Cases Decided in | | |
	1951–1957	1958–1964	1965–1971
Federal cases	0	1 (4.5%)	7 (20.6%)
Friendly cases	0	1 (4.5%)	8 (23.5%)
Expedited cases	0	2 (9.1%)	9 (26.5%)
Total cases	11	22	34

[1] One should be clear that the increase in federal cases was not completely or even largely a consequence of the decision in *Flast* v. *Cohen,* 392 U.S. 83 (1968). Four of the eight federal cases were brought before that decision.

TABLE 14-2

Amount of Activity by Three Major Separationist Groups
in Separationist, Adversary Cases in Seven-Year
Periods, 1951-1971

Number of Three Groups Participating	Cases Decided in		
	1951-1957	1958-1964	1965-1971
None	2 (18.2%)	6 (30.0%)	2 (9.1%)
One	6 (54.5%)	8 (40.0%)	7 (31.8%)
Two or three	3 (27.3%)	6 (30.0%)	13 (59.1%)
Total	11	20	22

Note: The unit of analysis here is the case, not the total number of group interventions. The 53 cases here analyzed were all of those of the 67 that were adversary cases in which separationists brought the action.

State—did not increase the percentage of cases in which they were involved, if only because they had little margin for increase. In only 16 of the entire group of 67 cases spanning the 1951–1971 period was there no sign of activity by at least one of the three groups. They had, in other words, established their activity and preeminence in the litigation on church and state by the early 1950s. Despite that early record of activity and intervention in the cases, however, the three separationist groups over time increased the volume of their activity per case. Especially if one looks only at the adversary cases brought by separationist interests, two or three of the leading groups increasingly entered, where formerly only one had (Table 14–2). The reader can also note that in Table 14–2, with the body of cases narrowed to adversary cases brought by separationists, the incidence of group activity does rise over time. The shift reflects the conscious cooperation and information-sharing of the three chief separationist groups. Finally, other separationist groups increasingly participated in these church-state cases, making for a richer, denser, more diverse texture of group participation. From 1951 through 1957 other separationist groups participated in only two (18.2 percent) of the separationist cases, but by 1965–1971, they were in 11 (44.0 percent).[2]

[2] The base for the percentages here is the total of 56 cases in which the plaintiff's interest was separationist: 11 from 1951–1957, 20 from 1958–1964, and 25 from 1965–1971.

Furthermore, between 1951 and 1971 the groups increased the strength of their voice in the origin of church-state litigation. As Table 14–3 suggests, the role of the groups, especially the national groups, increased significantly. The effect, of course, was to permit the groups to shape the general pattern and strategy of the litigation more effectively, for it is an axiom in constitutional litigation that the earlier a group enters a case the greater its potential control over it. This move to greater group participation in the origin of cases seems, in fact, to have begun in the middle third of the period, in advance of some of the other changes.

Over the period between 1951 and 1971, therefore, the work of the separationist groups grew in scope and complexity. The three leading groups entered the period already deeply involved in church-state litigation. They added to the politicization of church-state issues in these two decades by entering a new phase of more concentrated and cooperative action. At the same time other separationist groups stepped up their activities, ending the virtual monopoly of group participation that the three established groups had earlier enjoyed. More importantly perhaps, the groups—especially the national groups—increasingly took a role in originating the cases.

The groups, however, were not the only participants in these cases to change between 1951 and 1971. Plaintiffs themselves changed. The individual plaintiff continued to have a role in the litigation right up to 1971, symbolized best perhaps by the watchful and well-publicized presence of Madalyn Murray O'Hair. But over the years governmental officials and bodies joined the parade

TABLE 14–3

Separationist Group Activity in the Origin of Church-State
Cases by Seven-Year Periods, 1951–1971

Group Role in Origin of Cases	Cases Decided in		
	1951–1957	1958–1964	1965–1971
None	5 (45.5%)	8 (40.0%)	8 (32.0%)
Local group(s)	3 (27.3%)	5 (25.0%)	5 (20.0%)
Mixed local, national	3 (27.3%)	0	2 (8.0%)
National group(s)	0	7 (35.0%)	10 (40.0%)
Total	11	20	25

Note: The 56 cases are those in which the plaintiff interests were separationist.

to court. There were no governmental plaintiffs between 1951 and 1957, two (9.1 percent) between 1958 and 1964, and nine (26.5 percent) between 1965 and 1971. Their presence in the litigation reflects in part the increase in friendly suits; five of the eleven instances of governmental plaintiffs occurred in them. The other six reflect growing govermental activism in constitutional litigation.

More significant, perhaps, was the growing frequency with which the organized accommodationist forces participated in the church-state cases. Roman Catholic involvement, chiefly through the U.S. Catholic Conference, was apparent in only 16 of the 67 cases, half of those between 1965 and 1971. To be sure, that rate of activity showed no increase from 1951 to 1971, for one-half (34) of the 67 cases were indeed decided in the last seven year period. Nor was there any increase in the frequency with which the accommodationists entered litigation as intervenor defendants. What did change was the degree of activity represented by each accommodationist intervention. The defendant intervenors by 1965–1971 took almost twice as great a percentage of appeals (6 in 34 cases; 17.6 percent) as they had in 1951–1957 (1 in 11; 9.1 percent). Furthermore, accommodationist groups showed an increasing inclination to bring church-state litigation. There were only 5 instances in the 58 adversary cases of accommodationists initiating the litigation; 4 of the 5 fell between 1965 and 1971.

All in all, an increasing degree of political pluralism and a heightened politicality came to church-state litigation in the years of the 1950s and sixties. Naturally, one wonders why. It is tempting to suppose that constitutional litigation such as this has a growth pulse, a developmental energy of its own. Activity begets counteractivity, it is said, and the organization of one set of interests spurs the organization of others. An escalating spiral of political activity, an intensification of political conflict results. It is a common explanation, perhaps even a conventional wisdom of scholarly social science. One can find it developed in much of systems analysis and group theory.[3] But it is an explanation that is difficult to document, for it depends on deductive, logical suppositions as much as on empirical evidence.

In this particular instance, there is a good deal of common-sense appeal and some documentary facts to support the developmental explanation. There was, indeed, an increasing awareness among

[3] See, for example, the very influential work of David B. Truman, *The Governmental Process* (New York: Knopf, 1951).

the groups that their interests were being compromised by litigation whose goal was vindication rather than constitutional development, and in which the parties were making only the merest shadow of a constitutional argument. Furthermore, the groups increasingly perceived the new opportunities available to them in the judicial process. Legal realism and sociological jurisprudence created a new set of outlooks and expectations for the courts, a new awareness of their involvement in the political processes. Even the judges came to a new realism about their roles, and some of their decisions—especially those in *NAACP* v. *Button* and *Flast* v. *Cohen*—legitimated and invited group access to the courts. This argument therefore has a common-sense appeal that seems to validate the developmental explanation. But there are, unhappily, no time-series data to buttress it. That is, there is no perceptible sequence to all of the changes between 1951 and 1971. The developmental "chain" of events and influences, if there was one, occurred in so short a span of time that it escapes attention in the seven-year periods we have employed. By those time measures, the changes appear to have happened more or less simultaneously.

There is also a much less grandiose explanation for the changes in the process of litigating these issues after 1951. Those changes coincided with changes in the nature of the public policies under challenge. To some extent, the changing shape of this constitutional litigation reflected nothing more than a shift in the level of government involved (Table 14–4). Or, to put the same point a little differently, it reflected a shift in the ownership of the oxen being gored (Table 14–5). The shift from concern with local policy

TABLE 14-4

Policy-Making Levels Involved in Church-State Litigation
by Seven-Year Periods, 1951–1971

Level of Government Making Policy	Cases Decided in		
	1951–1957	*1958–1964*	*1965–1971*
National government	0	0	3 (6.3%)
State government	3 (23.1%)	10 (33.3%)	31 (64.6%)
Local government	10 (76.9%)	20 (66.7%)	14 (29.2%)
Total	13	30	48

Note: The total of 91 policy-making levels results from the fact that a significant number of the 67 cases involved two levels of policy at the same time.

TABLE 14-5
Policies Overturned, by Level of Policy, in Church-State
Litigation by Seven-Year Periods, 1951–1971

Governmental Level of Overturned Policy	1951–1957	Cases Decided in 1958–1964	1965–1971
State	0	5 (41.7%)	7 (46.7%)
Local	6 (100.0%)	7 (58.3%)	8 (53.3%)
Total	6	12	15

to state and national policy recruited new groups and intensified the commitments of old groups. It raised the stakes of judicial conflict, and it gave the entire process of litigation a new salience. It involved a level of government that was more active constitutionally, and that had at its command more constitutional expertise. And it expanded the opportunities for friendly suits and special, expediting procedures in the courts.

When policy disputes move from the fragmented, decentralized politics of local government to those of statewide government, the judicial processes meld more easily and more fully into the wider universe of policy processes and politics. One more illustration may help to support the point. Some 12 of all the 67 cases emerged directly and speedily from a battle in the state legislature, and 9 of those 12 happened within the 1965–1971 period. That is to say, in 9 of the 34 cases decided between 1965 and 1971, the bringing of a constitutional test case was a direct, uninterrupted extension of a battle the groups had lost in the legislature. The challenges to the Pennsylvania and Rhode Island parochaid statutes are especially illustrative. Alliances of groups in both states formed to repulse the bids for aid to religious schools. A substantial part of their argument against the legislation rested on its unconstitutionality, and they repeatedly affirmed their intention to test it if the bills passed. The bills did pass, and the group alliances, with very few changes, immediately brought litigation.

POLITICIZING CONSTITUTIONAL DEVELOPMENT

At least in this one area of American constitutional law, the process of constitutional litigation has become intensely political. Most

344

of the cases came not as individual suits for remedy but as well-organized pursuits of favorable constitutional rulings. They came, in other words, as *constitutional* litigation. And in varying degrees most of the actors and institutions in the judicial process recognized them as cases that not only raised important constitutional questions, but that also were bound to affect bitterly contested issues of public policy.

Preeminent in the politicization of church-state litigation have been the three leading separationist groups. They seized the initiative in framing and bringing church-state cases to the American courts, and thus in framing the agenda of questions the courts must decide. Only sixteen of these sixty-seven cases were untouched by their concerns. Moreover, the three groups altered the quality and nature of the litigation. They were far more attentive to strategic considerations, both in litigating cases (that is, insisting on full trial records) and in setting priorities among issues for litigation. They altered the nature of plaintiffs in some of these cases, preferring to work with religious, less aggressive, high-status plaintiffs. And they brought better and more experienced attorneys to the litigation. In short, they brought to the sixty-seven church-state cases a litigating skill, an ongoing concern and interest, and a constitutional purposefulness that lifted the litigation very much out of the ordinary.

So constant and intertwined have been the roles of the three separationist groups in this litigation that they have come to operate as a group "system." There is evidence of cooperation, ranging all the way from frequent informal contacts to the brief life of a formal, representative litigation consortium. And yet there has been repeated competition and, ultimately, a division of labor. The separationism of each of the three has different perspectives and meanings, and thus they have quite separate members and clienteles. They tend to be interested in different issues and so in different cases: the AU concern over Roman Catholic power serves as the chief example. They also go about litigating in different ways which reflect differences in their internal organizations and decision making. They differ even in their degree of attachment to the ultimate constitutional objective in bringing the cases. They differ, too, in their attachment to each other. The ACLU and AJC are drawn together by physical proximity, by overlapping personnel, and similarity of views and approaches, leaving AU somewhat isolated. The ACLU and AJC, for instance, remained less concerned

345

with Catholic influence than AU, more sedulous in pursuing entirely constitutional goals than AU, and more incremental in strategy and more anxious to win decisions than AU.

In brief, the major separationist litigating groups have been the major influence transforming church-state litigation in American courts. They have not only heightened its politicality; they have, as well, centralized and nationalized it. They have brought to it legal figures such as Leo Pfeffer, and they have centralized information and communication about church-state litigation. Local group involvement in these cases diminished between 1951 and 1971. Moreover, both local groups and other national groups supplemented rather than complemented the work of the three main groups; they were found in those cases in which the ACLU, AJC, or AU were already present. It is probably not misleading, therefore, to speak in this interest-group system of "major" effective groups and "minor" groups, whose impact on the litigation and judicial politics was peripheral and even minimal.

The three separationist groups were not alone, however, in seeking constitutional and policy goals in the judicial process. Plaintiffs, especially those who themselves originated church-state litigation, often acted at the price of personal financial sacrifice and obloquy in the community. Sometimes markedly zealous and socially unconventional, they were the rare individuals single-minded enough to pursue unpopular litigation. Inner directed, even eccentric, individuals thus joined well-organized national groups in setting the major outlines of constitutional litigation in church-state issues. At times, in fact, they jarred the strategic plans of the groups by their initiatives and forced the groups into uncongenial litigation.

Finally, the major accommodationist groups—especially those associated with Roman Catholicism—became increasingly active in these cases. Something approaching an "accommodationist bar" developed around the U.S. Catholic Conference and the person of William Ball. It accumulated an expertise and degree of communication about litigation that rivaled, in kind if not in degree, that of the separationist groups. Other groups, such as Citizens for Educational Freedom (CEF) and the National Jewish Commission on Law and Public Affairs (COLPA), also participated in a few cases. Struggling to find a role in litigation that never directly involved them at the origin, the accommodationist groups increasingly mobilized intervening defendants or assisted the governmental bodies defending the policy challenged. All in all, they left the defendants without aid of some type in only forty percent of the cases.

The presence of groups and plaintiffs with explicit constitutional goals is indeed one mark of a highly politicized body of litigation. It is not the only one, however. The litigation itself and the reverberations it sends out may also show the characteristics of political litigation. In these church-state cases one can point to:

the impact of the litigation upon the actors, especially in the form of community hostility;

the intensive and immediate impact of the litigation on policy considerations in the other policy-making institutions of government (the intertwining of parochaid legislation and litigation, for instance);

the voting patterns of judges, especially along religious lines, which suggest that they perceived the cases in terms of broader public policy interests and outcomes (one might also note the incidence of disqualifying and recusing among the judges of the trial courts);

the high appellate ratio in these cases. Somewhere between 40 and 50 percent of the total universe of church-state litigation in American courts apparently reached appellate levels. In 38 of the 67 appellate cases (56.7 percent) some party sought access to the U.S. Supreme Court; in 10 (14.9 percent) they achieved it;

the increasing incidence of advisory opinions and friendly suits, the purest forms of political jurisprudence.

This is a body of litigation, then, in which great issues of constitutional and public policy were fought out in an open, explicit way apparent to the major participants and to involved clienteles and institutions beyond the judiciary.

Within this universe of sixty-seven church-state cases in American appellate courts, the subset of cases involving elementary and secondary education were even more than usually political. Group participation was more frequent and more intense in the school cases. The separationists won far more victories in them; all but two of the twenty-nine proseparation decisions came in school cases. The divide between the school cases and the other church-state cases also apparently guided the votes of the Protestant and

347

unchurched judges whose votes were not related to their religious backgrounds. The school cases, moreover, were most apt to grow directly out of policy disputes in legislatures, and in the aftermath of decision the degree of defiance of the courts and the harassment of plaintiffs was greater in them. The school cases apparently added to the political and policy concerns over church-state relations additional policy concerns over elementary and secondary education. The coincidence of the interests of separationism and public education in these cases amplified the already audible policy overtones in the rest of church-state litigation.

Some constitutional litigation has always been self-conscious and purposive and thus political. Plaintiffs have always sought to promote broader interests and to shape public policy in litigation. The politicization of church-state cases represents, therefore, not a new phenomenon in American constitutional litigation, but rather an accentuation of what had always been the case in a far less common and systematic way. Whether this new degree of political jurisprudence in church-state cases is unusual by contemporary standards is not easy to say. The involvement of the NAACP and other groups in the equal protection cases of the post-World War II period is well documented.[4] At various points in the late 1950s and early 1960s, indeed, the NAACP was second only to the United States government in the number of cases it brought to the U.S. Supreme Court. Conventional wisdom and scholarly evidence also suggest that other areas of constitutional litigation—especially those in civil liberties—are similarly litigated, but direct comparison is difficult in the absence of data on entire constellations of constitutional litigation.

Nor is it easy to compare the role of litigating groups in church-state litigation with the role of other groups in other sets of cases. The information about group activity in these sixty-seven cases does, however, permit one to plead that the power of the groups here must be an important exception to some skepticism about the general importance of groups in litigation.[5] It leads one to sus-

[4] For a classic study of the NAACP in litigation, see Clement E. Vose, *Caucasians Only* (Berkeley and Los Angeles: University of California Press, 1959).

[5] Nathan Hakman, especially, has minimized the role of litigating groups. The fullest statement of his position can be found in his "The Supreme Court's Political Environment: The Processing of Noncommercial Litigation," a chapter in Joel B. Grossman and Joseph Tanenhaus, eds., *Frontiers of Judicial Research* (New York: Wiley, 1969); see, for example, p. 245. Hakman relies heavily on counts of amici and plaintiff party appearances

pect, indeed, that a fuller consultation with all parties to a body of litigation would reveal a degree of group participation well beyond what one might gather from the printed records of cases.[6] In any event, the major groups in church-state litigation between 1951 and 1971 mobilized, even monopolized, the resources of constitutional litigation: the talent, the money, the involved personnel, the skill and experience in litigation. They professionalized the litigation and they publicized it, stimulating additional activity in the cause of developing the constitutional law of church and state. Above all, they joined the necessary degree of motivation and concern to the necessary resources for litigation—a joining which very few individual litigants can or will achieve.

LIMITS TO POLITICAL JURISPRUDENCE

Political influence, even of a somewhat unusual sort, can be exercised within the judicial process. The separationist groups and individual plaintiffs in these cases prove that once again. But it is a special kind of political power or influence. Unlike that in the other two branches in the American political system, it does not depend on the mobilization of those traditional political resources needed to influence electoral politics: large sums of money and great blocks of loyal voters. It is far less dependent, therefore, on considerations of opinion, prestige, acceptance, or even acceptability. The special forms and rules of the judicial process itself define the special resources necessary for this influence.

Even the limits to political power and influence in the judicial

---

noted in the case reports and on questionnaires returned by attorneys in litigation. I would disagree with a number of Hakman's assumptions and procedures. Group roles extend (both in scope and importance) far beyond the formal ones of plaintiff and amicus curiae. Because they tend to assume a rather traditional legal role even in the most politicized constitutional litigation—see the findings in Chapter VII—the attorneys in the cases are not always the best source for information on the group or other political involvement in the case. A good deal of the Hakman terminology also suggests assumptions that are, in fact, questionable. For instance, the description of plaintiffs in group-sponsored cases as "pawns" or "symbols" suggests a generally inconsequential role, which the experience of these sixty-seven church-state cases would refute. Strong, initiative-taking litigants need not be incompatible with group activity of the most effective sort.

[6] For instance, in his *Constitutional Change* (Lexington, Mass.: D.C. Heath, 1972), Clement E. Vose discovered, many years after the fact, a degree of group activity in some of the great cases by examining archival materials.

process have their special judicial quality. Chief among them are the norms and expectations, the forms and procedures of the courtroom. While the American judiciary may on one level shape public policy by construing law and constitution, on a second level it still determines rights and equities, guilt or innocence, still gives meaning to various bodies of law. The judges continue, therefore, to meet old standards of formality, distance, and impartiality. Parties and interests to litigation must make their arguments in the traditional ways: by written brief or oral argument on the legal issues. Attempts to influence the decisions of judges are far more restricted than they are in legislative or executive agency politics. The latitude and proprieties of influence in the judicial process are tightly circumscribed by the widely honored traditions that encase it.

Beyond the limits that the judicial forum puts on the pursuit of interests in the judicial process, however, there are the less obvious limits imposed by the structure of public policy. That is to say, access to the judicial process and the subsequent opportunity to influence its decisions depend in great part on the procedures that are customary in the judiciary, and on the values and perceptions of the individuals, especially the judges, who people it. That much is now almost conventional scholarly wisdom. But in ways that are far less obvious, influence in the judicial process—at least in areas of constitutional law—depends also on the structure of the public policy dispute.

It is the very logic and structure of church-state policy that gives the initiatives in litigation to separationists. The public policy at issue—whether it is national, state, or local—involves some arrangement or liason between church and state to which the separationists object. It thus falls to them to challenge public policy in the courts, when and however they choose. Thus, the accommodationists brought only 10 of these 67 cases, and only 5 of the 58 adversary cases. Accommodationist groups and interests were forced into a defensive, reactive position in most of the litigation. Worse yet, the logic of litigation challenging public policy cast some governmental body, not the chief accommodationist groups, into the role of defendant. A major share of accommodationist effort went simply to finding entree into the very litigation that fundamentally threatened their interests. While the separationists worked to influence the course of constitutional development, the accommodationists struggled just for representation in the process.

350

Furthermore, the locale of the sixty-seven cases was also related to the nature of the public policy at issue. Parochaid legislation, and thus the parochaid cases, was limited largely to states with large Roman Catholic populations. And in a significant number of cases, the litigation itself was virtually an uninterrupted extension of a battle fought in the legislature to stop the passage of the policy in the first place. If the case began in a local policy dispute, moreover, those beginnings seemed to exacerbate the backlash on the plaintiffs. If the locale of the litigation was also the site of the policy jurisdiction—that is, if the litigation was brought in the confines of the jurisdiction in which the policy was made—the likelihood of unhappy consequences for the plaintiffs increased.

Finally, the nature of the policy itself seemed to determine the likelihood of compliance with appellate court decisions. If the policy was local rather than statewide or national, enforcement was fragmented, and noncompliance more feasible. Furthermore, if the policy did not involve the appropriation of funds, enforcement lost a sanction and noncompliance was again more feasible. Combining the two factors, therefore, enforcement and compliance were most feasible in instances of statewide policies that relied on appropriated funds. The fate of parochaid statutes—both statewide and involving substantial funding—best illustrates the point. Conversely, enforcement was most difficult and noncompliance most feasible in instances of local policies not dependent on appropriations (for example, prayer in public schools).

All of this is to argue that the basic nature of the judicial process and the public policy at issue—in addition to the interested groups and actors—determine much of what happens in the judicial process. It is the nature of the judicial institutions and the policy being contested that, above all, determines who will enter the judicial process and on what terms. They define the extent of the opportunities for litigating groups and plaintiffs.

THE CONSEQUENCES OF POLITICAL JURISPRUDENCE

The decisions of American appellate courts burst into an almost infinite variety of impacts and aftermaths. In the most politicized areas of constitutional law, a decision of the United States Supreme Court leaves untouched scarcely any of the major publics and processes involved with the policy. Not the least of the impacts, how-

351

ever, are those that circle back upon the judicial process and judicial institutions themselves. As the constitutional politics of church and state became more explicit in policy concern and accelerated in pace, they worked a number of changes in the life and labor of the American appellate courts.

The Increased Workload in the Courts

The sheer bulk of church-state cases increased geometrically between 1951 and 1971. There were more cases decided in the last one-third of that period than there were in the first two-thirds. Over that time the case burden also shifted from state to federal courts, taking advantage thereby of the speedy access to the U.S. Supreme Court. And nine of the ten cases decided by the Supreme Court were decided between 1961 and 1971. In their small way, therefore, the litigators of church-state issues added their bit to the already heavy and overloaded dockets of American appellate courts. They also added their part to the increasing burden on the Supreme Court that has prompted Chief Justice Warren Burger, among others, to suggest the limitation or abolition of the three-judge panels.

The Stimulation of Judicial Activism

Courts cannot ignore the demands placed upon them. As sophisticated groups and individuals bring litigation whose primary purpose is to overturn some public policy, they create enormous pressures on the courts to take precisely that activist step. Litigation of this sort both reflects and stimulates a general public expectation that courts will assert constitutional rights and restrictions over the public policies that emerged from the representative politics of the legislature. The power of appellate courts to resist these pressures is limited. If they spurn them completely, they risk a very serious danger of appearing timid and committed to the status quo. Even more serious, they risk losing support in that part of the public that expects an activist judiciary.

The effects of the activist pressures were, indeed, apparent in church-state litigation after 1950. It was in a church-state case (*Flast* v. *Cohen*) that the Supreme Court abandoned its long-time refusal to entertain suits in which the plaintiffs' only interest was the general one of a taxpayer.[7] In *Flast* the Court conceded, in

[7] *Flast* v. *Cohen*, 392 U.S. 83 (1968); *Frothingham* v. *Mellon*, 262 U.S. 447 (1923).

352

effect, that the federal courts would be more activist—less restrained or restricted—in enforcing assertions of constitutional rights and limits. It is perhaps also pertinent that the decision in *Flast* came in 1968, just two years after the Senate had passed its Judicial Review Bill of 1966.* The bill gave any citizen or taxpayer standing in federal courts to raise challenges under the First Amendment to a list of statutes making grants or loans to church-related institutions. The list included nine statutes that Congress had passed within the preceding decade, among them the National Defense Education Act of 1958, the Higher Education Acts of 1963 and 1965, legislation setting up poverty programs, and Congressional grants for elementary and secondary education.

The bill went through the Senate without extensive opposition. Its chief supporter, Senator Sam Ervin of North Carolina, supported it in the confidence that the courts would invalidate much of the legislation, but the bill also received the support of proponents who foresaw a constitutional clarification spurring additional programs of aid to education. The Department of Health, Education and Welfare, however, opposed it, and a raft of constitutional experts raised all manner of constitutional questions, especially the question of Congress's authority to legislate on what had apparently been, in *Frothingham,* the Supreme Court's interpretation of the references to "cases" and "controversies" in Article III of the Constitution.[9] The bill encountered slowly accumulating opposition in the House of Representatives, and never left the Judiciary Committee. The issue was, however, shortly mooted by the decision in *Flast*. The expanded constitutional role that the Senate had proposed to mandate, the Supreme Court took up voluntarily.

The Development of Special Routes for Constitutional Litigation

At least in the field of church-state relations, the pressures for speedy assertion of constitutional primacy over public policy have produced a new speed and even casualness in constitutional litigation. The special procedures for expediting litigation have probably taken some toll in the thought and attention given to legal argument, and they have often propelled litigation at such a speed that important interests never managed to enter. The more frequent

---

* S. 2097, 89th Congress, 2d Session (1966).

[9] Leo Pfeffer testified in favor of the bill before the Senate Judiciary Committee's Subcommittee on Constitutional Rights, chaired by Senator Sam Ervin. Pfeffer and Ervin later shared oral argument before the U.S. Supreme Court in *Flast* v. *Cohen,* the case that finally settled the issue.

resorts to friendly suit and advisory opinion, by dispensing with the adversary relationship of parties to litigation, have thereby risked compromising the adversary nature of the constitutional argument.

In short, these developments threaten the quality of the records and argument reaching appellate courts. The expedited and friendly cases do not bring experienced church-state (or even civil liberties) counsel to the litigation. They often pose hypothetical questions, and even when the questions are real, they may be "immature." The constitutionality of parochaid statutes, for instance, was challenged before the administrative facts and impacts of the policies could be known. Courts scrutinized the statutes more or less as they were printed rather than as they affected public policy. Finally, and ironically, the growth of these special processes often left major interests unrepresented in the judicial forum. (Political jurisprudence leads ultimately to a strangely unpolitical variant.) The danger is thus a combination of the worst of two worlds: political jurisprudence without the access and representation of the interests deeply concerned.

Acceleration of the Pace of Constitutional Change

Active, purposeful litigation rushes the appellate courts from one constitutional question to another. The courts have little or no breathing room, no time to rest or recover from the wounds of unpopular decisions, before a new issue comes hard upon the heels of the last one. The acceleration of litigation and the resulting compression of constitutional "time" also robs the appellate courts of time for maneuver. While courts may prefer to explore and refine an already opened issue in subsequent cases, well-organized litigators may rush them into new issues. Even the U.S. Supreme Court, despite the great degree of control it enjoys over its jurisdiction, must certainly feel the pressures generated by litigation with public awareness and support behind it. At least the Court honored a high percentage of group-sponsored requests for appellate jurisdiction in these church-state cases. Gone or diminished, therefore, are the opportunities to clarify a line of constitutional development and the opportunities to retreat somewhat from an unpopular or unwise decision.[10] Quite simply put, the courts lose some of their

[10] Note Walter Murphy's thesis on the Supreme Court's tradition of strategic retreat in the last chapter of his *Elements of Judicial Strategy* (Chicago: University of Chicago Press, 1964).

former control over the tempo of litigation, and therefore over the agenda of issues they must face. And thus they lose some of the strategic options they once had.

Erosion of Public Support for the Courts

The onslaught of purposeful constitutional litigation threatens the erosion of support for the courts by placing them on the horns of two dilemmas. First, the accelerated litigating of deeply-felt issues means an increase in the unhappiness over decisions— whichever way they go—and over the courts that make them. Moreover, a great share of constitutional cases arise as minorities assert their constitutional guarantees against the policy preferences of majorities. So it is often majorities that are unhappy, and whose confidence in the courts is eroded. If there is also a defiance of or noncompliance with the courts, courts may suffer further losses of prestige. Judges may even begin to worry about compliance and enforcement problems in subsequent decisions.

Furthermore, an accelerated pace of political jurisprudence makes the courts choose between the active litigators in American society and those who cling to older and greatly less political views about courts and judges. Litigating groups and plaintiffs increasingly expect the appellate courts to intervene in and decide policy questions. Implicitly, at least, they accept the fact of the judges' role in the political process, and they expect them to be judicial activists in that role. When they bring litigation, they do not often want judicial self-restraint. A great many Americans, on the contrary, cling to the belief that the courts are "above" or at least aside from the political processes. One can only imagine what their reactions might have been, to take only one example, as a state supreme court divided precisely along Catholic-Protestant lines in a celebrated case over public aid to religious schools. At the least such cases and especially such decisions threaten their general confidence in the judiciary.

These are considerations not easy to measure in reality. But two central facts are beyond dispute. The Supreme Court's public support as measured in the Gallup poll declined markedly in the 1960s (see Table 14–6). Moreover, the public reacted hostilely to the Court's decisions on prayer and Bible reading in the public schools. As late as October of 1971, only 27 percent of the American adult public approved of the 1963 and 1964 decisions. The prayer decisions, one should add, were not the only ones to merit

TABLE 14-6
Ratings Given to the United States Supreme Court
in Four Gallup Polls, 1963–1969

Ratings	1963	1967	1968	1969
Excellent and good	43%	45%	36%	33%
Fair and poor	41%	46%	53%	54%
No opinion	16%	9%	11%	13%

public disapproval in this period; the public was, for example, no more pleased with the Court's 1966 decision on the admissibility of confessions in criminal trials. But the American public did approve of a number of Supreme Court decisions, the ones on reapportionment and the dissemination of birth control information, for instance.

Opinion surveys, therefore, document both a declining public support for the Supreme Court and a public disapproval of a number of the most celebrated Supreme Court decisions of the time. Are these two aspects of opinion about the Court related? Every indication we have would suggest that they are. Scholarly studies suggest generally that the policy positions of individuals—and their consequent agreements or disagreements with decisions of the Court—are major determinants of general support levels for the Court. And, more specifically, opposition to the school prayer decisions correlated with disapproval and low levels of public support.[11]

These have been the major impacts of political jurisprudence on American appellate courts as the litigation on church-state questions reveals them. In and of themselves they do not constitute a judgment on political jurisprudence. That balance can be struck only after one looks at the full range of accomplishments and im-

[11] I am aware of three studies that make both the general point and relate it to public disapproval of the prayer decisions. They are: Walter F. Murphy and Joseph Tanenhaus, "Public Opinion and the United States Supreme Court: A Preliminary Mapping of Some Prerequisites for Court Legitimation of Regime Changes," a chapter in Grossman and Tanenhaus, eds., *Frontiers of Judicial Research;* John H. Kessel, "Public Perceptions of the Supreme Court," *Midwest Journal of Political Science* 10 (1966), 167–191; Kenneth M. Dolbeare, "The Public Views the Supreme Court," a chapter in Herbert Jacob, ed., *Law, Politics, and the Federal Courts* (Boston: Little, Brown, 1967).

pacts it has had, both in the judicial process and outside of it. Political jurisprudence doubtless has had its gains and successes, especially in the political access and equity it has afforded minorities with negligible influence in other areas. It may, as well, have raised the levels of political confidence and efficacy of individuals within these minorities. It may thus have even aided their personal integration into the American political system. Political jurisprudence may also have assisted the development of political innovation in an otherwise deadlocked political system. Its growth has, indeed, often been attributed to the failure of legislatures to come to grips with the great problems of the day. But whatever may have been the more general results of organized and purposeful constitutional litigation, it has altered not only the judicial processes themselves but the delicate fabric of public expectations and support that have for so long been the courts' major source of legitimacy and their first line of defense.

IN CONCLUSION

It is the pledge of the American Constitution that it will limit the ability of majorities to enact their goals and preferences into public policy. For a long time, however, even sizable minorities faced two barriers in claiming those constitutional protections. They often lacked the skills and resources, even the desire, to battle through the labyrinths of the judicial system. And even when the will and resources were there, the courts were chary with their hospitality. The federal courts, especially, demanded a degree of interest on the part of the plaintiff that effectively precluded many constitutional challenges to majoritarian policy. With appeal to the final constitutional authority thus limited, many constitutional wrongs went without remedy.

The onset of political jurisprudence in various areas of constitutional law changed all that. The courts broadened the rights of access; decisions such as those in *Flast* v. *Cohen* and *NAACP* v. *Button,* for example, insured a freer entry to the federal courts. And purposeful litigation resulting from the zealotry of individual plaintiffs and the exertions of litigating groups exploited this easier access to demand a more extensive judicial enforcement of the Constitution. Thus there has flowered in the judiciary a "minoritarian" politics that seeks for its authority and legitimacy, not coalitions of voters or aggregates of conventional political influ-

357

ence, but the weight of the Constitution itself. By their recourse to the judicial process and the Constitution, litigating minorities have increasingly been able to invoke the authority of the constitutional document as a limit on past and future public policy.

In the past the tendency has been strong to separate the constitutional politics of the judicial process from the politics of policy-making in the other two branches. As these sixty-seven church-state cases indicate, constitutional politics cannot be separated so easily from the rest of the political process. They are perhaps separable in law; they are not in politics. The separationist groups and plaintiffs seek constitutional interpretations, not out of constitutional curiosity, but to close off certain policy options. Accommodationists resist the constitutional probes in order to sustain or extend policy options. The invocation of the constitutional limit is a strategy or tactic in policy politics. And so the courts, by reason of their interpretation and application of constitutions, are involved in policy making. The constitutional limits restrict the making of policy just as surely as do the opinion and activity of majorities in the electorate.

In their special, very legal way, the courts thus offer an alternative or supplementary avenue for the influencing of public policy. Especially by providing a route by which minorities can restrict policy development, the courts add to the richness and complexity of American pluralist politics. They offer relatively equal access and thus a new mode of representation for some relatively powerless interests. In these church-state cases not only separationists generally, but virtually every shade and nuance of separationism found the entree to policy making on church-state matters through the courts that they could not otherwise find. The political role of separationism, depending as it did on constitutional limits, was ultimately defensive and without initiative in the formulation of policy. But influence there was, however defensive, and perhaps as much influence as one could justify a minority's having in a democratic polity.

As this church-state litigation suggests, however, the minoritarian politics of the judicial process is neither egalitarian nor formless. The resources that lead to power and influence in the judicial process are no more evenly distributed than the political resources that lead to power and influence in legislatures. The advantages of organization are as great in the judicial process as in the legislative. There is, moreover, a division of labor, a stability in interests and actors, a continuity of concern that structures the representation of interests and the political roles in the litigating of these constitutional issues. Especially at the higher reaches of the judicial process—and most especially in the United States Supreme Court—access is selective, the representations purposeful, the cases resonant with policy overtones. It is at that point that the order and structure imposed by both the discretion of the courts and the resources of the participants is most obvious. The nature and structure of influence in the judicial process is surely peculiar to it, and yet it is fully parallel in form and outline to the structure of influence we have taken for granted in legislatures and executives.

XV | EPILOGUE:
1971 TO 1974

The determined, even desperate, search for a permissible form of aid to religious schools surged well past 1971. The decisions of June 1971 were discouraging, to be sure. But as the plight of the parochial schools worsened, the quest for a constitutional way of helping them quickened. Test case followed legislation, and new legislation followed test case. The issue of parochaid thus dominated church-state politics between 1971 and 1974, as accommodationists within these three years exhausted virtually all politically feasible forms of aid to the religious schools.

The politics of litigating church-state issues that had matured and stabilized by 1971 also continued into the next few years. The role of the three chief separationist groups continued and, in general, trends in the process of litigation carried through to 1974 with few apparent alterations or deviations. Even the rate of litigation increased apace. High appellate courts decided 11 church-state cases from 1951 to 1957, 22 from 1958 to 1964, and 34 between 1965 and late June 1971. But in just the three years from late June 1971 to June 1974, there were at least 34.[1]

---

[1] The phrase "at least" means exactly that. Very probably some cases decided by then had not appeared in the usual published reports by the time this epilogue was written in November 1974. In identifying these cases for this period, I used the same criteria that were used to select the sixty-seven cases of the study. The thirty-four cases were these: *Allen* v. *Morton,* 495 F.2d 65 (1973); *Anderson* v. *Laird,* 466 F.2d 283 (1972); *Anderson* v. *Salt Lake City,* 475 F.2d 29 (1973); *Board of Education* v. *Bakalis,* 299 N.E.2d 737 (1973); *Brusca* v. *State Board of Education,* 405 U.S. 1050 (1972); *Cecrle* v. *Illinois Educational Facilities Authority,* 288 N.E.2d 399 (1972); *Clayton* v. *Kervick,* 285 A.2d 11 (1971); *Durham* v. *McLeod,* 192 S.E.2d 202 (1972); *Epeldi* v. *Engelking,* 488 P.2d 860 (1971); *Grit* v. *Wolman,* 413 U.S. 901 (1973); *Hunt* v. *McNair,* 413 U.S. 734 (1973); *Jackson* v. *California,* 460 F.2d 282 (1972); *Johnson* v. *Sanders,* 403 U.S. 955 (1971); *Manning* v. *Sevier County,* 517 P.2d 549 (1973); *Meyer* v. *Oklahoma City,* 496 P.2d 789 (1972); *Mikell* v. *Town of Williston,* 285 A.2d 713 (1971); *Miller* v. *Ayres,* 191 S.E.2d 261 (1972); *Miller* v. *Ayres,* 198 S.E.2d 634 (1973); *Panarella* v. *Birenbaum,* 343 N.Y.S.2d 333 (1973); *PEARL* v. *Levitt,* 413 U.S. 472 (1973); *PEARL* v. *Nyquist,* 413 U.S. 756 (1973); *People ex rel. Klinger* v. *Howlett,* 305 N.E.2d 129 (1973); *POAU*

THE CHURCH-STATE CASES, 1971–1974

No less than 13 of the 34 cases (38.2 percent) between 1971 and 1974 litigated some form of aid to religious schools (Table 15–1). Another 9 (26.5 percent) raised issues of aid for religious colleges and universities. More than 60 percent of the cases, in other words, reflected the determined efforts of those years to shore

TABLE 15-1

Nature of Church-State Issues in 34 Cases Decided
in High Appellate Courts, 1971-1974

	Number
I. Aid to Religious Organizations	
parochaid (various forms of aid to religious schools)	13
tuition loans or grants for attending religious colleges	5
bonds for construction of buildings at religious colleges	3
bus rides for pupils of religious schools	2
tax exemptions for religious organizations	1
"shared time" programs in schools	1
use of income from public lands for religious purpose	1
purchase of services at religious university	1
	27
II. Religious Influences in Public Places	
religious symbol (e.g., cross) on public lands	3
rental of public property to religious crusade	1
invocation said at high school commencement	1
compulsory chapel at military academies	1
articles in college newspapers criticizing religions	1
religious operation of public hospital	1
	8
Total	35[a]

[a] There are 35 categories in 34 cases because one case consolidated two very different issues.

v. *Essex*, 275 N.E.2d 603 (1971); *Pratt* v. *Arizona Board of Reagents*, 520 P.2d 514 (1974); *Public Funds for Public Schools* v. *Marburger*, 417 U.S. 961 (1974); *Sloan* v. *Lemon*, 413 U.S. 825 (1973); *State ex rel. School District* v. *Nebraska Board of Education*, 195 N.W.2d 161 (1972); *State ex rel. Rogers* v. *Swanson*, 219 N.W.2d 726 (1974); *State ex rel. Warren* v. *Nusbaum*, 198 N.W.2d 650 (1972); *State ex rel. Warren* v. *Nusbaum*, 219 N.W.2d 577 (1974); *Von Stauffenberg* v. *District Unemployment Compensation Board*, 459 F.2d 1128 (1972); *Weiss* v. *Bruno*, 509 P.2d 973 (1973); *Wiest* v. *Mt. Lebanon School District*, 320 A.2d 362 (1974); *Wolman* v. *Essex*, 409 U.S. 808 (1972).

up the troubled educational institutions of American religious organizations. No other concern in the vast terrain of church-state controversy had any impact of consequence. Viewed more generally, the dominance of issues involving aid to religious institutions reflected the unhappy times on which they had fallen. That dominance also highlights the shift in subject-matter concerns from the twenty years before (compare Table 10–2). The basic church-state conflict is enormously stable, but it manifests itself in ever-changing ways.

In several other revealing ways, the trends of 1971 and earlier were either accelerated or modified. The pace of accommodationist initiation of suits quickened, the result of two conspicuous influences. First, there grew up in the late 1960s an accommodationist hope that they might also invoke the then-fashionable "equal protection" argument, the doctrine that came to be known as "substantive equal protection." The nub of the argument was the assertion that the state owed it to parents of parochial school students to grant them the same degree of educational support it gave to parents of public school children. (That spate of cases lasted only until 1972, when the Supreme Court disposed of the contention in the *Brusca* case.) Second, and more important, the rise in the number of accommodationist suits appears to be related to a rise in the incidence of friendly suits. While the friendly suit is difficult to identify from the formal record, it is worth noting that among the accommodationist suits one state official sued another in four, that the state's bonding authority was at issue in two, and that in three a state official, as the defendant, argued the unconstitutionality of a state statute—all tell-tale signs of the friendly suit in most instances.

That upsurge in friendly suits is related to the acceleration of another trend: the shift from the defense of local public policy to the defense of state policy. Of these 34 cases, 24 (70.6 percent) involve state policy. That trend, in turn, reflects the shift in issues discussed above. Programs of aid to financially distressed schools and colleges must of necessity be state (or federal) programs, drawing on the taxing power and the policy scope of the states. Even some kinds of aid that had traditionally been local—such as free transportation to religious schools—became statewide as the problems became more acute and the politics of response more intense. The results of that newly concentrated involvement of the states are predictable: a greater number of friendly cases, a more

362

expert defense of accommodationist policies, and a greater likelihood of compliance with adverse decisions. Those consequences in turn surely mean a more intense and rapid litigation of church-state issues.

In one important respect—the politics of litigation—little changed after 1971. In 15 of the cases (44.1 percent) there were either amici curiae or intervenors. Leo Pfeffer was involved formally as a counsel of record in 5 cases, 2 of them in argument before the United States Supreme Court. The involvement of the American Civil Liberties Union, Americans United, and the American Jewish Congress also carried into the 1971–1974 period without relaxation. At least one of them participated actively in the sponsorship of 6 of the 9 cases that went to the United States Supreme Court for decision.[2]

THE PATTERNS OF DECISION

The even division between separationist and accommodationist outcomes also continued past June of 1971. In 3 of the 34 cases decided between 1971 and 1974, the outcomes were mixed. Of the remaining 31 cases, the separationist interests prevailed in 16. The even division of outcomes is the more remarkable because in this period 8 of the 9 U.S. Supreme Court decisions were separationist, and the Supreme Court had been equally separationist before June 1971. One might have expected the rate of total separationist victories to climb in a period in which the guiding Supreme Court precedents were so favorable and in which the social and political strength of organized religion was so clearly in decline. Why the divergence between Supreme Court decisions and decisions in the full universe of cases? (It is not, one should be clear, because of any marked unwillingness of other appellate courts to follow the Supreme Court's precedents.)

The explanation of the continuing victories for accommodationism lies in the issues brought to appellate courts. Of the 15 accommodationist victories, 4 were won in cases over aid to religious colleges and universities. The decisions of the Supreme Court in

---

[2] The qualifications and limitations of this paragraph result from the fact that this epilogue is based almost entirely on formal, printed sources. There are no data derived from interviews, as there are in the rest of the book. Hence, for example, it is not possible to identify cases in which Leo Pfeffer or the three separationist groups may have participated on a less formal basis.

Tilton v. *Richardson* and *Hunt* v. *McNair* generally supported those kinds of aid. A fifth dealt with a form of parochaid, and was in effect superseded by a Supreme Court decision in a later case. Of the remaining 10, one can only say that most raised unsettled issues—issues on which the Supreme Court had not spoken or on which, if it had, there was still room for the states to erect a higher wall of separation (bus rides to religious schools, for instance). Among them were questions of shared-time programs, prayer at voluntary commencement ceremonies, and the payment of unemployment taxes by religious organizations. There were even issues one might call frivolous: a charge, for example, that public colleges were establishing a "secular religion" by permitting the campus newspaper to attack organized religion. But they were all unsettled issues, and the earlier separationist precedents gave litigators hope that they might now be won.

There is, therefore, a dynamic in constitutional litigation: conspicuous success breeds failure. The separationist victories apparently encouraged subsequent suits that failed. Victories encouraged a reexamination of old issues on the grounds, one presumes, that appellate courts, having become generally more separationist, will be separationist in a specific instance. They also encourage the adventurous to test new issues, and thereby to probe the outer limits of the new separationism. Finally, they would also appear to lead one segment of litigants to believe that the new separationism is a literal and absolute separationism. The very success of separationism thus entices separationists into the constitutional territory of the accommodationists.

Another perspective on the growth of the law of separation is evident if one examines closely the kinds of cases that separationists won between 1971 and 1974. Between 1951 and 1971 almost all separationist victories came in cases on elementary and secondary education. Only the Eugene, Oregon, cross case and the Maryland case over aid to five colleges were exceptions. But no fewer than five of the separationist victories in 1971–1974 fell outside the school cases. Three concerned aid to students attending religious colleges, and one each involved compulsory chapel attendance at the military academies and government participation in a Christmas celebration with religious aspects. At the least, those five cases suggest an expansion of separationist doctrines despite the inability of the separationists to increase their winning percentage in the total group of cases.

364

Amid this testing and probing of the limits of separationism, the United States Supreme Court limited its concerns almost exclusively to the single issue of parochaid. It gave all of its separationist victories to parochaid cases. (In the ninth case it upheld South Carolina's bonds to underwrite buildings at religious colleges.)[3] The Court had, in fact, another one of its June decision days for church and state in 1973, deciding five cases on June 23, 1973. The rapid, concentrated concern of the Court over this one issue to the exclusion of others demonstrates once again its power to accelerate or retard the resolution of constitutional conflict. It also suggests that the Court not only responds to the central constitutional questions of the time. It defines and highlights them, as well.

THE LAW OF CHURCH AND STATE

Those decisions the Supreme Court renders are authoritative and important out of all proportion to their number, if only because of their force as precedents that bind all other American courts. The nine decisions of the Court from 1971 to 1974 added chiefly to the law on public aid to religious schools. In truth, however, there were no great constitutional innovations in those three years, since the Court's decisions largely expanded and refined doctrines it had set down in June of 1971. The years of 1971 to 1974 were largely years of completing an ongoing exploration rather than striking out on new paths.

In the three chief parochaid cases of June 25, 1973, the Supreme Court essentially extended its earlier rationales and rulings to new variants of aid to religious schools. In *PEARL* v. *Nyquist* the Court struck down three different kinds of aid to religious schools:

> direct grants to nonpublic schools for the "maintenance and repair" of school facilities, the grants being limited to schools whose pupils came from low-income families.
>
> tuition reimbursement to low-income families sending children to nonpublic schools.
>
> income tax deductions for parents not qualifying for the tuition reimbursement to low-income families.

[3] The eight separationist victories came in: *Brusca* v. *State Board of Education, Grit* v. *Wolman, Johnson* v. *Sanders, PEARL* v. *Levitt, PEARL* v. *Nyquist, Public Funds for Public Schools* v. *Marburger, Sloan* v. *Lemon,* and *Wolman* v. *Essex.* See note 1 of this chapter for citations.

365

In *PEARL* v. *Levitt* the Court voided another New York statute, the one reimbursing nonpublic schools for performing services (such as testing and examining) mandated by state law. In *Sloan* v. *Lemon* the Pennsylvania statute that fell was designed to repay parents for the tuition they paid to nonpublic schools. And in summary affirmations (without opinion)—one of them on that busy June day—the Court also upheld decisions voiding the Connecticut purchase of services plan, an Ohio tuition reimbursement statute, an Ohio tax credit plan, and a New Jersey plan to repay parents of children in nonpublic schools for textbook and other similar expenses.[4]

Suffusing the three parochaid cases of 1973 are the logic, the rationale, and the criteria the Court developed in June of 1971 and before. The old three-fold test still framed most of the rhetoric, both of lawyers and of the appellate courts. The tests pivoted on whether:

the policy had a clearly secular purpose;

its primary effect was either to advance or inhibit religion;

there was an excessive governmental entanglement with religion.

Thus, nonparallel tests of legislative motive, of policy consequence, and of interaction between means and ends governed the constitutional scrutiny. Not only were the tests less than precise, there also appeared to be a scissors effect in the application of any two of them. If legislatures tried to protect the secular purpose of the policy (and avoid the test of effect), they threatened the policy with entanglements. If they avoided entanglements, they increased the risk of advancing the cause of religion. Moreover, it turned out that the Supreme Court really employed the latter two tests more frequently than the first, perhaps one more example of its continuing failure to assess legislative motive or intent. At best, the tests struck many observers as vague and difficult of empirical application. At worst they seemed merely to offer separate doctrinal formulae for outcomes already chosen.

The only remaining parochaid decision (*Brusca* v. *State Board of Education*) was far less visible. The Court wrote no opinion in it. But, in its way it made a more distinctive mark on American

---

[4] The eighth parochaid case was *Brusca* v. *State Board of Education,* an accommodationist suit on equal protection grounds. No public policy (except perhaps inaction) was challenged in it.

constitutional law, for it marked the early end to the growing equal protection argument within the "no establishment" doctrine. That assertion had gained momentum when it was accepted by the West Virginia Supreme Court in a transportation case in 1970.[5] The incipient constitutional doctrine was, however, ended when the Court affirmed summarily the decision of the three-judge district court in *Brusca*. That decision ended, therefore, the major doctrinal counteroffensive of the accommodationists in the 1960s and seventies.

Finally, in its ninth decision, the Court in *Hunt* v. *McNair* expanded gingerly on its earlier views on public aid to religious colleges and universities. (The decision was 6 to 3, a vote larger in margin than the 5 to 4 of its *Tilton* decision.) In the *Hunt* case the Court maintained its distinction between elementary and secondary education on the one hand and higher education on the other. But in *Hunt,* as in *Tilton,* the Court spoke carefully and on narrow grounds. It applied the three-pronged test of the parochaid cases, but found (chiefly) that the effect of the aid was not to advance religion. The main consideration seemed to be the religious nature of the college rather than the force of the policy. So, with colleges and universities becoming less and less religious in fact, it seemed more and more doubtful that aid to them might advance the cause of religion.

IMPACTS AND AFTERMATHS

Between the 1971 and 1973 decisions of the United States Supreme Court on aid to religious schools, individual states enacted one, two, and even three policies in an attempt to find the acceptable one. Their work is reflected in the post-1971 decisions in the appellate courts, and most of it is detailed in Chapter XIII. The complex of problems that beset the religious schools only worsened with time, however. Certainly the judicial decisions were not encouraging, and the falling number of religious vocations, the migration of middle-class Catholics out of the city parishes, and the preference of many younger Catholic parents for public education all spelled continued financial crisis. And to these problems in the early seventies was added the impact of rising rates of inflation.

---

[5] *State ex rel. Hughes* v. *Board of Education.* The U.S. Supreme Court rejected both appeal and certiorari petitions in 1971.

A glimmer of hope for religious education shone briefly after the 1972 elections. President Richard Nixon had publicly pledged his full help during the campaign, and then he had won an overwhelming victory with a coalition of voters that included large numbers of ordinarily Democratic Catholics. It seemed at the time that the possibility of federal aid was at an all-time high, and advocates of help mobilized in late 1972 for the push for federal legislation. CREDIT (Citizens Relief for Education by Income Tax), an organization whose leadership overlapped that of Citizens for Educational Freedom, built its policy preference into its name and that name's acronym. Then in late April of 1973 the secretary of the treasury, George Schultz, proposed a tax credit plan as one part of a larger package of reforms of the tax laws. The administration's tax credit plan would have allowed parents to claim credit against their tax liability for a sum equal to one-half of the tuition they paid to nonpublic schools up to a maximum of $200 per child. The credit would have been scaled down for parents with incomes above $18,000.

Then the Supreme Court decisions of late June 1973 snuffed out all hope. Even Congressional advocates of the tax credit legislation agreed that it was no longer a possibility. Gloom reigned among the supporters of religious schools, even though it stopped short of despair. It was clear now that they could not count on public funds, and that they were now cast back on their own resources and on those of their supporters. At least auxiliary services and the child benefit theory had emerged unscathed from the decisions of the 1970s, and a number of state legislatures moved quickly to expand aid to the schools within these possibilities. New York, for example, decided to refund the fuel taxes the religious schools paid in transporting their pupils, and it also extended the maximum distance it required some local school districts to transport parochial school students. In other states there was a small upsurge of interest in shared-time (dual enrollment) programs. But these were palliatives, and the leadership of the nation's religious schools predicted greater sacrifices in the years ahead.

There was still, ironically, one untested alternative in all of this: the voucher plan. "Ironically" because it was that very policy option that had brought Citizens for Educational Freedom into being, and because one of its earliest proponents, Father Virgil Blum, was still active in accommodationist councils. But political opposition to the voucher plan intensified in the 1970s, for those were increasingly bad times for public education, too. Educational administrators and teachers, and their national organizations, opposed the plan because of its financial implications for public education, and civil rights organizations saw it shoring up alternatives to integrated education. They fought bitterly against attempts of the U.S. Office of Education to set up a pilot project for the voucher plan. So, with all of their politically possible options struck down by the Supreme Court, the accommodationist forces found themselves unable to try the one policy that might have passed the tests of the Supreme Court.

Parochaid may have dominated church-state politics between 1971 and 1974, but it did not hold a monopoly. Church-state issues rise and fall, but they are not easily put to rest. The matters under litigation in those years are illustrative. But in addition to the new litigation, the impact of older decisions lingered. Another proposed amendment to the United States Constitution to permit voluntary prayer in public places got strong support in 1973. Despite the urgings of the American Legion and ad hoc organizations, such as Citizens for Public Prayer and the National Back to God Movement, it made little progress in the Congress, however. The climate of opinion in the 1970s was hardly as supportive of public religiosity as it was in the 1950s.

Even the specific aftermaths of the sixty-seven cases in this book were slow to taper off. Nowhere was that slowness more evident than in the only two cases between 1951 and 1971 in which separationists won victories in cases having nothing to do with elementary and secondary education. In Maryland, whose high court had earlier invalidated aid to religious colleges (the *Horace Mann League* case), the legislature in 1971 passed a law to aid all seventeen of the state's private institutions of higher education with direct grants. In the fall of 1974 a three-judge federal district court in Baltimore upheld, by a 2–1 vote, the plan as it applied to four religious colleges. The U.S. Supreme Court (5–3) refused shortly thereafter to halt payment of the funds, while leaving open the possibility of a full review of the decision. The cross on Skinner's Butte in Eugene, Oregon, remained physically on the butte and legally in the Oregon courts. After the state supreme court's ruling in 1969, the Lane County Circuit Court ordered the removal of the cross. Then in the next year the citizens of Eugene voted to make the cross a memorial to war veterans, and the defendants subsequently moved to set aside the original decree in view of the cross's new purpose. The trial on the motion was finally held in late 1974, and by the end of the year all parties were awaiting a decision. The litigation over the cross had, of course, begun in that same court in May of 1965.

After all of the analysis of the process of litigating church-state cases, one central question remains: where is the law of church and state? The political activity of the participants in the process has a goal and a purpose. Whether their concern was the judiciary or the more conventional political arenas, the ultimate question for all of them is one of success or failure in shaping the constitutional law of church and state.

In applying that highest standard of effectiveness, there are two ways of looking at the almost twenty-five years—the constitutional "generation"—between 1951 and 1974. If one looks only at the cases themselves, it appears to have been a separationist generation. Separationists won substantial victories in the two overriding questions of the period: religious practices in the public schools, and public aid to the religious schools. Only in the affirmation of the constitutionality of tax exemptions did the accommodationists score a remotely comparable victory. That kind of scorekeeping grows from the realities of American society in the 1940s and 1950s. Alliances between church and state were normal and expected, and any separationist decision in the courts was a conspicuous victory against the consensus of the status quo. Viewed in those terms, the period between 1951 and 1974 was a time of separationist struggles in the courts to break the accommodationist grip on so much of public policy in the country.

At the same time, the period can be seen as a time of the first systematic application of the "no establishment" clause. Various state courts had already made excursions into church-state questions, to be sure, but with the silence of the United States Supreme Court, that clause was uncharted constitutional territory. American courts, therefore, decided the meaning of those faintly archaic words of the First Amendment without the guidance of a structure of authoritative precedents. And the contending groups litigated with greater freedom, too, as a result of the late unfolding of the law of church and state. As a result, what emerged in those years was a process and substance of constitutional explication that served both the imperatives of the constitutional document and the realities of contemporary American society.

370

APPENDIX I
The Universe of Cases

The central data for this book are the events and actors in the sixty-seven cases deciding constitutional issues of the separation of church and state under the state and the United States constitutions. It should be clear from the start that the sixty-seven cases are not a sample. They are all of the cases—the complete universe meeting the criteria of selection. This appendix is intended to clarify those criteria.

The criteria used in defining the universe of cases were three. To qualify for selection a case:

1) must have been decided finally between 1951 and June 28, 1971, the date of the Supreme Court's historic decisions on aid to religious schools and universities;

2) must have been decided in the highest appellate court of a state or in either a Federal Court of Appeals or the United States Supreme Court;

3) must have raised and decided a substantial constitutional question of church-state separation.

Taken together, the three criteria identify those cases in a twenty-year period that reached the stature of precedent in American constitutional law on the separation of church and state.

The first two criteria are not difficult to apply. Any case decided on substantive church-state grounds in the specified appellate courts between 1951 and 1971 is eligible. But a word of justification for the criteria may be in order. The time span embraces a generation of almost feverish litigation on church and state, beginning with *Zorach* v. *Clauson* in 1951 and extending to the Supreme Court's spate of decisions in late June of 1971, including those of *Lemon* v. *Kurtzman* and *Tilton* v. *Richardson*. To the extent that one can define any periods in the development of an area of constitutional law, these twenty years appear to qualify because of the increased incidence of litigation, the coincidence with greater legislative activity on church-state issues, and the bracketing of the years by historic decisions of the United States Supreme Court. An argument might be made that the "period" ought ideally be extended another four years, back to 1947 and the case of *Everson* v. *Board of Education*. Whatever intellectual merit such an argument might have, I have rejected that option for practical, operational reasons. Working in the 1960s, it was difficult enough to find participants and jog memories about cases decided in 1951 (which often originated in the late 1940s). The problems would have been vastly greater, and probably insurmountable, had the beginning date been pushed back another four years.

As for the criterion of high appellate consideration, it, too, resulted from a combination of logic and pragmatism. If the purpose in selecting the cases was to identify those cases that added to the body of constitutional precedents on church-state questions, then one had to look to reported appellate cases. The only apparent anomaly in the criterion involves the inclusion of intermediate federal appellate courts and the exclusion of similar state courts. I made that decision for a number of reasons. The decisions of the federal courts of appeals have been fully reported for some time; only some of the state intermediate appellate courts are so reported. Furthermore, states differ vastly in whether or not they have an intermediate appellate court level; and, among those that do, their jurisdictions differ greatly. Furthermore, during the twenty-year period of this study a number of states created intermediate appellate courts. Finally, in most states the highest appellate court remains the forum for the final decision of constitutional issues. In view of all these considerations it seemed wise to limit state cases to those that reached the highest state appellate court.

The chief problems in applying the criteria surrounded the third—that the cases must have decided a substantial constitutional question of church-state separation in the appellate consideration. It is often the nature of constitutional cases to raise a handful of constitutional issues within the same set of facts, and often issues of church-state separation become entwined with other constitutional issues. The hard question in these instances was whether or not the separation issue was the "central" issue, that is, whether the interests of the parties, the facts of the case, and the treatment of the issues by the appellate courts made it basically a "separation" case.

372

In making those decisions a number of cases raising separation questions, among others, were eliminated: for example, the Sunday closing cases (such as *McGowan* v. *Maryland,* 366 U.S. 420, 1961, and the three other cases decided with it) seem to me fundamentally to raise issues of commercial rights and interests, of free exercise of religion, and of the legitimacy of a secular "day of rest." Certainly these issues have been more salient in the decisions of appellate courts than the church-state questions. By the same token, the Maryland case on the constitutionality of a religious oath of office (*Torcaso* v. *Watkins,* 367 U.S. 488, 1961) seems to be primarily concerned with questions of "free exercise" of religion; and the banning of the movie, "The Miracle," in New York (*Burstyn* v. *Wilson,* 343 U.S. 495, 1952) primarily concerned the position of movies under the First Amendment's guarantees of free expression.

There are other, even more difficult decisions: instances in which the church-state issue is clearly present but where it may not be "strong" or assertive enough for consideration. Take, for example, the Florida case of *Koerner* v. *Borck* (100 So.2d 398, 1958). A deceased lady had willed to the city of Orlando a sum of money to be used to build a chapel in a public park; after her death relatives challenged the will on a number of grounds, including one that the grant for the chapel was invalid because it was unconstitutional under the "no establishment" clause and the Fourteenth Amendment. In deciding that cases such as *Koerner* did not deal primarily with separation I have asked the following questions:

> are the interests of the plaintiffs primarily those of church-state separation?
>
> has the appellate court rested its decision at least in significant part on the church-state question?
>
> has the appellate court dealt with the church-state issue in constitutional terms (either a state constitution or the United States Constitution) rather than on statutory or other nonconstitutional grounds?

Since in the *Koerner* case the answer to the first two questions was "no," it was excluded. The interests of the plaintiffs clearly had little to do with church-state matters, and the Florida Supreme

373

Court, perhaps recognizing that the separation argument was a throw-in, passed the question rather quickly in its opinion.

The largest group of cases eliminated in the application of this third criterion are those decided on nonconstitutional grounds. There are first of all those cases decided on nonsubstantive grounds; *Flast* v. *Cohen* (392 U.S. 83, 1968) is undoubtedly the best known of them. It began as a challenge of the use of Elementary and Secondary Education Act funds for religious schools, but it was decided in the U.S. Supreme Court solely on the issue of the citizen's standing to bring the suit in vindication of a constitutional right. Similarly, other church-state cases were rejected because the supreme court of the state decided the case solely on the appropriateness of the remedy sought (*O'Callahan* v. *Aikens,* a Georgia case reported at 126 S.E.2d 212, 1962), or the failure to exhaust remedies (*State ex rel. Sholes* v. *University of Minnesota,* 54 N.W.2d 122, 1952). In other cases the state courts brushed aside the constitutional questions in preference to decisions on statutory grounds. Among those cases were *School District* v. *Houghton* (128 A.2d 58, 1956), *Quinn* v. *School Committee of Plymouth* (125 N.E.2d 410, 1955), and *Dilger* v. *School District* (352 P.2d 564, 1960). One case, *Squires* v. *City of Augusta,* was included in the study even though it was technically decided on legislative grounds, and that decision merits special explanation. First of all, the constitutional issues had been raised by all parties in *Squires* through all steps of the planning and execution of the litigation. Furthermore, the Maine Supreme Court in its majority opinion took up and "decided" the constitutional issue in extended dicta; the dissenting opinion also fully aired the constitutional question.

Finally, it must be clear that this universe of cases does not include cases arising under the "free exercise" clause of the First Amendment or under similar state constitutional provisions. There are no cases, in other words, that fall into the conventional category of issues of religious freedom. In cases raising questions both of separation and of free exercise I have had to decide with which issue the case was primarily concerned. Cases dealing largely or entirely with the following kinds of questions of religious freedom have been excluded: disagreements within religious sects or congregations, the rights and position of groups such as Jehovah's Witnesses or the Muslims, conscientious objection and selective service, resistance of religious groups such as the Amish to compulsory school attendance, state-enforced medical care or precaution (such as vaccination) over religious objections, religious requirements for parents adopting children, and issues of abortion and contraception.

The sixty-seven cases included in this study, therefore, embrace all the precedents that have entered the constitutional jurisprudence on church-state relations in the twenty years from 1951 to 1971. Any generalizations about the growth of that body of constitutional law in those decades are generalizations about these cases. A list of the sixty-seven cases and their legal histories follows.

1. *Abernathy* v. *City of Irvine*
   355 S.W.2d 159 (1961)
   371 U.S. 831 (1962)

2. *Americans United* v. *Independent School District No. 622*
   179 N.W.2d 146 (1970)
   430 U.S. 945 (1971)

3. *Aronow* v. *United States*
   432 F.2d 242 (1970)

4. *Berghorn* v. *Reorganized School District No. 8*
   260 S.W.2d 573 (1963)

5. *Board of Education of Central School District No. 1* v. *Allen*
   273 N.Y.S.2d 239 (1966)
   276 N.Y.S.2d 234 (1966)
   228 N.E.2d 791 (1967)
   389 U.S. 1031 (1968)
   392 U.S. 236 (1968)

6. *Board of Education for Independent School District No. 52* v. *Antone*
   384 P.2d 911 (1963)

7. *Bowerman* v. *O'Connor*
   247 A.2d 82 (1968)

8. *Brown* v. *Orange County Board of Public Instruction*
   128 So.2d 181 (1960)
   155 So.2d 371 (1963)

9. *Calvary Bible Presbyterian Church* v. *Board of Regents*
   436 P.2d 189 (1967)
   393 U.S. 960 (1968)

10. *Carden* v. *Bland*
    288 S.W.2d 718 (1956)

11. *Chamberlin* v. *Dade County Board of Public Instruction*
    143 So.2d 21 (1962)
    374 U.S. 487 (1963)
    375 U.S 802 (1963)
    160 So.2d 97 (1964)
    377 U.S. 402 (1964)
    379 U.S. 871 (1964)
    171 So.2d 535 (1965)

12. *Clayton* v. *Kervick*
    267 A.2d 503 (1970)
    403 U.S. 945 (1971)

13. *Commissioner of Education* v. *School Committee of Leyden*
    267 N.E.2d 226 (1971)
    404 U.S. 849 (1971)

14. *Community Council* v. *Jordan*
    432 P.2d 460 (1967)

15. *DeSpain* v. *DeKalb County School District 428*
    255 F.Supp. 655 (1966)
    384 F.2d 836 (1967)
    390 U.S. 906 (1968)

16. *DiCenso* v. *Robinson*
    316 F.Supp. 112 (1970)
    403 U.S. 602 (1971)

17. *Dickman* v. *School District No. 62C, Oregon City*
    366 P.2d 533 (1961)
    371 U.S. 823 (1962)

18. *Engel* v. *Vitale*
    191 N.Y.S.2d 453 (1959)
    206 N.Y.S.2d 183 (1960)
    176 N.E.2d 579 (1961)
    368 U.S. 924 (1961)
    370 U.S. 421 (1962)
    186 N.E.2d 124 (1962)

19. *General Finance Corporation* v. *Archetto*
    176 A.2d 73 (1961)
    369 U.S. 423 (1962)

20. *Hartness* v. *Patterson*
    179 S.E.2d 907 (1971)

376

21. *Horace Mann League of U.S. v. Board of Public Works*
    220 A.2d 51 (1966)
    385 U.S. 97 (1966)

22. *Hunt* v. *McNair*
    177 S.E.2d 362 (1970)
    403 U.S. 945 (1971)

23. *In Re Proposal C*
    185 N.W.2d 9 (1971)

24. *Johnson* v. *Presbyterian Homes of Synod of Florida*
    239 So.2d 256 (1970)

25. *Kintzele* v. *City of St. Louis*
    347 S.W.2d 695 (1961)

26. *Lemon* v. *Kurtzman*
    310 F.Supp. 35 (1969)
    397 U.S. 984 (1970)
    403 U.S. 602 (1971)

27. *Lewis* v. *Allen*
    159 N.Y.S.2d 807 (1957)
    207 N.Y.S.2d 862 (1960)
    200 N.E.2d 767 (1964)
    379 U.S. 923 (1964)

28. *Lien* v. *City of Ketchikan*
    383 P.2d 721 (1963)

29. *Lincoln* v. *Page*
    241 A.2d 799 (1968)

30. *Lowe* v. *City of Eugene*
    451 P.2d 117 (1969)
    459 P.2d 222 (1969)
    397 U.S. 591 (1970)
    397 U.S. 1042 (1970)
    398 U.S. 944 (1970)

31. *Lundberg* v. *County of Alameda*
    298 P.2d 1 (1956)
    352 U.S. 921 (1956)

32. *Mangold* v. *Albert Gallatin Area School District*
    307 F.Supp. 637 (1969)
    438 F.2d 1194 (1971)

33. *Matthews* v. *Quinton*
    362 P.2d 932 (1961)
    368 U.S. 517 (1962)

34. *McVey* v. *Hawkins*
    258 S.W.2d 927 (1953)

35. *Miller* v. *Cooper*
    244 P.2d 520 (1952)

36. *Murray* v. *Comptroller of Treasury*
    216 A.2d 897 (1966)
    385 U.S. 816 (1966)

37. *Murray* v. *Curlett*
    179 A.2d 698 (1962)
    371 U.S. 809 (1962)
    374 U.S. 203 (1963)

38. *Nohrr* v. *Brevard County Educational Facilities Authority*
    247 So.2d 304 (1971)

39. *Perry* v. *School District No. 81, Spokane*
    344 P.2d 1036 (1959)

40. *Rawlings* v. *Butler*
    290 S.W.2d 801 (1956)

41. *Rhoades* v. *School District of Abington Township*
    226 A.2d 53 (1967)
    389 U.S. 11 (1967)
    389 U.S. 846 (1967)

42. *Schade* v. *Allegheny County Institution District*
    126 A.2d 911 (1956)

43. *Schempp* v. *School District of Abington Township*
    177 F.Supp. 398 (1959)
    184 F.Supp. 381 (1959)
    364 U.S. 298 (1960)
    195 F.Supp. 518 (1961)
    201 F.Supp. 815 (1962)
    374 U.S. 203 (1963)

44. *Seegers* v. *Parker*
    241 So.2d 213 (1970)
    403 U.S. 955 (1971)

45. *Sills* v. *Board of Education of Hawthorne*
    200 A.2d 817 (1963)
    200 A.2d 615 (1964)

46. *Snyder* v. *Town of Newtown*
    161 A.2d 770 (1960)
    365 U.S. 299 (1961)

47. *Southside Estates Baptist Church* v. *Board of Trustees*
    115 So.2d 697 (1959)

48. *Spears* v. *Honda*
    449 P.2d 130 (1968)

49. *Special District for Education and Training of Handicapped Children* v. *Wheeler*
    408 S.W.2d 60 (1966)

50. *Squires* v. *Inhabitants of City of Augusta*
    153 A.2d 80 (1959)

51. *State* v. *Nusbaum*
    115 N.W.2d 761 (1962)

52. *State* v. *Williamson*
    347 P.2d 204 (1959)

53. *State Board of Education* v. *Board of Education of Netcong*
    270 A.2d 412 (1970)
    401 U.S. 1013 (1971)

54. *State ex rel. Chambers* v. *School District No. 10*
    472 P.2d 1013 (1970)

55. *State ex rel. Hughes* v. *Board of Education*
    174 S.E.2d 711 (1970)
    403 U.S. 944 (1971)

56. *Stein* v. *Oshinsky*
    224 F.Supp. 757 (1963)
    348 F.2d 999 (1965)
    382 U.S. 957 (1965)

57. *Stone* v. *Salt Lake City*
    356 P.2d 631 (1960)
    365 U.S. 860 (1961)

58. *Swart* v. *South Burlington Town School District*
    167 A.2d 514 (1961)
    366 U.S. 925 (1961)

59. *Tilton* v. *Richardson*
    312 F.Supp. 1191 (1970)
    403 U.S. 672 (1971)

60. *Truitt* v. *Board of Public Works*
    221 A.2d 370 (1966)

61. *Tudor* v. *Board of Education*
    100 A.2d 857 (1953)
    348 U.S. 816 (1954)

62. *Vermont Educational Buildings Financing Agency* v. *Mann*
    247 A.2d 68 (1968)
    394 U.S. 957 (1969)
    396 U.S. 801 (1969)

63. *Walz* v. *Tax Commission*
    292 N.Y.S.2d 353 (1968)
    246 N.E.2d 517 (1969)
    397 U.S. 664 (1970)

64. *West Morris Regional Board of Education* v. *Sills*
    279 A.2d 609 (1971)
    404 U.S. 986 (1971)

65. *Wooley* v. *Spalding*
    293 S.W.2d 563 (1956)
    309 S.W.2d 42 (1957)
    365 S.W.2d 323 (1962)

66. *Zellers* v. *Huff*
    236 P.2d 949 (1951)
    261 P.2d 643 (1953)

67. *Zorach* v. *Clauson*
    86 N.Y.S.2d 17 (1948)
    87 N.Y.S.2d 639 (1949)
    89 N.Y.S.2d 232 (1949)
    89 N.Y.S.2d 923 (1949)
    90 N.Y.S.2d 750 (1949)
    90 N.E.2d 68 (1949)
    96 N.Y.S.2d 564 (1950)
    99 N.Y.S.2d 339 (1950)
    102 N.Y.S.2d 27 (1951)
    100 N.E.2d 463 (1951)
    343 U.S. 306 (1952)

APPENDIX II
Sources

The usual bibliographic note would not suggest the ways in which I gathered the data on which this study rests. It draws on a considerable range of sources beyond the printed page, and I will describe them briefly in this appendix.

Data on the origins of a case and the parties, attorneys, and local groups initiating it come largely from visits to the site. I have travelled from Maine to Florida and Alaska to Hawaii in pursuit of the events and personalities in these sixty-seven cases. While at a site I tried to interview the parties and attorneys (those for the plaintiffs more than those of the defense), to examine court records and newspaper accounts, and to seek general background from knowledgeable local informants. In a number of instances, especially those involving the early cases, reconstructing the events of a case was mostly a search for anybody close to the case who could remember the events of fifteen or twenty years earlier.

This on-site interviewing resulted in approximately 275 interviews with people involved in this litigation. Whenever possible the interviews were face to face, although in a few instances they were conducted over the phone, or later by letter with enclosed questionnaire. In almost every instance, too, I examined full court files both in the trial and the appellate courts. For more general background information the newspaper files, indexes, and clippings of local libraries, or of the newspapers themselves (their "morgues" or libraries) were invaluable. In the aggregate, however, probably no single source of information was more useful than the attorney of the plaintiffs in the litigation. A personal interview with him had my highest priority in visits to the site of a case.

Secondly, I have relied heavily on the files and archives of the three major groups sponsoring litigation in church-state issues: the American Civil Liberties Union, the American Jewish Congress, and Americans United for Separation of Church and State. All three organizations have kept substantial files on past cases; the files of the American Jewish Congress are especially useful, both for their comprehensiveness and completeness, and for the thorough way in which they have been indexed and cross-referenced. The papers of the American Jewish Congress and Americans United are available at their headquarters in New York and Washington, respectively. The ACLU keeps papers only for the five most recent years; materials earlier than that are given to and housed in the Princeton University library.

In addition to researches in these three organizations' materials, I have also sought information on the involvement of these and other groups through interviews. They have included interviews with leaders of the three groups above, as well as the Citizens for Educational Freedom, the United States Catholic Conference, the National Jewish Commission on Law and Public Affairs, and a number of state affiliates of the American Civil Liberties Union. Finally, I have drawn on interviews with attorneys and individuals especially active in this area of constitutional law.

Many of the remaining data come from more conventional sources. Data on the backgrounds and characteristics of judges deciding these cases have been gathered from a number of sources: the usual biographical directories (such as the regional versions of *Who's Who* and the older *Directory of American Judges*), the files of newspapers, libraries, and state historical societies, and the files of other scholars. (I have not used either personal interviews with or questionnaires mailed to the judges.) Census data and data of the 1957 religious census of the National Council of Churches have been used to describe the sites of the litigation.

One last word should, perhaps, be said about two published listings of litigation on church-state relations. The *Civil Liberties Docket,* edited by Ann Fagan Ginger for the Meiklejohn Institute in Berkeley, California, reported current litigation in all civil liberties fields. Its listings of church-state cases from its origin in 1955 to 1966 is, unfortunately, rather incomplete. Beginning in 1966 the American Jewish Congress' Commission on Law and Social Action began to publish (approximately semiannually) a listing of all church-state litigation (including cases on religious freedom as well as those on separation). It carries the simple title of *Litigation Docket.* It is virtually complete, and it contains brief summaries of the facts, lists of attorneys and all parties, and information on participating groups in each case. It is an invaluable tool for the scholar in the field, and it also constitutes a major tool for groups involved in the litigation.

APPENDIX III
Definitions and Criteria

Scattered throughout the text and tables of the book are a series of terms, the operational definitions of which are not self-evident. Rather than clutter the text with the definitions, especially since many of the terms recur in other chapters, they are gathered in this appendix, where they can be available to the working specialist without interrupting the progress of other readers. They are arranged here in alphabetical order.

Catholic interests (*involved in cases*). Those cases noted as having Catholic interests involved are characterized by identifiable Roman Catholic interests in the controversy of the case that are separate from the interests of all other organized religions. Thus, cases involving aid to private religious schools meet the test and are included. Those concerning tax exemptions for all religions are not.

College, type of. The categories here are self-explanatory, except for "private prestige." That group includes Amherst, Brown, Carleton, Chicago, Claremont, Columbia, Cornell, Dartmouth, Duke, Harvard, Johns Hopkins, Northwestern, Oberlin, Pennsylvania, Princeton, Reed, Rochester, Smith, Stanford, Swarthmore, Vanderbilt, Vassar, Washington U., Wesleyan, and Yale. The list is not exhaustive; it is only a sorting of actual college affiliations.

Group Roles. For an extensive explanation of the three-fold categories of amicus curiae, intermediate, and sponsorship, see the discussion in the text of Chapter IV.

Law School, type of. Only one category needs explanation: "prestigious." It includes the law schools of the following universities: Chicago, Columbia, Cornell, Duke, Harvard, Michigan, New York, Northwestern, Pennsylvania, Stanford, Vanderbilt, Virginia, and Yale.

Occupation. The occupational categories used here (as in Table 6–1) are those of the U.S. Bureau of the Census, and all of its rules for placing specific occupations into categories have also been employed.

Plaintiffs. In coding and analyzing the characteristics of the plaintiffs in the separationist-adversary cases, it was necessary to reduce the multiple plaintiffs (where they occurred) to a single "plaintiff" per case. In doing so three rules were used. First, where there were two or more individuals as plaintiffs, the leader or organizer among them was selected as the single plaintiff. Second, if there was no leader or organizer, I constructed an average or modal "plaintiff" from the characteristics of all of the actual plaintiffs. Finally, where there were both individual plaintiffs and group plaintiffs (or an organization or corporation) in the same case, the individuals alone were used for the purpose of this analysis.

Protestants, Liberal and Conservative. The liberal Protestants have been defined to include Episcopalians, Lutherans, Presbyterians, Congregationalists, Evangelical and Reformeds, Unitarians, and Universalists. (That definition ignores, for lack of information, the differences among the various Lutheran organizations and synods.) The conservative Protestants include Baptists, Methodists, Disciples of Christ, Dutch and Christian Reformeds, Bible Presbyterians, and members of the Assembly of God. The distinction between liberal and conservative or traditional Protestants is, therefore, entirely theological.

Regions (of the United States). The usage in this study adopts the four regional definitions of the U.S. Bureau of the Census. The Northeast includes New England, New York, Pennsylvania, and New Jersey. The North Central is composed of Michigan, Ohio, Indiana, Wisconsin, Illinois, Minnesota, Iowa, Missouri, the Dakotas, Nebraska, and Kansas. The South includes Maryland, West Virginia, Kentucky, the Deep South, and Oklahoma and Texas. The West begins with Montana, Wyoming, Colorado, and New Mexico, and includes all states west of them.

Selection of Judges. The Missouri plan refers, as it usually does, to those various selection systems in which the governor appoints from the nominees of a special panel. "Election" refers to both partisan and nonpartisan elections in which the usual electorate elects the judge. "Appointment" refers to those selection systems in which the governor or the legislature or both select the judge (even though the process of legislative choice is called "election" in several states).

Socio-Economic Status. The one time that SES categories are used (Table 6–2), they are the author's rough estimates based chiefly on the education, the occupation, and the place of residence of the individuals involved.

States, by Percentage of Pupils in Catholic Schools. The states by quartile (the highest percentages in the first quartile), and in order within quartile are as follows:

First: Rhode Island, Pennsylvania, New Hampshire, New York, Wisconsin, New Jersey, Massachusetts, Illinois, Missouri, Minnesota, Ohio, Delaware, and Connecticut.

Second: Louisiana, Maryland, Iowa, Nebraska, Michigan, Kentucky, Vermont, Indiana, Hawaii, North Dakota, Maine, and Kansas.

Third: California, Montana, South Dakota, New Mexico, Florida, Oregon, Colorado, Washington, Nevada, Idaho, Wyoming, Texas, and West Virginia.

Fourth: Arizona, Virginia, Mississippi, Arkansas, Alabama, Tennessee, Oklahoma, Utah, Alaska, Georgia, South Carolina, and North Carolina.

INDEX

Abernathy v. *City of Irvine,* 70, 165, 212, 315

Abraham, Warren, 199

accommodationists (*see also* defendants), 8–9, 31, 342

Adams, John, 84

adversary cases (*see also* litigation), 231–57; changes in, 340; number of, 231–36, 246; origins, 236–45; outcomes, 252–56; pairs of, 240–43; in Supreme Court, 245–52

advisory opinions, 273–75

Alabama Civil Liberties Union, 295

Alexander Meiklejohn Institute, 232, 382

Allen v. *Morton,* 360

Alltucker, John, 195

amendments, constitutional (*see also* Constitution, U.S.), 308–15

American Association for the Advancement of Atheism, 49

American Civil Liberties Union, 8–9, 31–47, 56, 57–59, 87, 134, 138, 149, 153, 159, 161–62, 165, 184, 247, 262, 275, 280, 293, 305, 314–15, 324, 327, 329, 333, 339, 363, 381–82; affiliates, 37; amicus curiae, 124–25; appeals, 98–101, 121–22; attorneys, 167–69, 172–73; capacity for litigation, 73–80; cases, 60–63; Church-State Committee, 37, 40–41, 53; *Civil Liberties,* 36; compliance, role in, 300–303; decision making, 39–41; diversity within, 35–36; goals in litigation, 92–95; litigation decisions, 42–45; origins, 31; public relations, 123–24; records of fact, 114–20; relations with other groups, 80–86; role in litigation, 64–72, 345–46; separationism, 32–33, 36–37; strategies in litigation, 95–125, 127, 129; success in litigation, 125–27; test cases, 103–14

American Jewish Committee, 39, 47, 162, 280

American Jewish Congress, 31–47, 44, 51, 56–59, 86–87, 145, 153, 189, 234, 247, 272, 280, 303, 305, 314–15, 327, 329, 339, 363, 381–82; amicus curiae, 124–25; appeals, 98–102, 121–22; attorneys, 167–69, 172–73; capacity for litigation, 73–80; cases, 60–63; Commission on Law and Social Action, 42, 159; compliance, role in, 300–303; decision making, 38–41; diversity within, 35; goals in litigation, 92–95; litigation decisions, 45–47; *Litigation Docket,* 70, 74, 79, 161, 232–35, 382; origins, 31; public relations, 123–24; records of fact, 114–20; relations with other groups, 80–86; role in litigation, 64–72, 345–46; separationism, 33; strategies in litigation, 95–125, 127–29; success in litigation, 125–27; test cases, 103–14

Americans United, 31–47, 56, 57–59, 86–87, 135, 150, 153, 163, 165, 175, 184, 203, 223, 247, 275, 309, 314–15, 327, 329, 339, 363, 381–82; amicus curiae, 124–25; appeals, 98–102, 121–22; attorneys, 42, 167–69, 172–73; capacity for litigation, 73–80; cases, 60–63; *Church and State,* 34, 46, 54, 65, 95; compliance, role in, 300–303; decision making, 38–39, 41; diversity within, 35–36; goals in litigation, 92–95; litigation decisions, 45–46; origins, 31; public relations, 122–23; records of fact, 114–20; relations with Baptists, 52; relations with Scottish Rite Masons, 54–55; relations with other groups, 80–86; role in litigation, 64–72, 345–46; Roman Catholicism, concern with, 33–35,

387

389

Library of Congress Cataloging in Publication Data

Sorauf, Francis Joseph, 1928–
    The wall of separation.

    Includes index.
    1. Ecclesiastical law—United States.   2. Church and state in the United States.   I. Title.
KF4865.S6   342'.73'085   75-3476
ISBN 0-691-07574-3